# Special Events

# The Wiley Event Management Series

**SERIES EDITOR: DR. JOE GOLDBLATT, CSEP**

*Dictionary of Event Management, Second Edition*
by Dr. Joe Goldblatt, CSEP, and Kathleen S. Nelson, CSEP

*Special Events, Third Edition*
by Dr. Joe Goldblatt, CSEP

*Corporate Event Project Management*
by William O'Toole and Phyllis Mikolaitis

*Event Risk Management and Safety*
by Peter E. Tarlow, Ph.D.

# Special Events

**TWENTY-FIRST CENTURY GLOBAL EVENT MANAGEMENT**

**THIRD EDITION**

Dr. Joe Goldblatt, CSEP

Julia Schiptsova
Contributing Editor, Third Edition

**JOHN WILEY & SONS, INC.**

*Library of Congress Cataloging-in-Publication Data*

Goldblatt, Joe Jeff, 1952-
   Special events : twenty-first century global event management / Joe Goldblatt.—3rd ed.
     p. cm.— (Wiley event management series)
   Includes index.
   Includes bibliographical references and listings of online and multi-media sources.
   ISBN 0-471-39687-7 (cloth : alk.paper)
   1. Special events—Management. I. Title. II. Wiley events.

GT3405 .G65 2001
394.26′068—dc21                               2001026946

*A public celebration is a rope bridge of knotted symbols strung across an abyss. We make our crossings hoping the chasm will echo our festive sounds for a moment, as the bridge begins to sway from the rhythms of our dance.*

**Ronald Grimes, *Beginnings in Ritual Studies* (1982, p. 231)**

# Dedication

In 1913 my great-grandfather wrote to my maternal grandfather these words of encouragement as he prepared to wed my grandmother:

> *Dear Alcibiade,*
> *I write today to wish you and Leah all the happiness there is in married life. That your lives will be long and happy and that in case there happens to be some little troubles in your youth you will be steadfast in your love to one another. If you do this you will conquer all and happiness will soon return.*

Their long and happy marriage produced two daughters, Rosa and Bertha, and seven grandchildren. These two proud Southern women often assembled our family around an elegant table for the purpose of celebrating a beautiful family. With eternal gratitude I dedicate this book to my remarkable mother and aunt. They first introduced me to the traditions and rituals of celebration. Through their steadfastness and love, the first seeds of celebration were planted deep within me. The evidence of their enduring influence is apparent in the pages of this book.

# Special Dedication

This book is dedicated to the members of the New York City Fire Department (NYFD); the New York City Police Department (NYPD); the staff and rescue workers of the United States Pentagon; the thousands of rescue workers in New York, Pennsylvania, and Washington, DC; the families of those who lost their loved ones; and the sacred memories of those individuals whose lives are forever enshrined in our global consciousness. May we always remember these acts of heroism, commemorate the sacrifices that were made, and commit to turning our sorrows into future celebrations through a renewed commitment to global understanding and lasting peace.

Furthermore, the author has directed that a portion of the author's proceeds will support various charitable organizations that provide support for the families of the victims of the September 11, 2001 tragic events.

# Contents

# Foreword

It is with great pride and humility that I write this foreword. As a professional newspaper journalist for nearly a quarter of a century, this is my first attempt at executing this form of writing. But being the persuasive and charming person that he is, Joe didn't ask me to do this—he told me. And he would not take "no" for an answer.

"You've known me all your life," Joe told me. "And you're a writer, a very good one too. So write."

I reside in and am a native of the city of New Orleans, where every week of every month there are dozens of special events taking place. Of course, like residents in other parts of the country, we celebrate the usual national and religious holidays. But here in New Orleans—in Louisiana—it is just as important to us what we celebrate as how we celebrate.

And playing vital roles in the success of any celebration in my hometown are two important elements, music and food. You can rarely have one without the other.

My culture celebrates and pays tribute to what some may view as the oddest of things, but for the Louisiana native, it seems perfectly natural. We have local festivals honoring such foods as andouille sausage, crawfish, crabs, catfish, shrimp, chili, pecans, strawberries, and gumbo.

In New Orleans, baptisms, deaths, marriages, graduations, birthdays, anniversaries, and even school fairs are celebrated like they are no place else on earth. No one visiting this unique and diverse city should be shocked to see a group of jazz musicians playing a lively tune after a funeral.

We celebrate and honor all forms and types of music, paying tribute to musicians of every race, class, and culture through every venue imaginable: on street corners, in hotel lounges, in neighborhood bars, under tents, in school auditoriums, and in concert halls.

From January 6, we celebrate the start of the Carnival season with an event called "Twelfth Night," named for the twelve days after the celebration of Christmas. For the next few weeks, prior to the start of the 40 days of Lent, we celebrate by attending daily parades and parties throughout the metropolitan New Orleans area.

And as private organizations plan and execute elaborate, colorful, and festive parades and balls, those who are not members of these groups can still enjoy the celebration of the Carnival season in their own way by simply being a spectator.

Just about every weekend in the fall and spring, school fairs abound. Gone are the days of such activities as fish ponds, ball throws, and strongmen competitions. To get the largest crowds, fair planners have to offer would-be fair goers a variety of everything: food, games, arts and crafts, refreshments, and live music. And booking the most popular, local band can become a year-round job.

So you can see why it as important to those interested in special events, either as planners or attendees, to keep in mind that why people celebrate and how people celebrate are of equal importance. From national conventions to school fairs, from major sporting events to local football or baseball jamborees, keeping organized while knowing what the public wants is critical. I say this knowing quite well that the author of this book is the utmost authority on how to organize an event, large or small. This book will help you fully understand the why and how of celebration and so much more.

If anyone epitomizes the title of "professional event manager," it is Joe Goldblatt. I have known him for nearly fifty years, and together we have celebrated hundreds of family events. He has an uncanny and dare I say, brilliant, knack for making a quiet, family dinner into a memorable event. He is a special events master through and through, never passing up a chance to liven things up, to transform the tedious and mundane into the spectacular.

From his childhood of performing magic tricks that included making Leah, his little sister, disappear from inside a special box, to his recent career in academia, Joe has many gifts that few possess. In the midst of sadness, he can make people smile. A happy occasion for Joe becomes a indelible memory. And Joe has no problem laughing at himself as he recalls the times from our own childhood when he was the instigator of a practical joke but then laughed the loudest when the joke was on him.

Writing this foreword has been a wonderful opportunity to briefly share with you my view of what special events have meant to me and to the family Joe and I experienced as children. So now it is time for you to celebrate and to make your own special memories, both personally and professionally, as you join our family and follow my cousin Joe into the magical, memorable world of professional event management.

Eva Jacob Barkoff, Community News Editor
*The Times-Picayune Newspaper,* East Jefferson Bureau
New Orleans, Louisiana

# Preface

"I am bringing shrimp, crabs, and crayfish." Thus, my Aunt Bertha wrote to my mother (her sister) in 1967 telling her of an upcoming visit she would make to our home in Texas. My mother, a native Cajun who raised her family in Texas, was surely excited about the upcoming visit of her only sibling. I am also certain her mouth was watering in anticipation of the seafood that would soon arrive with Aunt Bertha, who we lovingly called "Aunt T."

I felt a similar sense of anticipation when John Wiley & Sons' senior editor, JoAnna Turtletaub, phoned me to ask if I would serve as series editor for a new project entitled the Wiley Event Management Series. According to JoAnna, through research, Wiley had identified the fact that the special events field was expanding rapidly and needed new books to meet current and future educational demands of the profession. The first book in the series would be the third edition of *Special Events,* which historically was the first academic textbook in the field. This book would be followed by three or four books per year, to keep pace with the tremendous growth being experienced by the field. The development of a series or canon of books in the emerging profession of event management marks a new and major milestone in an ancient tradition (celebrating) and a modern profession (event management).

The first edition of this book was entitled *Special Events: The Art and Science of Celebration.* This title reflected the ritual and ceremonies, as well as the emerging technologies associated with this field. The second edition approached the field from a business standpoint, and the title became *Special Events: The Best Practices in Modern Event Management.* However, the third edition has now addressed the major issue of the twenty-first century, and that is the global environment in which events are now conducted. Therefore, the new subtitle is *Twenty-First Century Global Event Management.*

In the preceding edition I noted that the profession was experiencing dramatic growth and a move toward standardization through professional certification the Certified Special Events Professional [CSEP]) program sponsored by the International Special Events Society). This growth has continued and even escalated, giving further evidence of the need for an expanding body of knowledge. Examples of this growth are the George Washington University (GWU) Event Management Certificate and master's degree programs. In the second edition of this book I noted that GWU's program enrolled 200 students annually. Now, only three years later, GWU educates more than 4,000 professional event managers annually. The new subtitle of this book, *Twenty-First Century Global Event Management,* also reflects how the profession (and, some would argue, all professions) is changing. Today, GWU's Event Management Program enrolls students from more than thirty different countries, and graduates hold distinguished and important positions around the world.

The future is bright indeed for event managers equipped with the essential tools of experience and education. For the first time since the early development of the profession, classified advertisements appear regularly in major daily newspapers seeking event managers. To further assist employers, event management headhunting agencies recruit and match meeting planners and event managers with employers. For the first time in the history of the profession, event management is being formally recognized as something that is valuable and unique and that is desirable as a career.

# A Bright Future for Event Managers

The future of the event management profession is ripe with promise. This is due to several factors. First, the growth in two-income families has propelled growth in the service industry. In record numbers, husbands and wives are turning to event managers to handle the details of their social life-cycle events. Second, the United States has become a nation of specialists. Those with specialized training, such as event management, are in demand by people and organizations that require specific expertise. As the event management profession grows through education, people employed as event managers will be in greater demand. Finally, the event management profession incorporates multitasking skills that form a generic management base. For example, event managers must be marketing, human resource, and financial specialists to produce effective events successfully on a continuous basis. Those trained in this field are able to use these highly portable skills to succeed in other professions, such as public relations or general business, where event management may fall under the category of "other duties assigned." As the economy continues to be unpredictable and the labor force reinvents itself on a daily basis, event managers are well positioned to anticipate and even prosper from these changes. A 1995 article in *M & C Magazine* described how, due to layoffs or downsizing, many traditional meeting planners were using their meeting planning skills in other fields to earn new income. Event managers are even better positioned, as they are more broadly trained than meeting planners and this training and experience will enable them to succeed more quickly in locating a new position if required.

According to the Public Relations Society of America (PRSA), more than 150,000 people practice public relations. Event management, according to PRSA, is one of the fastest-growing and most important trends in this modern profession. Public relations is a discipline that grew out of journalism and psychology. Although well trained in writing and research, few of its current practitioners have event management training, and this means new opportunities for trained event managers.

Related profession is represented by the 12,000 television and radio stations in the United States. According to the National Association of Broadcasters (NAB), the majority of these stations have one or more people responsible for live station promotions. These events are usually managed by those with a marketing background but little or no logistics experience. Once again, this means opportunities for you in this expanding field.

In my own profession of higher education there are more than 3,000 institutions, and each produces numerous events, ranging from convocation to commencement. Each university or college has at least one person or many people who produce events full time and many more who are involved part time.

# The Challenge of Change

The multitude of changes that took place in the special events community during the recession of the late 1980s and early 1990s can be grouped into three broad categories. First, the uncertain economic times had reduced spending for events, and firms that produced only mega or big ticket events were either out of business, merging, or slowly reinventing themselves. Second, technological changes, such as the rapid adoption of the facsimile, computer, modem, Internet, and other marvels of the modern age placed greater stress on the special events community to accelerate delivery of ideas and events themselves. Finally, competition had magnified as the special events field turned from a local business into a global one, and through downsizing, literally hundreds and perhaps even thousands of former event professionals working for corporations and government agencies were now freelancing and competing with the more established firms.

These three trends—economic uncertainty, rapid technological advancement, and increased competition—produced a major paradigm shift within the event industry. This shift occurred during the mid-1980s as the event industry was feeling overly confident and expanded rapidly. Now the industry was in an era of economic uncertainty, technological change, and escalating competition and did not know how to cope or plan. This period, reflected by an uncharted course within and outside the industry, is where I began my research to provide tools that would not only expand but also sustain this industry and help it meet the challenges ahead. The paradigm had shifted from an unformed group of professions known as special events personnel into an emerging discipline encompassing many professions known as *event management*.

These professions are now required to prepare for the social, economic, and political challenges that confront established professions, such as medicine, accounting, and law. Event management has moved from infancy to adolescence and is now entering adulthood. In business terms, it has moved from birth to growth to maturity and now faces complacency, which could be followed by decline or by reinvention and sustained growth through education and strategic planning. The latter is what this book aims to do with your commitment as a professional event manager.

# How These Trends Affect You

The growth in the rapidly emerging discipline of event management has been unprecedented during the last 50 years and has certainly accelerated during this decade. Those event managers who respond to challenging economic times with sound financial practices will produce consistently profitable events. Those event managers who anticipate and adapt emerging technologies to support their emerging discipline will certainly produce more efficient and perhaps more profitable events. Those event managers who set quality standards and find the right market niche will help ensure that competition is kept in check. These three trends—economic uncertainty, rapid technological advancement, and increased competition—are *positive* signs for event managers, which is why this book is essential for your career and business. The first of these trends represents a unique opportunity to reinvent or perhaps for the first time actually define a profession. Second, these trends provide us with unparalleled technological innovations to produce more efficient, higher quality, and more profitable events. Finally, growing competition allows us to improve and focus on individual strengths through serving niche markets. These three trends and the paradigm shift they form provide you with an exciting platform from which to relaunch or build your career.

# Under Construction: A Blueprint for the Professional Career

All careers are constantly under construction. However, the more successful careers, including event management, follow a general blueprint to match actions to the final product. Although some careers happen by accident, most are the result of a passion for a specific type of work, training, practice, professional networking, and that most ephemeral of experiences—timing.

My definition of a perfect job is to find something you like to do so much that you would do it for nothing. Once you have found this type of job, the next challenge is to find someone to pay you to do it. Event management is exactly this type of profession. This passion for helping people celebrate runs deep among serious event managers. Some even see their work as part ministry rather than solely as a commercial profession.

# Education: Your Unique Journey

To fully realize the potential of this paradigm shift, you must begin your own unique journey. This book is the first step in a continuous educational process that you and millions of others are embarking on as businesses reinvent themselves at the speed of light. The changes identified in each field require skilled managers, marketers, and researchers with state-of-the-art and science tools. Only through continuous education can you make sure that you remain sharp enough to make your dreams come true.

> *Two woodsmen decided to engage in a competition to see who could be first to chop down two mighty trees. At the appointed time one woodsman began to chop furiously, swinging the axe forcefully against the large tree. After several minutes the woodsman glanced over to the other woodsman and noticed that he was sitting against the tree cradling his axe. The first woodsman wiped the sweat from his brow and walked over to his challenger and asked why he was sitting down. "I am taking time to sharpen my axe," said the wise challenger. One hour later the first woodsman was still furiously wielding his axe as he heard the sound "Timber!" and watched as the second woodsman felled his tree. Is there any doubt how the second woodsman won this competition?*

Sharpening your skills through participation in professional organizations, attending educational programs, and networking with your peers is extremely important. This importance can be translated into bottom-line results. According to the U.S. Bureau of the Census, the more you learn, the more you will earn. This is reflected among event managers whose educational attainments are significantly better than those of the average public, and perhaps as a result their incomes are significantly greater as well.

The findings in a 1999 study of members of the International Special Events Society (ISES) showed that event managers now earn between $25,000 and $100,000 as compared with a median U.S. salary of approximately $23,000. More than one-third of U.S. event managers earn between $50,000 and $100,000. Correspondingly, the majority of event managers has earned baccalaureate degrees, and more than 20 percent has earned graduate degrees as well. The baccalaureate diplomas ranged from advertising to zoology. However, nearly 25 percent have degrees in business administration, demonstrating the importance of a solid grounding in this discipline. Noticeably absent were degrees in event management. Through specialization in this profession, you literally have the same opportunities that physicians, attorneys, accountants, and other professions enjoyed over a century ago. The major difference is that these traditional professions were composed solely of males; and it required decades before women were admitted or given even marginal respect. By contrast, the event management profession was an equal opportunity career from the beginning.

# Global Opportunities

There are numerous global business opportunities for event managers. Traditionally, a client develops close rapport with his or her event manager. Simultaneously, the event manager develops expertise into the client's organizational culture, including the key employees who compose the decision-making core. Therefore, it is only natural that when an event held this year in New York is held the following year in New Mexico or even Norway, the event manager will be asked to travel to that destination to maintain continuity. This important organizational or institutional memory is an important asset for event managers to develop.

Another asset that must be developed for the global marketplace is an understanding of the cultural, economic, and political nuances of each destination where an event is being held. Members of the International Congress and Convention Association (ICCA) told me that an event manager who wants to do business in Europe, Asia, or Latin America needs to spend significant time learning the business practices and cultures of each country. Learning the language is considerably easier than understanding why people in that country make certain decisions and how those decisions may be influenced positively or negatively by the actions of the event manager.

According to the members of ICCA, event managers who are planning global careers should speak and write one or more languages in addition to English. The most popular languages are French, Spanish, and German. As the Pacific Rim economy continues to develop, Japanese and Mandarin Chinese will be added to this list. Furthermore, it was suggested by ICCA members that global event managers must allow sufficient time to develop relationships with their global trading partners, as these contacts develop slowly and cannot be rushed. The goal is to establish a long-term partnership built on mutual trust.

# Event Management: A Multidisciplinary Profession

The most interesting finding of the ISES study was that only 50 percent of event managers' work time was invested in the management of events. This explains the multidisciplinary nature of this emerging discipline. Whether you currently are an administrative assistant or the chief executive officer (CEO), chances are that at some time you have had to organize a meeting or other event. You probably used transferable management skills to accomplish this project. However, you soon realized that specialized training was also needed to produce an effective event. Many students who apply for admission to event management programs tell me that although managing events was but one of their job responsibilities, it was the one they most enjoyed. Therefore, they are seeking further training in this profession to improve their chances for long-term success doing something they truly enjoy. In learning these highly portable skill sets, they are simultaneously increasing their opportunities for long-term career success in many other professions as well.

As I counsel these students I realize that the emerging discipline identified in this book as the profession of event management is part of a much larger movement. Millions of career professionals and those just starting their careers are in search of work that is meaningful, financially rewarding, and, yes, fun. With the elimination of long-term security in most jobs, workers are now in search of a career path that satisfies deeper longings in addition to financial compensation. They are turning to event management because it allows them to combine people, travel, creativity, and the tangible reward of seeing a project through to completion into a satisfying and rewarding career. In their eyes I see the excitement of real new opportunities and feel their determination to succeed in this profession. Through your efforts and those of thousands of others, humankind's oldest tradition is being transformed rapidly into the modern profession known as event management.

The Profile of Event Management study has been conducted for more than six years, and it has identified some important trends that will be analyzed further in this book.

- Event managers are committed to continuing education, with more than 85 percent stating that they will continue their education throughout their careers.
- The most frequent type of continuing education will be industry seminars (held at conventions). However, nearly 10 percent will enroll in formal certificate programs that lead to professional certification.
- Event managers are more technologically savvy than ever before. In the last two years, Internet use has grown from 50 percent to more than 80 percent.
- Event managers earn more, with nearly 30 percent earning between $50,000 and $100,000.
- Women continue to outnumber men and earn more at all economic levels except $100,000 and above, where they earn only 5 percent less than men in this category. By contrast, in related but narrow professions, such as meeting planning, women event planners continue to earn 15 percent less than men, although they outnumber men significantly.
- Event managers produce corporate human resource events more frequently than other types of events. This may be due to the demand for high quality employees during a period of full employment in North America. Corporate human resource and corporate marketing events account for over one-third of events produced by professional event managers.

Events are also a major catalyst for tourism in North America. According to the Travel Industry Association (TIA), 31 million U.S. adults attended a festival while on a trip away from home. The majority of tourists attended an arts or music festival, and their household incomes were significantly higher than those of other U.S. travelers. Dr. Colleen May of the Ohio Department of Tourism reports that 3,150,000 persons attended special events in Ohio in 1999. In fact, May reports that special events are the leading motivator for Ohio day-trip tourists and overnight travelers.

The TIA study reported that more than one-fifth of all U.S. adults attended a festival while on a trip away from home and that event travelers differ from all U.S. travelers in a number of ways. First, event travelers traditionally travel as families, are college graduates, and have two or more wage earners in the household. Perhaps most important is that persons who attend events earn significantly more ($53,000 versus $47,000) than other types of travelers in the United States. Therefore, family events, such as arts or music, ethnic, folk or heritage, county or state fair, parade, food festival, religious festival, or other types, attract better educated, higher-income families to destinations.

These and other findings are explored in further detail in this book. Six years of research coupled with the case studies included in the new third edition provide a new and improved resource to help you rapidly advance your career. During these six years of research and despite the numerous changes in the field, one thing has remained constant, as reflected in the title of the book. The term *special events* continues to represent extraordinary moments in our lives. The third edition retains the original title but issues a new challenge to practitioners. Through this book you may indeed have an impact on global advancement of this field in the twenty-first century.

Therefore, I welcome you to the third edition of *Special Events* as together we enter an unprecedented period of growth and change for the profession. Just as Mama welcomed Aunt Bertha with her culinary treasures, I welcome you to Chapter 1 of *Special Events: Twenty-First Century Global Event Management,* as together we sample, taste, and treasure new experiences rooted in old traditions.

*Dr. Joe Goldblatt, CSEP*

# Acknowledgments

My extended global event management family helped ensure that the third edition of *Special Events* would reflect the many threads within the profession. From the warm description of my celebration roots (in the *Foreword* to the book) to the hundreds of technical details that were researched, verified, checked, and rechecked by scholars in the field, this book is the result of many hearts and many hands.

The visionary who first identified the significant growth of this profession and accepted the challenge of providing education for its practitioners and students is JoAnna Turtletaub, senior editor of John Wiley & Sons, Inc. Ms. Turtletaub is indominable, inspirational, and incomparable in her zeal for excellence in professional publishing. Her commitment to this profession is valued by its members around the world.

A few years ago a young woman walked into my office without an appointment and announced that she had come all the way from Latvia to see me. She became one of my brightest students and most trusted advisors. Her talent is far greater than her years, and I am extremely grateful that she agreed to serve as my coordinating editor for this edition of *Special Events.* Julia Schiptsova, the contributing editor of this third edition, brought greater intellectual rigor, commanding arguments, and a global perspective to this book. It is because of her intellectual talent that this book rises to a new level in its third incarnation. I am most grateful for her charm, hard work, and even bullying me from time to time to ensure the book would achieve the success that she knew was possible.

Ms. Schiptsova was assisted and ably supported by an extremely talented person whose intellectual skills and business savvy improved the book greatly. I offer my sincere thanks to Alexey Khripunov for his many contributions to this volume. The appendixes were checked, researched, and compiled by Jill Zeigenfus. She is a future leader in the profession.

My family allowed me the precious hours to do what I most enjoy, sharing ideas with others, in order that I could revise the book for a new generation of readers. I am truly blessed to have been given a wonderful wife, Nancy, and two fine sons, Max and Sam. These gifts grow more valuable every day, and I am grateful that they somehow manage to find my activities interesting and important. My family is the support system for my traditions, rituals, and ceremonies, and it is because of them and through them that I am able to write this and other books.

The exquisite photographs that illustrate the book are the work of Monica Vidal, a great photographic artist. The special events industry is fortunate to benefit from the talent of this gifted chronicler of our profession.

The foreword was lovingly written by an award-winning journalist, Eva Barkoff. She is well acquainted with the author as she is my cousin with whom I share thousands of family memories of celebration.

A hardworking, extremely bright, and dedicated group of students from The George Washington University Event Management Program contributed numerous hours of research to produce the book: Cassaundra Brown, Danika Foster, Maggie Gallant, Arnold Guanko, Youn Joo Han, Virginia Hoekenga, Stacey Martin, Holly Persinger, Jerra Quinton, Alyson Rappaport, Jessica Soren, and Jill Zeigenfus. These young men and women represent a bright future for the event management profession, and I truly look forward to their further achievements in the years to come.

Finally, the following people contributed their ideas, inspiration, and support to help Julia and me improve the third edition of *Special Events*. To them, we raise our cup in a loyal toast of gratitude and friendship.

| | | |
|---|---|---|
| Eva Barkoff | Linda Higgison | Jason Quinn |
| Jaclyn Bernstein | Robert Hultsmeyer | Tom Rossi |
| Dr. John Bowen | Bertha Jacob, deceased | Dr. Frank Satterthwaite |
| Dr. Clif Boyle | Sam Jacob, deceased | Dr. Irv Scheider |
| Tatiana Chernauska | Johnson & Wales | Dr. Oleg Schiptsov |
| Sara and Frank Cohen | University | Patti Shock |
| Alice Conway | Glenn Kasofsky | Carolina Sicilia |
| Dr. Joanne Crossman | Dr. Richard Kosh | Dr. Lisa Sisco |
| Sally Elstrod | Leah and Stephen | Robert Sivek |
| Linda Faulkner | Lahasky | Dr. Doug Smith |
| Keven Fountain, J.D. | Louise Lynch | Mary Ellen Smith |
| Max Darwin Goldblatt | Nancy Lynner | Dr. Wright K. Smith |
| Max Goldblatt, deceased | Dr. Patt Manheim | Frank Supovitz |
| Rosa Goldblatt, | Lena Malouf | The George Washington |
| deceased | Robert J. Miller | University |
| Sam deBlanc Goldblatt | Dr. Bill Millett | Stephen Joel |
| Gary Gray | Doris Morales | Trachtenberg |
| Dr. Joseph Arthur | Kathy Nelson | Dr. Brunetta Wolfman |
| Greenberg | Leah Pointer, deceased | Dr. John Yena |
| Earl Hargrove, Jr. | Dr. Alexander | |
| Jack Hartzman | Portnyagin | |
| Dr. Donald E. Hawkins | Catherine H. Price | |

# Special Events

# Theory of Event Management

# CHAPTER 1

# Welcome to Twenty-First-Century Global Event Management

**IN THIS CHAPTER YOU WILL LEARN HOW TO:**

- Recognize and understand the demographic changes affecting global event management growth
- Utilize the psychographic changes affecting event length, purpose, and outcomes to improve performance
- Identify new and emerging career opportunities
- Understand why education has become the most important factor in event management growth
- Identify industry certification programs
- Advance your career throughout the twenty-first century

The professional event management host knows that the word "Welcome!" is an essential part of the guest experience at any event. Therefore, I warmly welcome you to the third edition of *Special Events*. However, in the global spirit of the third edition, allow me to add the following:

- Benvenuto! (Italian)
- Bienvenidos! (Spanish)
- Bien venue! (French)
- Dobro pozhalovat! (Russian)
- Fun ying! (Cantonese Chinese)
- G'day! (Australian English)
- Hos geldin! (Turkish)
- Huan ying! (Mandarin Chinese)
- Kali meta! (Greek)
- Kwaribu! (Swahili)
- Laipni ludzam! (Latvian)
- Sabah al kher! (Arabic)
- Shalom! (Hebrew)
- Urseo oh se yo! (Korean)
- Velkomst! (Danish)
- Willkommen! (German)
- Youkoso! (Japanese)

With the rapid development of the Internet, the world as we once knew it vanished quickly. The local or regional nature of the event management business was replaced with lightning speed by global connections throughout the world. I discovered this while seated at my home computer receiving e-mail messages from distant lands. "Thanks for your excellent book—it changed my perspective about the profession," wrote one industry member from the Far East. These types of messages were quickly followed by requests for information and ultimately, offers to fly me to lands that I had only read about prior to the development of the Internet. Indeed, the Internet has had the same (or perhaps a greater) influence as that of Gutenberg's printing press. The World Wide Web has woven the event management profession together into a new global community. As a result of this new "web," each of us now has far greater opportunities for career and business development than we previously imagined or aspired.

During the past decade (since the first edition of *Special Events*) the field of event management has seen numerous changes, and Table 1-1 summarizes

**Table 1-1**  A Decade of Change

| Event Aspect | From: | To: |
|---|---|---|
| Event organization | Amateur | Professional |
| Event guests | Younger | Older |
| Event technology | Incidental | Integral |
| Event markets | Local | Global |
| Event education | Nonessential | Essential |
| Event evaluation | Narrow | Comprehensive |

these paradigm shifts. These six aspects of the profession reflect how the event management field has experienced sweeping change in the past decade. The letters above the massive doors to the National Archives in Washington, DC announce "Where past is prologue." And so it is with our profession of event management. To go forward, we must first reflect on the historical roots of a field of study.

# From Special Events to Event Management

The term *special events* may have first been used at what is often described as the "happiest place on earth." In 1955, when Walt Disney opened Disneyland in Anaheim, California, he turned to one of his imagineers, Robert Jani, and asked him to help solve a big problem. Each day at 5:00 P.M., thousands of people, in fact almost 90 percent of the guests, would leave the park. The problem with this mass exodus was that Walt's happiest place on earth remained open until 10:00 P.M. This meant that he had to support a payroll of thousands of workers, utilities, and other expenses for five hours each day with no income.

To correct this problem, Robert Jani, then director of public relations for Disneyland and later the owner of one of the most successful event management production companies in the world, Robert F. Jani Productions, proposed the creation of a nightly parade that he dubbed the "Main Street Electric Parade." Dozens of floats with thousands of miniature lights would nightly glide down Main Street, delighting thousands of guests who remained to enjoy the spectacle. This technique is used today in all Disney parks, with perhaps the best example at Epcot, where a major spectacular is staged every night. According to the producers, this spectacle results in millions of dollars of increased spending annually.

One of the members of the media turned to Robert Jani during the early days of the Main Street Electric Parade and asked, "What do you call that program?" Jani replied, "A special event." "A special event, what's that?" the reporter asked. Jani thoughtfully answered with what may be the simplest and best definition of a *special event:* A special event is that which is different from a normal day of living. According to Jani, nowhere on earth does a parade appear on the main street every night of the year. Only at Disneyland, where special events are researched, designed, planned, managed, coordinated, and evaluated, does this seemingly spontaneous program take place every night. Jani, who would later produce National Football League Super Bowl half-time spectaculars as well as the legendary Radio City Music Hall Christmas Show, among many other unique events, was a man whose motto was "Dream big dreams and aim high."

## ANTHROPOLOGICAL BEGINNINGS

Some 35 years later in the first edition of this book, I defined *special events* as a unique moment in time celebrated with ceremony and ritual to satisfy specific needs. My definition emerged from that of anthropologist Victor Turner, who wrote: "Every human society celebrates with ceremony and ritual its joys, sorrows, and triumphs." According to Turner and other researchers who I had studied in my exploration of anthropology, ceremony and ritual were important factors in the design, planning, management, and coordination of special events.

Five years later, after interviewing nearly 150 experts in special event management for my first book, I discovered that while special events represents many professions, one person is always at the helm of this large vessel. That person is the *event manager.*

# Growth Opportunities

Only four decades ago, when an orchestra was needed to provide music for a wedding or social event, one consulted an orchestra leader. Very often, the orchestra leader would provide references for additional talent to enhance the event. Mike Lanin, president of Howard Lanin Productions of New York City, tells the story of a meeting his father, Howard Lanin, the renowned society maestro, had with a client in Philadelphia during the late 1920s. Having already asked Lanin to provide music for her daughter's coming-out party being held at the Bellvue-Stratford, the client asked that he provide decor as well. When Lanin asked how much the client would like to spend, the client replied, "Just make it lovely, Howard—just make it lovely." Lanin immediately realized that to make this huge ballroom "lovely" might require an investment of five figures. With inflation, the cost of such an undertaking today would well exceed six figures. But Lanin was fortunate to have earned his client's total trust. Without further discussion, the orchestra leader and decorator went to work. Few clients of any era would offer such an unlimited budget. But more and more often, special events professionals such as the Lanins are being asked to provide more diversified services. And although orchestra leaders may have been comfortable recommending decorations and other services and products for social events three decades ago, they and others with specific areas of expertise found that when it came to events designed for advertising and public relations opportunities, they required specialized assistance.

Public relations is a proud ancestor of the celebrations industry. Less than 50 years ago, the modern profession of public relations and advertising became an accepted tool in American commerce. When a corporation wished to introduce a new product, increase sales, or motivate its employees, its corporate leaders turned to public relations and advertising professionals to design a plan. Today, the celebrations industry includes tens of thousands of hard-working professionals, who for the first time in the industry's history are truly working together to offer their clients the excellent services and products they deserve. As an example of the growth of event management in the public relations field, consider this comment from the first person in the United States to receive a master's degree in public relations, Carol Hills of Boston University: "My students are extremely interested in events. They recognize that public relations and events are inseparable. Event management is certainly a growth area in public relations practice."

According to the International Council of Shopping Centers (ICSC) in New York, marketing directors who produce events for local and regional shopping centers can earn in the high five figures. Marketing professionals have recognized the need for specialized training and the benefits of certification within their industry. Events help attract and influence consumers to purchase specific products and services from small retail stores up to major regional shopping centers with hundreds of shops. In this age of entrepreneurism, the creation of new business is far greater than the growth of established firms. With each new business created, there is a new opportunity to celebrate through a grand opening or other special event. There are over 1 million new businesses created annually in the United States that may require an event manager to produce an opening celebration.

An *event manager* is a person responsible for *researching, designing, planning, coordinating,* and *evaluating* events. You will learn about each of these phases in the pages to come. However, the logical question one may ask is: What is the event management profession?

# The Event Management Profession

*Event management* is a profession that requires public assembly for the purpose of *celebration, education, marketing,* and *reunion.* Each of these overarching activities is encompassed by the profession of event management.

...be argued that like tourism, event management is actually ...y industries, increasingly as data are gathered and scientific ... becomes more apparent that event management represents ...nowledge.

...xperts in the field of professional certification, all profes-...ed by three unique characteristics: (1) the profession must ... of knowledge, (2) the profession typically has voluntary ... result in certification, and (3) the profession has an ac-...uct or ethics. The profession of event management meets ...ations.

...explore further the definition of event management. The term *public assembly* means events managed by professionals who typically bring people together for a purpose. Although one person can certainly hold an event by himself or herself, arguably it will not have the complexities of an event with 10 or 10,000 people. Therefore, the size and type of group will determine the level of skills required by a professional event manager.

The next key word is *purpose.* In daily lives events take place spontaneously, and as a result are sometimes not orderly, effective, or on schedule. However, professional event managers begin with a specific purpose in mind and direct all activities toward achieving this purpose. Event managers are purposeful about their work.

The third and final key component consists of the four activities that represent these purposes: *celebration, education, marketing,* and *reunion.*

## CELEBRATION

Celebration is characterized by festivities ranging from fairs and festivals to social life-cycle events. Although the term *celebration* can also be applied to education, marketing, and reunion events, it serves to encompass all aspects of human life where events are held for the purpose of celebration.

When one hears the word *celebration,* an image of fireworks or other festivities typically is imagined. In fact, the word *celebration* is derived from the Latin word *celebrate,* meaning "to honor." Another commonly accepted definition is "to perform," as in a ritual. Therefore, celebrations usually refer to official or festive functions such as parades, civic events, festivals, religious observances, political events, bar and bas mitzvahs, weddings, anniversaries, and other events tied to a person's or organization's life cycle or of historical importance.

## EDUCATION

From the first event in kindergarten or preschool to meetings and conferences where many adults receive continuing education throughout their entire adult life, educational events mark, deliver, test, and support growth for all human beings. This growth may be social, such as the high school prom, or it may be professional, such as a certification program. Regardless of the purpose, a public assembly is either primarily or secondarily educationally related.

The term *educate* is also derived from Latin; the term *educate* means to "lead out." Through education events, event managers lead out new ideas, emotions, and actions that improve society. Examples of education events include convocations, commencements, alumni events, training at a corporation, meetings and conferences with specific educational content, and a fairly new activity known as *edutainment.* Edutainment results from the use of entertainment devices (such as singers and dancers) to present educational concepts. Through entertainment, guests may know, comprehend, apply (through audience participation), analyze, and even evaluate specific subject matter. It may be used to lead out new ideas to improve productivity.

## MARKETING

Event marketing, according to *Advertising Age,* is now an intrinsic part of any marketing plan. Along with advertising, public relations, and promotions, events serve to create awareness and persuade prospects to purchase goods and services. These events may be private, such as the launch of a new automobile before dealers or the public, as in Microsoft's Windows 95 program. Retailers have historically used events to drive sales, and now other types of businesses are realizing that face-to-face events are an effective way to satisfy sales goals. The appearance of soap opera stars at a shopping center is an example of many types of promotions used to attract customers to promote sales.

## REUNION

When human beings reunite for the purposes of remembrance, rekindling friendships, or simply rebonding as a group, they are conducting a reunion activity. Reunion activities are present in all the event management subfields because once the initial event is successful, there may be a desire to reunite. The reunion activity is so symbolic in the American system that President Bill Clinton used this theme for his inaugural activities.

# Event Management Subfields

The desire and need to celebrate are unique characteristics that make us human. The humorist Will Rogers is reported to have said: "Man is the only animal that blushes . . . or needs to!" Human beings are the only animals that celebrate, and this not only separates us from the lower forms but perhaps raises us to a transcendent or even spiritual level. The growth of event management subfields certainly reflects this extraordinary capability of celebration to transform humans and entire industries.

As noted earlier, anthropology historically has recognized a four-field approach to this established discipline. However, the profession of event management is encompassed by many specialized fields: *advertising, attractions, broadcasting, civic, corporate, exposition, fairs, festivals, government, hospitality, meetings, museums, retail,* and *tourism.* Event managers may specialize in any of these fields; however, rarely is an event manager expert in more than a few of these specializations. For example, a director of event management for a zoological society may plan events for the zoo, and some of those events may involve retail promotions. Therefore, a knowledge of education and marketing as well as administration and risk management is important.

These subfields are not scientifically categorized—there are many linkages between them. However, the following list provides an overview into the possibilities for event managers as they seek to chart their future course of study. Once trained in the fundamentals of event management, event managers must specialize or concentrate their studies in one or two event subfields. By concentrating in two areas, event managers are further protected from a downturn in a specific market segment, as they have been trained in two different subfields. For example, if association meeting planners suddenly realized that they were no longer in demand, due to outsourcing, cross-training in corporate event management may allow them to make a smooth transition to this new field. Use the following descriptions of subfields as a guide to focus your market or future employment options.

## CIVIC EVENTS

Beginning with the U.S. bicentennial celebration in 1976 and continuing with the individual centennial, sesquicentennial, and bicentennials of hundreds of towns and cities, Americans have created more events than at any other time in the history of the republic. In both Europe and Asia, celebration is rooted in long-standing religious, cultural, and ritual traditions. The United States has not only blended the traditions of other cultures but has created its own unique events, such as the annual Doo-Dah Parade in Pasadena, California. Anyone and everyone can participate in this event, and they do. There is a riding lawn mower brigade, a precision briefcase squad, and other equally unusual entries. As the United States matures, its celebrations will continue to develop into authentic made-in-the-U.S.A. events.

## EXPOSITIONS

Closely related to fairs and festivals is the exposition. Although divided into two categories—public and private—the exposition has historically been a place where retailers meet wholesalers or suppliers introduce their goods and services to buyers. Some marketing analysts have suggested that it is the most cost-effective way to achieve sales, as people who enter the exposition booth are more qualified to buy than is a typical sales suspect. Furthermore, the exposition booth allows, as do all events, a multisensory experience which influences customers to make a positive buying decision. A major shift in this field has been to turn the trade show or exposition into a live multisensory, event with educational and entertainment programs being offered in the various booths. Like many others, this field is growing. Although some smaller trade shows have consolidated with larger ones, just as many or perhaps more shows are being created each year. This spells opportunity for savvy event marketers who wish to benefit from this lucrative field.

## FAIRS AND FESTIVALS

Just as in ancient times, people assembled in the marketplace to conduct business, commercial as well as religious influences have factored into the development of today's festivals, fairs, and public events. Whether a religious festival in India or a music festival in the United States, each is a public community event symbolized by a kaleidoscope of experiences that finds meaning through the lives of the participants. This kaleidoscope is comprised of performances, arts and crafts demonstrations, and other media that bring meaning to the lives of participants and spectators.

These festivals and fairs have shown tremendous growth as small and large towns seek tourism dollars through such short-term events. Some communities use these events to boost tourism during the slow or off-season, and others focus primarily on weekends to appeal to leisure travelers. Regardless of the reason, fairs (often not-for-profit but with commercial opportunities) and festivals (primarily not-for-profit events) provide unlimited opportunities for organizations to celebrate their culture while providing deep meaning for those who participate and attend.

## HALLMARK EVENTS

The growth of the Olympic Games is but one example of how hallmark events have grown in both size and volume during the past decade. From America's Cup to Hands Across America to the centennial celebration of the Statue of Liberty, the 1980s were a period of sustained growth for such mega-events. Although television certainly helped propel this growth, the positive impact of tourism dollars has largely driven the development of these events. Ironically, the world's fair movement appears to have ebbed, perhaps due to the fact that the inventions that previous world's fairs showcased (space travel, computers, teleconferencing) have become commonplace and there is no need to offer further predictions because these supposedly future happenings actually occurred before the fairs opened. This provides an opportunity to reinvent, revive, and perhaps sustain this hallmark event.

## HOSPITALITY

In the hospitality industry, hotels throughout the world are expanding their business interests from merely renting rooms and selling food and beverages to actually planning events. Nashville's Opryland Hotel may have been the first to create a department for special events as a profit center for the corporation. They were followed by Hyatt Hotels Regency Productions, and now other major hotel chains, such as Marriott, are exploring ways to move from fulfilling to actually planning and profiting from events.

## MEETINGS AND CONFERENCES

The Convention Industry Council, an organization that represents over two dozen organizations in the meeting, conference, and exposition industries, states that the annual contribution to the U.S. economy by these industries is over $80 billion. Since widespread use of the jet airplane in the 1950s, meetings and conferences have multiplied by the thousands as attendees jet in and out of cities for three- and four-day events. These events are primarily educational seminars that provide networking opportunities for both association members and corporate employees. Whether a corporate or association event, the globalization of the economy has produced significant growth in international meetings, and as a result, event managers are now traveling constantly both domestically and internationally.

## RETAIL EVENTS

From the earliest days of the markets of ancient times, sellers have used promotions and events to attract buyers and drive sales. The paradigm has shifted in this subindustry from the early 1960s and 1970s, when retailers depended on single-day events to attract thousands of consumers to their stores. Soap opera stars, sports celebrities, and even live cartoon characters during a Saturday appearance could increase traffic, and in some cases sales as well. Today, retailers are much more savvy and rely on marketing research to design long-range promotional events that use an integrated approach, combining a live event with advertising, publicity, and promotions. They are discovering that cause marketing, such as aligning a product with a worthy charity or important social issue (e.g., education), is a better way to build a loyal customer base and improve sales. This shift from short-term quick events to long-term integrated event marketing is a major change in this subindustry.

## SOCIAL LIFE-CYCLE EVENTS

Bar and bas mitzvahs, weddings, golden wedding anniversaries, and other events that mark the passage of time with a milestone celebration are growing for two important reasons. As the age of Americans rises due to improvements in health care, there will be many more opportunities to celebrate. Only a few years ago a fiftieth wedding anniversary was a rare event. Today, most retail greeting card stores sell golden anniversary greeting cards as but just one symbol of the growth of these events.

In the wedding industry it is not uncommon to host an event that lasts three or more days, including the actual ceremony. This is due to the great distances that families must travel to get together for these celebrations. It may also be due to the fast-paced world in which we live, and that often prevents families and friends from uniting for these milestones. Whatever the reason, social life-cycle events are growing in both length of days and size of budgets.

Funeral directors report that business is literally booming. Coupled with the increase in number of older U.S. citizens is the fact that many people are not affiliated with churches or synagogues. Therefore, at the time of death a neutral location is required for the final event. Most funeral chapels in the United States were constructed in the 1950s and now require expansion to accommodate the shift in population. New funeral homes are being constructed and older funeral homes are being expanded.

In the first edition of this book I predicted that in the not-too-distant future, funerals might be held in hotels to provide guests with overnight accommodations as well as to provide a location for social events. Now I predict that in some large metropolitan areas due to aging demographics, funeral home construction will be coupled with zoning decisions regarding hotel and motel accommodations to provide a total package for out-of-town guests. With the collapse of the traditional family of the 1950s and the proclivity that Americans have for relocation, it is not unreasonable to assume that weddings, funerals, and reunions are those events central to our lives for reconnecting with family and friends. Perhaps one growth opportunity for future event managers will be to design a total life-cycle event environment providing services, including accommodations, for these important events in a resort or leisure setting.

Social life-cycle events have always been important. While conducting focus group research at a local nursing home, a 97-year-old woman told me: "When you get to be my age, you forget almost everything. What you do remember are the important things: your daughter's wedding, your fiftieth wedding anniversary, and other milestones that make life so meaningful." Increasingly, due to limited time availability, people are turning to event managers to organize these important milestone events.

## SPORT EVENTS

One example of the growth in popularity in professional sports is the rapid development of sports hall of fame and museum complexes throughout the United States. The 1994 World Cup soccer craze generated excitement, visibility, and in some cases, significant revenue for numerous destinations throughout the United States. Before, during, or following the big game, events are used to attract, capture, and motivate spectators, regardless of the game's outcome, to keep supporting their favorite team. In fact, the line has been blurred between sport and entertainment, due largely to the proliferation of events such a pregame giveaways, postgame fireworks and musical shows, and even promotions such as trivia contests during the game.

## TOURISM

Since the U.S. bicentennial in 1976, when literally thousands of communities throughout the United States created celebrations, event tourism has become an important phenomenon. According to a study I conducted in 1994, those communities that do not have the facilities to attract the largest conventions are turning increasingly to event tourism as a means of putting heads in beds during the off-season and weekends. Whether it is in the form of arts and crafts shows, historical reenactments, music festivals, or other events that last anywhere from 1 to 10 days, Americans are celebrating more than ever before and profiting from event tourism. From taxpayers to political leaders to business leaders, more and more stakeholders are becoming invested in event tourism. According to a 1999 study by the Travel Industry Association of America, one-fifth of adults visited a special event (fair, festival, other) while on vacation.

# Stakeholders

Stakeholders are people or organizations who have invested in an event. For example, the stakeholders of a festival may include the board of directors, the political officials, the municipal staff, the participants (craftspeople), the utility companies, and others. The event manager must scan the event environment to identify both internal as well as external stakeholders. An internal stakeholder may be a member of the board, the professional staff of the organization, a guest, or other closely related person. External stakeholders may include media, municipal officials, city agencies, or others. A stakeholder does not have to invest money in an event to be considered for this role. Emotional, political, or personal interest in a cause is evidence of investment in an event.

# The Event Management Professional Model

From defining the profession, to identifying the principal activities conducted within this profession, to listing some of the subfields where event managers work, this is not intended to be a comprehensive analysis. Rather, it is a framework within which you can begin to see a pattern emerge. This pattern is reflected in Figure 1-1, a model that depicts the linkages between the definition, activities, subfields, and stakeholders. It will be useful to you as you begin or continue your studies in event management, as it provides a theoretical framework supporting the organization of this profession.

THE PROFESSION

EVENT MANAGEMENT

The function that requires human assembly for the purpose of
celebration, education, marketing, and reunion

⇓

THE PROFESSIONAL TITLE

EVENT MANAGER

The person responsible for researching, designing, planning,
coordinating, and evaluating an event

⇓

SUBFIELD SPECIALIZATION

Examples of subfields: civic events, conventions, expositions, fairs and festivals,
hallmark events, hospitality, incentive travel, meetings and conferences,
retail events, reunions, social life-cycle events, sport events, and tourism

⇓

STAKEHOLDERS

Individuals or organizations financially, politically,
emotionally, or personally invested in an event

**Figure 1-1**
Goldblatt Model for the Event Management Profession

# Change: The Only Constant
# in Event Management

A six-year study entitled *The Profile of Event Management* (Chicago, Illinois:
International Special Events Society, 1999) has identified many significant
changes in the event management profession. Many of these shifts were identified in Table 1-1; now let's explore these changes further and see how they
may affect your career.

## DEMOGRAPHIC CHANGE

Within the next decade, nearly 70 million Americans will turn 50 years of age.
As a result of the graying of America, not only will millions of Americans celebrate a major milestone (middle age) but event managers will be forced to rethink the types of events they design. For example, as Americans age it is likely
that they will experience more health problems, such as loss of hearing and

vision and restriction of movement. Therefore, event managers must respond to these changes with improved resources, such as large-type printed programs, infrared-assisted listening devices, and event ramps and handrails to accommodate persons with physical challenges. The good news is that as people age, so do their institutions, creating a multiplier effect for the number of celebrations that will be held. The other news is that event managers must anticipate the requirements the aging population will have and be prepared to adapt their event design to satisfy these emerging physical and psychological needs.

## PSYCHOGRAPHIC CHANGE

Tourism researchers have identified the adventurist or allocentric tourist as the fastest-growing market in leisure travel. This projection is further evidenced by the rapid growth in ecotourism programs throughout the world. In both developed and developing countries, event managers must rethink the approach to events to preserve the high-touch experience for guests. This need for high levels of stimulation may be a direct response to the decade-long fascination with the Internet, which is essentially a solitary endeavor. The Internet may have directly or indirectly created an even greater demand for high-touch, in-person, face-to-face events. By understanding the psychographic needs of event guests and providing high-touch experiences, event managers may in fact have greater opportunities for maximizing the outcomes that guests desire.

## CAREER OPPORTUNITIES

Table 1-2 lists 15 established event management careers. No one can determine accurately how many more careers may be added to this list in the near-, mid-, or long-term future. However, using the demographic and psychographic cues identified in this chapter, the event manager may begin to imagine what is most likely to develop in terms of future careers.

The aging population in North America will certainly require a strong health care system to provide a comfortable lifestyle. This growth in the field of health care will inevitably create new positions for event managers in tourism, recreation, leisure, and education, related directly to serving older people with programs tailored to their physical abilities and personal interests.

The rapid technological development we have experienced in the past decade will probably continue and even accelerate. Therefore, professional event managers must meet the technological challenges of the twenty-first century through a commitment to continuing education. As these new technology platforms emerge, event managers must improve their skills continually to meet these fierce challenges or risk being left behind as technology advances.

Will we see the emergence of an *eventologist,* one who combines high touch and high tech to provide a virtual and live event enabling the guest to achieve high levels of customization, speed, and service through appropriate technology and greater emphasis on satisfying the personal needs of each person? Although

**Table 1-2** Fifteen Event Management Positions and Background and Experience Typically Required

| Event Management Position | Background and Experience Typically Required |
|---|---|
| Attraction event manager | Organization, marketing, logistical, human relations, financial, negotiation |
| Catering director | Food and beverage coordination, organization, financial, supervisory, sales, negotiation |
| Civic event manager | Organization, legal and regulatory research ability, human relations, financial, marketing, logistical, negotiation |
| Convention service manager | Organization, supervisory, financial, logistical, human relations, negotiation |
| Family reunion manager | Human relations, marketing, financial, organization, supervisory, negotiation |
| Festival event manager | Organization, financial, marketing, volunteer coordination, supervisory, entertainment, cultural arts, negotiation |
| Fundraising event manager | Research, fundraising, proposal writing, marketing, human relations, volunteer coordination, financial |
| Political event manager | Affiliation with a cause or political party, volunteer coordination, financial, marketing, human relations, fundraising |
| Public relations event manager | Writing, organization, research, financial, marketing, human relations, public relations, logistical, negotiation |
| Retail event manager | Marketing, advertising, organization, financial, human relations, logistical, negotiation |
| School reunion event manager | Research, organization, financial, marketing, negotiation, volunteer coordination |
| Social life-cycle event manager | Human relations, counseling, organization, financial, negotiation |
| Sport event manager | General knowledge of sport, organization, financial, marketing, negotiation, volunteer coordination, supervisory |
| Tourism event manager | Organization, political savvy, financial, marketing, research |
| University/college event manager | Organization, financial, supervisory, marketing, logistical, human relations, negotiation |

we cannot predict with total accuracy what will occur one year from today, much less five years from this moment, we must be prepared by accepting responsibility for harnessing the new technologies to best serve event guests.

## GENDER OPPORTUNITIES

Although studies of gender in event management consistently indicate that females out number men in this profession, recent studies *(Profile of Event Management)* also indicate that more men are beginning to enter the profession. For a variety of reasons, it is essential that the profession attract both men and women.

In those fields where females have dominated (e.g., teaching, nursing) salaries have flattened. Historically, females have been significantly undervalued in the world of work as compared to male workers. In fact, in the meeting planning profession, females, according to the annual salary study of the American Society of Association Executives continue to earn 15% less than their male counterparts, despite the fact that they significantly outnumber males in the profession.

Males will continue to enter the profession, due to the rich array of career opportunities that await them and the lucrative salaries that are being established. However, to achieve long-term success, the profession must provide upward mobility for all workers. Upward mobility is tied only partially to compensation. Greater upward mobility specifically requires that as an event management employer, you must provide advancement, lifestyle, and training opportunities for event workers, to enable them to achieve professional growth within specific event organizations. Without these internal opportunities, event managers will continue to seek new employment and take with them the institutional memory and experience they have gained while working for your firm.

## EDUCATIONAL OPPORTUNITIES

When the second edition of *Special Events* was written in 1996, I identified 30 to 40 colleges and universities that offered courses, degrees, and certificates in event management–related studies. In a study commissioned in 1999 by the Council for Hospitality, Restaurant, and Institutional Education (CHRIE), I identified over 140 institutions of higher education that offer educational opportunities related to event management.

Finally, the technological advancement we have experienced is directly responsible for the contraction and consolidation of global markets. To ensure future success and career advancement, an event manager must embrace the global market as an opportunity rather than a challenge. Through research, focus, and sensitivity to cultural differences, the professional event manager will be able to reap infinite benefits from the new global economy. In this book, we provide a strategic plan for learning how to identify and conquer these markets to ensure further long-term personal and professional growth. Perhaps the fastest growth has been in the development and delivery of distance learning programs. At George Washington University, over 4000 annual registrations are received for the certificate program; however, the fastest-growing delivery system is for distance learning students in 24 countries throughout the world.

## CERTIFICATION

Historically, modern professions have used voluntary professional certification as a means to slow or discourage regulatory bodies (such as local and state governments) from creating licensing requirements. When a profession can demonstrate the ability to regulate itself effectively, government is less likely to interfere. The event management profession first addressed the issue of certification in 1988, when the International Special Events Society announced formation of the Certified Special Events Professional (CSEP) task force. This organization studied a wide variety of certification programs to determine which one would serve as a valid model for the event profession. Ultimately, the Canadian model emerged as the best template from which to construct the CSEP program.

The Canadian government, through the Alberta Tourism Education Council (ATEC), conducted an in-depth study that produced two vocational standards: event manager and event coordinator. ISES merged these two standards into a single comprehensive position entitled *event manager* and utilized the ATEC research to develop a body of knowledge for this new vocation. The four knowledge domains identified by ATEC and ratified by ISES are administration, coordination, marketing, and risk management.

This book is based on the CSEP certification program and provides an excellent study manual for the CSEP certification program. This book and the *International Dictionary of Event Management,* 2nd ed. (Wiley, NY, NY, 2000) are the major texts required to study successfully for the CSEP examination.

# Developing Your Career

Now that event management is emerging as a professional career, it is essential that you manage your growth carefully to sustain your development for many years to come. There are numerous challenges in developing any professional career, whether medicine, law, or event management. Identifying these challenges and developing a strategic plan to address these challenges is the most effective way to build long-term success. The four primary challenges that professional event managers encounter are time, finance, technology, and human resources. They are the four pillars upon which you will reconstruct or construct a successful career (see Figure 1-2). This chapter will help you transform these challenges into opportunities for professional growth as well as better understand the emerging resources available in this new profession.

## MASTERING YOURSELF

The first person to be managed is you. Your ability to organize, prioritize, supervise, and delegate to others is secondary to being able to manage your time and professional resources efficiently and effectively. Once you are sufficiently well managed, you will find that managing others is much easier. Managing yourself essentially involves setting personal and professional goals and then devising a strategic plan to achieve them. This involves making choices. For example, you may want to spend more time with your family, and that will

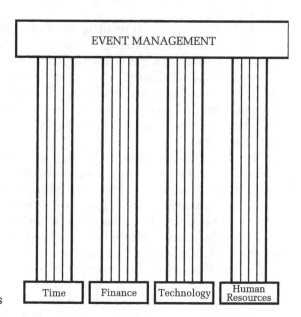

**Figure 1-2**
Four-Pillar Approach: Foundation for Success

determine in what field of event management you elect to specialize. Certain fields will rob you of time with your family and friends, especially as you are building your career; others will allow you to work a semiregular schedule. Association or corporate meeting planning may require that you work 9:00 A.M. to 5:00 P.M. for 40 weeks of the year and 7:00 A.M. to 10:00 P.M. or later during convention preparation and production. Hospitality event management positions, by contrast, may require long hours every day for weeks on end. After all, the primary resource of the event manager is time. It is the one commodity that once invested, is gone forever. Setting personal and professional goals has a direct correlation with the type of work you will perform as an event manager. Hopefully, the fruits of your labors will represent an excellent return on your investment.

## MASTERING TIME MANAGEMENT

One key element in effective time management is the ability to use your time effectively by distinguishing between what is urgent and what is important. Urgency is often the result of poor research and planning. Importance, however, results from a knowledge of priorities of time, resources, and the overarching goals of the event. I recognized this principle upon selling my business, when for the first time in my adult life I was able to distinguish between my personal and professional time. Too often, the event manager—one who usually loves what he or she is doing for a living (thereby distinguishing this person from most of the working population of the world)—combines personal and professional time to his or her detriment. In my own experience, I carefully analyzed the capacity for personal and professional time each week and learned that only 168 hours are available. Of these hours, 56 are invested in sleeping and 21 in eating, leaving 91 hours for work and personal commitments. For nearly 15 years I had used between 70 and 80 of these valuable hours for work-related activities, leaving only 10 or so per week for my family and myself. With this analysis complete, I set about matching my time to my new goals.

One of the reasons I sold my business was to spend more time with my family and improve myself both mentally and physically. Therefore, I realized that by working smarter instead of longer, I could accomplish in 50 hours the tasks that it had formerly taken me 25 percent more time to do. This new plan would allow me to spend additional time with my family and work toward achieving other personal goals that I had set.

Effective time management must begin with setting personal and professional priorities, especially as this profession is one with a high degree of burnout. Finding a healthy balance between the worlds of work, family, leisure, recreation, and spiritual pursuits is essential to your long-term success as an event manager. This book will not only help you find this balance but also show you how to integrate time management principles into every aspect of your event management professional career. This integration of time management principles will ultimately allow you more hours for recreation, leisure, and self-improvement, while providing increased earnings with fewer working hours. The following suggestions for event time management will help you develop an effective system suitable for your personal and professional style:

1. Budget your time and relate this budget directly to your financial and personal priorities. For example, if you value your family life, budget a prescribed period of time to be with your family each week.
2. Determine by an analysis of your overhead what your time is worth hourly. Remind yourself of the value of your time by placing a small sign with this amount on it near your telephone and condense extraneous phone calls and other activities that are not profit producing.
3. Make a list of tasks to complete the next day before you leave the office or go to bed. Include all telephone calls to be made in this list and carry it with you for ready reference. In the age of cellular communications, you can return calls from anywhere. As each task is completed, cross it off triumphantly. Uncompleted tasks should be moved to the next day's list.
4. Determine whether meetings are essential and the best method for communicating information. Many meetings may be conducted via telephone conference call rather than in person. Other meetings may be canceled and the information communicated through memoranda, newsletters, or even video or audio recordings.
5. When receiving telephone calls, determine if you are the most appropriate person to respond to the caller. If you are not the most appropriate person, direct the caller to the best source. For example, when

people contact you for information about the event management industry, refer them immediately to the International Special Events Society (1-800-688-ISES). Tell them that if they have additional questions, you will be pleased to answer them after they contact ISES.

6. Upon opening mail or reading facsimiles, handle each item only once. Respond to casual correspondence by writing a note on the document and returning it with your business card. Not only is this efficient but it is also good for the environment. Respond to business documents upon receipt by setting aside a prescribed time of day to handle this important task.

7. Have your mail sent to you through an overnight service when traveling for more than three business days. This allows you to respond in a timely manner.

8. Prepare a written agenda for every meeting, no matter how brief. Distribute the agenda in advance and see that each item includes a time for discussion. When appropriate, ask the meeting participants to prepare a written summary of their contributions and deliver them to you prior to the start of the meeting. This will assist you in better preparing for the contributions of the meeting participants.

9. Establish a comprehensive calendar that includes the contact name, address, and telephone number of people with whom you are meeting. Use computer software contact information programs to take this information on the road with you.

10. Delegate nonessential tasks to capable assistants. The only true way to multiply your creativity is to clone yourself. A well-trained, well-rewarded administrative assistant will enhance your productivity and even allow you occasionally to take some well-deserved time off.

## MASTERING FINANCE

Becoming a wise and disciplined money manager is another pillar upon which you can construct a long-term career in event management. During your event management career you will be required to read and interpret spreadsheets filled with financial data. You cannot entrust this to others. Instead, you must be able to understand their interpretations of these data and then make judgments based upon your final analysis. Many event managers are uncomfortable with accounting. When interviewing students for admission to the event management program at George Washington University, I noted that over 90 percent said that they were not comfortable with their financial or accounting skills.

Sharon Siegel, executive vice-president of Deco Productions of Miami, Florida, has owned her company for several years and understands well the importance of prudent financial management. "Watching your overhead is extremely important," says Sharon, "especially if you are constructing and storing props." Siegel, former owner of Celebrations, merged her company with an entertainment firm and provides full-service destination management services, including design and fabrication of decorations. To help control overhead, her firm is located in the building that houses her husband's large party rental operation. Not only does this protect the bottom line, but it improves gross income through referral business generated through the party rental operation.

Sound financial practices allow savvy event managers to better control future events by collecting and analyzing the right information through which to make wise decisions. In this book we look at many ways in which you may become more comfortable with accounting and as a result help greatly improve your profitability, to ensure a long, prosperous future in this profession. The following techniques for event management financial success will assist you with establishing your own framework for long-term profitability.

1. Set realistic short-, mid-, and long-term financial goals.
2. Seek professional counsel.
3. Identify and use efficient financial technology.
4. Review your financial health regularly and systematically.
5. Control overhead and build wealth.

## MASTERING TECHNOLOGY

New advances from the fax machine as well as new technologies from integrated systems digital networks (ISDNs) to the Internet (see sidebar) and e-mail are transforming the way in which event managers conduct business. As an example, most résumés that I review describe computer skills and software literacy. Although this is a basic requirement for most administrative jobs, it is surprising that many event managers are still somewhat intimidated by the computer age.

Overcoming this intimidation through the selection of proper tools to solve daily challenges is an essential priority for modern event managers. These basic tools may include software programs for word processing, financial management, and database management.

Word processing skills allow the event manager to produce well-written proposals, agreements, production schedules, and other important documents for daily business easily and efficiently. Many successful event managers incorporate desktop publishing software with word processing tools to produce well-illustrated proposals and other promotional materials.

Earlier we discussed the importance of prudent financial management. Financial spreadsheet software allows modern event managers to process quickly, efficiently, and accurately hundreds of monthly journal entries and determine instantly profit or loss information from individual events. These same software systems also allow you to produce detailed financial reports to satisfy tax authorities as well as to provide you with a well-documented history of income and expense. Most important, the use of electronic financial management tools will enable you to determine instantly your cash flow

## Navigating the Internet for Event Management Success

Millions of people are currently using the Internet to satisfy their information, marketing, and other personal and professional needs. It is predicted that this number will soon rise to 1 billion. Will the Internet reduce or eliminate the need for human assembly? On the contrary, futurists such as Alvin Toffler and William Hallal predict that this unprecedented information technology will increase the desire for public assembly, as hundreds of millions of people assemble virtually and find common interests that require public assembly to fully satiate their needs.

The Internet is a complex network of millions of computers that sends and receives information globally. Initially conceived by the Department of Defense Advanced Research Projects Agency, the Internet was installed as a highly stable network with no single point of origin. Initially, only the government, university scientists, and technical people used the Internet to share information, due to its inherently technical interface. With the invention of the *browser,* a software program that allows the ability to view parts of the Internet graphically (known as the World Wide Web), the Internet is now the fastest-growing communications device in the world. Not since the invention of the printing press has communications been so rapidly transformed.

To use the Internet, you will need to identify a local access server, such as one of the major online subscription services or one of hundreds of local access firms. Once you are admitted to cyber (meaning "to steer") space, you may easily navigate between thousands of sites (or *home pages*) using search engines which allow you to search for information that has been indexed.

In the event management profession there are hundreds of home pages on the Internet system (see Appendixes 1 and 2 for some examples). Viewing sites with a browser on the World Wide Web using the point-and-click method is easy and fun. Many of the pages contain *hyperlinks,* which are a way to access more information. After you click your mouse on a highlighted key word *(hypertext)* on a home page, a related home page appears.

One of the easiest and fastest ways to conduct research is through the Internet system. For example, the event manager who desires to identify sources for entertainment may either review a variety of home pages related to this subject or visit a *chat room*—a live link across the Internet—to query other people who are interested in the same subject.

ISES members use an electronic bulletin board system not on the Internet to post services they need when developing proposals or researching other destinations. The bulletin board is similar to a chat room in that it allows the participants to communicate asynchronously. By comparison a chat room is a synchronous conversation in real time.

If you can wait a day or two to retrieve the information you require, the bulletin board may be a feasible option. However, if you need the information now, you will want to go directly to the chat room or home page.

Regardless of what service you use, the Internet system is the event manager's most dynamic tool in transforming tomorrow's events through unlimited education and research. Get connected, log on, navigate, and surf the event management superhighway to find greater success.

position to further ensure that at the end of the month, you have enough income to cover bills and produce retained earnings for your organization.

Learning to use these systems is relatively simple, and most event managers report that they are impressed with the ease and efficiency of this technology compared to the days of pencil or pen entries in financial journals. There are numerous brand names available for purchase, and I encourage you to determine at the outset your financial management needs and then select software that will cost-effectively meet those needs now and for the immediate future.

A database system will allow you to compile huge amounts of information, ranging from vendor to prospective client to guest lists and organize this information for easy retrieval. Event managers coordinate hundreds of resources per year and the ability to store, organize, and retrieve this information quickly and cost-efficiently as well as securely is extremely important for business operations and improved earnings.

There are numerous software systems available and many that may be customized to fit the individual needs of your organization. However, event managers may fail to recognize the time required to enter the data initially and the discipline required to continue to add to the original database in a systematic manner. According to Dan Mummaw, event manager from Lansing, Michigan, effectively using information technology requires commitment from the entire team. "We asked everyone in the office to pitch in and help us build the database. It was difficult at first and some people actually left the organization, but in the final result we are a more effective and profitable organization," says Mummaw.

Whether for human, financial, or organizational purposes, information technology is the critical link between an average organization soon in decline or a great event management firm with expansive growth potential. The following procedure for using event management technology provides an approach for acquiring the right technology to match your needs.

1. Identify the technology needs within your organization.
2. Review and select appropriate technology.
3. Establish a schedule for implementation.
4. Provide adequate training for all personnel.
5. Review needs systematically and adapt to new technology.

## MASTERING HUMAN RESOURCE SKILLS

Empowering people is one of the most important human resource skills the event manager must master. Thousands of decisions must be made to produce successful events and the event manager cannot make all of them. Instead, he or she must hire the right people and empower them to make a range of important decisions.

The empowerment of event staff and volunteers is contrasted with the primary reason for failure by most event management concerns. According to informal interviews with dozens of event management entrepreneurs, the greatest challenge is not creativity but financial administration. Perhaps this is why in many companies the chief financial officer (CFO) is one of the best compensated at the executive level.

As event managers become more educated in finance, human resource management, and other business skills, they are actually demonstrating entrepreneurial skills to their present employers. Many employers actually reward entrepreneurs (or as they are commonly referred to, *intrapreneurs*) as they exhibit the skills needed to manage a complex competitive environment autonomously.

Therefore, one of the benefits of mastering skills in event management is the ability to learn how to run your own business effectively to improve your performance as an employee. In addition, you may be improving your opportunity to one day own and operate your own successful event management consulting practice. Managing your financial affairs requires education, professional counsel, and discipline.

## THERE IS NO SUBSTITUTE FOR PERFORMANCE

When meeting with his team and listening to their assurances of improving profits, Harold Gineen, former chairman of ITT, would invoke the most sacred of all event management business principles: "There is no substitute for performance." Four pillars of long-term success in event management—time, financial, technology, and human resource management—must be applied to achieve consistent success. Setting benchmarks to measure your achievements will help you use these pillars to build a rock solid foundation for your event management career. According to Sharon Siegel and many of her colleagues, all event managers are ultimately measured only by their last performances. Steadily applying these best practices will help ensure many stellar event performances to come.

# Challenges and Opportunities

Three important challenges await you in developing a long, prosperous professional career in event management. Each of these challenges is related to the other. The environment in which business is developed, the rapid changes in available resources, and the requirement for continuous education form a dynamic triangle that will either support your climb or entrap you while limiting your success. You will find that your ability to master each of these challenges dramatically affects your success ratio throughout your career.

## BUSINESS DEVELOPMENT

Every organization faces increased competition as the world economy becomes smaller and you find that you no longer compete in a local market. Performing a competitive analysis in your market area is an important step in determining your present and future competitors and how you will differentiate yourself to promote profitability. One way to do this is to thoughtfully consider your organization's unique qualities. After you have identified these qualities, compare them to the perception your current and future customers have of other organizations. Are you really all that different from your competitors? If you have not identified your unique differentiating qualities, you may need to adjust the services or products you provide to achieve this important step. Following is a guide to best practices in competitive advantage analysis.

1. Audit your organization's unique competitive advantage: quality, product offering, price, location, trained and experienced employees, reputation, safety, and so on.
2. Survey your current and prospective customers to determine their perception of your unique attributes compared to competing organizations.
3. Anonymously call and visit your competitors and take notes on how they compare to your unique competitive advantage.
4. Share this information with your staff and adjust your mission and vision to promote greater business development.
5. Review your position systematically every business quarter to determine how you are doing and adjust your plan when necessary.

Whether you are the owner, manager, or employee, maintaining a competitive advantage in event management is the secret to success in long-term business development. Combine this technique with constantly reviewing the trade and general business literature as well as information about general emerging trends to maintain your most competitive position.

Relationship marketing is increasingly important since the development of affinity programs by retailers in the 1950s. Modern organizations are just now learning what buyers and sellers in ancient markets knew hundreds of years ago. All sales are based on relationships. Implied in that relationship is the reality that the buyer and seller like, respect, and trust one another. The higher the price, the more important this process becomes. Therefore, event managers must use events to further this important process.

According to *Advertising Age* and other major chroniclers of global marketing relationships, relationship marketing is the fastest-growing segment in the entire marketing profession. The event manager must invest the same time that larger organizations do to understand how to use events to build solid relationships that promote loyalty, word-of-mouth endorsement, and other important attributes of a strong customer and client relationship.

## RESOURCE DEVELOPMENT

As more and more organizations create their own home pages on the World Wide Web, consumers will be exposed increasingly to infinite resources for event management. Your challenge is to select those resources that fit your market demand and cultivate them to ensure the highest consistent quality. One of the reasons that brand names have grown in importance is due to consumers' desire for dependability and reliability. Positioning yourself and your organization as a high-quality, dependable, and reliable service through your careful selection of product offerings will further ensure your long-term success. Whether you are selecting vendors or determining what quality of paper upon which to print your new brochure, every decision will reflect your taste and more importantly that of your customers. Determine early on through research who you are serving and then select those resources to match their needs, wants, desires, and expectations. This may be accomplished as follows:

1. Identify through research the market(s) you are serving.
2. Establish a database to collect information about the needs, wants, desires, and expectations of your customers.
3. Regularly review new products (some event managers set aside a specific day each month to see new vendors) and determine if they meet the standards set by your customers.
4. Match the needs, wants, desires, and expectations to every business development decision. For example, do your customers prefer to do business with you in the evening? If so, stay open late one night per week.
5. Regularly audit your internal procedures to make certain that you are developing new business by positioning your products and services as quality, dependable, and reliable resources for your customers.

## LIFELONG LEARNING: A USER'S GUIDE

If the 1950s were the age of innocence in event management, the 1990s and well into the new millennium may be described as "the renaissance." You are part of an era of unprecedented learning and expansion of knowledge in the field of event management. This book will serve as your primer to direct you to additional resources to ensure that you stay ahead rather than behind the learning curve in this rapidly changing and expanding profession. One way to do this is to establish learning benchmarks for yourself throughout your career. Attending one or two annual industry conferences, participating in local chapter activities, or setting aside time each day to read relevant literature (see Appendixes 3 and 4) about the profession will certainly help you stay current. Perhaps the best proven way to learn anything is to teach someone else what you have learned. Collecting information that can later be shared with your professional colleagues is an excellent way to develop the habit of lifelong learning. Consider the following techniques for lifelong learning:

1. Budget time and finances to support continuing education on an annual basis.
2. Require or encourage your employees to engage in continuous event management education by subsidizing their training. Ask them to contribute by purchasing books that are related to the course work.
3. Establish a study group to prepare for the Certified Special Events Professional (CSEP) examination.
4. Set aside a specific time each week for professional reading. Collect relevant information and then highlight, clip, circulate, or file this information at this time.
5. Attend industry conferences and expositions to expose yourself to new ideas on an annual basis. Remember that upon returning to your organization you will be required to teach what you have learned to others. Therefore, become a scholar of your profession.

When you audit the business environment, select resources that demonstrate your quality, dependability, and reliability, and engage in a program of lifelong learning, you will be far ahead of your current and future competitors. This book will help you understand the profession of event management as both an art and a science, requiring not only your creativity but also your exacting reasoning ability. However, any book is only a catalyst for future exploration of a field of study. As a result of using this book to promote your future growth, you will have established the rigor required to become a scholar of event management and an authority in your organization. To maintain your position, you will not only need to return to this book as a central reference but begin a comprehensive file of additional educational resources. This book provides several appendix resources from which you may assemble this base of knowledge. Upon completing this book use Appendix 1 to enlarge your comprehension of the profession by contacting the organizations listed to request educational materials to improve and sustain your practice. Doctors, lawyers, and accountants as well as numerous other established professions require continuous education to meet licensing or certification standards. Our profession must aspire to this same level of competence. This will occur through your use of this book and commitment to future educational opportunities.

# Getting Focused

Although ISES has identified nearly two dozens professions within the events industry, you must soon decide how you will focus your studies. After reading the preface and this chapter, you should be able to comprehend the macro-profession of event management through brief descriptions of the many subfields. Now is the time to begin to focus your studies on one or two specific subfields, such as tourism, meetings, festivals, reunions, and social life-cycle event management. Use the list of event management positions described in Table 1-2 as a tool to get focused, and select the one or two areas where you wish to concentrate your studies.

Did you note the similarities in background and experience in each position? The key to your success in this business (or any other for that matter) is a thorough grounding organization, negotiation, finance, and marketing. Human relations experience is also essential, as is the related volunteer coordination skill. Increasing in importance is your ability to design, conduct, and analyze research. Throughout the book each skill is discussed in detail. However, you must now begin to focus on how you will apply these skills to your particular career pursuits.

Event management is a profession that provides skills for use in a variety of related disciplines. Grounded in the science of management, you will also learn skills in psychology, sociology, and even anthropology as you further develop your career. As you move from one subfield to another, these foundational skills will serve you well. They are the portable elements of this curriculum that you may take with you and apply to a variety of different types of events.

# How to Use This Book

### SELF-EDUCATION: THE READING LOG

Each chapter of this book represents the sum of many years of professional reading by this author. Therefore, as you approach a new chapter, look for related writings in industry trade and professional journals as well as general media such as the daily newspaper. As you identify these readings save them for your study time. When you complete your two 20-minute study periods, give yourself a bonus by reading the related reading and then noting in your reading log the title, author, date, and a short description. Developing this habit during your study period will begin a lifelong process that will reward you richly throughout your career. Make certain that you develop a filing system for these readings for future reference and use the reading log as a classification system for easy reference.

### BENCHMARK CHECKLISTS

Self-improvement is the goal of every successful person. It is a continuous process. To ensure continuous self-improvement and business improvement requires utilizing an old tradition in a new context. The term *benchmarking* was first used by Xerox Corporation to describe the way its corporate leaders reinvented its organization to compete more effectively. This process was so successful that Xerox won the most coveted award in corporate America, the

Malcom Baldrige Award for Quality. The principles of benchmarking are simple; however, the application requires commitment and discipline.

Benchmarking is a management process in which you study similar organizations to determine what systems they are using that can become quality benchmarks for your own organization. Once you have identified these benchmarks, your organization's goal is to meet or exceed these standards within a specified period of time.

The checklists throughout this book are your benchmarks. They are the result of 25 years of study of successful individuals and organizations in the profession of event management. Your goals should be to develop the rigor to meet or exceed these standards during your event management career.

## CRITICAL CONNECTIONS FOR CAREER ADVANCEMENT

In addition to the numerous tables, charts, and models in this book, each chapter includes four critical connections to help you rapidly advance. The very nature of special events is to connect people through a shared activity, and therefore each chapter includes specific instructions for global, technological, resource, and learning connections. Make certain that you carefully review these sections at the end of each chapter to expand, reinforce, and ultimately expand your connections in the twenty-first century global event management profession.

## THE APPENDICES

This important part of the book is designed to provide you with extensive resources in one location to use throughout your professional life. Review these listings and determine what gaps you currently have in your operations, marketing, or other areas, and use these resources to begin to ensure closure. Furthermore, as event management is an emerging discipline and rapidly expanding profession, you may notice gaps in the appendixes that you can fill. Send me your resources at joe.goldblatt@jwv.edu and you will be acknowledged in the next edition.

## ROLE AND SCOPE

This book's role is to expand the knowledge base in the emerging discipline of event management. The scope of its task is to provide concrete techniques to immediately improve your practice as an event manager. Your career needs will ultimately determine how you use this book to improve your business. However, if you are sincerely interested in expanding the knowledge base in event management through your pursuit, your practice will improve in equal proportion to your level of commitment. This is so important that it bears repeating. If you are interested in expanding the body of knowledge in event management, your skills will improve in equal proportion to your level of commitment.

Therefore, as in most profession, the harder you work, the more you will learn. And as is also true in all professions, the more you learn, the more you will earn. I encourage you to become a scholar of this fascinating profession, and as suggested earlier, read this book as though some day, somewhere, you will be requested to teach others. I challenge you to achieve mastery through these pages so that those you will influence will leave this profession even better prepared for those who will follow.

I, like you, am a student of this profession. There are new learning opportunities every day. Over a decade ago, I stood outside a hospital nursery window gazing lovingly on our newborn son, Sammy. Only a few hours earlier, I had telephoned my cousin Carola in New Orleans at one o'clock in the morning to announce his birth and, choking back tears, to tell her and the family that he would be named for my uncle, her father, who had recently died. Celebrating this new life together, we laughed out loud about the "curse" that might come with my son's name. Would he be as funny, charming, irascible, and generous as my Uncle Sam? His potential was limitless. Confucius declared several thousand years ago that "we are cursed to live in interesting times indeed." Like Sammy, regardless of what road you take in the infinitely fascinating event management profession, you can be assured of finding opportunity in very interesting times. In the closing lines of his best-seller *Megatrends* (1982, Warner Books) John Naisbitt exalted the world he had spent years analyzing: "My God, what a fantastic time in which to be alive." The future that you and your colleagues will create will carry the curse of Confucius, the joy of Naisbitt, and the final assurance of the French poet Paul Valery, who wrote: "The trouble with the future is it no longer is what is used to be." Your future is secure in knowing that overall there are 150 million new births annually in the world and, therefore, just as many events (and many more) to manage.

# Career Advancement Connections

## GLOBAL CONNECTION

Connect globally with event managers throughout the world through an Internet list serve such as Event Management, which is managed by Leeds Metropolitan University in Great Britain. World of Events provides a global forum for discussion of event management topics by both researchers, academics, students, and practitioners throughout the world *(www.worldofevents.net)*.

## TECHNOLOGY CONNECTION

Develop an interactive Web-based data management system to enable you to collect and access your event management data from throughout the world. The best system for achieving this is to create an intranet-based database that can be accessed by an authorized event manager from any remote point on earth. It is critical to protect your valuable data. The protection can be enforced by setting different levels of access: to review data only, to add data, or to delete and modify data.

## RESOURCE CONNECTION

The Data on Meetings and Events (DOME) Internet database and search engine lists hundreds of research reports with links to research providers. The DOME staff also designs and conducts original research studies to benefit the events industry. Visit DOME at *www.domeresearch.org.*

Over 150 colleges and universities throughout the world offer courses, curriculums, degrees, certificates, and other resources. The George Washington University (GW) Event Management Program is the world's largest and most comprehensive educational program leading to professional certification in event management (12 colleges from Brazil to Barcelona have licensed the GW program). For a free list of these programs, visit *www.gwu.edu/emp.*

## LEARNING CONNECTION

Construct a one-, three-, five-, and 10-year plan or blueprint to identify your career goals and path. Assess your current skill and experience level and list the educational, practical, and theoretical resources that you will need to achieve your goals and objectives. Read *Dollars and Events: How to Succeed in the Special Events Business* (1999, Wiley) by Joe Goldblatt and Frank Supovitz, *What Color Is Your Parachute? 2001: A Practical Manual for Job-Hunters and Career-Changers* [*What Color Is Your Parachute* (paperback)] (2000, Ten Speed Press) by Richard Nelson Bolles, and *What Color Is Your Parachute Workbook: How to Create a Picture of Your Ideal Job or Next Career* by Richard Nelson Bolles (1998, Ten Speed Press).

# CHAPTER 2

# Models of Global
# Event Management

**IN THIS CHAPTER YOU WILL LEARN HOW TO:**

- Recognize and use the five phases of the modern event management process
- Identify the strengths, weaknesses, opportunities, and threats of your event
- Create an accurate blueprint for your event
- Conduct a comprehensive needs assessment
- Complete a gap analysis for your event
- Communicate effectively with event stakeholders

All successful events have five critical stages in common to ensure their consistent effectiveness. These five phases or steps of successful event management are *research, design, planning, coordination,* and *evaluation* (see Figure 2-1). In this chapter we explore each phase, to enable you to produce successful events every time.

# Research

Excellent event research reduces risk. The better research you conduct prior to the event, the more likely you are to produce an event that matches the planned outcomes of the organizers or stakeholders. For many years public relations professionals and other marketing experts have realized the value of

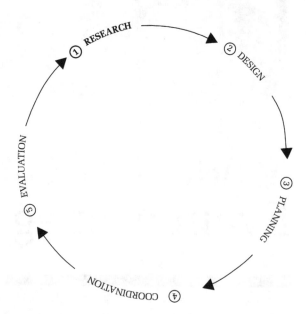

**Figure 2-1**
Event Management Process

using research to pinpoint the needs, wants, desires, and expectations of prospective customers. Government leaders regularly conduct feasibility studies prior to authorizing capital investments. These feasibility studies include exhaustive research. An event is a product that is placed before the public with the reasonable expectation that they will attend. Therefore, it is imperative that you conduct careful and accurate consumer research to reduce the risk of nonattendance.

I have interviewed hundreds of leading event management professionals and they have stated their belief that more time must be devoted to research and evaluation of events. According to these experts, if more time were devoted to these phases of the event management production process, then ultimately less time and expense would be needed to complete the intervening steps.

The three types of research that are used for preevent research are quantitative, qualitative, or a combination or hybrid of both. Matching the research type to the event is important and is determined by the goals of the research, the time allowed for conducting the research, and the funds available.

## MARKET RESEARCH TECHNIQUES

Before bringing a new product or service to market the inventor or manufacturer will conduct market research to determine the needs, wants, desires, and expectations of the target market. Whether your event is a new or a preexisting product, market research is required to determine how to obtain the very best position in a sometimes crowded marketplace. Typically, qualitative and, in most cases, focus group research is used for this purpose.

Market research will help you determine the target or primary market as well as the secondary and tertiary markets for your event. Market research will also enable you to study the service levels expected by guests as well as the perceptions by internal stakeholders of the services currently being delivered. By studying the market in depth, you are able to spot emerging trends, develop new service delivery systems, and solve minor problems before they become major catastrophes.

One example of this is the event manager who discovered through research that attendees could not register for the upcoming convention during normal business hours due to workplace regulations. Therefore, she invested in an answering service for six months prior to the meeting to accept registrations between the hours of 5:00 P.M. and 8:00 A.M. This new service was a major success, and registrations for the conference increased markedly.

## QUANTITATIVE VERSUS QUALITATIVE RESEARCH

### Quantitative Preevent Research
Event managers primarily use quantitative research to determine demographic information such as gender, age, income, and other pertinent facts about the future market for an event. This research is relatively inexpensive to conduct

and easy to tabulate and analyze with computers. Figure 2-2 provides a model of a typical quantitative preevent research survey.

Whether you use a written survey, in-person interview, or telephone interview method of construction, the research survey is of prime importance. To achieve the greatest possible response, offer a reward such as "enclose your business card and we will share the research findings with you," or offer an immediate incentive such as enclosing a $1 bill.

Questions may be developed in two different styles. Question 4 uses a *Likert scale* to allow a respondent to select the response that states his or her opinion precisely. Question 5 uses a *semantic differential scale* to allow a respondent to select a continuum between two opposing adjectives. The number that the respondent circles indicates the likelihood of attending or not attending an event.

---

The following survey will enable the organizers of XYZ event to determine the feasibility of producing the following event. Your participation is important in this effort. Answer all questions by checking the appropriate box. Return this survey by January 1, 2001.

1. Gender?     ☐ Male     ☐ Female

2. Age?     ☐ Under 25     ☐ 26–34     ☐ 35–44     ☐ 45–60     ☐ 61 and over

3. Income?     ☐ Under $24,999     ☐ $25,000–44,999     ☐ Over $45,000

4. If the event were held during the summer I would: *(Likert scale)*
   ☐ Not attend     ☐ Maybe attend     ☐ No opinion     ☐ Probably attend     ☐ Positively attend

5. If the event were held during the fall I would: *(semantic differential scale)*
   Not Attend     ☐ 1     ☐ 2     ☐ 3     ☐ 4     ☐ 5     Positively attend

6. If you checked number 1 above please describe your reasons for nonattendance in the space below: *(open-ended question)*

   _____

   _____

   _____

Return this survey by January 1, 2001 to:
Alan Shawn Feinstein Graduate School
Johnson + Wales University
8 Abbott Park Place
Providence, Rhode Island 02903
or fax to 401-598-4738

To receive a *free copy* of the survey results please include your business card.

---

**Figure 2-2**
Quantitative Preevent Survey Model

## Qualitative Preevent Research

Market research consultants rely on qualitative research to probe for hidden meanings in quantitative studies. Qualitative research tells the research organization what is beneath the numbers in quantitative research and therefore is an important step in the research process. This type of research may take the form of a focus group, participant/observer research, or a case study. Selecting the proper methodology depends on your goals, the time available, and the funding.

The *focus group* is typically comprised of 8 to 12 people of similar background and experience who assemble for the purpose of discussion. A trained facilitator leads the group through specific questions that will provide clues to the goals or outcomes desired from the research. A focus group may be one hour in length, although in most cases they last between 90 minutes and two hours. In some instances, a room with a one-way mirror is used to allow the other stakeholders to observe participants for subtle changes in body language, facial reactions, and other gestures that may reveal information in addition to their verbal opinion. The focus group is audiotaped and the tapes are later transcribed and analyzed to identify areas of agreement or discord.

The *participant/observer* style of qualitative research involves placing the researcher in a host community to participate in and observe the culture of those being studied. For example, if you desire to determine whether or not a certain destination is appropriate for relocation of an event, you may wish to visit, participate, and observe for an extended period of time before making a decision. Interviews with key informants are essential to this research.

The third type of qualitative research is entitled the *case study.* In this style a preexisting event is singled out as a specific case to be studied in depth. The event may be studied from a historical context, or the stakeholders may be interviewed to determine how personality, skill, and other factors drive the success of the event. The case study enables the event researcher to draw conclusions based on the research gleaned from a comparable event.

## Cost

Qualitative research is generally more expensive than quantitative research due to the time that is involved in probing for deeper, more meaningful answers than only digits. The cost of training interviewers, the interviewer's time, the time for analyzing the data, and other costs contribute to this investment. Although the cost is greater, many event managers require both qualitative and quantitative studies to validate their assumptions or research their markets.

## Combined Research

In most cases event managers use a combination of quantitative and qualitative research to make decisions about future events. This combined research allows the event manager to obtain large volumes of information in a cost-efficient manner using the quantitative method and then probe for hidden meanings and subtle feelings using the qualitative approach.

Effective quantitative research has elements of qualitative research included to increase the validity of the questions. Event managers should use a small focus group or team of experts to review the questions before conducting a survey. These experts can confirm that a question is understandable and valid for the research being conducted. Table 2-1 provides a simple way for event managers to determine what research methodology is most effective for their purpose.

The goals and required outcomes of the research, combined with the time frame and funding available, will ultimately determine the best method for your preevent research. Regardless of the type of research you conduct, it is important that you take care to produce valid and reliable information.

## VALIDITY AND RELIABILITY: PRODUCING CREDIBLE PREEVENT RESEARCH

All research must be defended. Your stakeholders will ask you bluntly, "How do you know that you know?" If your research has high validity and reliability, you can provide greater assurance that your work is truthful. Validity primarily confirms that your research measures what it purports to measure. For example, if you are trying to determine if senior citizens will attend an event, you must include senior citizens in your sample of respondents to ensure validity. Furthermore, the questions you pose to these seniors must be understandable by them to ensure that their responses are truthful and accurate.

Reliability helps prove that your research will remain truthful and accurate over time. For example, if you were to conduct the same study with another group of senior citizens, would the answers be significantly different? If the answer is "yes," your data may not be reliable. Designing a collection instrument that has high validity and reliability is a challenging and time-consuming task. You may wish to contact a university or college marketing, psychology, or sociology department for assistance by an experienced researcher in developing your instrument. Often, a senior-level undergraduate student or graduate student may be assigned to help you develop the instrument and collect and analyze the data for college credit. The participation of the university or college will add credibility to your findings. Software applications such as Microsoft Excel should be used for analyzing data. For more complex analysis you may use statistical applications such as SAS, Minitab, and SPSS.

**Table 2-1**   Selecting the Appropriate Preevent Research Method

| Goal | Method |
| --- | --- |
| Collect gender, age, and income data | Written survey |
| Collect attitudes and opinions | Focus group |
| Examine culture of community | Participant/observer |
| Identify comparable characteristics | Case study |
| Collect demographic and psychographic data | Combined methods |

## INTERPRETING AND COMMUNICATING RESEARCH FINDINGS

Designing and collecting preevent research is only the beginning of this important phase. Once you have analyzed the data carefully and identified the implications of your research as well as provided some recommendations based on your study, you must present the information to your stakeholders. The way that you do this will determine the level of influence you wield with stakeholders.

If the stakeholders are academics or others who have a research background, using tables or a written narrative may suffice. However, if, as is most often the case, stakeholders are unsophisticated with regard to research, you may instead wish to use graphs, charts, and other visual tools to illustrate your findings. To paraphrase Confucius, "One picture is certainly worth a thousand numerals." To present your preevent research findings effectively:

1. Determine your audience and customize your presentation to their personal communication learning style.
2. Describe the purpose and importance of the research.
3. Explain how the research was collected and describe any limitations.
4. Reveal your findings and emphasize the key points.
5. Invite questions.

Distributing a well-produced written narrative with copies of the information you are presenting (such as graphs from slides) will be helpful to the stakeholders, as they will require more time for independent study before posing intelligent questions. In the written narrative include a section describing the steps you have taken to produce research that demonstrates high validity and reliability and list any independent organizations (such as a university or college) that reviewed your study prior to completion.

Communicating your research findings is an essential phase in the research process. Prepare, rehearse, and then reveal your data thoughtfully and confidently. Summarize your presentation by demonstrating how the findings support the goals and objectives of your research plan.

## THE FIVE W'S: HOW TO PRODUCE CONSISTENTLY EFFECTIVE EVENTS

Too often students will ask me *what event* they should produce for a class project instead of *why* they should produce the event in the first place. Following the economically rocky early 1990s, corporations, associations, governments, and other organizations began to analyze carefully why a meeting or event should occur. This solid reasoning should be applied to every event decision.

The first step is to ask: "*Why* we must hold this event?" There must be not one but a series of compelling reasons that confirm the importance and viability of holding the event.

The second step is to ask: "*Who* the stakeholders will be for this event?" Remember that stakeholders are both internal and external parties. Internal stakeholders may be the board of directors, committee members, staff, elected leaders, guests, or others. External stakeholders may be the media, politicians, bureaucrats, or others who will be investing in the event. Conducting solid research will help you determine the level of commitment of each of these parties and better help you define who this event is being produced for.

The third step is to determine *when* the event is being held. You must ask yourself if the research-through-evaluation time frame is appropriate for the size of this event. If this time period is not appropriate, you may need to rethink your plans and either shift the dates or streamline your operations. *When* may also determine where the event may be held.

The fourth step involves determining *where* the event will be held. As you will discover in this chapter, once you have selected a site, your work becomes either easier or more challenging. Therefore, this decision must be made as early as possible, as it affects many other decisions.

The fifth and final "W" is to determine from the information gleaned thus far *what* the event product is that you are developing and presenting. Matching the event product to the needs, wants, desires, and expectations of your guests while satisfying the internal requirements of your organization is no simple task. "What" must be analyzed carefully and critically to make certain that the why, who, when, and where are synergized in this answer.

Once these five questions have been answered thoroughly, it is necessary to turn your deliberations to *how* the organization will allocate scarce resources to produce maximum benefit for the stakeholders. SWOT (strengths, weaknesses, opportunities, threats) analysis provides a comprehensive tool for ensuring that you review each step systematically.

## SWOT ANALYSIS: FINDING THE STRENGTHS, WEAKNESSES, OPPORTUNITIES, AND THREATS

Before you begin planning an event, SWOT analysis usually must be implemented to underpin your decision making. SWOT analysis assists you in identifying the internal and external variables that may prevent the event from achieving maximum success.

### Strengths and Weaknesses

The strengths and weaknesses of an event are primarily considerations that can be spotted before the event actually takes place. Typical strengths and weaknesses of many events are shown in Table 2-2. The strengths and weaknesses may be uncovered through a focus group or through individual interviews with the major stakeholders. If the weaknesses outnumber the strengths and there is no reasonable way to eliminate the weaknesses and increase the strengths within the event planning period, you may wish to postpone or cancel the event.

**Table 2-2** Event Strengths and Weaknesses

| Strengths | Weaknesses |
|---|---|
| Strong funding | Weak funding |
| Good potential for sponsors | No potential for sponsors |
| Well-trained staff | Poorly trained staff |
| Many volunteers | Few volunteers |
| Good media relations | Poor media relations |
| Excellent site | Weak site |

## Opportunities and Threats

Opportunities and threats are two key factors that generally present themselves either during an event or after it has occurred. However, during the research process they should be considered seriously, as they may spell potential disaster for the event. *Opportunities* are activities that may be of benefit to an event without significant investment by your organization. One example is that of selecting a year in which to hold an event that coincides with your community's or industry's 100th anniversary. Your event may benefit from additional funding, publicity, and other important resources simply by aligning yourself with this hallmark event. Other possible beneficial outcomes, sometimes indirect, such as the potential of contributing to the event host's political image, are considered opportunities.

*Threats* are activities that prevent you from maximizing the potential of an event. The most obvious threat is weather; however, political threats may be just as devastating. Local political leaders must buy into your civic event to ensure cooperation with all agencies. Political infighting may quickly destroy your planning. A modern threat is that of terrorism. The threat of violence erupting at an event may keep people from attending. A celebrity canceling or not attending can also create a significant threat to the success of an event. Typical opportunities and threats for an event are listed in Table 2-3.

**Table 2-3** Event Opportunities and Threats

| Opportunities | Threats |
|---|---|
| Civic anniversary | Hurricanes and tornadoes |
| Chamber of Commerce promotion | Political infighting |
| Celebrity appearance | Violence from terrorism |
| Align with environmental cause | Alcoholic consumption |
| Tie-in with media | Site in bad neighborhood |
| Winning elections | Celebrity canceling or not attending |
| Devoloping more loyal employees | |

You will note that although strengths and weakness are often related, opportunities and threats need not be. Once again, in making a decision to proceed with event planning, your goal is to identify more opportunities than threats. All threats should be considered carefully and experts should be consulted to determine ways in which threats may be contained, reduced, oreliminated.

SWOT analysis (see Figure 2-3) is a major strategic planning tool during the research phase. By using SWOT analysis an event manager can not only scan the internal and external event environment but can proceed to the next step, which involves analyses of the weaknesses and threats and provide solutions to improve the event planning process.

The research phase of the event administration process is perhaps most critical. During this period you will determine through empirical research whether you have both the internal and external resources essential to make a decision to produce an effective event. Your ability to select the appropriate research methodology, design the instrument, and collect, analyze, interpret, and present the data will ultimately determine whether or not an event has sufficient strength for future success. The first pillar of the event management process—research—rests squarely in the center of the other four supporting columns. Although each is equal in importance, the future success of an event depends on how well you conduct the research phase.

| S = strengths | | |
|---|---|---|
| 1. Strong funding | Internal | |
| 2. Well-trained staff | Internal | |
| 3. Event well respected by media | External | |
| W = weaknesses | | Existing conditions |
| 1. Weak funding | Internal | |
| 2. Few human resources | Internal | |
| 3. Poor public relations history | External | |
| O = opportunities | | |
| 1. Simultaneous celebration of a congruent event | External | |
| 2. Timing of event congruent with future budget allocation | Internal | |
| T = threats | | Future/predictive conditions |
| 1. Weather | External | |
| 2. New board of directors leading this event | Internal | |

**Figure 2-3**
SWOT Analysis

# Design: Blueprint for Success

Having researched your event thoroughly and determined that it is feasible, time may now be allotted to use the right side of the brain—the creative capacity—to create a general blueprint for your ideas. There are numerous ways to begin this process, but it is important to remember that the very best event designers are constantly visiting the library, attending movies and plays, visiting art galleries, and reviewing periodicals to maintain their inspiration. This continuous research for new ideas will further strengthen the activities you propose for an event.

## BRAINSTORMING AND MIND MAPPING

Too often in volunteer-driven organizations the very best ideas are never allowed to surface. This occurs because well-meaning volunteers (and some not so well-meaning volunteers) tell their colleagues that "this will never work" or "this is impossible at this time." Although their opinions are certainly valid, the process of shooting down ideas before they are allowed to be fully developed is a tragic occurrence in many organizations. Creativity must be encouraged and supported by event managers because ultimately, the product you will offer is a creative art. Creativity is an essential ingredient in every event management process.

Therefore, when beginning the design phase of this event management process, conduct a meeting where creative people are encouraged to brainstorm the various elements of the event. The event manager is the facilitator of this meeting, and in addition to various creative stakeholders, you may choose to invite other creative people from the worlds of theater, dance, music, art, literature, and other fields. At the outset of the meeting, use a flipchart to lay out the ground rules for the discussion. In large bold letters write "Rule 1: There are no bad ideas." "Rule 2: Go back and reread rule 1."

You may wish to begin the session with an activity that will stimulate creativity. One activity I've used is to place an object in the center of the table and invite participants to describe what it might become. For example, a shoebox might become a tomb, a rocket, or a small dwelling. As each person offers his or her ideas, the others should be encouraged to be supportive.

Once you have completed these warm-up activities, members should be given simple suggestions regarding the "why" of the event. From these suggestions they should be encouraged to provide creative ideas for "who, when, where, what, and how." As the facilitator, if one member (or more than one member) tends to dominate the discussion, ask him or her to summarize and then say "thank you" as you quickly move on to others to solicit their ideas. Use the flipchart to list all the initial ideas, and do not try to establish categories or provide any other organizational structure.

Mind mapping allows an event manager to begin to pull together the random ideas and establish linkages that will later lead to logical decision making. Using the flipchart, ask each member of the group to revisit their earlier ideas and begin to link them to the four W's and ultimately help you see how the event should be developed. Write "Why?, Who?, When?, Where?, What?", and "How?" in the center of a circle on a separate page of the flipchart. From this circle draw spokes that terminate in another circle. Leave the circles at the end of each spoke empty. The ideas of your team members will fill these circles, and they will begin to establish linkages between the goal (Why?, Who?, When?, Where?, What?, and How?) and the creative method. Table 2-4 is an example of a successful event mind-mapping activity.

Mind mapping is an effective way to synthesize the various ideas suggested by group members and begin to construct an *event philosophy*. The event philosophy will determine the financial, cultural, social, and other important aspects of the event. For example, if the sponsoring organization is a not-for-profit group, the financial philosophy will not support charging high fees to produce a disproportionate amount of funds, or the tax status may be challenged. Mind mapping allows you to sift through the ideas carefully and show how they support the goals of the event. By your doing this, an event philosophy begins to emerge. Those ideas that do not have a strong linkage or support the philosophy should be placed on a separate sheet of flipchart paper for future use. Remember Rule 1?

## THE CREATIVE PROCESS IN EVENT MANAGEMENT

Special events require people with the ability to move easily between the left and right quadrants of the cerebellum. The right side of the brain is responsible for creative, spontaneous thinking, while the left side of the brain handles the more logical aspects of our lives. Event managers must be both right- and left-brained to be able to function effectively. Therefore, if you have determined that one side of your brain is less strong than the other, you must take steps to correct this to achieve maximum success in event management.

The majority of this book is concerned with logical, reasoning activities. Therefore, assuming that one of the aspects of event management that you find attractive is the creative opportunities afforded in this profession, I will provide some insight into ways to develop your creativity to the highest possible

**Table 2-4**  Event Management Needs Assessment

| Why? | + | Who? | + | When? | + | Where? | + | What? |
|---|---|---|---|---|---|---|---|---|
| What is the compelling reason for this event? Why must this event be held? | | Who will benefit from this event? Who will they want to have attend? | | When will the event be held? Are the date and time flexible or subject to change? | | What are the best destination, location, and venue? | | What elements and resources are required to satisfy the needs identified above? |

= How?

Given answers to the five W's, how do you effectively research, design, plan, coordinate, and evaluate this event?

level. Remember that developing creativity is a continuous process. The reason that some corporations put their advertising accounts out for review to other agencies periodically is to be sure that the current agency is working at its highest possible creative level. As an event manager, you too must strive for constant review of your creative powers to make certain that you are in high gear. Following are some tips for continuously developing your creativity:

1. Visit one art gallery each month.
2. Attend a live performance of opera, theater, or dance each month.
3. Read great works of literature, on a continuing basis.
4. Enroll in a music, dance, literature, visual arts, acting class, or discussion group.
5. Apply what you are discovering in each of these fields to event management.

Perhaps the best way to stretch your creativity continually is to surround yourself with highly creative people (see Figure 2-4). Whether you are in a position to hire creativity or must seek creative types through groups outside the office, you must find the innovators in order to practice innovation.

## MAKING THE PERFECT MATCH THROUGH
## NEEDS ASSESSMENT AND ANALYSIS

Once you have completed the brainstorming and mind-mapping activities satisfactorily, it is time to make certain that your creative ideas perfectly match the goals and objectives of your event. This is accomplished through *needs assessment and analysis*.

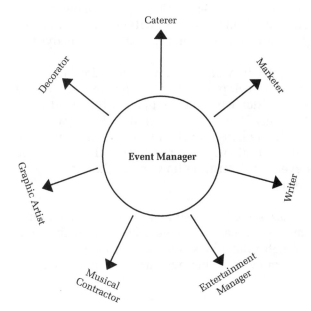

**Figure 2-4**
Creative Influences

Needs assessment and analysis enables you to create an event that closely satisfies the needs of your stakeholders. You actually began this process by asking "Why?" and "Who?". Now it is time to take it one giant step forward and survey the stakeholders to determine if your creative solutions will satisfy their needs. To accomplish this part of the design phase, develop your ideas into a series of questions, query the key constituents for the event, and determine if the various elements you have created—from advertising to decor, from catering to entertainment, and everything in between—meet their expectations. Once you are confident that you have assessed the needs of the stakeholders adequately and confirmed that you have through analysis determined how to satiate these needs, you are well prepared to confirm the final feasibility of your event design.

## Is It Feasible?

*Feasibility* simply means that you have looked at the event design objectively to determine if what you propose is feasible given the resources available. This is the final checkpoint before actual planning begins and, therefore, must be given adequate time for review. Municipalities often engage professional engineers or other consultants to conduct lengthy feasibility studies before approving new construction or other capital expenditures. Although you may not need a battery of consultants, it is important for you to review all previous steps thoroughly when determining the feasibility of an event plan.

The three basic resources that will be required are financial, human, and political. Each of these resources may have varying degrees of importance, depending on the nature of the event. For example, a for-profit or large hallmark event will require significant financial investment to succeed. On the other hand, a not-for-profit event will rely on an army of volunteers, and, therefore, the human element is more important. A civic event will require greater political resources to accomplish. Therefore, when assessing and analyzing feasibility, first determine in what proportions resources will be required for the event. You may wish to weigh each resource to help prepare your analysis.

**Financial Considerations**    You will want to know if sufficient financial resources are available to sustain development and implementation of the event. Furthermore, you must consider what will happen if the event loses money. How will creditors be paid? You will also want to know what resources you can count on for an immediate infusion of cash should the event require this to continue development. Finally, you must carefully analyze the cash flow projections for the event to determine how much time is to be allowed between payables and receivables.

**The Human Dimension**    In assessing the feasibility of an event, you must not only know where your human resources will come from but how they will be rewarded (financially or through intangibles such as awards and recognition). Most important, you must know how they will work together as an efficient event team.

**Politics as Usual**   The increasingly important role of government leaders in event oversight must be viewed with a practiced eye. Politicians see events as both good (opportunities for publicity, constituent communications, and economic impact) and bad (drain on municipal services and potential for disaster). When designing civic events it is particularly important that you understand and enlist the support of politicians and their bureaucratic ministers to ensure smooth cooperation for your event. Furthermore, for all events it is essential that you carefully research the permit process to determine if the event you have designed is feasible according to the code within the jurisdiction where the event will be held.

## The Approval Process

The research and design phases add to the event history once an event is approved. The approval process may be as simple as an acceptance by the client or as complex as requiring dozens of signatures from various city agencies that will interact with the event. Regardless of the simplicity or complexity of this step, you should view it as an important milestone that once crossed assures you that the plan has been reviewed and deemed reasonable, feasible, and has a high likelihood-to-succeed ratio. All roads lead to official approval, whether in the form of a contract or as individual permits from each agency. Without official approval, an event remains a dream. The process for turning dreams into workable plans requires careful research, thoughtful design, and critical analysis. This could be called the "planning to plan phase" because it involves so many complex steps related to the next phase. However, once the approval is granted, you are on your way to the next important phase: the actual planning period.

# Planning Effective Events

The planning period is typically the longest period of time in the event management process. Historically, this has been due to disorganization. *Disorganization* is best characterized by frequent changes resulting from substitutions, additions, or even deletions due to poor research and design. Ideally, the better the research and design, the simpler and briefer the planning period will be. Since events are planned by human beings for other human beings, this theory is fraught with exceptions. However, your goal should be to develop a smooth planning process based on careful research and design procedures. The planning phase involves using the *time/space/tempo laws* (see Figure 2-5) to determine how best to use your immediate resources. These three basic laws will affect every decision you make; how well you make use of them will govern the final outcome of an event.

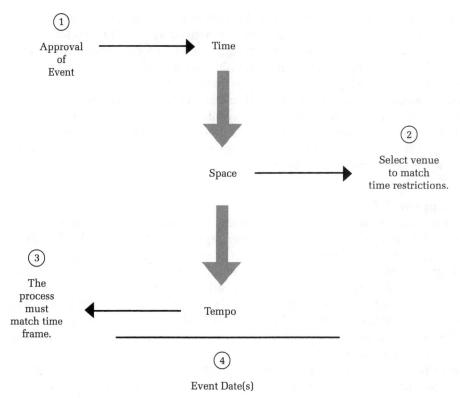

**Figure 2-5**
Time/Space/Tempo Laws

## TIMING

The law of timing refers to how much time you have in which to act or react. The first question that many event managers ask the client is: When would you like to schedule the event? The answer to that question tells you how much time you have to prepare. Often, that timetable may seem incredibly short.

The length of time available for planning and for actual production will dramatically affect the cost and sometimes the success of the event. Equally important, as you discovered earlier, is how you use your time. The Greek philosopher Theophrastus said, "Time is the most valuable thing a human can spend."

Mona Meretsky, president of COMCOR, a Fort Lauderdale corporate events firm, notes that when budgeting her time to prepare a final cost estimate for a client, she realizes that the time she invests will exceed the number of billable client hours because she is a perfectionist. She will "take as much time as is required for each event to make certain that the details are attended to. It pays off in the long run. I've never had a corporate client not come back." Budgeting your time, as shown by Meretsky, is not an exact science but rather a dynamic experience that must be governed by the importance of each event.

When budgeting your time for a proposed event, some independent event managers estimate the amount of time necessary for preevent client meetings, site inspections, meetings with vendors, ongoing communications and contract preparations, actual event time from time to arrival through departure, and postevent billable time. You may wish to allocate your billable time to follow the five phases of the event process: research, design, planning, coordination, and evaluation.

You can only estimate the time involved in these tasks and therefore must add a contingency time factor to each phase. Mona Meretsky believes that using a 10 percent contingency factor will help you cover extra time required but not originally projected.

Like Mona Meretsky, Audrey Gordon, sole proprietor of Audrey Gordon Parties of Chicago, admits that her actual time often exceeds her projected time. "A bar mitzvah could, if necessary, be planned in one eight-hour day. The worst case scenario is days of planning, as people usually change their minds often."

By paying careful attention to the research and design phase, you will be able to budget your time more precisely. This is particularly true for the event itself. This part of planning involves when to arrive for a particular event, when to cue the appropriate musician or performer, when to take breaks, and of course, when to stop. Planning the time of an event is as important as managing your planning time.

Mona Meretsky says, "I request that my personnel be set up for our events one hour in advance. In Florida guests often arrive early, and we must be ready when they are."

Audrey Gordon, owner of a one-person firm, must rely on legions of vendors to produce her social life-cycle events. Her planning must be careful and precise, even to the point of listing what song is to be played at a specific time. The net result of her exhaustive preparation is that the guest is able to relax and enjoy the event, as every element happens logically, sequentially, and on time.

The moment the client approves the date of an event, the event manager must begin assessing how the planning period will affect other business operations. Therefore, the law of timing sometimes requires that when an unreasonable time frame is allotted to produce an event professionally, the event manager must decline to accept the opportunity. The ultimate factor that will govern every decision regarding timing is made when you ask yourself: "Given this amount of time, can I produce an event that displays the quality and professionalism I am known for without losing equal or possibly larger opportunities?" Your answer will determine whether the light turns green, fades to yellow, or becomes red.

## SPACE

The law of space refers to both the physical space where an event will be held and the time between critical decisions pertaining to the event. The relationship of timing to space is one that is constant throughout the entire event process.

In the 1988 Super Bowl half-time show in Jack Murphy Stadium, Radio City Music Hall Productions designed an elaborate half-time show featuring 88 grand pianos. Suddenly, without warning, the day before the actual production, the producer was instructed that his setup time for the production was reduced to only a few minutes. Further complicating matters, the groundskeepers at the stadium raised serious concerns that the movement of the pianos onto the field would affect the turf on which the second half of the game would be played. In this example and numerous others, the actual physical space governs the time required for various elements of the event.

When selecting a *venue* for an event, the location and physical resources present will significantly affect the additional time that must be invested. If you select a historic mansion with elaborate permanent decor, less time will be required to decorate the site. By comparison, if you select a four-walled venue such as a hotel or convention center (where you are literally renting the four walls), significant time and expense must be invested to create a proper atmosphere for the event.

Burt Ferrini, event manager at Northeastern Illinois University in Chicago, recognizes the importance of space. As the manager of commencement exercises, Ferrini must coordinate thousands of people in a space most are not familiar with. Furthermore, he must ensure that the event runs precisely on time. "I prepare individual schedules for each group of participants and then after rehearsing them individually I blend them together in a master schedule. Breaking the large event down into component parts and then reassembling it on the day of the event helps ensure a smooth ceremony."

When considering the space for an event, some event managers prepare an elaborate checklist to review each element carefully. The checklist should reflect the goals and objectives of the event and not merely replicate a form you have copied for convenience. One of the primary considerations when selecting space is the age and type of guest who will be attending. Older guests may not be able to tolerate extreme temperatures, and this may preclude you from selecting an outdoor venue. For events with young children, you may or may not wish to select a site in a busy urban setting. Go back to the research and needs assessment phase and review why this event is important and who the stakeholders are. Then select a venue specifically to match their needs, wants, and expectations.

The terms *ingress* and *egress* are important concepts when reviewing a potential venue. *Ingress* defines the entrances or access to the venue, and *egress* refers to the exits or evacuation routes. When considering ingress and egress you must consider not only people, including those with disabilities, but also vehicles, props, possibly animals, and indeed any element that must enter or exit the site. You must also keep in mind the time available for ingress or egress, as this will determine the number of portals (doors) that may need to be available for this purpose.

Parking, public transportation, and other forms of transportation, including taxis, limousines, and tour buses, must also be considered when analyzing a site. These considerations should include the number of parking spaces, including those for the disabled, the availability and security/safety of public transportation, and the time required to dispatch a taxi.

## TEMPO

The final law of event planning is concerned with the rate or tempo at which events take place during both production planning and the event itself. From the moment the client approves an agreement or authorizes you to proceed with planning to the final meeting, you must be aware of the projected rate at which events will happen. Improved technology such as fax and online services has dramatically accelerated the process and the demands of clients to "do it now." However, "now" is often not as efficient as later. When an event manager is pressured to deliver a product before it is fully developed, the results may be less than exemplary. Therefore, as you manage the rate at which tasks will be completed and events will occur, it is important to consider if each action is being performed at the best time. "Maybe" is not an acceptable response. To determine if this is the best moment for this task to be handled, ask yourself if you have sufficient information and resources to implement it. If not, try to delay the action until you are better prepared.

Establishing the proper tempo is not an exact science. Rather, like a conductor of an orchestra, you must allow your personal taste, energy, and experience to guide you as you speed up or slow down the tempo as required. Analyzing the event site and estimating the time required for a project, the event manager is better able to set the tempo or schedule for the setup, production, and removal of the equipment. Without this advance analysis, the event manager becomes an orchestra conductor without benefit of a score, a musician without benefit of a maestro.

Understanding the needs of guests also helps establish and adjust the tempo during an event. If the guest is concerned primarily with networking, a leisurely time frame should be followed to allow for plenty of interaction. For example, while the transition from cocktails to dinner may be brisk when the program is more important than networking, the transition may be slowed when the emphasis is on the connections the audience members make among themselves.

Paul Demos, longtime director of catering at the Chicago Hilton and Towers Hotel, matches the type of service to the needs of the guests. "The number of courses, whether wine is served, the dress style of the guests," according to Demos, all govern the ultimate tempo of the event and type of service required.

These three basic laws, as old as human creation itself, govern the planning of all events. To become an expert event manager you must master your ability to manage time in the most minute segments. You must develop the vision to perceive the strengths, weaknesses, opportunities, and threats of every space. Finally, you must be able to analyze the needs of your guests to set tempos that will ensure a memorable event.

## GAP ANALYSIS

Too often, event managers proceed by rote memory to produce an event in a style with which they are most familiar. In doing this they often overlook critical gaps in the logical progression of event elements. Identifying these gaps and providing recommendations for closure is the primary purpose of *gap analysis.*

This planning tool involves taking a long, hard look at event elements and identifying significant gaps in the planning that could weaken the overall progression of the plan. An example is an event manager who has scheduled an outdoor event in September in Miami Beach, Florida. September is the prime month of the hurricane season. The event manager has created a wide gap in his or her plan that must be closed to strengthen the overall event. Therefore, finding a secure indoor location in case of a weather emergency would be a good beginning toward closing this gap.

Use a critical friend—a person whose expertise about the particular event is known to you—to review your plan and search for gaps in your logical thinking. Once you have identified the gaps, look for opportunities to close them. By implementing the findings from SWOT and gap analysis, you are able to begin executing your plan. This execution phase is known as coordination.

# Coordination: Executing the Plan

As the light turns green, the tempo accelerates and you are now faced with coordinating the minute-by-minute activities of the event itself. I was once asked, "What does it take to be a competent event manager?" "The ability to make good decisions," I swiftly answered. You realize now that it requires much more than good decision-making ability; however, it is also true that during the course of coordinating an event you will be required to make not dozens but hundreds of decisions. Your ability to use your professional training and experience to make the correct decision will affect the outcome of the entire event. While it is true that event managers should maintain a positive attitude and see problems as challenges in search of the right solution, it is also important that you apply critical analysis to every challenge that comes your way. Following is a simple but effective way to make these decisions.

1. Collect all the information. Most problems have many sides to review.
2. Consider the pros and cons of your decision in terms of who will be affected.
3. Consider the financial implications of your decision.
4. Consider the moral and ethical implications of your decision.
5. Make a decision and do not look back.

# Evaluation: The Link to the Next Event

The event management process, as shown in Figure 2-6, is a dynamic spiral that is literally without end. The first phase—research—is connected with the last—evaluation. In this phase you will ask: "What is it we wish to evaluate, and how will we best accomplish this?" Events may be evaluated by each part of the event management process or through a general comprehensive review of all phases. It is up to you and your stakeholders to decide what information you require to improve your planning and then implement effective strategies to accomplish this phase.

Perhaps the most common form of event evaluation is the written survey. Usually, the survey is conducted immediately following the event, to collect the satisfaction level of the participants and spectators. As with any evaluation method, there are pros and cons to immediate feedback. One bias is the immediate nature of the feedback, which prohibits a respondent from digesting the total event experience before providing his or her feedback.

Another form of evaluation is the use of monitors. A *monitor* is a trained person who will observe an element of the event and provide both written and verbal feedback to the event manager. The event monitor usually has a checklist or survey to complete and will then offer additional comments as required. The benefit of this type of evaluation is that it permits a trained, experienced event staff member or volunteer to observe the event objectively while it is taking place and provide instructive comments.

The third form of event evaluation is the telephone or mail survey conducted after the event. In this evaluation the event manager surveys the spectators and participants after the event through either a mail or a telephone survey. By waiting a few days after the event to collect these data, the event manager is able to glean from the respondents how their attitudes have changed and developed after some time has passed since participating in the event.

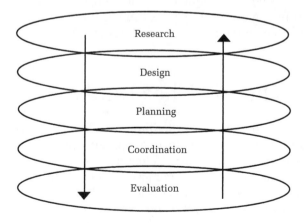

**Figure 2-6**
Event Management Process

A new form of evaluation that is growing in popularity is the pre- and postevent survey. This evaluation allows an event manager to determine the respondents' knowledge, opinions, and other important information both before and after their attendance at an event. This is especially helpful when trying to match expectations to reality. For example, an event guest may state upon entering an event that he or she expects, based on the advertising and public relations, to enjoy nonstop entertainment. However, upon completing the exit interview, the guest registers disappointment because of the gaps in the programming. This type of evaluation helps event organizers close gaps between overpromising and underdelivering certain aspects of an event. Registration mail-in rebates and other incentives may be offered for filling out both surveys.

Regardless of the form of evaluation you use, it is critical that you not wait until the end of the event to find out how you are doing. If you were to attend any banquet where I am responsible for the event, you might be surprised to see me wandering from table to table and asking guests how they are enjoying dinner. In doing this, I am able to uncover gaps in execution of the plan. One guest might say: "I ordered vegetarian and was served meat." I am able to correct this error immediately. If I had waited until the person had filled out an evaluation form, it would have been too late.

Take the temperature of your guests hourly to make certain that you are on target in meeting your goals and objectives. By doing this you are able to reset your course immediately and ensure that together you will arrive at the same destination—a successful event.

This event management process is the conceptual framework for every effective event. The process is dynamic and will require selectivity by the event manager to determine where to begin and how to proceed to best accomplish the objectives. One event may be past the research stage and the event manager retained merely to coordinate the elements. Still another may be midway through the planning phase. The effective event manager will immediately recognize that the event process cannot be complete or totally effective unless each phase is considered carefully. It matters not where you begin the process. It is essential that every phase be considered, visited, and understood.

# Communications: The Tie That Binds

Event management is a profession whose success or failure ratio often depends on people's ability to communicate effectively with one another. It does not matter whether this communication is oral, written, electronic, or all three. What is important is that event managers become practiced communicators in order to maintain clear communications with all stakeholders. Regardless of the communication channel that you are using, you want to make sure that you make your point clearly and establish the right priorities in your message.

Often, both visual and auditory noise will provide a barrier to open communication. Visual noise includes those visual distractions that take place when you are trying to communicate with others. Auditory noise may be music, traffic, or other distractions that interfere with others' ability to hear and concentrate on what you are saying. Remove all noise before trying to communicate with others. Find a quiet place to meet, remove visual distractions, and verify and confirm that those you are communicating with comprehend what you are sharing.

Written communications are essential not only for record keeping but also for purposes of mass distribution. It is impossible to transmit verbally to 1000 people an event update without distortion. (Remember the children's game "gossip"?) Use memorandums, briefing statements, bulletins, and other documents to communicate effectively to one or many others. Memorandums should include an "Action Required" statement to inform the reader how best to respond and in what time frame.

Bulletins must be sporadic or you run the risk of becoming the person who cried "wolf" once too often and now are ignored by everyone. Newsletters are a particularly effective tool for communications; however, use caution, as they are extremely labor intensive.

Perhaps one of the best ways to communicate is through a meeting. When scheduling a meeting, make certain that you prepare an agenda in advance that lists the items for discussion. Distribute this document in advance of the meeting to those who will attend and ask them to comment. This will help them prepare for the meeting. Use the agenda to guide the meeting and as the leader serve as a facilitator for discussion. Using a flipchart will help you capture ideas while sticking to the agenda. One extremely effective device is to assign the meeting participants prework so that they come to the meeting prepared and ready to make specific contributions. Make sure that your meeting does not take much longer than initially planned; otherwise, you will give the impression of being a disorganized person who does not value your own time and the time that others will invest in the meeting.

Alternative communication techniques include producing audiotapes and videotapes as well as using teleconferencing through compressed video (telephone lines). Since the average person commutes 20 or more minutes twice daily to the office, this is an excellent time to put your meeting or information on audiotape, add a little music, and share your ideas. The major drawback to this alternative is that the communication is one-way. Videotapes also allow you to express your thoughts creatively with photos, interviews, and music and to show the tape before a large group of people creating excitement in numbers. Two-way video using existing telephone lines and a compressed system is an effective way to present data, visuals, and some person-to-person interaction. It is also relatively inexpensive compared to traditional satellite uplink/downlink technology.

The use of computer online chat rooms has grown in popularity due to the rapid expansion of the Internet technologies. When using chat rooms, avoid personal issues and conduct postings in a businesslike manner. Personal issues may be addressed through other mediums, such as telephone calls. Chat rooms are excellent information exchange opportunities and you will find that your colleagues will provide you with new resources for producing better events.

# Synergy: Linking Administration, Coordination, Marketing, and Risk Management

The Walt Disney Company is the only organization of its size with an executive board position titled Vice-President for Synergy. Due to the diversity in the Disney product line (theme parks, retail stores, movies, recordings, sport, television), the leaders of this successful organization believe that one person must be responsible for ensuring that there is synergy among all aspects of the business operation.

Up to one year in advance, before Disney rolls out a new movie, the retail stores are developing new products, the theme parks are planning new live shows, and the other aspects of the corporation are preparing for joint promotion and distribution of the new product. This kind of synergy allocates Disney's scarce resources in the most efficient manner.

Your event also has scarce resources. These resources include your ability to administrate, coordinate, market, and manage the risk for the event. You must link these four competencies together carefully and thoroughly throughout the event process in order to produce the very best and most profitable event product.

The administration process of an event serves as the foundation for the resources you will select and manage during the coordination process. Poor administration will later undermine your ability to coordinate the event. Strong coordination will result in better marketing results. Unless your operations people are aware that today's tickets are discounted, all the advertising in the world will be wasted. The link between coordination and marketing, and for that matter administration, is vital. Finally, legal, ethical, and risk management issues form a strong river current that runs through every decision you make in event management. If your marketing team leader overpromotes or promotes an event inaccurately, he or she will place those who must coordinate event operations at a great disadvantage. In subsequent chapters we introduce each of these competencies in detail, but at this early stage it is important for you to recognize the connection between them. Together, they weave a strong tapestry that will help shield you from future problems and provide a rich understanding of how all team members must work together productively.

## GLOBAL CONNECTION

Internet online discussions help to establish communication among event management organizations and various other event stakeholders. This will also help to reduce operations costs, especially for international events. Since international events usually require longer time for logistical preparations, it is important to use the fastest methods of communication to facilitate the planning stage.

## TECHNOLOGY CONNECTION

With the development of the Internet, many event management organizations started using Internet-based applications that allow secured sharing of information among multiple parties. One example is George Washington University's interactive data- and information-sharing site, Prometheus *(www.prometheus.gwu.edu)*. Another example is Microsoft Outlook *(www.microsoft.com)*, where participants can exchange files as well as conduct online team activities. Using such password-secured Web sites, you can post files and exchange information from anywhere in the world.

## RESOURCE CONNECTION

Contact event management industry associations to stay abreast of quickly developing industry trends. The International Special Events Society (ISES, *www.ises.com*) is committed to continuous education in the event management community.

## LEARNING CONNECTION

In this chapter you have covered the five stages of each event. To enhance your understanding of the chapter, complete the following activity:

You are managing a new European car launch in the United States. Over 5000 attendees are expected to be at the event over a three-day period. The event will include various elements, such as a car show, indoor test driving, and a gala reception. The contract requires that you develop the complete event program and implement it. This event requires a lot of creativity and excellent organization skills. You need to produce the event and to be able to execute it flawlessly. What tasks will you perform in each of the five stages?

# PART TWO

# Event Administration

Event
Administration

**Facing Page**
The National Building Museum in Washington, DC provides a dramatic setting for this elegant and exotic themed dinner. *Photograph courtesy of Monica Vidal.*

# CHAPTER 3

# Developing and Implementing the Event Plan

**IN THIS CHAPTER YOU WILL LEARN HOW TO:**

- Conduct comprehensive research for your event
- Identify key sources of information for planning
- Design a program creatively
- Develop an appropriate theme
- Establish and manage an effective strategic plan
- Develop and manage the timeline for an event

The administration of a professional event is the first competency that must be mastered in the certified special events professional body of knowledge. Comprehensive administration is the foundation for all successful events. The administration of an event provides you and the stakeholders with data with which to design the dream that will produce the deliverables you desire. The term *event* originated from the Latin term *e-venire. E* in Latin means "out" and *venire* means "come." Therefore, events are, in fact, "outcomes."

During the administration process the event manager must make certain that data identified during research are used to drive the design and ultimately to produce the measurable outcomes required by event stakeholders:

$$research\ (data) + design = planned\ successful\ outcomes$$

Research without the important phase of design will result in a dry, one-dimensional, and perhaps boring event. To produce a multidimensional and multisensory event experience that transforms guests, you must research as well as design the event outcome. The research and design phases ultimately produce the tools with which you can construct a blueprint of the event plan. The final event plan is, in fact, a direct reflection of the research and design phases.

## STRETCHING THE LIMITS OF THE EVENT

Whereas research is either inductive or deductive in form and often proceeds in a linear fashion, the design phase is weblike and often kaleidoscopic. Just as the Internet provides you with literally millions of resources for event design, your own mental process must mirror this technology. During the design process the professional event manager considers every possibility and challenges every assumption determined during the research phase. This pushing of the research envelope is essential if you are to produce innovative, highly creative, unique special events that will exceed the expectations of guests.

B. Joseph Pine and James H. Gilmore state in *The Experience Economy* (Allston, MA: Harvard Business School Press, 2000) that "You are what you charge for." If you are to steadily increase the value of your work as an event researcher, designer, planner, coordinator, and evaluator, you must strive continually to collect the best information and resources to produce a solid plan that satisfies the needs, wants, desires, and ultimately, expectations of event guests.

## DESIGNING THE EVENT ENVIRONMENT

Like a playwright who molds his or her play to create a setting that a theater's limited confines can accommodate, event managers face a similar challenge each time they are called upon to create an environment. Whether the site is a palatial mansion or a suburban park, the challenges remain the same. How can the site be adapted to meet the needs of guests? Ballrooms with their four bare walls, department stores filled with products, and even main streets upon which parades are staged offer the same problems and opportunities as those confronting playwrights and set designers.

When creating an environment, the special events professional must again return to the basic needs of the guests. The final design must satisfy these needs to become successful. Lighting, space, movement, decor, acoustics, and even such seemingly mundane concerns as rest rooms all affect the comfort of the guests and so play vital roles in creating a successful environment.

# Five-Card Draw: Playing the Five Senses

When attempting to satisfy the needs of guests, remember that the five senses are most powerful tools. Like five winning cards in the event manager's hand, combining the five senses—tactile, smell, taste, visual, and auditory—to satiate the needs of guests is the primary consideration when designing the event environment. The olfactory system creates instant emotional and creative reactions within your guests. How many times have you walked into a room, noticed a familiar smell, and suddenly experienced déjà vu? Event management pioneer Jack Morton says that smell is the most powerful sense because of the memories it produces. In fact, smell may generally be the strongest sense in terms of generating emotional response; however, this will vary among individual guests. Therefore, as the event manager you must actively seek to employ in your environmental design elements that will affect all the senses.

When designing a "Gone with the Wind" banquet, you may erect a backdrop that immediately conjures memories of Tara, play music from the famous movie's theme, and even have Rhett and Scarlett look-a-likes at the door to greet and touch your guests. However, that magnolia centerpiece on the table is sadly missing one element. When you add a light scent of Jungle Gardenia perfume, the event suddenly becomes a total sensory experience.

Just as some guests are sensitive to certain stimuli, such as smell or auditory, other guests have a primary sense that they rely upon. Due to the influence of television, many baby boomers may rely primarily on their visual sense. When designing the environment, this is important to recognize when you are trying to communicate your message quickly. Use the senses as instruments to tune the imagination of guests. Be careful to avoid playing sharp or flat notes by overdoing it. Find the perfect sensory melody and guests will become involved in your event creatively and emotionally.

The following procedures will enable you to survey guests to determine their level of sensitivity as well as their primary sensual stimuli in order to create an effective event sensory environment.

1. Use a focus group to determine the primary sensory stimuli of your guests.
2. Identify any oversensitivity or even allergies guests may have that could be irritated by certain sensory elements.
3. Use the draft diagram of the event environment to identify and isolate the location of certain sensory experiences.
4. Share this design tool with typical guests and solicit their attitudes and opinions.
5. Audit the venue to determine the preexisting sensory environment and what modifications you will be required to implement.

## SOUNDSCAPING

To communicate with the guests at an event, you must design a sound system and effects that are unique and powerful enough to capture their attention. Do not confuse powerful with loud, however. Poignant background music at a small social event has as much power as a booming rock beat at a retail promotion. As with other components of event production, successful use of sound requires gauging and meeting the needs of the audience.

Sound by itself is a most powerful sensation. When asked which of her senses she would like to have returned to her, the late Helen Keller, blind and deaf since birth, explained that the ability to hear is more important than the ability to see. The eyes can deceive, but the way in which others speak and the thoughts they share reveal much about personality and intentions. Sound unlocks our imagination and allows us to visualize images buried in our subconscious. When planning the sound design for your event, many questions need to be considered. What is to be the dominant sensory element for the event? Sound may be the dominant sensory element for your event; for example, if live music or extensive speeches are the major component of your event, your investment in high-quality sound production may be paramount.

How will sound help support, reinforce, or expand the guests' perceptions of the event? Consider the theme of your event and devise ways in which sound can be used to convey that theme to the guests. For example, if you are planning a Polynesian theme event, the use of recorded island-type music at the entrance will help communicate that theme.

Are the architectural conditions in the venue optimal for sound reproduction? This question is most important considering the number of new sites being created every day. The majority of these sites were not designed for optimum sound reproduction, and the event planner or sound designer must therefore consider how to improve the sound conditions in the venue. In the five special events markets, sound design, like lighting, is growing tremendously. In the social market, not only are live bands used more than ever, but with the addition of new electronic instruments, the repertoire of a small live band can be increased manyfold. Moreover, the rise of the disc jockey format and the more frequent use of videotape requires that the sound quality must be better than ever before. As the sophistication of the audio components available to the average consumer has increased, the sound systems for retail events have had to improve in quality as well to match the sound many guests can experience in their living rooms. Whether it be a fashion show or a visit with Santa, excellent sound is required to give the event credibility and value in the eyes (or ears) of the guest. Millions of dollars' worth of merchandise may be on display, but if the sound system is poor, the guest perceives less value and is less inclined to buy.

Meetings and convention events also place more importance on sound reproduction for their programs. Gone are the days when a meeting planner was content to use the hotel house speakers for live music. Today, many musical groups carry their own speakers, mixing boards, and operators.

## VISUAL CUES

Baby boomers and subsequent generations, raised in front of television sets, may require strong visual elements to assist them with experiencing your event. This includes using proper signs to orient the guest and provide clear direction. Additional visual elements that must be considered are the proper and repetitive use of key design elements such as the *logo*. A logo is the graphic symbol of the organization sponsoring the event. Not only must this symbol be represented accurately, but it must always appear in the same manner to benefit from repetitive viewing and establish consistency to promote retention.

## TOUCH

Whether you are considering the cloth that will dress the banquet table, the napkins, or the printed program, touch will immediately convey the quality of the event environment. To establish this sense, use several different textures and while wearing a blindfold, touch the various elements to determine what feelings are promoted. When handling the cloth, do you feel as though you are attending a royal gala or a country picnic? When holding the program, are you a guest of the king or the court jester? Use this blindfold test to help you narrow your choices and effectively select the right fabric, paper, or other product to properly communicate the precise sense of touch you desire.

## SMELL

Earlier we discussed the use of a perfume such as Jungle Gardenia to stimulate the sense of memory through smell. Remember that throughout the event environment a series of smells may be present that will either create the correct environment or confuse and irritate the guest. When conducting the site inspection, note if the public areas are overdeodorized. This smell is often a clue that these chemicals are being used to mask a foul smell. Instead, you may wish to look for venues whose aromas are natural and the result of history, people, and of course, natural products such as plants and flowers.

Some people are extremely sensitive to strong odors. Therefore, when using the sense of smell, do not overdo it. Instead, establish neutral areas where the smell of a scented candle, flowers, or food odors is not present, to provide the nose with a respite from this stimulation. However, establishing individual areas that have a strong aroma of pizza baking or chocolate melting is also important to both attract and convey the proper atmosphere. You may, for example, wish to incorporate the smell of barbecue into your western-themed event or pine trees into your Christmas wonderland. Again, when establishing these areas of smell, try and isolate them so that the guests can return to a neutral zone and not feel overwhelmed by this sense.

## TASTE

The sense of taste will be discussed later; however, the event manager must realize that the catering team members play a critical role in establishing a strong sensory feeling for the event. Consult in advance with the catering team and establish the goals and objectives of the food presentation, and then determine how best to proceed in combining the other four senses with the sense of taste to create a total olfactory experience for the guests. Keep in mind the age, culture, and lifestyle of the guests. Older guests may not be as sensitive to taste, whereas other guests may require spicier food combinations to engage the sense of taste. The taste sense historically has been linked with a strong sensual experience. Play the taste card for all it is worth and you will transform guests from spectators to fully engaged participants who will long remember the succulent event you have designed.

## BLENDING, MIXING, AND MATCHING FOR FULL EFFECT

Make certain that you carefully select those event design sensory elements that will support the goals and objectives of the event. Do not confuse or irritate guests by layering too many different senses in an effort to be creative.

Rather, design the sensory experience as you would select paint for a canvas. Determine in advance what you hope to achieve or communicate and then use the five senses as powerful tools to help you accomplish your goals.

## BELLS AND WHISTLES: AMENITIES THAT MAKE THE DIFFERENCE

Once you have established the atmosphere for your event environment and satisfied the basic needs of all guests, you have the opportunity to embellish or enhance their experience by adding a few well-chosen amenities. An amenity is best defined as a feature that increases attractiveness or value. In today's added value-driven business environment, amenities are more important than ever before. These amenities may range from advertising specialty items given as gifts at the beginning or the end of the event, interactive elements such as virtual environments, and even child care.

A popular way to stretch the budget is to transform the guests into decor elements. This is accomplished by distributing glow-in-the-dark novelty items such as necklaces, pins, or even swizzle sticks. As guests enter the darkened event environment, their glowing presence suddenly creates exciting visual stimuli. Firms such as Liquid Light in Los Angeles specialize in customizing these items with the slogans, logo, or name of the sponsoring organization.

Another effective amenity that is growing in popularity is the virtual event environment. Using virtual reality software, guests are able to experience many different environments at the same time. Wearing specially constructed goggles, the guest is propelled visually to the top of a skyscraper, where he or she does battle with evil demons or may stroll casually through a virtual trade show environment pausing to visually inspect a variety of different booths. These systems have become integral to the success of high-tech industries and are gaining in importance in assisting guests in maximizing their time while at an event by providing the opportunity to visit several different environments in a short time period.

Whether dealing with glow-in-the-dark jewelry or virtual reality software, the needs, wants, and desires of guests must be evaluated consistently to determine if the communications media you are using are effective and efficient. Using feedback from specific populations will help you achieve this purpose rapidly.

# Identifying the Needs of Your Guests

Once you have gathered all the quantitative data from the site inspection, it is time to analyze your findings and determine what implications emerge for your event environment design. Most important considerations include the legal, regulatory, and risk management issues that are uncovered during site inspection.

## PROVISION FOR GUESTS HAVING DISABILITIES

If the venue is not in full compliance with the Americans with Disabilities Act, you may need to make certain modifications in your design. See Chapter 9 for a complete discussion of compliance with this act.

## IMPLICATIONS OF SIZE, WEIGHT, AND VOLUME

Let us assume that your design requires massive scenery and that the ingress to your venue is a door of standard width and height. How do you squeeze the elephant through the keyhole? The answer is, of course, "very carefully." Seriously, make certain that your design elements can be broken down into small units. Using component parts for the construction process will enable you to design individual elements that will fit easily through most doorways.

Weight is an important consideration, as many venues were not built with this factor in mind. Before bringing in elements that have extraordinary weight, check with the facility engineer to review the construction standards used in the venue and then determine if the stress factor is sufficient to accommodate your design. Furthermore, shifting weight can cause serious problems for certain venues. Therefore, if you are using a stage platform and simply placing a heavy prop, you may not experience any problems. However, if on this same platform you are showcasing 50 aerobic dancers performing high-energy routines, the platforms may not be sufficiently reinforced to handle this shifting weight. In addition to reviewing the stress weight that the area can accommodate with the engineer or other expert, conduct independent tests yourself by actually walking across the stage or examining the undergirdings to ensure that what goes up will not come down.

The final consideration is volume. The fire marshal determines the number of persons that can be safely accommodated in the venue. You, however, greatly influence this number by the seating configuration, the amount of decor, and other technical elements that you include in the final event environment. Less equals more. Typically, the fewer design elements you incorporate, the more people you can accommodate. Therefore, when creating your total event design, first determine the number of people you must accommodate. Subtract the number of square feet required for the guests and the remainder will determine the volume of elements that contribute to the event environment.

### Example: Calculating and Sizing the Event Environment

1. Identify the total number of persons and multiply the square feet (or meters) required for each person. For example:

$$\begin{array}{r} 50 \text{ couples} \\ \times\ \underline{10 \text{ square feet per couple}} \\ = 500 \text{ square feet} \end{array}$$

2. Subtract the total number of square feet required for the couples from the total space available. For example:

1000 square feet available for dance floor
−   500 square feet required by couples
────────────────────────────────────────
=   500 square feet available for props, tables, chairs, and other equipment

Do not do this in reverse. Some event managers create a lavish design first, only later to find that the number of guests will not allow them to install this design.

## SECURING THE ENVIRONMENT

Just as the fire marshal is responsible for determining occupancy, the police and local security officials will determine how to secure an environment to reduce the possibility of theft or personal injury. When considering the theme and other important design elements, remember that people will be walking under, over, and within this environment, and their safety must be paramount in your planning. Providing adequate lighting for traversing the event environment, securing cables and other technical components with tape or ramps, and posting notices of "Use Caution" or "Watch Your Step" are important considerations when designing beautiful as well as safe event environments.

Theft, sadly, is a major concern in designing an event environment. Do not make it easy to remove items from the event environment. Secure perimeter doors with guards or provide bag check stations at the entrance to discourage unscrupulous persons from easily lifting valuable event elements. This is especially important when designing expositions where millions of dollars of merchandise may be on display for long periods of time. Furthermore, do not allow event participants to store merchandise or personal goods such as purses in public areas. Instead, provide a secure area for these elements, to ensure a watchful eye.

## TRANSPORTATION AND PARKING FACTORS

The venue may or may not provide easy vehicle ingress. Therefore, well in advance you must locate the proper door for load-in of your equipment, the times the dock is available for your deliveries, and other critical factors that will govern your ability to transport equipment and park your vehicles. Another consideration for transportation relates to approved routes for trucks and other vehicles. In some jurisdictions, such as Washington, DC, truck and large vehicular traffic is strictly regulated. Once again, confer well in advance with transportation and venue officials to determine the most efficient route.

Whether you are parking your vehicles in a marshaling facility or on the street, security must be considered as well as easy access. Some venues may not be located in the safest of neighborhoods, and therefore securing your vehicles and providing safe and fast access to them are important. Well-lit fenced-in areas are best for parking; however, the proximity of the vehicles to the loading area of the venue is the prime concern.

You may think that transportation and parking have little to do with creating a proper event environment, but these two considerations should be given significant attention. Many events have started late or suffered in quality due to late or lost vehicles and inefficient load-in operations. Remember, you may design the most incredible event environment, but until it is shipped, loaded in, and installed properly, it is only your idea. Proper transportation and installation will turn your idea into a dynamic event environment.

# Manage the Event Environment and They Will Come Back

Understanding the basic needs of the guest is of paramount importance, especially when you are working with a smaller budget than you would like. In circumstances where the budget is severely restricted, there are ways, using your imagination, to stretch limited funds. Use your budget to enhance the beginning and the end, as these are what the guest will most remember. Following are some considerations for managing the design of an event environment.

## ENTRANCES AND RECEPTION AREAS

The event manager must immediately establish the theme of the event with environmental design. The use of proper signs, bearing the group's name or logo, and appropriate decor will reassure guests that they are in the right place. Consider the arrival process from the guests' point of view. They received the invitation some time ago and probably did not bring it with them to the event. Therefore, they are relying on memory to guide them to the right building and the right room. Once they have located parking, they ask the attendant to direct them to XYZ event. The attendant is rushed, having to park several hundred cars for perhaps as many as six different functions and cannot recall the exact location of the affair. Should the guests stumble upon your site and not recognize it because the logo is absent or the entrance does not communicate the theme of the party, they will become confused and lost. Providing your own personnel in costume or professional wardrobe will help guests locate your event, as will proper signage. Upon arrival, guests should have an "Ah-ha!" experience, knowing that they have arrived at the right place at the right time. You can offer guests this experience and create a positive impression by proper design of the reception area at which they are greeted. When guests must wait in long lines, they often begin to resent the event or its hosts. You must plan for these delays and offer solutions.

Figures 3-1 to 3-4 demonstrate how to place greeters, or "damage control" hosts, to handle problems in the reception area. In Figure 3-1 the guests have begun to form a second row at the reception table. When this occurs, greeters should immediately invite the second-row guests to step forward to the additional tables set behind the primary tables. Having extra tables available will be perceived by guests as an added courtesy and will help ease heavy arrival times. Note that the guests at the primary tables enter between them so as not to conflict with the guests at the additional tables.

Figure 3-2 shows a solution to the problem of guests arriving without an invitation and without their names appearing on the list of invitees. To avoid embarrassment and delay, the guest is invited to step forward to the courtesy table, conveniently isolated from the general crowd flow. There the problem can be resolved quietly and courteously, or the guest may be ushered out a back door without disrupting the event.

The scenario depicted in Figure 3-3 is one that every experienced event planner has known. During heavy arrival time, such as the second half-hour of a one-hour cocktail party preceding the main event, long lines of guests are forming while those staffing the reception tables are trying to greet arrivals quickly and efficiently and keep the line moving. Professional greeters can make the guests' wait less annoying. Their job is simply to greet the guests in

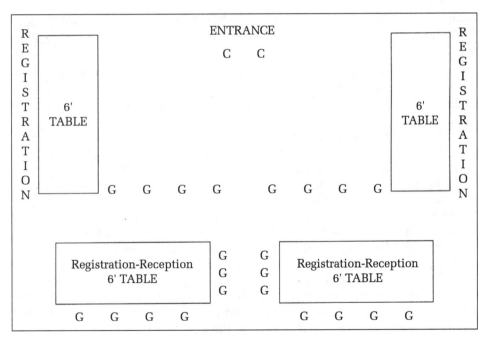

**Figure 3-1**

Registration–Reception Setup with Secondary Tables Supporting a Primary Table (G, guest; C, control)

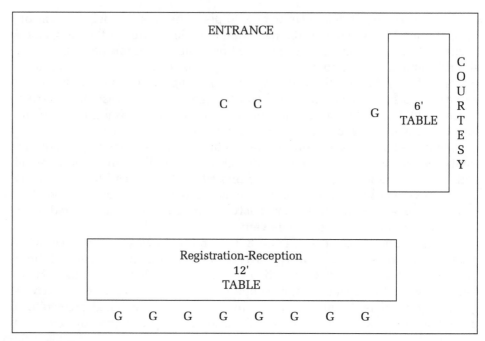

**Figure 3-2**
Registration–Reception Setup with a Secondary Courtesy Table (G, guest; C, control)

line, quietly thank them for coming, and answer any questions they may have while waiting. Often, professional performers, such as strolling mimes, clowns, jugglers, or magicians, may be used in this area to entertain, thereby distracting guests while they wait in line.

When you expect long lines over a brief period, the best arrangement is a variation of Figure 3-1. By using two additional courtesy tables, positioned at an angle as shown in Figure 3-4, you may alleviate crowding. The reception setup integrating the professional greeter into the flow of guest traffic further ensures the ease and comfort of guests.

In Figure 3-4 you can keep guests moving forward and handle disputes at the same time. The hosts and hostesses at these courtesy tables should be trained to resolve disputes quickly and know when to refer a guest to a supervisor for further assistance. Most disputes can be remedied simply, requiring no more than preparation of a name badge, a payment, or other minor business. If handled at the primary table, such tasks become cumbersome. Experienced planners know that the floor plan for the reception area should facilitate guests arrivals and is critical to the success of the event. The way in which a guest is first received at an event determines all future perceptions that he or she will have about the event program you have designed. Take time to plan this area carefully to ensure an efficient and gracious reception.

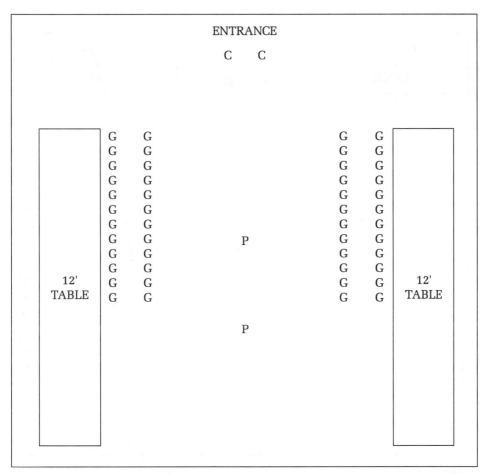

**Figure 3-3**
Reception Setup Integrating the Professional Greeter into the Flow of Guest Traffic (G, guest; C, control; P, professional greeter)

## FUNCTION AREAS

The reception area may create the first impression, but the main function area will determine the effectiveness of the overall design. This is the area in which guests will spend the most time, and this is the area where your principal message must be communicated to guests in a memorable manner. Traditional space designs are currently being rethought by meeting planners as well as psychologists to develop a more productive environment. Paul Radde is a psychologist who has pioneered the development of physical space planning for conferences that provides a more optimum environment in which to learn. Radde has, often to the chagrin of various hotel setup crews, determined that speakers prefer and often deliver a better talk when there is no center aisle. In

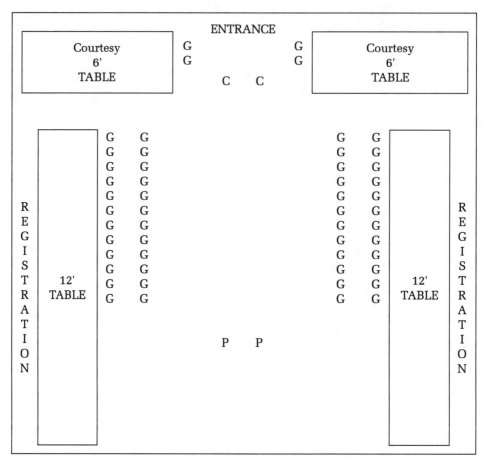

**Figure 3-4**
Reception Setup Using Two Additional Courtesy Tables Positioned at an
Angle (G, guest; C, control; P, professional greeter)

the traditional theater- or classroom-style setup shown in Figure 3-5, all of the
speaker's energy escapes through the center aisle. When this lane is filled with
live bodies, the speaker's interaction is increased, as is the human connection
among audience members themselves.

Figure 3-6 demonstrates the optimum setup, complete with wide aisles on
each side to allow for proper egress. With this setting, each row should be at
least 6 inches farther apart than in Figure 3-5, to allow for more efficient
egress. Some fire marshals prohibit the arrangement in Figure 3-6 because
some audience members will be seated too far from an aisle. An excellent alternative is shown in Figure 3-7, in which the front two rows are solid, with
side aisles beginning behind the second row.

Perhaps the best adaptation is shown in Figure 3-8. In this arrangement all
rows except the first five are sealed, and the center aisle is easily reached by

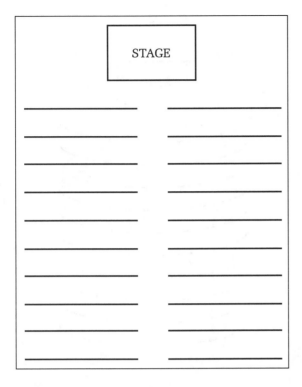

**Figure 3-5**
Traditional Theater- or Classroom-Style Setup

latecomers in the rear of the auditorium. Planning an effective seating arrangement is only the beginning. Masking tape or rope on stanchions can be used to seal the back rows, as shown in Figure 3-8, encouraging guests to fill in the front rows first.

Once filled with guests, the tape is removed. After 30 years of watching audiences head for the back rows, I experimented a few years ago with this method to determine if I could control seating habits without inconveniencing the audience unduly. Much to my delight, several audience members have thanked me for this subtle suggestion to move up front. Without this direction the audience becomes confused and retreats to old habits.

Interestingly, once a guest claims a seat, he or she will return to it throughout the event. However, unless I have predetermined that they will sit up front by making the back rows unavailable, all of the coaxing and bribing (I once placed dollar bills under front-row seats) will not move the audience from the back-row comfort zone.

## INNOVATIVE SITES

The purpose of creatively designing your environment is to provide a dynamic atmosphere within which your guest may experience the event. Decorator Terry Brady knows all too well how important such an atmosphere can be, as he once staged a banquet in a tractor–trailer. The guests were escorted up the

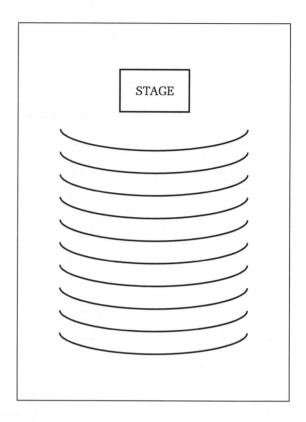

**Figure 3-6**
Optimum Theater- or Classroom-Style Setup

steps and dined inside an actual tractor–trailer decorated by the Brady Company's team of artists. The goal of this creative design was to surprise and intrigue guests, who were picked up in limousines and brought to this isolated and inelegant site. Inside the tractor–trailer, they found luxurious decor, complete with chandeliers, tapestries, and fine linens. Brady recalls that the total tab for the 40 guests, including catering, service, and decor, was roughly $16,000. Not every client will allocate upward of $400 per person for an event. Nonetheless, the event planner is increasingly faced with the challenge of finding innovative, creative environments in which to stage their events. Curators of museums and public buildings in record numbers throughout the United States have begun setting fees and offering their buildings to groups that wish to host a reception or meeting in a novel atmosphere. With these new opportunities for use of public space come increased challenges for decorators, who must now cope with the increased demand for atmospheric props in place of flats, banners, murals, and other more traditional scenic devices. Table 3-1 includes a sampling of ideas for unusual sites in which to hold special events. Use this list to brainstorm with your event stakeholders to determine the best venue for your next event. The possibilities for exciting, innovative, and offbeat event sites are infinite. It is important, however, that your

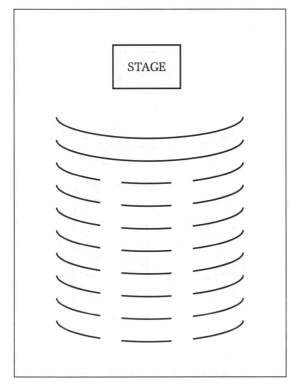

**Figure 3-7**
Modified Theater- or Classroom-Style Setup

selection be logical and practical in terms of location, parking, setup, budget, and use of space.

One important book, entitled "New York's 100 Best Party Places: Weddings, Special Occasions, Corporate Events," by S. Stuman and H. Sheets (2000, City & Co.) lists 100 event sites in New York City. The publication may be obtained by telephoning (212) 737-7536. In a northern California-based publication entitled *Perfect Places* by Lynn Broadwell and Jan Brenner (2001), venues ranging from historic homes to modern museums are described, with careful attention to both aesthetic and logistical detail. This publication may be obtained by calling (510) 525-3379. A companion book by Broadwell is entitled *Here Comes the Guide* (2001), and focuses on sites for weddings. According to Broadwell, writing in *ISES Gold* (1994): "Twenty years ago event sites were a rare commodity. What's changed? Everything."

Wherever you turn, you will find new products and new services available to help you transform an environment for a creative special event. Many unusual products can be found at gift shows (trade shows featuring new and unusual gift items), antique stores and shows, flea markets, used and classic clothing stores, hotel closeout sales, and other businesses selling off stock. The ISES worldwide resource directory lists additional groups and organizations that can help create an environment for your next special event.

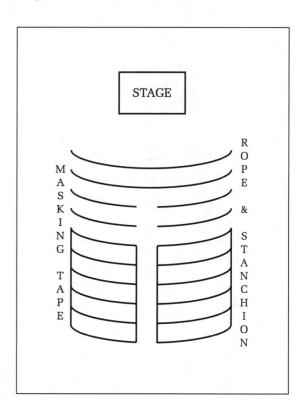

**Figure 3-8**
Modified Theater- or Classroom-Style Setup
with Roped-Off Rear Section

## AMENITIES AND FURNISHINGS

The possibilities for linens, silverware, glassware, centerpieces, and even costumes for servers are greater in the profession today than ever before. Sites, sources, and suppliers for these items can be found in journals such as *Event World, Special Events,* and various industry newsletters. See Appendixes 4 to 6 for dozens of additional resources.

### Edible Centerpieces and Displays

The centuries-old European custom of including elaborately designed food displays as part of the decor is finally becoming popular—indeed, in some regions, de rigueur—in the United States. This important area of setting design can range from fancy carved crudités for the hors d'oeuvres to elaborate centerpieces carved from thick dark chocolate. Today's special events professionals are as concerned with the aesthetic appeal of food selections as they are with taste. In fact, food presentation has become an artform in the United States, one in which annual competitions are held in areas ranging from ice sculpture and sugar works to chocolate and pastry design. When incorporating food into an overall design, remember that ultimately, most food is intended to be eaten. The display must be accessible to guests and still look appealing after guests are served. If possible, a server should offer the first guests who visit the display a serving of the decorated or carved item. This will help encourage other guests to help themselves. You may wish to prepare two versions of an item: one for show on an elevated, lighted platform, and one for serving, placed within reach of guests. This will allow every guest to appreciate the work of your culinary artists throughout the event.

## Decorating the Environment

The decorating profession has undergone a rapid transformation since the days when Howard Lanin's client told him: "Just make it lovely." Today, making it lovely involves a specialized professional in touch with the latest styles and products with which to create specific environments that will satisfy guests' individual needs. Today's designers are creating more profound, if only temporary, works of art to frame special events. Sixty years ago special events were most often held either in private rooms, private clubs, churches, public sites, or hotels. Modern decorators are faced with the challenge of turning almost any conceivable space into a suitable environment for a special event. From football fields to tractor–trailers, today's decorators must display more imagination, creativity, and skill than ever before to keep pace with changing styles and trends. The designer/decorator's craft is one of transformation. Turning a polo field into a castle, a ballroom into the land of Oz, or a black tent into an extraterrestrial fantasy, decorators transport guests from the ordinary to the extraordinary by creating a world of fantasy.

Regional customs and geographic location may determine to some extent what types of products are used for some events. Very often, for example, a client in Florida will request a mariachi theme, and a client from the Southwest will desire a Polynesian holiday. But expanded delivery services, which allow suppliers to express-mail almost anything overnight, have enabled designers and decorators to obtain almost any product for a special event, regardless of location.

One challenge that decorators face is designing an environment that will satisfy both primary and secondary audiences. Creating designs and products that will translate to television, film, and still photography is becoming increasingly important. Consequently, when formulating design ideas, consider both the primary and secondary audiences—who will view this event and in what format? Perhaps the design will be detailed in such a way that it will show well in close-up photography. Many stock decor items available in today's events marketplace did not exist 60 years ago. Synthetic fibers and plastics have become increasingly sophisticated, enabling the fabrication of countless imaginative pieces. Even as these lines are written, products continue to be developed, providing greater selection at lower cost. Trying to describe all the products and techniques available to the event practitioner is impossible. The following discussions will introduce you to some of the more popular products and the imaginative ways that some innovative special events planners use them. Their continual exploration of new ways to satisfy clients' needs is the ultimate key to creative design.

**Table 3-1**   Event Sites

### In Transit

| | | |
|---|---|---|
| Aircraft carrier | Hot-air balloon | Space shuttle |
| Blimp | Monorail | Stationary caboose |
| Concorde | Moving railroad train | Subway platform |
| Concorde SST | Orient Express | Tractor–trailer |
| Cruise ship | Paddle-wheel steamboat | Trolley |
| Double-decker bus | Roller coaster | Yacht |

### Design by Mother Nature

| | | |
|---|---|---|
| Apple orchard | Christmas tree farm | National forest |
| Arboretum | Dude ranch | Pasture |
| Botanical center | Formal garden | Rose garden |
| Caverns | Greenhouse | Summer camp |
| Central Park | Meadow | Underneath a waterfall |

### Music, Music, Music

| | | |
|---|---|---|
| Rave night club | Grand Ole Opry stage | Symphony hall |
| Estate of deceased music star | Opera house | Television set of |
| Gazebo or bandshell in a park | Recording studio | *American Bandstand* |

### On Stage

| | | |
|---|---|---|
| Circus center ring | Famous actor's dressing room | Theater green room |
| Circus museum | Professional theater—lobby | Theatrical museum |
| Comedy nightclub | backstage, on-stage | |
| Community theater | | |

### At the Movies

| | | |
|---|---|---|
| Any movie theater | Former movie or television | Former movie set (such as |
| Drive-in movie | location (such as the Bridge | Universal Studios' back lot or |
| Estate of a deceased | in Madison County or | Granada Studios tour) |
| film star | Southfork Ranch in Dallas | Historic movie theater |
| | | Radio City Music Hall |

### Food, Glorious Food

| | | |
|---|---|---|
| Apple orchard | Cornfield | Kitchen of a bakery |
| Bottling plant | Distillery | Vineyard |
| Cannery | | |

### Infamous

| | | |
|---|---|---|
| Alcatraz | Microbrewery | Saloon in a ghost town |
| Former speakeasy | Nightclub | |
| Homes of famous outlaws | | |
| (now, often museums) | | |

### Stately

| | | |
|---|---|---|
| Castle | Convent | Monastery |
| Cathedral | Mansion | |

**Table 3-1**  *(Continued)*

### *The Child in You*

| | | |
|---|---|---|
| Amusement park | Clown alley at a circus | Laser tag center |
| Arcade | Fairgrounds | Puppet theater |
| Children's museum | Family entertainment center | Virtual reality center |
| Children's theater | | |

### *Wild Places*

| | | |
|---|---|---|
| Animal shelter | Pet kennel | Wild animal park |
| Aviary | Stable | Zoo |
| Local animal farm or ranch | | |

### *In Scholarly Pursuits*

| | | |
|---|---|---|
| University/college dining hall | University/college private dining facility (president's dining room) | University/college theater, meeting room, chapel |
| University/college library | | |

### *In Glass Cases*

| | | |
|---|---|---|
| Aquarium | Medical museum | Science museum |
| Art museum | Natural history museum | Sculpture museum |
| Aviation museum | Planetarium | Textile museum |
| Historical society museum | Potter's studio | |

### *Behind the Scenes*

| | | |
|---|---|---|
| Aircraft hanger | Empty swimming pool | Movie sound stage |
| Baseball dugout | Football locker room | Presidential library |
| Current embassy | Former embassy | Television studio |
| Diplomatic reception rooms at the U.S. Department of State | | |

### *The Winner Is You*

| | | |
|---|---|---|
| Basketball court | Hockey rink | Racetrack |
| Fifty-yard line of a football field | Home plate on a baseball diamond | Roller rink |
| Swimming pool | Miniature golf course | Former Olympic Games venue |

### *Ghoulish and Ghastly*

| | | |
|---|---|---|
| Abandoned hospital morgue | Cemetery | Mausoleum |
| Abandoned hospital operating room | Funeral home | Tombstone manufacturer |

### *Highly Scientific*

| | | |
|---|---|---|
| Astrological observatory | Computer laboratory | General science laboratory |

## Interactive Decor

Today's guests want to be more than just spectators at a special event—after all, movies and television provide plenty of opportunities to watch fantastic special effects and see gorgeous set designs and wonderful performances. To provide more than just a passive viewing experience, the event designer must create an environment that allows the guests to participate—to be actors in the decorator's dream world.

In Atlanta, I experimented with this idea of interactive decor with an audience of prestigious and somewhat jaded professional catering executives. The challenge was to show these hospitality professionals something new, working, as always, within a specific budget. The theme of the banquet was "Starship NACE" (National Association of Catering Executives). As the guests entered the foyer, they passed between two 25-inch color television monitors that featured a close-up view of an extraterrestrial's face. As each guest passed, the alien greeted him or her by name and offered a warm welcome to the event. I stood in the shadows, out of sight, and watched the guests' reactions—they suddenly stopped and laughed, clearly baffled by how an image on a screen could recognize and greet them. In actuality, an actor was hidden in a side room. As each guest stepped into the reception area, a technician using a two-way radio revealed the name to the actor, who in turn announced the name on television. Fog machines were set a few feet beyond the television monitors; just as the guests were recovering from one experience, they would receive a small blast of dry chemical fog to surprise them again. Throughout the cocktail reception, a prerecorded endless-loop cassette tape featuring space sounds and a professional narrator making preboarding announcements was played. When the time came to open the ballroom doors for dinner, four astronauts dressed in white jumpsuits, with NACE embroidered on their breast pockets, and blue and white space helmets, also featuring the NACE emblem, appeared in front of each door. As the doors were slowly opened, more fog seeped from the ballroom into the cocktail area. The guests entered the ballroom via a tunnel constructed of black pipe and drape and hundreds of miniature white lights. They tiptoed over a moonscape atmosphere, created by thousands of Styrofoam peanuts covered by ground cloth. Walking through that tunnel, the guests were entering another world. Once inside the ballroom, a robot welcomed the guests from the dance floor and instructed them to "be seated quickly, as the starship would be departing soon." "Also Sprach Zarathustra," the music used in the movie *2001: A Space Odyssey,* played in the background, and the sound effects of sonic blasts were added, projected through four speakers to create a true sense of surround sound. One-dimensional scenic pieces of planets were hung from the walls, and miniature strobe lights created the effect of starlight.

Later chapters explore how the use of video and live action helped to provide constant interaction for the guests attending this event. At this point it is sufficient to understand the importance of creating a design that will meet the needs of the guests. Today, any site can be transformed through decor, using a variety of products and techniques. Regardless of the site and the decoration details, however, the designer's objective remains the same: satisfying the guests. To accomplish this goal, the designer must involve the guests in the event as much as possible through their senses, their activities, and their emotions. Site design can facilitate such involvement, as the "Starship NACE" event demonstrates.

In another example of interactive decor, my firm was involved in designing a theme event entitled "A Dickens of a Christmas," in which the streets of Victorian London were recreated to bring the feeling of Charles Dickens's England to a hotel exhibit room. Since one of Dickens's best-known tales is *A Christmas Carol,* we decided to employ a winter setting and scattered artificial snow throughout the hall. I was delighted to see the usually staid guests kicking the snow throughout the room as they traveled down each lane, participating actively in the setting. We also included a group of street urchins (actually, professional boys and girls with extensive Broadway credits), who were instructed to attempt to steal food from the lavish buffets throughout the room. Each time they snatched a scone, the waiters would grab them and say, "All right, if you want to eat, you must sing for your supper!" The children then proceeded to sing a 10-minute medley of holiday carols. The guests reacted first with surprise when the waiter reprimanded the children and then, within seconds, became emotionally involved as the adorable and talented children sang for their supper. A life-sized puppet of Ebenezer Scrooge was also used. As guests wandered by his house (a display piece), he popped his head out and shouted, "You're standing on my kumquats! Get out of my garden now! Bah, humbug!" The guests, of course, loved this Christmas nemesis. Those who were recognized by the puppeteer were called by name, much to their delight and the delight of their friends. Mr. Scrooge created gales of laughter, once again emotionally stimulating the guests.

The potential for effective design is truly greater than ever. To succeed, the guest must be involved sensuously, physically, and emotionally. The Bible tells us that "There is nothing new under the sun." My friend Cavett Robert, chairman emeritus of the National Speakers Association, has said, "Much that is described as 'new' is actually old wine in new bottles." These maxims apply to the decor industry because with every advancement of new technology, the basic principles of satisfying the guest's sensual, physical, and emotional needs remain unchanged.

## INSIDE THE WORLD OF EVENT DESIGN

Hargrove, Inc., of Lanham, Maryland, was founded in the late 1930s by Earl Hargrove, Sr. Hargrove specialized in what was then called *window trimming,* decorating store windows of retail establishments in the Washington, DC, area to promote sales. With the advent of television, Hargrove's clients began to funnel their advertising dollars into the new medium, and his business soared. When Hargrove's son, Earl Jr., returned home from a stint in the Marine Corps in the late 1940s, he joined his father's company. Earl Jr. wanted to pursue the new and lucrative field of convention and trade show display and exposition decorating, but his father wanted to remain solely in the specialty decorating market. Although they separated for a time, Earl Jr. pursuing the convention market and Earl Sr. struggling in the specialty decorating market, they eventually rejoined forces.

Their longevity in the Washington, DC, events arena is best symbolized by their association with the national Christmas tree located beside the White House. In 1949, Earl Hargrove, Jr. placed the star high atop the tree; in that same year, he and his father renewed their business partnership, and a new brilliance in special events decor began. Today, that partnership includes many more members of the Hargrove family, a talented team of employees, and a large warehouse-studio filled with thousands of props, scenic items, and parade floats. When Earl Hargrove, Jr. began in partnership with his father, he discovered the lucrative market for Washington social events. He recalls receiving an order in the early 1950s to decorate a country club for which the total bill was $350. Times certainly have changed, both in terms of budget and available products with which to decorate. Today, a third-generation Hargrove, Chris, directs a sales team that provides decor for major casinos, corporations, and associations as well as private individuals who seek decor for their bar and bas mitzvahs, weddings, and other celebrations. Chris believes that his mission in the social-event field is to bring the client's theme to life through decor. Doing so today, however, is trickier than in past years, in part because of more stringent fire regulations. According to Chris, "Three states have particularly tough fire laws governing interior decor, and others are following. Every product we use must be flameproofed, which in the balloon industry, for example, is very difficult to accomplish, largely due to high manufacturers' costs." When Earl Jr. began with his father, the available materials were paper, cloth, and wood. Today, he and Chris enjoy many more options, including foam, fiberglass, a wide selection of flameproofed fabrics, and a full range of plastics, to mention only a few. Forty years ago, the guest was content merely to view the decoration. Today, Chris is challenged to give the guest a feeling of participation and interaction with the element of the decor.

He designs sets for themed events using devices such as time tunnels, which the guests walk through to enter the main event, or three-dimensional props that the guests may touch. Both Hargroves agree that a successful decorator must offer a full range of services and products to be successful. Hargrove, Inc. will rent out a single prop or create an entirely new themed event. This diversity has proven successful for over 40 years. The Hargroves, along with other professional decorators, suggest that although there are millions of new decorating ideas for special events, not all of them are practical. Therefore, it is always important to consider the following when choosing decorations:

1. What will the venue (site, building) allow in terms of interior/exterior decor?
2. What are the policies regarding installation? What are the policies or laws of the local municipality regarding decorating materials?
3. What is the purpose of the decor?
4. Are you conveying a specific theme?
5. Is there a specific message?
6. What period or style are you attempting to represent?

7. What are the demographics and psychographics of your attendees?
8. Are they spectators or participants?
9. What are the budgetary guidelines for the decor?
10. How long will it be in use?
11. Which existing scenic pieces can be modified to fit your theme or convey your message?

## Parades and Float Design

Starting with the original Cherry Blossom parade in Washington, DC, the Hargrove artists have been recognized as leaders in the U.S. float design and construction industry. Many nationally known parades, including the annual Miss America parade in Atlantic City and the 1987 We the People parade in Philadelphia, celebrating the bicentennial of the U.S. Constitution, have featured Hargrove floats. Designing, building, transporting, and operating floats can be a costly enterprise. But the rewards for the sponsor, in terms of publicity, can be priceless, provided that the right steps are taken. The following questions should be addressed before contracting to design a float.

1. What does the parade committee or organization allow in terms of size, materials, and thematic design?
2. Under what meteorological conditions and in what climate will the float be used? (Some float builders specialize in designs suitable for particular climates.)
3. Will the float appear on television?
4. What investment will the sponsor make?
5. What constraints are imposed by the parade itself regarding construction, size, weight, materials, and themes? (For example, spatial constraints may limit a float's dimensions.)
6. What message does the sponsor wish to convey?
7. Where will the floats be stored prior to the parade?
8. What is the physical environment of the parade route?

When asked why he continues to pursue this extremely labor-intensive sector of the decorating profession, Earl explains with a story: "A few years ago, I was in Atlantic City with the Miss America Parade, and a man in the convention pipe-and-drape industry saw me watching my floats go down the boardwalk. He said: 'Earl, why don't you get out of the float business and just concentrate on the convention draping part? That's where the profits are.' Well, I didn't answer him, but I knew at that moment how different our company is from all the others. This guy was the unhappiest guy in the world. He didn't really love what he did. On the other hand, we do what we love to do, and I hope it shows in our work."

Parade floats are a perfect example of the need to consider the ultimate viewership of your design. Corporations sponsor floats in an effort to develop positive publicity and influence consumers to buy their products and services. Since only a few parades are televised nationally, most floats need only ensure that the sponsor's theme is conveyed to the live audience viewing the event. Many floats include people—pageant queens, actors, actresses, costumed characters, and celebrities—in their design. When planning the float design, it is essential to consider their place in the display. The wardrobe color of the person riding on the float, for example, will affect the total look of the float and therefore is an important design concern. Additionally, the lighting at the time of the parade will determine to some extent which colors and materials will best convey your message.

As I noted above, it is essential to review the parade organization's requirements for parade floats before making any design choices. In most cases it will be appropriate to feature the float sponsor's name prominently in the design. The manner in which you incorporate the sponsor's name or logo into the float design will affect the integrity of the display itself. Be careful to make the sponsor's name and/or logo a cohesive part of the design whenever possible rather than merely tacking a loose sign on the side as though it were an afterthought. Your ability to incorporate the sponsor's message into your final design in a seamless manner will determine the effectiveness of the float in the eyes of both the viewer and the sponsor. Whether it's themed decor for social events or major parade floats for the Philadelphia Thanksgiving Day parade, the Hargrove family, starting with the founder, Earl Sr. and continuing today with Earl Jr. and Earl III (Chris), bring innovations to the art and science of decor. They are serious businessmen concerned with profit and growth, but they are guided ultimately by the feeling that they bring a special magic to special events. The Hargroves still ensure the placement of the star high atop the national Christmas tree; perhaps this is a symbol of the bright, shining influence their art has shone upon the special events universe.

### Say It with Flowers

A major floral decorator on the East Coast, Angelo Bonita, of Floral Events Unlimited by Angelo Bonita, is fond of describing his work for social and corporate events as "combining floral, food, and props to create 'still lifes.' " His family owned a nursery business in Pennsylvania when he was young, and Angelo became an expert not only in how best to grow plants, but also in the wide range of possibilities in floral design. Bonita, who has designed events in Asia, the Middle East, and the United States, believes that "clients and their planners will place a new emphasis on casual elegance and that American style: originality."

Flowers are usually more costly than stock rental decorations (props) because of their perishable nature. According to some designers, the markup for floral is often four times the cost. If the cost of the floral centerpiece is $20, the designer will sell it to the client for $80 to recover his or her labor, materials, and overhead costs, plus retain a margin of profit.

John Daly, CSEP, president of John Daly, Inc., of California, began his successful design firm with floral products. He suggests that when designing vertical centerpieces, the following guidelines should be observed: "The centerpiece height should not exceed 14 inches unless it is loose and airy, therefore see-through, over the 14-inch mark. This, of course, does not apply to the epergne arrangement. An epergne is a flower holder, such as a candelabra or mirrored stand, that raises the flowers from the table. When using the epergne, the base of the floral arrangement should begin at least 24-inches above table height."

Daly believes that event design has truly matured into both a fine art and science because of the new materials available and the speed at which they can be obtained. Today, a wider range of floral products is available because of the advances in transportation and shipping. With the advent of overnight delivery systems, Daly can have virtually any product he wishes for any event in any location. As designer for events in Seoul, Korea and on the Virgin Islands, this advantage has increased his ability to use fresh and exciting ideas in many far-off event sites.

### It's a Balloon

Balloon decor can range from a simple balloon arch to more elaborate designs, such as three-dimensional shapes or swags of balloons, intertwined with miniature lights, hung from the ceiling. Balloons can create special effects, such as drops, releases, and explosions. Balloon drops involve dropping balloons over the audience from nets or bags suspended from the ceiling. Releases including setting helium-filled balloons free outdoors from nets, bags, or boxes, all commercially available. Explosions might include popping clear balloons filled with confetti, or popping balloons mounted on a wall display to reveal a message underneath.

From centerpieces to massive walls of balloons, such as the U.S. flag displays that Treb Heining created for the city of Philadelphia, balloon art has become an established part of the special events industry. Organizations such as the National Association of Balloon Artists (NABA) and Pioneers Balloon Company's Balloon Network are working to educate both balloon professionals and their clients to the uses of this artform as well as to ensure greater responsibility in employing it.

Howard Zusel, owner of A-1 Entertainment of Chicago has staged enormous corporate theme events for tens of thousands of guests. Zusel stocks a large inventory of amusement- or carnival-type props and equipment. From popcorn poppers to moon bounce equipment, Zusel's firm is one of the leading purveyors of these products in the Chicago area. For corporate events, Zusel works closely with the corporation to create a workable floor plan or site plan. Each of his props and amusement devices is positioned to attract and engage the guest. Because of his total understanding of the components of a successful event, Zusel's firm also provides themed entertainment to bring the props to life. All personnel are properly uniformed and neatly groomed to meet and serve the guests. Zusel annually dispenses hundreds of thousands of balloons; in the carnival and amusement business, they are a basic decor item. Balloon design is not, however, limited to carnival or amusement themes.

In fact, although the balloon may be rooted in this tradition, it has "taken off," enjoying a soaring acceptance and prominence in the decor industry. Balloon art has become an integral part of event decor largely because of the innovations of Treb Heining of California. From creating an enormous birthday cake for a tenth-anniversary celebration at a shopping mall to supervising the balloon effects for the opening and closing ceremonies of the Los Angeles Olympic games, Heining has been at the forefront of his profession for many years. He began by selling balloons at Disneyland in Anaheim, California, and later begun to use the same products for decoration at both social and corporate events. He has designed the massive balloon drops for the Republic National Conventions, incorporating the balloon-holding nets in the decor prior to the actual drop.

In recent years there has been much discussion regarding the effect of balloon releases on the environment. Marine biologists have determined that wind currents cause balloons to drift out over bodies of water, where they lose velocity and eventually fall into the waters below. They are concerned that sea animals may ingest these products and become ill or die. Although there is presently no conclusive evidence that balloon releases have harmed marine animals, what goes up must eventually come down, and both the balloon professional and his client must act responsibly. Electric power companies in some jurisdictions throughout the United States have reported incidences where foil balloons have become entangled in power lines following a release, causing power failures due to the conductivity of the metallic balloon. All balloon professionals disapprove of foil balloon releases as well as releases where a hard object is included in or on the balloon itself. Although it is impossible to regulate a balloon's final destination after a release, it is possible to design and stage releases that will not adversely affect the environment. A tethered release—where the balloons are released on long tethers and now allowed to float freely—may be one alternative. In some jurisdictions the Federal Aviation Administration requests notice of balloon releases in order to advise pilots in the area.

## Tents: Beyond Shelter Is Decor

One example of a new adaptation of a classic environment is in the tenting industry. Developments in materials and workmanship in this industry have multiplied the design possibilities of tents. One three decades ago, the standard tent available for a special event was a drab olive U.S. Army tarpaulin. Flooring was rarely considered, and lighting was most elementary. Today, however, thanks to major innovators such as Harry Oppenheimer, CEO of HDO Productions, the tenting industry has truly come of age. Oppenheimer sees his service as "essentially solving a space problem. For that special occasion, such as a fiftieth anniversary, you don't have to build a family room to accommodate your guests. You can rent a tent with all of the same comforts of a family room." Oppenheimer believes the successful tenting professional prepares for the unforeseen, imagining the structure in snow, wind, rain, and perhaps hail. Most professionals in the tenting industry will not only carefully inspect the ground surface but will also bore beneath the surface to check for underground cables and pipes that might be disturbed by the tent installation. When Oppenheimer receives an inquiry for tenting from a prospective client, he first dispatches an account executive from his firm to meet with the client in person and view the site. Once the site has been inspected, the account executive is better prepared to make specific recommendations to the client. HDO Productions uses a computer network to track the client's order. The computer will first tell HDO if equipment and labor are available to install the tent on the date requested. The computer then lists the number of employees needed for the installation as well as prints the load sheet for the event.

Today's tent fabrics are more likely to be synthetic than muslin. Synthetics provide a stronger structure that is easier to maintain and aesthetically more pleasing. Oppenheimer particularly likes such innovations as the Parawing tent structure, which can be used indoors as well as outdoors in venues that need aesthetic enhancement to mask unfinished portions or obnoxious views. The addition of lighting to these sail-like images will make the event even more aesthetically pleasing. Heating, air conditioning, and flooring are also now available for tented environments. Each of these important elements can help ensure the success of your tented event. A competent tenting contractor will survey your installation area and determine if flooring is advisable, or perhaps essential, because of uneven topography. Listen carefully to his or her recommendations. I had the misfortune of watching 3000 women remove their fancy dress shoes as they sank ankle deep in mud under a tent. The client refused to invest in flooring, although the additional cost was quite minimal. A pouring rain arrived just before the guests stepped under the canopy and flooded the public areas of the tent. It is a wonder the client did not have to replace 3000 pairs of ruined shoes. From wooden floors to Astroturf, your tent contractor can recommend the most cost-efficient ground surface for your event. In some instances the location for the tent may require grading or other excavation to prepare the land for effective installation. A preliminary evaluation and recommendation are provided by many tent contractors at no charge in order to prepare a proper bid for an event.

Heating or air conditioning can increase the comfort of your guests, thus helping increase attendance at your tented event. Once again, your tent contractor will assist you in determining whether to add these elements and what the cost will be. If you elect to air-condition or heat your tent, make certain that the engineer in charge of the temperature controls remains on-site during the entire event. The temperature will rise as the tent fills with guests, so the heating or air conditioning must be adjusted throughout an event to ensure comfort. When you use a tent, you not only take responsibility for ensuring the comfort and safety of the guests, but in some jurisdictions you are actually erecting a temporary structure that requires a special permit. Check with local authorities.

A tent provides a special aesthetic appeal; like balloons bobbing in the air, white tent ropes seemingly touching the clouds signal event to your arriving guests. Few forms of decor make as immediate and dramatic an impression as a tent does. With a competent tent contractor, the problems you might anticipate are easily manageable, and the possibilities for an innovative event, year-round, are limitless.

### Decor Costs

When hiring a design professional for an event, expect to cover not only the cost of labor, delivery, and the actual product, but also the consultation fee of the designer. In some cases this consultation fee may be included in the final bid for the job. If you are soliciting many different proposals, it is best to outline your budget range for the project to the prospective designers up front. This openness may dictate the selection of products for your event. Labor is a major component of design charges because the designer-decorator's craft is so time consuming.

The complexity of the design will affect costs, as will the amount of time available for installation. The longer the time allowed for installation, the fewer persons required. I have seen decor budgets double when less than one hour was allotted for installation of a major set. Allow enough time for the designers to do their work from the very beginning, alleviating the need for extra last-minute labor to complete the job. While many variables are involved in pricing decor, a typical margin of profit above the direct cost of materials and labor is 40 percent. This does not include the general overhead associated with running a business, including insurance, rent, promotion, vehicles, and the like. Therefore, today's designers must be very careful when quoting prices to ensure that costs are recovered adequately and allowing for a profit. When purchasing design services, remember that each designer possesses a unique talent that may be priceless to your particular event. This perception of value may, in your estimation, overrule the pricing formulas described above.

# Themed Events

The theme party or theme event originated from the masquerade, where guests would dress in elaborate costumes to hide their identity. From these masquerade events a variety of themes were born. Today, it is typical to attend western, Asian, European, South and Central American themed events, as often themes are derived from destinations or regions of the country or world. Robin Kring, author of *Party Creations: A Book of Theme Design* (Denver, CO: Clear Creek Publishing, 1993), says that "theme development and implementation are really very easy. Themes can be built on just about any item you can think of."

Themes usually are derived from one of three sources. First, the destination will strongly influence the theme. When guests travel to San Francisco, they want to enjoy a taste of the city by the bay rather than a Texas hoedown. The second source is popular culture, including books, movies, and television.

Whether the theme is a classic *(Gone with the Wind)* or topical *(Toy Story),* the idea is usually derived from popular culture. The third and final source are historical and current events. Themes reflecting the Civil War, World War II, or the landing of a human on the moon, as well as the collapse of the Berlin Wall, have strong historical or current significance and may be used to develop themes. See the examples of themed events in Table 3-2.

An important consideration when planning theme parties is to understand the history of the group. Themes can be overused and it is important that you rotate themes to maintain the element of surprise. When planning theme parties, ask your client the following questions:

1. What is the history of your theme parties? What did you do last year?
2. What is the purpose or reason for this event?
3. Is there a specific theme you wish to communicate?
4. To convey the theme, is food and beverage, decor, or entertainment most important for your group's tasks?
5. Remembering that first and last impressions are most important, what do you want the guests to most remember from this event?

The answers to these questions will provide you with ample instructions to begin your planning of a terrific themed event. The list of themes in Table 3-2 is by no means exhaustive. However, it does reflect a sample of the top themes in current use in American events. When selecting a theme, make sure you are certain that the theme can be communicated easily and effectively through decor, entertainment, food and beverage, and of course, invitation and program design.

## BIG THEME SUCCESS WITH SMALL BUDGETS

Even the slightest budget can enjoy big results through a carefully planned theme event. First, you must decide what elements are most important because it is not likely that you will be able to fund equally everything you desire. If your guests are gourmets, the largest percentage of the budget will be dedicated to food and beverage. On the other hand, if they are creative, fun-loving people who are only slightly interested in the menu, you will want to shift your expenditure to decor and entertainment. Make certain that the first impression (entrance area) is well decorated, as this not only sets the tone for an event but is often the most photographed area. Next, include a series of surprises, such as a dessert parade or the arrival of a guest celebrity as your auctioneer, to keep guests on the edge of their seats.

Finally, share your resources with others. Check with the director of catering at the hotel and find out if other groups are meeting in the hotel before, during, or following your stay. Ask for permission to contact their event manager and determine if you can produce the same event and split the costs for decor and entertainment. You will find that you can afford 50 percent more by allocating your scarce resources in this manner.

**Table 3-2**  Themes from Popular Culture, History, and Current Events

| Theme | Audience | Elements |
|---|---|---|
| The Wild Wild West | All ages; very popular with men | *Decor:* hay bales, western-style bar, western jail set for photos, saloon with swinging doors<br>*Entertainment:* gunslingers, lariat act, whip act, knife-throwing act, medicine man magic show, western band, western dancers, fiddle ensemble, harmonica act, strolling guitarist, cowboy singer on live horse, steer, and trainer<br>*Food and beverages:* barbecue, hamburgers, biscuits, baked beans, rattlesnake, fowl, fresh pies |
| South of the Border | All ages; international guests; events held in states or areas bordering Mexico | *Decor:* small bridge over the Rio Grande River; customs officials and signs at the entrance; bright yellow lighting inside entrance; carts with vendors in Mexican attire selling novelties; cacti; colorful blankets of southwestern design; umbrella tables with tequila logo on top<br>*Entertainment:* mariachi musician, flamenco and folk dancers, folk artists weaving baskets and other handicrafts<br>*Food and beverages:* tacos, fajitas, refried beans, rice, chili, tamales, guacamole, margaritas |
| The New Millennium | Younger guests; men and women; businessmen and businesswomen; scientists; engineers; scholars | *Decor:* large video projection screens projecting star pattern at entryway, followed by a darkened tunnel with thousands of miniature lights and spacelike sound effects; dance floor covered in light fog with pulsing lights; internet stations on personal computers set throughout the room<br>*Entertainment:* robots, actors in astronaut costumes, and actors in alien costumes; high-tech band performing space-associated music<br>*Food and beverages:* space food preset at each setting with freeze-dried ice cream and jellybeans representing various vitamins |
| Mardi Gras | Younger guests; especially appropriate for New Orleans events | *Decor:* two large papier-mâché heads or floats framing the entrance; one doubloon given to each guest to exchange for a drink; purple, green, and gold balloons; exterior facades of Bourbon Street landmarks<br>*Entertainment:* quick-sketch artists; jazz band, including second-line parade; Mardi Gras revelers throwing beads |

**Table 3-2** *(Continued)*

| Theme | Audience | Elements |
|-------|----------|----------|
| | | *Food and beverages:* mufalata sandwiches; seafood, including crawfish and oysters; gumbos; red beans and rice; shrimp Creole, biscuits; po' boy sandwiches; snowball; king cakes; hurricane-style drinks |
| Riverboat | All ages, especially older audiences | *Decor:* small gangplank bridge leading to doorway; life preserver over doorway with name of event displayed; inside main function room is casino, theater, long bar, colorful pennants, and flags |
| | | *Entertainment:* Dixieland jazz band, banjo players, close-up magicians masquerading as gamblers |
| | | *Food and beverages:* southern cuisine, including ribs, pork, fried chicken, grits, mint juleps, bourbon served in souvenir shotglasses |
| Paris Nights | All ages, especially younger audiences | *Decor:* entryway marquee with chaser lights representing a Paris nightclub; in the center of the room a three-dimensional replica of the Eiffel Tower outlined in miniature lights; ficus trees on the perimeter with miniature lights; backdrops or sets of typical Parisian facades, including the Louvre, the Follies Bergère, and the Comédie Française |
| | | *Entertainment:* quick-sketch artists, cancan dancers, cafe orchestra, chanteuse |
| | | *Food and beverages:* crepes, cheeses, pastries, wines, champagne |
| Hooray for Hollywood | All ages | *Decor:* sign announcing "The Hollywood Palladium"; red carpet with rope and stanchion on either side; follow spotlights sweeping the carpet; inside the function room, film props such as directors' chairs, cameras, lights, backdrops, a wind machine, and other props |
| | | *Entertainment:* a team of young male and female fans screaming as the guests arrive; a recording studio for instant sing-alongs; improvisational movie set area with instant replay; photo area with guests wearing wardrobe items from famous movies |
| | | *Food and beverages:* menu items from Hollywood |

**Table 3-2**   *(Continued)*

| Theme | Audience | Elements |
|---|---|---|
| Broadway Bash | All ages | *Decor:* large entrance sign proclaiming "Opening Night Starring [the name of the guests]"; fake ticket booth distributing programs; guests enter through stage door and actually walk onto the stage<br>*Entertainment:* actors portraying ticket sellers, ticket takers, stage doorman, actors; Broadway orchestra in pit performing selections from top Broadway shows; musical comedy performers performing popular Broadway songs; photos taken with Broadway look-alikes<br>*Food and beverages:* New York cuisine, including Coney Island frankfurters, New York strip steak, Manhattan clam chowder |
| Rock Around the Clock | Younger audiences; baby boomers | *Decor:* giant jukebox facade serves as entranceway; interior transformed into gymnasium complete with basketball hoops at each end of dance floor and school name and logo on dance floor; bright ribbon in the school colors swagged from the ceiling; mirror ball for lighting effect<br>*Entertainment:* 1950s, 1960s, 1970s rock 'n' roll; hula hoop contest; servers on roller blades; a phone booth–stuffing contest; a '57 Chevy for photos<br>*Food and beverages:* beer, pizza, hot dogs, hamburgers, malts, French fries, cherry Cokes |
| Dickens of a Christmas | All ages | *Decor:* entryway with Covent Garden design; fake snow scattered throughout; cemetery area with the tombstones of Marley and famous British writers; facades of London landmarks, including the Tower of London, Big Ben, and Parliament<br>*Entertainment:* a team of strolling urchins sings for their supper; a Salvation Army worker plays harp; Father Christmas poses for photos; a woman strolls, selling live geese in cages<br>*Food and beverages:* cider, ale, beer, wassail, holiday punch |
| Rave Party | Generation X; teenagers | *Decor:* fencing, salvage, industrial equipment<br>*Entertainment:* punk rock band; DJ with lighting effects<br>*Food and Beverages:* fast food |

## TRENDS IN THEME EVENTS

Interactive events are transforming couch potatoes into fully participatory guests. David Peters of Absolute Amusements in Florida annually produces hundreds of interactive events, ranging from the Team Excellence Olympics for Xerox Corporation to school picnics. Peters features unusual interactive equipment such as sumo wrestling (where the participants wear giant foam rubber suits), the Velcro wall (where the participants wear Velcro-covered jump suits and jump and land in various positions on a large wall covered with Velcro), and virtual surfing (where surfers stand on boards attached to electronic terminals and see themselves on a large video monitor as they roll, slide, and sometimes tumble into the virtual ocean). When designing interactive events, keep in mind the safety of the participants. Alcohol will, of course, increase the margin of risk for a guest. Some event managers require guests to sign hold-harmless waivers to acknowledge the risk involved with the activity.

Your event environment is the opportunity to explore dozens of opportunities in decor, entertainment, and other elements to make every moment unique and memorable. Every event manager has essentially this same opportunity. But understanding how the various pieces fit together to solve the puzzle that is the event environment, you provide a finished picture that will be remembered by your guests for years to come. Your ability to design, balance, and mold this collage will be rewarded by the guests' total immersion in the environment, leaving an indelible impression for many years. Remember, this is one reason you are so valuable. You are the artist and scientist who creates and plans this unique moment in time.

# Sustainable-Event Management: Conserving the Environment

When I addressed the Nature Conservancy, a major U.S. environmental research and educational organization that focuses on environmental issues, I was impressed with how these leaders use events to communicate the important message of conservation. You can use every event as an opportunity to stress environmental sensitivity. Whether implementing a recycling plan or selecting products that do not harm the ecosystem, the event manager has an implied responsibility through sustainable event planning to produce events that are environmentally sensitive.

## ENVIRONMENTAL SENSITIVITY

Environmental sensitivity is important for two major reasons. First, it is the right thing to do. When allocating scarce resources for an event, remember that no resource is as scarce as the environment in which we live, work, and play.

Second, clients are increasingly requesting that every event meet or exceed certain environmental standards. Major corporations have been criticized by their customers for not demonstrating enough sensitivity to the environment. Therefore, when these corporations retain you to manage an event, they want you to reflect their renewed commitment to environmental concerns.

The best way to accomplish this is to clearly define the organization's environmental policy and then incorporate these policies into your event environment design and operations. Event sponsors who practice recycling in all likelihood will want recycling bins at an event they sponsor. Event sponsors who do not use foam products for disposable serving utensils will not want you to specify these items in your catering orders. Meet with the key environmental policy person for the organization sponsoring your event and determine with his or her help how to incorporate such policies within the event environment.

Why not create your own policies? To ensure that events enjoy sustainable growth, it is important for you to establish your own environmental policies that will demonstrate to prospective event sponsors your knowledge and sensitivity regarding these issues. These policies need not be repressive. However, they must be consistent. Do not alter your policies merely to satisfy the budget considerations for the event. Instead, seek creative solutions such as finding a sponsor for the recycling station to make certain that your environmental ideals are well protected at every event.

## RECYCLE YOUR SUCCESS

In the exposition event field a growing trend is the recycling to local schools of leftover materials such as paper, pens, pencils, and other reusable supplies. Usually, these items end up in the dumpster when only a few blocks from the venue there may be a school with children who cannot afford these basic supplies. You may wish to incorporate this program in your agreements to inform your sponsor of your policy of recycling your success to help others.

Many event sponsors recycle leftover food products to local homeless shelters or food distribution agencies. This assures your guests that you are committed to sharing the success of your banquet with those less fortunate. Some venues require the recipients to sign a hold-harmless form; however, regardless of the legal technicality, this opportunity to feed others should be seized for every event.

Still another way to recycle your success is to build into your event a project to benefit a local organization. Some event organizers provide a day before or after the event to clean up a local playground, paint a school, or perform some other community service using the skills of the attendees at the event. To arrange this activity, contact the volunteer center in the local community. The office of the mayor is a good place to start to locate the local volunteer coordinating organization. Tell the office what resources you are bringing to their destination and then apply your success to help others.

# Inspiration and Perspiration

A famous novelist once stated that writing is 10 percent inspiration and 90 percent perspiration. Although the design phase provides inspiration, it also expands and tests the limits of research. At the conclusion of the design phase the event manager should have a clear idea of the needs and desires of event stakeholders. The goals and objectives that were identified in the research phase represent the skeletal structure in the anatomy of an event, and the flexible elements identified in the design phase represent the musculature needed to move event research forward. Now it is time to add the cardiovascular system to give and sustain life for the event. This is the beginning of the event's life, and the primary organ that will sustain this life is the *event strategic plan.*

## EVENT STRATEGIC PLANNING

The event strategic plan (ESP) provides the definition for event stakeholders of the steps, people, time frame, and other critical elements needed to ensure that an event reaches a successful outcome. Your ESP can be compared to the tracks driving a locomotive. Without tracks the train cannot reach its destination. Without a workable plan an event cannot achieve the optimum outcome and arrive at the destination that you and the stakeholders desire.

The planning phase is a direct result of the data collected during research and the color, luster, and texture mixed into the process during design. The plan must be reasonable (as confirmed during the research phase) and match the expectations of the stakeholders (as identified during the design phase). The planning phase involves the key informants or leading stakeholders who will manage the event. During the planning meeting it is important to involve those people who not only will have the responsibility but also the authority to make decisions. The plan will reflect those decisions, and these important stakeholders must be included to ensure that they take ownership in the creation of the plan. The following key informants should be involved in the planning process:

- Admissions coordinator
- Advertising coordinator
- Assistant event manager
- Audiovisual coordinator
- Caterer
- Decorator
- Entertainment coordinator
- Event coordinators
- Event manager
- Exposition coordinator
- Facility manager
- Fire department
- Food and beverage coordinator
- Insurance coordinator
- Legal advisor
- Lighting, sound, and technical production coordinator
- Logistics coordinator
- Marketing coordinator
- Medical coordinator
- Municipal, state, and federal officials
- Police
- Public relations coordinator

- Registration coordinator
- Risk management coordinator
- Safety coordinator
- Security coordinator

- Sponsorship coordinator
- Transportation coordinator
- Ushering coordinator
- Volunteer coordinators

## PLANNING TO PLAN

Tom Kaiser, author of *Mining Group Gold* (Burr Ridge, IL: Irwin Professional Publishing, 1995), suggests that prior to any meeting the participants should be assigned prework to prepare them to participate actively in the meeting. The scope and level of the prework is determined by the event manager based on the skills and responsibilities of the planning team members. The planning team members should, however, be prepared to contribute empirical information in addition to their opinions as a result of their preparation.

The planning process begins with the announcement of the planning meeting. This announcement should include a time and date for the meeting that is convenient for the planning team members. One of the most common mistakes is to schedule this meeting without advance consultation with the participants. An effective planning meeting requires that the planning team members be fully committed to the process. This commitment requires advance approval of the date, time, location, and format. Another common mistake is not allowing sufficient time for the first meeting. Prior to scheduling the first meeting you should assemble a small group of senior members of the team to actually plan the planning process. This planning to plan (or preplanning) is a critical part of the ESP process.

Most event managers require several planning meetings to establish the final timeline and thorough event plan. During the preplanning meeting you should reach consensus on how many planning meetings will be needed and when and where they should be scheduled. The location and length of the planning meeting will have a direct impact on the efficiency you achieve. It is important to locate a site for the meeting that is convenient for the participants, yet free of distraction. It is also important to remind stakeholders that they will need to leave beepers, cell phones, and other personal distractions outside the meeting.

The length of the meeting will ultimately influence the productivity. The maxim "less is more" is appropriate for planning meetings. Limit meetings to 90 minutes maximum. If the meeting must last longer than 90 minutes, schedule frequent breaks. The agenda for the ESP meeting will guide the team toward their eventual goal: the production of a workable and sustainable plan. Therefore, the agenda should be developed during the preplanning process and distributed to the full team in advance of the first planning meeting. Following is a typical agenda for the ESP meeting:

    I. Welcome and introduction of team members
    II. Review of goals and objectives of event

    **III.** Review of critical dates for event
    **IV.** Reports from team members from prework
     **V.** Discussion of event preproduction schedule
    **VI.** Consensus regarding event preproduction schedule
   **VII.** Discussion of production schedule
  **VIII.** Consensus regarding production schedule
    **IX.** Final review of plan to check for any illogical elements, gaps, over-sights, or other
     **X.** Adjournment

## CONFIRMING VALIDITY, RELIABILITY, AND SECURITY

After the planning meeting or meetings, conclude that the event manager must make certain that the event plan is valid, reliable, and easily communicated to a wider group of stakeholders. Prior to distribution of the plan, make certain that your event plan passes the "grandmother test." Show the plan to those stakeholders who were not directly involved in the planning process. Ask these stakeholders pointed questions, such as: "Is this logical? What is missing? Does the plan support the goals and objectives of the event?"

Once the plan is validated and prior to distribution to a wider group of stakeholders, make certain that there are no security implications of this release. For example, if a very important person (VIP), such as a high-ranking elected official or celebrity, is included in the plan, you may wish to assign the individual a pseudonym or limit the distribution of the plan to preserve the security for your event.

## THE TIMELINE

The tracks that your event train will travel to reach its successful destination are reflected in the instrument known as the *event timeline*. The event timeline literally reduces to writing the major decisions that will be included in the event from the beginning of research through the final tasks involved in evaluation. Often I am asked: "When does the event timeline begin?" After many years of experience and literally thousands of event experiences, I can state that it must begin with the first inquiry about the potential or prospective event. For example, the first telephone call from a prospective client researching your availability to manage an event or from an event manager who is researching information about your catering services may quickly lead to design, planning, coordination, and finally evaluation.

Therefore, I suggest that you begin the construction of the timeline when you first hear that unmistakable sound that telegraphs curiosity and enthusiasm or that twinkle in the eye that immediately and firmly announces that a potential spectacular is hiding just around the corner (from research and design). In fact, the only distance between you and that ultimate realization of the event may be a few hours, days, weeks, or months. To best control this period, it is essential that you construct a realistic time frame.

Another reason that many events fail is due to an insufficient time frame to effectively research, design, plan, coordinate, and evaluate an event. When time is not sufficient to research an event properly, you may end up paying more later, due to insufficient or incorrect information. When time is not sufficient to design an event, you may overlook some of the more creative elements that will provide you with the resources to make the event magical and therefore memorable.

Each event manager should construct a timeline that begins with the research phase and concludes with the evaluation phase. The timeline should cover each aspect and component of the event. It should include the start and ending times for each activity or task. It must be comprehensive and incorporate the individual timelines established by auxiliary organizations such as vendors and government regulations. The event manager should carefully collect individual timelines from all vendors and other service providers. The timeline should detail the elements or components that appear in other peoples timelines. This process of purging and merging the various timelines into one master production instrument is essential for communication between all parties.

Prior to distribution of the final copy, the event manager should seek consensus among all stakeholders before codifying the final results. The timeline must be acceptable to all stakeholders. One way to ensure the careful review and approval of each critical stakeholder is to require that they initial their acceptance upon the final document. The final timeline should be distributed to all stakeholders as well as appropriate external officials (i.e., police, fire, media) to ensure timely service and provide effective damage control. By providing media and other external stakeholders with accurate information in a timely manner, you may avoid problems with innuendo and hearsay that cause erroneous reporting of your event planning process.

The way you depict your timeline ultimately will determine its effectiveness in communication to the broadest possible number of event stakeholders. Table 3-3 shows a typical event timeline in summary form. Although the information in Table 3-3 is presented in summary form, it demonstrates that the timeline must be a comprehensive instrument that provides a separate row for each task, list of participants, start and end dates and time. For example, in the *evaluation* phase, only the quantitative survey evaluation is listed as the task to be performed. In fact, as you will discover later in the book, evaluation is a comprehensive process, and in this phase you will also evaluate factors ranging from finance to timing. Each of these factors will be listed on a separate task line with specific participants assigned to supervise this process.

The timeline provides the event manager and event stakeholders with a precise tool for managing the event. It is the comprehensive map that results from the event planning process. Just as with any map there may be shortcuts; the entire map must be depicted to ensure accuracy to provide the traveler with the best choices for gaining efficiency during the journey. The same may be said of the timeline. Once you have created this master planning document, in subsequent meetings you may adjust the timeline to gain speed and save

**Table 3-3** Event Timeline Summary

| Phase | Task(s) | Participants Event and Responsible Persons | Start Date and Time | End Date and Time |
|---|---|---|---|---|
| Research | Collect and analyze three years of event history or review comparable events | Key stakeholders and informants: event manager, financial manager, marketing manager, and volunteer coordinator | June 1, 9 A.M. | June 14, 5 P.M. |
| Design | Collect ideas from similar events; brainstorm with key informants and vendors | Event manager, key informants, vendors, creative staff | June 15, 12 noon (luncheon) | June 16, 5 P.M. |
| Planning | Preplan planning meetings, announce/schedule planning meeting, assign prework, facilitate planning meeting, develop timeline | Event manager, key informants, critical stakeholders, key advisors | June 18, 9 A.M. | June 29, 5 P.M. |
| Coordination | Identify prospective vendors, contract vendors, develop final production schedule, implement production schedule | Event manager, event coordinators, vendors, key external stakeholders | July 1, 9 A.M. | August 1, 5 P.M. |
| Evaluation | Prepare and distribute surveys, collect data, tabulate data, analyze data, prepare report of findings and recommendations, submit final report | Event manager, evaluation team, client representative | Sept. 1, 9 A.M. | Sept. 30, 5 P.M. |

time and money but assuring that you will also ultimately reach your destination in order to achieve your goals and objectives.

The process of planning from preplanning through the essential corrective planning during the coordination phase forces the event manager and his or her team to logically assemble the best ideas to produce added value for the client. In addition, the planning process must result in a document or instrument that will guide and memorialize the journey of the stakeholders. From a legal standpoint, the timeline, organizational chart, and production schedule can be used to show illogical planning, or even worse, gaps in the planning process. During my experience as a expert witness in numerous trials involving negligence by event professionals, these three documents are often used by attorneys to prove that the event manager and his organization did not meet or adhere the standard of care generally accepted in the modern profession of event management.

As the modern profession of event management transforms into the twenty-first-century global marketplace, event managers must not only meet and exceed the standard of care that is generally accepted in developed countries but also use these instruments to begin to communicate a global standard for the worldwide event industry. Through standardized planning instruments and processes event management will join other well-developed professions, such as medicine and engineering, in establishing protocols that will lead to better communication, increased safety, and higher-quality performance wherever event managers research, design, plan, coordinate, and evaluate professional events.

# Career Advancement Connections

## GLOBAL CONNECTION

When planning events in countries outside North America, the following considerations must be incorporated to ensure a smooth planning process:

- Some countries and cultures incorporate a more rigid planning framework. Ask the experienced event organizers in the country where you are working to offer their insights as to the best way to organize and lead your planning team.
- In many countries the event manager holds the title of professional congress organizer (PCO). This person is usually responsible for multiple functions, including financing the event as well as marketing the overall program. When working with a PCO, determine in advance the range of his or her responsibilities regarding the planning phase. Some PCOs adhere to the requirements identified by the International Association of Professional Congress Organizers (IAPCO). For more information about IAPCO, visit their Web site at *www.iapco.org*.

## TECHNOLOGY CONNECTION

Although planning software is increasingly global in configuration, nuances in languages can lead to critical oversights and even errors. Therefore, it is important for you to appoint a local technology consultant to assist you with technology planning within the country where your event will be held. The following suggestions will further expedite your technology connections in the global event marketplace:

- Use the World Wide Web to research, confirm, and communicate inexpensively prior to your first site inspection. For more information about useful Web sites, see the Web directory lists in Appendix 2.

- Make certain that your planning process includes a thorough review of the technological capability of the venue and destination where the event will be held. Not all phone systems are created equal. In many developing countries, you may have difficulty with sending and receiving large files due to bandwidth limitations. Consult with local technology experts to plan in advance to overcome these challenges.
- The technological infrastructure of many event venues in countries outside North America is superior to systems in place in the United States and Canada. When planning the meeting site, keep in mind the critical importance of technology and select the site based on the technological capabilities to support your event.
- Plan to use technology to create a 24-hour seven-day time band for your event. Your event can easily begin with online marketing and registration; this can lead to chat rooms prior to the event, and be followed after the event with new online chat rooms. Furthermore, you can create a password-protected site for persons to log into your event when they cannot be there in person. You can also develop this site as a electronic commerce area and sell products, services, and access to information to create new revenue streams for your event budget.

## RESOURCE CONNECTION

To identify resources for the planning phase, remember the following key points:

- Determine what needs to be planned. If you are planning to plan, you may use the Data on Meetings and Events *(www.domeresearch.org)* Web site to find out about comparable events or visit ExpoWorld.net *(www.expoworld.net)* to find specific resources in the exposition field.
- If you need models of comparable events such as the complete planning guide for the National Football League Super Bowl or the Goodwill Games Opening Ceremony, visit the George Washington University Gelman Library Event Management and Marketing Archives *(www.gwu.edu/gelman).*
- If you use software to create a planning matrix such as a PERT chart *(www.criticaltools.com)* or a Gantt chart, make certain that you select the model that will be easiest to communicate to each of your stakeholders.

## LEARNING CONNECTION

Answer the following questions and complete the following activities.

1. Who are some of the key informants for your event, and why should they be included in the planning meeting?
2. What information should you send to the key informants prior to the first planning meeting?

3. How can you make certain that the planning meeting includes the input and consensus of all participants?
4. Write a memorandum to announce the first ESP meeting and assign prework to the participants.
5. Create a schedule for the planning process and show the linkages between the planning steps and the goals and objectives of the event.

---

**Facing Page**

The event designer is part of a wide range of human resources required to plan and execute every event. *Photograph courtesy of Monica Vidal.*

# CHAPTER 4

# Management of Human Resources and Time

**IN THIS CHAPTER YOU WILL LEARN HOW TO:**

- Improve human resource management
- Recruit excellent staff and volunteers
- Orient and train staff and volunteers
- Develop policies, procedures, and practices
- Motivate your event staff and volunteers
- Improve time management
- Benefit from diversifying your staff
- Create and evaluate the organization chart
- Reward good performance

As I mentioned previously in this book, human resources and time are among the four most critical components of success for every event manager. If you can manage your time and your people in today's event environment, your chances to survive and succeed as an event manager in the modern fast-paced world skyrocket. It is never too late to start using new time management techniques, invent new employee reward programs, or sit down with your employees to develop enhanced vendor contract procedures. The opportunities are endless if you are creative and open for positive criticism. It is very important to evaluate the existing situation objectively and think of what in your internal organization needs the most improvement and what you can do to contribute to this improvement.

# Human Resource Management

The event management industry is primarily a service industry, and therefore its vital part consists of intangible things such as customer service. You cannot touch it or smell it, but it exists, and moreover, it can make your events a disaster or a complete success. You are being paid for creating memorable positive experiences, and you and your staff are the critical resource that makes a guest's experience memorable. Issues such as your human resource organization, training, and employee retention are vital if you are to remain competitive. For example, most event management organizations offer similar services, but it is their people that make the difference. Members of your association are not very likely to attend next year's convention if they had a bad experience this year, and without trained and experienced people it is impossible to succeed. That is why you should always remember that you and your colleagues are the most important asset of any event management organization. You are the locomotive that makes the event management train move forward.

The global human resource sector endured major changes during the past several years. With the rapid growth of the global economy the employee turnover in many fields, including the event management field, increased tremendously. An average of five-year employee retention decreased to less than a year and a half per employee. This high turnover became a constant challenge to human resource and department managers. Under these circumstances it is more important than ever to motivate your employees and offer various soft benefits in addition to monetary rewards. Benefits such as travel, employee meals, subsidized parking in big cities, employee appreciation events, employee performance awards, training, and company-paid memberships in industry associations are no longer a rarity. In many cases you can encourage your employees greatly by creating growth and learning opportunities, supporting promotions, and creating valuable titles.

## CELEBRATING YOUR SUCCESS

The effective event leader looks for opportunities to celebrate the individual and the success experienced by your organization. Registration way ahead of last year? Break out the champagne! Mary confirmed that $10,000 sponsorship? Blow up the balloons and cut the cake that reads "Way to Go, Mary!" Your team has won an award for your recent event? Celebrate with dinner and dancing for the entire team. Your team will readily recognize that every good deed can get rewarded if you take the time to notice and mark the occasion.

You may wish to appoint one person from your organization as the internal event specialist in charge of these celebrations so that you can readily delegate these tasks and be assured that each one is handled by a capable person. Too often, event employees are like the shoemakers' children in that their managers plan wonderful events for others but scrimp on their own behalf. Your internal events should be models for all external events and your team should feel proud not only to be part of your celebration but to have made a positive contribution to the event. This is especially true of volunteers who work long hours for no financial remuneration.

It is extremely important to diversify staff to better represent your guests as well as provide new, creative viewpoints to develop your events. This will help the event management profession to grow and develop successfully. Currently, female representation in the profession is much higher than male. However, this may change in the future to better represent parity between men and women. More minorities in the United States will also join the exciting field of event management and bring their magnificent ethnic ceremonial traditions from African, Asian, Hispanic, and other cultures. The fusion of diverse cultures can weave a beautiful and strong tapestry to best display the potential of global event management.

One excellent suggestion for promoting diversity within organizations was offered by Judith McHale, president of Discovery Communications. In cases where managers are slow to recognize the importance of promoting women and others who are underrepresented in management, McHale recommends that diversity goals be made part of their bonus package. "That, at the end of the day, has a pretty positive impact" suggests McHale (*Washington Post,* March 18, 2001).

## VOLUNTEER COORDINATION

Volunteers are the life blood of many events. Without volunteers these events would cease to exist. In fact, the vast majority of events is entirely volunteer-driven. The profile of the volunteer has changed dramatically during the past two decades and it is important that the event manager recognize this change.

The emergence of the two-income family has meant that half of the volunteer force in the United States (women) is no longer available to work as full-time volunteers. Furthermore, since many people have more than one job and must carefully balance school, children's activities, and other commitments with their volunteer responsibilities, it is increasingly difficult to attract volunteers to assist with events.

Effectively recruiting, training, coordinating, and rewarding volunteers is a vital part of many event management operations. Although challenging, the following recommendations will help you streamline this critical function.

### Recruitment

Many event managers are now turning to corporate America to recruit legions of volunteers for their events. First, the corporation is asked to serve as an event sponsor, and as part of its sponsorship the corporation may provide key executives to give advice and counsel or a team of 100 volunteers or more to manage the beverage booths, games, or other aspects of the event. A good source for volunteer leadership through corporations is the office of public affairs, public relations, or human resources. Toni McMahon, executive director of the Arts Council of Fairfax County and producer of the International Children's Festival, goes right to the top. "I start with the chief executive officer. If I can get this person to buy into the event, others will surely follow," says Toni. Her track record speaks for itself, with literally dozens of major corporations providing hundreds of volunteers for this annual event.

Other sources for volunteers are civic and fraternal organizations. Part of the mission of these organizations is community service, so they will be receptive to your needs. A related organization is that of schools, both public and private. In many school districts across the United States, high school students are required to complete a minimum number of community service hours in order to graduate. And don't overlook colleges and universities. Many institutions of higher learning have dozens of student organizations that also have a service mission and may be willing to participate in your event.

The key to attracting these groups is the WIFM ("What's in it for me?") principle. When you contact these organizations, learn a little bit about their needs and then use the objectives of your event to help them fulfill their needs. The service aspect is a natural. Ron Thomas, CEO of the Tennessee Walking Horse National Celebration, coordinates dozens of community organizations, such as the Kiwanis, who provide concessions for his events. Their activity is the major fundraising aspect of the organization each year. They know exactly what's in it for them: cash. This cash enables them to do good work all year long. Determine what's in it for them and you will quickly find volunteers standing in line to help your event succeed.

## Training

All volunteers must be trained. This training need not be time-consuming, but it must be comprehensive. One way to reduce the amount of time required is to publish a handbook for volunteers that summarizes the policies and procedures of the event. Training may take the form of a social gathering such as an orientation, or it can be formalized instruction in the field at the actual event site. It does not matter how you deliver this training, as every group of volunteers will require a different method in order to help them learn. However, what is important is that you test for mastery to make certain that they are learning and applying the skills you are imparting. Testing for mastery can be done through a written exam, observation, or a combination of both.

## Coordination

The on-site management of volunteers entails coordinating their job performance to ensure that you are accomplishing the goals of the events. Depending on the skill level of the volunteers, you must assign team leaders or supervisors in sufficient number to oversee their performance. Remember that the coordination of volunteers involves coaching and mentoring. Make certain that your team leaders or supervisors are skilled in these areas.

## Rewarding Excellent, High Quality Performance

Don't wait until the end of the event to say "thank you." Some organizations publish volunteer newsletters while others host holiday parties to thank the volunteers for their help during the annual summer festival. Giving volunteers early, frequent, and constant recognition is a critical component in developing a strong and loyal volunteer team. You may wish to create an annual contest for Volunteer of the Year or some such recognition to encourage good-natured competition among your team members. Make certain that you carefully research with your volunteers how to effectively recognize and reward their service to the event.

## CONTRACTING TEMPORARY EMPLOYEES

You may incorporate cost-efficient human resource management with cost control by contracting temporary employees for peak seasons. This will allow you to keep in place only those employees who you need all year long. This will also help you to retain your permanent staff longer since you will be in a better position to extend your resources to a smaller number of permanent staff. The biggest downside of this strategy is the challenge of attracting qualified personnel for short-term assignments. You can minimize the risk of having to deal with unprofessional behavior by hiring hospitality and event students from your local colleges and universities or by establishing long-term trusting relationships with a specialized staffing agency. Your collaboration with local schools can be based on offering shorter- and longer-term professional internships. Such programs can also be helpful for screening your potential future employees.

# Time Management

Your return on your event investment is in direct proportion to your ability to manage your time efficiently and meet various deadlines. This is so important that it bears further explanation. If you have only eight hours to produce an event that normally requires 12 or more hours, you can either lose money or make money by how you plan and use the available time. For example, you may ask yourself what resources can be consolidated, what meetings combined, and what tasks delegated to allow you to remain focused on your eight-hour deadline. You can hire extra labor, purchase additional resources, schedule more meetings, and try to handle all the details yourself. The choice is yours.

These principles of time management are first applied in your daily life. How you spend your time performing everyday activities directly influences how you achieve your goals during your event management career. The ability to manage your time does not decrease as the number of assignments and tasks that you are involved in increases. The opposite is true. The busier you get and the more things you have planned, the more efficient you are in your time management and the more projects you manage to complete. It simply proves the famous Parkinson rule, stating that "a task can be accomplished within the amount of time assigned for its accomplishment," and getting a time extension on a project would normally push back the time of its accomplishment. Although in many situations it is true, you should, however, be careful and not overestimate your capacity. Always remember that it is better to underpromise and overdeliver.

# The Organizational Chart

Although not all event management organizations have their organizational charts in document form, all organizations have an internal structure that determines important things such as promotion, growth, and simply regulates everyday operations. Even if you have never seen an organizational chart, you

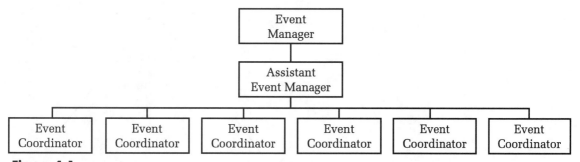

**Figure 4-1**
Flat Traditional Organizational Structure

know whom you report to, who reports to you, and at what level of responsibility and authority you are at a certain point in time. However, it is important to be able to evaluate organization charts from the employer and employee standpoints. Figure 4-1 represents a typical "flat" organizational structure with little opportunity for growth and significant power in two managers' hands. Although these structures exist, it is important to realize that employee retention under this structure is likely to be low since most people would like to see a potential for growth and promotion within their organization. If they do not find it, it they will soon start looking for other opportunities outside your

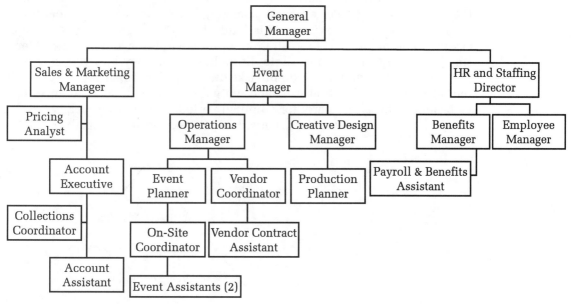

**Figure 4-2**
Dynamic Organizational Structure

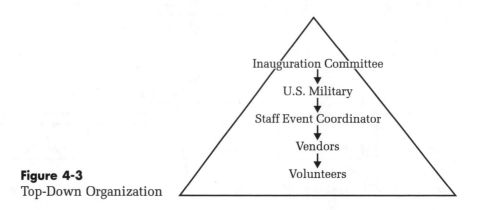

**Figure 4-3**
Top-Down Organization

organization. In its turn, the few managers in such organizations share high power and probably will keep their positions for a lengthy time period. However, if the organization structure for some reason cannot be changed, you can develop loyalty in your employees by creating incentive programs, improving work environment, and increasing compensation. Figure 4-2 represents a more dynamic and complex organizational structure that offers its employees better growth potential, higher titles, and more focused work assignments. In this kind of organization you can offer your employees cross-training opportunities that will add to their professional growth. You can clearly see identifiable departments, which will make it easier to form teams.

Less frequently, you can find other types of organization structures (see Figures 4-3 and 4-4). For example, some organizations have one subordinate reporting to three supervisors. This kind of situation rarely works out successfully and often leads to frustration for both employee and manager. Many small event organizations run into difficulties when they hire very few people to complete a vast variation of tasks due to limited financial resources. If the relationship is built on trust and mutual cooperation, such alliances can be beneficial for either party for a limited period of time. However, when the company gains more business, the situation needs to be changed. If an em-

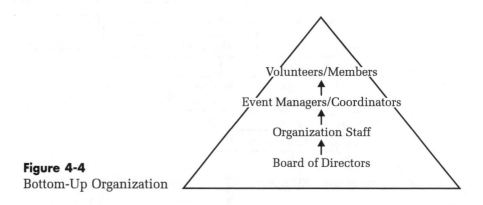

**Figure 4-4**
Bottom-Up Organization

ployee is overscheduled with work and is not physically able to complete it due to the lack of help, this employee will probably quit and look for another job. You have to remember that valuing your employees, investing in their development, and building their loyalty in the long run will be more financially rewarding to you than saving money on employee incentives and generating extra costs for recruiting and training.

# Developing Policies, Procedures, and Practices

Everyone benefits from well-written policies and procedures. First, the internal stakeholders benefit from having a clear process through which to make decisions. Second, the external stakeholders benefit from using a tool to help them understand the organization and the decision-making process of the event team. Finally, the guests themselves benefit. Although they may never see a copy of the policies and procedures, in the event of a life-threatening emergency thanks to this document lives may be saved.

This document is used in a variety of ways. It may be given to all full-time staff and volunteers as a reference tool. It may be distributed to members of the board of directors to guide the development of future policies. Most important, it may be used by the event manager to implement the board's policies through carefully developed procedures.

Policies are conceived and approved by the sponsoring organization's trustees. Typically, this is the owner of the event, such as a private businessperson, a corporate board of directors, or the trustees of a not-for-profit group. The policies that are developed and approved reflect the vision and mission of the organization, as well as comply with local, state, provincial, and federal laws.

Procedures are the implementation tactics for policy. Policy may be broad, overarching rules of conduct, whereas procedures are the regulations that administrators or event managers use to implement policy. Both policies and procedures are essential to produce and sustain successful events.

Many events have well-crafted policies and procedures that can serve as a model for an organization. Contact another event organization of similar size and scope, and ask it to share a copy of its policies and procedures. In addition, ask the company how they most effectively communicate these policies and procedures to its stakeholders.

Carefully review your vision and mission statement, and use your event strategic plan as a litmus test for every policy and procedure you create. Appoint experts in a variety of event fields, including volunteer coordination, risk management, sponsorship, and others to help you review and create the final draft of your policies and procedures.

Convene a focus group comprised of typical event stakeholders to make certain that what you have written can be implemented easily and effectively. Next, survey a wider group to sample their opinion. This group should include external stakeholders such as government, police, fire, and other officials.

Make certain that your policies and procedures are fully in compliance with local, state, provincial, and federal laws. Retain an attorney to review your document to ensure compliance. Your document may be beautifully written, but unless it is in full compliance with all laws, it will be of no value.

Finally, regularly evaluate and revise your policies and procedures. Laws change, events mature, and other changes require that your policies, procedures, and practices document be revisited annually to look for gaps and provide updates to close these gaps. One example of this is the massive revisions that were required following the implementation of the Americans with Disabilities Act. Following is an example of a typical event policy and procedure.

I. *Media conferences.* Media conferences will be held prior to the annual event and at other times as required. *(Policy)*
   A. The event manager will schedule the media conference with staff. *(Procedure)*
      1. The public relations coordinator will implement the media conference. *(Practice)*
   B. Participants will include but not be limited to credential members of the media, members of the board of trustees, and invited guests.
      1. Credentials will be required for admission to the media conference.
      2. The public relations coordinator will issue these credentials.
   C. The chair of the board of trustees will serve as the official spokesperson for the event organization at all media conferences. In the absence of the chair, the event manager will serve in this position.
      1. The official spokesperson will prepare in advance a copy of his or her written remarks and distribute for comment to the board.
      2. An audiorecording will be made of each media conference.
         a. The public relations coordinator will be responsible for recording the media conference and providing a written transcription.

# Career Advancement Connections

## GLOBAL CONNECTION

Appoint people from different cultural and ethnic backgrounds who will contribute to the success of your event. You can learn more about other national traditions as well as incorporating them into your theme by researching the Center for Popular Culture at Bowling Green State University *(www.bgsu.edu/departments/popc/center.html)*. However, diversity also presents potential challenges, and you should encourage training, orientation, and other employee assistance to support mutual respect and understanding.

## RESOURCE CONNECTION

Use the Microsoft Organization Chart to practice constructing a top-down or bottom-up event organization chart. Also visit the American Society for Training and Development Web site *(www.astd.org)* for additional resources.

## TECHNOLOGY CONNECTION

As technology becomes more affordable, one of the growing trends is to use tele- and videoconferencing for group projects and team building activities. In many cases this helps to save money on travel expenses and improve productivity.

## LEARNING CONNECTION

Draft an organizational chart of your event organization or another event organization with which you are familiar. Evaluate this chart from a long-term perspective and answer the following questions:

1. What are promotional and growth opportunities for employees based on this chart?
2. What can be done to this chart to increase employee retention?
3. What kind of cross-training programs can be incorporated in the organization to make employees more valuable and at the same time create additional learning opportunities for the employees?
4. What teams can be formed within the organization based on your chart?

# CHAPTER 5

# Financial Administration

**IN THIS CHAPTER YOU WILL LEARN HOW TO:**

- Understand basic event management financial and accounting terminology
- Maintain event financial records
- Understand and interpret the event balance sheet and income statement
- Calculate the break-even point and profit margin for your event
- Forecast projected revenues and expenses for your event
- Estimate reliable budget goals for your event
- Plan and allocate your event budget

The most common deficiency I have identified in all event managers relates to the area of financial management. Event managers by nature rely on the right side of the brain and often ignore the important logical thinking abilities that help ensure long-term success. Regardless if you use the services of a professional bookkeeper and/or accountant, knowledge of financial management is essential to the practice of modern event management. This knowledge is not difficult to master and with the development of modern software systems it is actually simple and, many say, fun to practice. Whether or not you enjoy financial management is not the issue. Few people enjoy studying for and taking their drivers' license exams. However, can you imagine what the streets would be like without this base line of knowledge? Wrecks, death, and destruction everywhere might result from this lack of rigor. Financial ignorance can just as easily wreck a creative, successful event management business and destroy one's reputation as well as produce serious legal implications. This chapter is essential if you are planning not only to make money but to keep it as well. Additionally, as your business ages along with you, this chapter will help you learn how to work a little less and earn a little more.

# Budgeting

The budget represents an action plan that each successful event manager must carefully develop. Budget preparation is probably the most challenging part in financial management since the entire preparation is usually based on limited information or assumptions. To complete the budget preparation, you should come up with estimates based on assumptions.

The event budget is the most important tool you will use to manage the financial decisions within your event management business. Each event represents a separate budget. All individual budgets are combined into an annual budget. Your daily business operations also require an annual budget to reflect your earnings and expenses. The expression "staying within the budget" should be used by event managers every day and within every project.

Each event budget represents the financial philosophy of the event. Since different events are designed for the different purposes, they may fail into one of the following categories:

1. *Profit-oriented events.* In this type of event, revenue exceeds expenses. Typical examples are events produced by corporations for the purpose of generating new sales.
2. *Break-even events.* In this type of event, revenue is equal to expense. A good example is an association conference. In this case, event professionals should budget the event, keeping the break-even assumption in mind. Admission fees should be calculated at the rate that will cover all expenses and break even.
3. *Loss leaders or hosted events.* These events are designed from the very beginning to lose money. A good example of such events is a university graduation or governmental celebration. These events are usually organized for the purpose of promoting a cause or agenda and not designed to break even or generate a profit.

If your event is a charitable endeavor, your financial philosophy will be markedly different than if it is a commercial venture. First, determine what the financial philosophy of your event is before you begin the budget process.

A budget represents the income and expenses of your organization or the individual event. An event budget is based on the following factors:

1. Marketing projections and estimates
2. The general history of previous identical or similar events
3. The general economy and your forecast for the future
4. The income expenses you reasonably believe you can expect with the resources available (return on investment)
5. Type of financing that you chose to use to finance your event (borrowed funds, prepayments, existing funds)

## FINANCIAL HISTORY

The best financial history is that which occurs over a three-year period. In some cases it is not possible to construct a precise history and the event manager must rely upon what is known at the time the budget is prepared or on estimates. In still other cases the event manager will have to rely on events of similar size and scope to develop the budget because his or her event is a first-time venture and no history exists. Not only is it important to base your budget on history, it is equally important that you develop controls to begin collecting financial data on the event budget you are currently preparing. These data will become the next event's historic information and help you construct a better budget.

The longer you are in the event management industry, the more accurate your estimates will be. A good technique used for developing income projections is *high–low*. The logic is that an event manager compares two scenarios: the best and the worst. Next, the manager decides whether the losses that may occur under the worst-case scenario are bearable and if so, accepts the projects. If not, the project is refused. This method is especially beneficial to small and middle-sized event management businesses that operate under financial constraints and do not have much margin for error.

## THE GENERAL ECONOMY

The economy is chaotic, unpredictable, and some economists would add, a disaster waiting to happen. You, however, must not be a victim to these predictions but instead use general economic data to assist you with the development of your budget. Reams of secondary data are available about the local, state, and national economy from offices of economic development as well as the U.S. Department of Commerce. No event takes place in a vacuum. Whether you are managing the International Special Olympics in New Haven, Connecticut, or the local food and wine festival, your event's success will be affected by the general economy. Indicators of strong economic health usually include low unemployment, a steady rate of inflation, and healthy retail sales. Other indicators include new home building activity, new industry, and capital investments by local, state, or federal government. Before locking in your final budget, consult with an economist from a local college or university, a representative from the local office of economic development, or the editor of the business section of your local newspaper and ask for his or her opinion on the health of the economy.

## REASONABLE PROJECTED INCOME

The Greek word *logos* (or logic) means to "act reasonably." A budget based on certain logical assumptions of projections of income is one that is within reason. To logically project revenue based on the resources available, market research as well as a general knowledge of the economy must be considered. For example, if your city festival is being held this year on the local payday from the area's largest industry, does that mean you can reasonably expect that spending will be increased for your event? The only way to test this theory is with research. You may wish to contact other events of similar size and scope and evaluate their experience with similar circumstances. Furthermore, you may wish to survey some of the workers to determine if they are more likely to attend the event this year and if so, if they will be inclined to increase their spending due to the coincidence of their payday and event date. Making reasonable assumptions about projected revenue is one of the most important decisions that you must handle as you begin the budgeting process. Gather all the facts, seek objective opinions and counsel, and then conservatively project the revenue you hope to achieve.

## TYPICAL INCOME CATEGORIES

Due to the wide range of events represented by the subfields within the event management profession, it is difficult to list categorically every type of income. However, there are some general items that most budgets include:

- Advertising revenues
- Concession sales
- Donations
- Exhibit or exposition booth rental fees
- Gifts in kind (actual fair market financial value)
- Grants and contracts
- Interest income from investments
- Merchandise sales
- Registration fees
- Special events ticket sales
- Sponsorship fees
- Vendor commissions (hotels)

## EXPENSES

When preparing your budget, the first thing you will note under the expense category is how many more items are listed as compared to income. My late father-in-law, a successful businessman, once told me, "The income comes in through one or two doors, but the expense can leak out of many doors." In the strange economic times of the mid-1990s, organizations placed greater emphasis on monitoring expenses because it was easier to control costs than to project revenue. My father-in-law also reminded me that Benjamin Franklin observed some 200 years ago, "A penny saved is a penny earned." Developing solid, predictable expense categories is critical to sound financial management. These expense items often come from historical data or comparing your event to others of similar size and scope. The actual amount budgeted for each expense line item is what you and your advisors believe to be reasonable based on the information known at the time the budget is prepared. Therefore, the more you know, the more precise your budgeting for expenses. This is another reason why record keeping is so vital to the success of your financial management operations. The general expense categories for most events are as follows:

- Accounting
- Advertising
- Advertising specialties
- Audiovisual equipment rental
- Audiovisual labor
- Automobile mileage reimbursements
- Automobile rental
- Awards and recognition
- Brochure and other collateral design
- Brochure and other collateral mailing
- Brochure and other collateral mechanical preparation
- Brochure and other collateral printing
- Complimentary registrations or admission
- Consultants
- Decor
- Entertainment
- Evaluations
- Food and beverage
- Gratuities
- Guest transportation

- Insurance
- Legal counsel
- Licenses
- Lighting equipment rental
- Lighting labor
- Local, state, provincial, and federal taxes
- Materials shipping/freight fees
- Miscellaneous or other
- Percentage of administrative overhead
- Permits
- Photocopying
- Photography
- Postage
- Proceedings editing, design, and printing
- Public relations
- Registration contract labor
- Registration materials
- Report preparation and publishing
- Research
- Risk management corrections
- Signs
- Site office furniture rental
- Site office supplies
- Site rental
- Site telephone expense
- Sound equipment rental
- Sound labor
- Speakers' fees and/or honoraria
- Speakers' travel
- Staff travel
- Videography
- Volunteer appreciation activities and gifts

## STRUCTURING ACCOUNT CODES

Each income or expense item must have a corresponding account code. Accounts are those general budget categories where items of similar type and impact on the overall budget are grouped together for more efficient analysis. For example, in the administration category the following items would appear.

- Decor
- Insurance
- Site telephone expenses

Under the account category "staff/volunteers," the following items would be grouped together:

- Staff accommodations
- Volunteer accommodations
- Volunteer appreciation activities and gifts

Each account code has a numerical listing to make it easy to find individual entries. The general categories start with the 100 series. For example, administration would be 100, marketing would be 500, and so on. Each item would have a separate sequential numerical listing as follows:

| | |
|---|---|
| 100 | Administrative |
| 500 | Marketing |
| 501 | Advertising |
| 502 | Advertising specialties |
| 503 | Brochure and other collateral design |
| 504 | Brochure and other collateral mechanical preparation |

505    Brochure and other collateral mailing
506    Brochure and other collateral printing
507    Public relations

## FINDING AND SUPERVISING AN ACCOUNTANT

Contact your local chamber of commerce to obtain a referral for an accountant who may be familiar with event budgets or service businesses. Once you have prepared a draft budget, seek the counsel of the accountant to review your budget and help you with establishing the various line items and account codes. Your accountant will be able to interpret the tax codes for you to make certain that your accounts match the terms and requirements for the local, state, provincial, and federal tax authorities.

Make certain that you discuss billing and fees with your accountant. You may retain the accountant to handle specific operations or to coordinate all of your financial procedures. Obviously, the cost will greatly fluctuate based on the number of tasks you ask the accountant to perform. Using accounting software may help you reduce your costs and provide you with better, faster information.

## ACCOUNTING SOFTWARE

Since the invention of the spreadsheet program for computers, accounting has never been the same. Commercial software packages such as Quicken have allowed small businesspeople to record their journal entries quickly, accurately, and cost-effectively. What once required many hours with a pencil and eraser has, thanks to modern computer science, been reduced to a fraction of the time. Microsoft Excel is also very useful in budgeting and creating financial projections. I encourage you to spend some time familiarizing yourself at least with basic functions of this software.

Although time-efficient, using commercial software does require certain additional safeguards. First, make certain you always backup your data on a floppy diskette and store this information in a safe, fireproof location. Next, regularly send a copy of your data to your accountant so that he or she can prepare your monthly, quarterly, and annual financial reports. Finally, consult with your accountant to determine the best type of software to invest in because to a large extent you will be partners and you should be using software that will allow you to communicate effectively on a regular basis.

# Producing Profit

The financial purpose of every for-profit business is to produce a fair net profit. The term *profit* means the earnings over and above all expenses.

$$\text{profit} = \text{revenue} - \text{expenses}$$

Not-for-profit organizations do not, for obvious reasons, use the term *profit.* Instead, they refer to this excess of income over expenses as retained earnings. In fact, the earnings are not retained for long as they are required by the tax code to reinvest them in their business operations rather than distribute them to shareholders as some for-profit businesses do.

Producing a fair net profit is both challenging and possible for event management businesses. The challenge is that event managers must work with a wide range of clients and it is difficult to budget for each event carefully to ensure a net profit. There are too many variables to ensure that this happens every time. However, if the business is to remain healthy at year end, a net profit must result from the business activities.

Although there is no average for net profit, let us consider for the purposes of discussion that your financial goal is to achieve an annual net profit of 15 percent. To do this you must guard all fixed overhead expenses carefully. All expenses can be divided into two major categories: (1) fixed overhead expenses and (2) variable expenses. Although both of these categories are expenses, the methods you use to manage and control them are different. To understand how you can minimize your expenses, you should be able to make a distinction between these two groups of expenses.

## FIXED OVERHEAD EXPENSES

Fixed overhead expenses of an organization are those predictable items such as rent, salaries, insurance, telephone, and other standard operating expenses required to support the event management business. The better you are able to achieve a lower cost of sale, the greater net profit you will achieve. To lower your cost of operations, it is imperative that you try to reduce your fixed overhead expenses. Many event management firms have suffered great losses or have even gone out of business entirely because they tried to expand too rapidly. Expansion brings increased cost of sales, and increased cost of sales means that you must produce much greater income. As we discussed earlier, due to the volatility of the world economy, this is not always possible. Once you have cut your fixed overhead expenses to a level that allows you to maintain quality but at the same time produce a fair net profit, you must return your attention to *variable* or *direct expenses.*

Fixed expenses of an individual event do not depend on the number of participants. For example, rent is a fixed expense. Rent expense usually does not vary when the number of participants increases or decreases slightly. Similar is the expense of live music. If an event manager contracts a local band to entertain guests, the cost of this entertainment is fixed. Variable costs are the costs that depend on the attendance: for example, food and beverages. Food and beverage expenses for 100 people will be approximately twice as large than if only 50 people attended the event.

The following example will help you to understand the difference. The event manager of a middle-sized corporation has to budget expenses for a reception. He or she is not sure about the exact number of guests; however, the minimum and the maximum number of guests are known. The minimum number is 200 guests and the maximum 400. The catering company has provided the event manager with its price quote of $25 per person for food and $15 per person for beverages. The event manager creates the expense calculation shown in Table 5-1.

## VARIABLE EXPENSES

Variable expenses are more difficult to predict because often they are purchased last minute from vendors and the prices may fluctuate. Variable or direct expenses include audiovisual rentals and labor, registration materials, proceedings design and printing, and other items with a total cost that is reliant on the final number ordered and your ability to negotiate a fair price. Due to last minute registrations and an increase in walkup guests for a variety of events, it is extremely difficult to wait until the last minute to order certain items. Printing as well as advance notice for audiovisual equipment rental and labor requires a sufficient window of time to deliver a quality product. This means that your ability to use historical data to project the volume of items you will need or to order less with an option to obtain additional supplies rapidly will greatly help you reduce your variable or direct expenses. In addition, your ability to negotiate the best deal for your event organization will also have tremendous impact on these items.

## NET PROFIT VERSUS GROSS PROFIT

Event managers endeavor to produce a fair net profit. The difference between net profit and gross profit is the percentage of fixed overhead expenses that was dedicated to producing a specific event. Fixed overhead expenses dedicated to the individual event include a percentage of staff salaries and benefits, a percentage of the office expense, and other shared expenses. This percentage will fluctuate, but by using time sheets you can easily calculate the staff time directed to the event, and the other expenses, such as rent, insurance, and telephone, may be given a percentage based on the time recorded from the time sheets.

**Table 5-1** Fixed and Variable Expenses

| Number of people | 200 | 400 | |
|---|---|---|---|
| Food $25 per person | $5,000 | $10,000 | Variable |
| Beverages $15 per person | 3,000 | 6,000 | expenses |
| Rent expense | 2,000 | 2,000 | Fixed |
| Entertainment expense | 1,000 | 1,000 | expenses |
| Total expenses | $11,000 | $19,000 | |

## BREAK-EVEN POINT

To understand the break-even calculation, you have to understand one more term: *contributional margin,* the difference between the revenue received from a single person and the variable costs incurred for one person. For example, if an event management company receives revenue of $50 per person but the total variable cost for one person is $40 ($25 food and $15 beverages), the contributional margin is $10 per person:

$$\text{contributional margin} = \text{revenue per person} - \text{variable costs per person}$$

The final step to calculate the break-even point is to divide the total fixed costs to the contributional margin:

$$\text{break-even point} = \frac{\text{total fixed costs}}{\text{contributional margin}}$$

For example, if the total fixed costs are $3000 and the contributional margin is $10, the break-even point is 300 people:

$$300 = \frac{\$3000}{\$10}$$

or

$$300 \times \$50 = \$15,000$$

If fewer than 300 people attend the event, it loses money. It turns profitable once the attendance exceeds 300 people. Therefore, the break-even point is achieved when you collect $15,000 in revenue. Table 5-2 demonstrates the break-even analysis.

**Table 5-2**   Break-Even Analysis

|  | Loss | Break-Even | Profit |
|---|---|---|---|
| Number of people | 290 | 300 | 310 |
| Revenue: | | | |
| $50 per person | $14,500 | $15,000 | $15,500 |
| Expenses: | | | |
| Variable expenses: | | | |
| Food $25 per person | 7,250 | 7,500 | 7,750 |
| Beverages $15 per person | 4,350 | 4,500 | 4,650 |
| Fixed expenses: | | | |
| Rent expense | 2,000 | 2,000 | 2,000 |
| Entertainment expense | 1,000 | 1,000 | 1,000 |
| Total expenses: | $14,600 | $15,000 | $15,400 |
| Profit (revenue–expenses) | $(100) | $— | $100 |

# Cutting Costs

Your ability as an event manager to cut costs rapidly to ensure consistent profits is one that will serve you well throughout your career. To decide which costs may be cut without sacrificing the integrity of the entire event, you must begin with the budgeting process by prioritizing expenses. Seek counsel from your stakeholders and honestly determine what in the worst-case scenario, if certain items must be cut from the budget, they would like to preserve and which should go to ensure a profit. Although this is a difficult decision process, it is wise to make such decisions free from internal and external pressures during the final days of the event management process. Typically, these costs are associated with variable or direct expenses. Therefore, the expenditure is not made until later in the event management process. Cutting your event's costs is one way to help improve your cash flow.

# Ensuring Positive Event Cash flow

It is not enough to just have profitable operations. Many event management companies were unsuccessful because they were always out of cash. These companies showed profit on their books but had an empty checking account. This situation is called *insolvency*. The best way to avoid insolvency is to execute sound cash flow management.

Cash flow is the liquidity that allows you to pay your bills, including salaries, in a timely manner. When this liquidity is gone, your reputation may not be far behind. To ensure a positive event cash flow, two measures are necessary. First, you must prearrange with your vendors payment terms and conditions that will allow you to collect the adequate revenues to honor these obligations. Second, you must diligently collect those funds that are due and payable to you in a timely manner in order to meet your obligations to your vendors.

Payables are those financial accounts that you have established with vendors. These are funds that are due and payable according to the agreements you have arranged with individual vendors. Receivables are those funds due to your event organization by a certain date. Aging receivables are simply those funds that were not collected at the time they were due. Following are simple techniques for collecting event management receivables.

1. Log on your calendar the day the receivable is due.
2. Telephone early in the morning to ask when your payment will be processed.
3. If possible, arrange to pick it up.
4. If it is not possible to pick it up, offer to provide an express-mail service.
5. Courteously, but firmly, request payment until received.

One of the challenges with the value of event management services is that there is often rapid depreciation as soon as the curtain rises. Consider this scenario. Your client has invested $50,000 with your firm to produce a gala awards dinner. Midway through the dinner the client's spouse notices a cigarette burn in the tablecloth. Later he or she comments on "skimpy" floral arrangements. Finally, he or she complains loudly about the inferior music and food. Before long the client locates you and wants to discuss the bill. Ironically, only three hours earlier the client walked through the ballroom and told you effusively how beautiful everything looked. Buyers of event management services and products are not usually experts in your profession. That is why they have retained you. Because the purchase of event management services and products is sometimes an emotional decision, the buyer may easily be influenced by others. *The only leverage you have as the professional provider of these services is to collect your full fee as soon as possible because the value of your performance will rapidly deflate otherwise.* The old maxim "people only value what they pay for" is absolutely true in this profession as well as medicine and other established professions.

Effective management of accounts receivable is only half of the equation needed for solid cash flow. The second half requires that you become knowledgeable about typical accounts payable agreements and learn to negotiate for the best possible payment terms. The best policy is to collect cash as fast as possible but pay off your bills on the last day allowed by the contract.

# Accounts Payable: Finding the Best Terms

When establishing relationships with vendors it is important that you learn as much as possible about the size, scope, and nature of their business. You will want to know if they own or lease their equipment. You will also want to know when they may have periods of slow business. Their "off season" can produce favorable terms and perhaps discounts for your event. You will also want to know if the vendor could benefit from exposure through your event. Some event managers have a stringent rule about not letting vendors promote themselves directly to their clients. However, it is my belief that these hard and fast rules may prevent you from providing your client with the products and services your vendor may be able to offer. In one example a video production company telephoned me after a major corporate event and asked permission to contact the corporate headquarters to provide their services directly. Not only did I encourage them to do so, I wrote letters to my client and others on their behalf. As a result of this courtesy and flexibility, this firm will work with me on price in the future for other clients who I may serve. Therefore, beware the dangerous word *always,* as it may cause you to provide less service than possible.

The key to negotiating excellent terms with vendors is first to establish professional friendships and conduct business in an atmosphere of mutual respect. The more you know about your professional partners (vendors) and the more they know about you, the easier it is to do business. There are typical accounts payable customs and traditions in the event management profession; however, your ability to make friends and provide assistance to your vendors will alter these customs to your benefit.

## TYPICAL ACCOUNTS PAYABLE CUSTOMS

One accounts payable custom is for the vendor to require a deposit of 50 percent of the final contracted cost as a deposit and receive the full balance plus any additional agreed upon charges immediately following the event. Entertainment vendors, especially those representing major celebrities, are even more stringent. They may require full payment in the form of a certified check prior to the first performance as a guarantee.

Another accounts payable custom is for the vendor to require a small deposit (as low as 10 percent) and then invoice you for the balance due net 10 or 30 days after the event. The final custom allows you to pay your balance on account. In this custom, typically you are a regular good customer of the vendor and they are allowing you to pay off the balance monthly or within a reasonable amount of time without interest, late charges, or other penalties. Sometimes, vendors even provide small discounts if you pay off your balance faster than required. There is a special terminology for that. For example, if a vendor offers you a 3 percent discount if you pay off your balance within the first 10 days, you may hear the following formula: "3/10, net 30." This means that if you pay off the balance within 10 days, you receive 3 percent off your total bill; otherwise, you have to pay the entire balance within the next 30 days.

The final custom is for the vendor to extend credit to your organization, allowing you to authorize purchases and be invoiced at a later date by the vendor. This is the best scenario, as you are able to negotiate credit terms well in advance. Although most accounts are due within 30 days of the date of the invoice, I have heard of some arrangements where the vendor will extend credit for 60 or even 90 days to maintain the account. It is up to you to negotiate the best possible terms.

## NEGOTIATING ACCOUNTS PAYABLE

Always negotiate from a position of strength. Strength in the area of accounts payable means that you have collected as much information as possible about the vendor with whom you need to negotiate. The answers to the following questions will enable you to negotiate favorable terms for your accounts payable.

1. How important is your business to this vendor?
2. During what time period is your business most needed?
3. Are your clients the types of organizations your vendor would like to do business with? How well funded/capitalized is your vendor?

4. How does your vendor market his or her services and products? How sophisticated are your vendor's business operations?
5. What are your vendor's standard and customary accounts payable terms?
6. Most important, are there other clients of this vendor you can speak with to determine what types of terms they are receiving?

Once you have the answers to these questions, it is time to ask your vendor for more favorable terms. To do this you will need to provide your vendor with documentation about your own business health. Testimonials from recent clients, a list of accounts receivable, and other financial data will also help you create a favorable impression. Once you have established your credibility with the vendor, ask for the most favorable terms. You might ask for credit and 90 days. The vendor may counter with 30 days and you then agree on 60 days. Do not play hardball. Remember, this vendor will be servicing your clients, and maintaining their goodwill is of supreme importance. However, you have a responsibility to your event organization to negotiate the most favorable terms and must remain firm in your pursuit of what you believe to be a fair agreement.

Your vendor may ask for a trial period, after which he or she may extend better terms once you have demonstrated your ability to meet your obligations consistently and provide the benefits your vendor expects. I cannot emphasize enough how important your relationships with your vendors are in the full spectrum of your event operations. The following story is typical of many businesses in the event management profession.

## CONTROLLING PURCHASES

The most common device for approving purchases is the *purchase order* (PO). No purchase should be authorized without an approved purchase order. This form specifies the product or service approved for purchase, the number of units, the price per unit, and the total amount due, including taxes and deliveries. The type of shipping and date and time of arrival should also be clearly specified. It should also state the payment terms. Instruct all your vendors by letter that you will only be responsible for purchases preceded by a valid purchase order. Include the following statement on each purchase order: *"Vendor may not substitute or alter this order without the written permission of the purchaser."*

This statement helps you avoid the creative vendor who is out of red tablecloths and believes that you will accept blue instead at the same price. Finally, the purchase order must have a signature line that grants approval and the date of the approval. The purchase order is the most important tool you have to control your purchases and therefore monitor those numerous doors where expenses leak and potentially drain your event economic engine. Since your PO is a very important financial document that can hold you or your company liable, it is important to ensure a safe procedure for issuing and approving all purchase orders. All your vendors should be informed as to who in your company is authorized to sign purchase orders. A PO signed by the authorized person should be mailed to a vendor at the beginning of the transaction. This PO procedure is very important and it can help save you money when you compose the final invoice.

# Common Event Financial Challenges and Solutions

The event management profession is a business, and not unlike other businesses, there are common problems and solutions. When event management business owners assemble for annual meetings and conferences, they can be heard discussing many of the same challenges year after year. As one wag said, "The problems don't change, the solutions only become more difficult." Perhaps by reviewing the following examples you will be able to anticipate some of these challenges and thereby take measures to avoid them entirely.

- **Challenge:**  Negotiating employees' salaries and benefits.
  *Solution:*  Collect information from ISES or from firms in similar market areas. Use this information to determine a market basket figure from which you can negotiate up or down based on the potential value of the employee to your firm.
- **Challenge:**  Proper compensation for event management salespeople.
  *Solution:*  Three methods are customary. First and most prevalent is the *draw against commission.* This approach requires that you provide the salesperson with a small stipend until his or her commissions have equaled this amount. After he or she has equaled the amount of the draw, the stipend stops and the salesperson receives only sales commissions. The second approach is *straight commission.* In this case usually the salesperson has existing accounts and is earning commissions immediately. Typical commissions range between 3 and 7 percent of the gross sale. Therefore, a salesperson who produces $500,000 in gross revenue will earn $35,000. The final custom is to offer the salesperson a *salary plus bonuses* based on sales productivity. This bonus is typically awarded after the salesperson reaches a certain threshold in sales, such as $1 million. A typical bonus is 1 or 2 percent of sales. A salesperson earning a salary of $50,000 could earn an additional $20,000 based on a 2 percent bonus on $1 million in sales.

    Straight salary as compensation is the least desirable because it provides no financial incentive and salespeople are typically driven by financial incentives. Whatever arrangement you agree upon, do not change it for one year. You will need one year of financial data on which to base your review and future course of action.

- **Challenge:**   Client is slow to pay balance of account.

  *Solution:*   Inquire how you can help expedite payment. Can you pick up the check? Is there a problem, and could the client pay the largest portion now and the rest later? Are other vendors being paid? Does the client have a history of slow payment? What leverage do you have? Can you suspend services until the balance is paid or payment on account is made? Could you speak with one of the owners or principals and solve this problem? Can you find a creative solution like the one that Andy Stefanovich of Opus Event Marketing, Richmond, Virginia, found? Andy had his dog send collection notice, complete with begging for food and a paw print.

- **Challenge:**   Out of cash.

  *Solution:*   With prudent management of accounts payable and receivable, this problem should not occur. Assuming that a business emergency has caused this unfortunate situation, you must immediately contact vendors and notify them of your intent to pay. Then notify all past due accounts receivable and accelerate collection. Reduce or stop spending with regard to fixed overhead. Next, contact your lenders to access a line of credit based on your receivables until you have sufficient cash to meet your expenses.

- **Challenge:**   Vendor promotes himself or herself to your client directly.

  *Solution:*   Do you have written policies and procedures outlining what is and what is not permissible by your vendor? Realistically, how will their promotion injure your business? Can you negotiate with your vendor to receive a commission from any future sales to this client since you were the first contact?

- **Challenge:**   Employee is terminated, starts own business, and takes your clients.

  *Solution:*   Does the employment agreement forbid this practice? Assuming that it does, you can have your attorney send a cease and desist letter. This rarely helps because the client has no constraints on who they do business with. Either way you lose. Instead, suggest to the former employee that he or she may wish to provide you with a commission on the first sale he or she makes with your former client as a courtesy for providing the first introduction. This way you can release the client and also receive some compensation for your effort in first identifying the account. If the former employee refuses to provide you with a commission, chances are that his or her bad business ethics will eventually alienate him or her from enough industry colleagues that it will limit the amount of sales that he or she is able to achieve and reduce significantly the level of services received from vendors who are suspicious of his or her behavior.

These common challenges and typical solutions should serve as a guide or framework to guide your decision making. Although most of the solutions in modern business still rely on common sense, I have noticed that there is nothing as uncommon in today's business environment as common sense. You will want to test each of these solutions with your business advisors (attorney, accountant, mentor) before implementing it to make certain that it addresses your particular problem and provides the most logical solution. There is no such thing as a general solution for a specific problem. All business problems are specific in nature, and you must seek a solution that addresses your precise problem.

# Foreign Exchange Rates

It is important in this global world that you understand exchange rates, their fluctuations, and the differences that international exposure brings to your financial operations. Remember that although large international event management companies depend greatly on global changes that occur regularly in various countries, middle-sized and small event management companies are also affected by these changes. Event management today is a global economic enterprise. Food and beverages that you purchase in the United States or elsewhere are often produced outside of the country where it is sold. Payments that your organization makes or receives from overseas can be conducted in either local or foreign currency.

The *foreign exchange rate* is the price of one currency expressed in another currency. For example, DKK 6.79/1 USD means that for 1 U.S. dollar (USD), the market requires 6.79 DKK (Danish krona); USD 0.1472/DKK means that for 1 Danish krona, the market requires 14.72 U.S. cents. The currency exchange rates change every day, sometimes even several times per day. Changes are usually not significant for small and middle-sized businesses and affect mainly large banks and investment companies. Exchange rates are generally affected by market conditions and government policy, and also by national disasters (especially for small countries).

## MARKET CONDITIONS

The general rule is that currencies of countries with strong economies are in greater demand than currency of countries with weak economies. If the economy of country A is getting stronger and stronger but the economy of country B is getting weaker and weaker, the exchange rate between the currencies of these countries will favor the currency of country A.

## GOVERNMENT POLICY

The currency of countries with strong governments that originate predictable policy is always preferred over the currencies of countries whose governments have unpredictable policies. Even during the close 2000 U.S. presidential election between George W. Bush and Al Gore, the U.S. dollar exchange rate was not greatly affected because the United States is known for its predictable domestic and foreign policy. Major financial newspapers, such as the *Financial Times* and *Wall Street Journal,* contain daily information about currency exchange rates and projections. You should monitor journals to forecast the economic conditions in countries where you will be doing business.

Changes in exchange rates affect all companies. Large businesses are affected directly; small businesses are affected indirectly. In one example of this, a large event management company based in the United States signs a contract with a U.K.-based corporation to produce a large event in London. The U.S. event management company is paid in pounds sterling. The total cost of the contract is £400,000. The contract is signed on June 1 and the event is to be held on December 21. The contract says that the U.K. company must make a 50 percent advance payment in June with the balance payable on the day of the event. On June 1 the exchange rate between the U.S. dollar and the British pound is USD 1.658/£. If the exchange rate between the pound and the dollar stays unchanged until December 21, the income statement of the event would appear as shown in Table 5-3. Note that since the event management company is U.S.-based, all expenses that it incurs are in the U.S. dollars and total $500,000.

The gross profit is calculated to be $163,000. This represents a 25 percent profit margin ($163,000/$663,200). Obviously, the project looks very attractive. The question is how attractive the project would be if the exchange rate were to change by December 20. Suppose that due to the strong economy in the United States, you predict that the U.S. dollar will appreciate (its value will increase). Now suppose that the exchange rate in December will be $1.5/£. Table 5-4 shows how this change could dramatically reduce your margin of profit. Due to the exchange rate change in December, £200,000 will be worth only $300,000 but total expenses are still $500,000 (since they occurred in U.S. dollars). Therefore, the gross profit dropped to $131,000 and the profit margin dropped to 20 percent.

The more expensive the U.S. dollar becomes, the less profit the U.S. organization makes from its overseas events that are paid in foreign currency. This means that the U.S. organization can purchase fewer dollars for the

**Table 5-3**   Income Statement: No Exchange Rate Fluctuation

|  | U.K. Pound | U.S. Dollar |
|---|---|---|
| Revenue |  |  |
|     50% advance on June 10 | £200,000.00 | $331,600.00 |
|     50% payment on December 20 | 200,000.00 | 331,600.00 |
|       Total | 400,000.00 | 663,200.00 |
| Total expenses | n/a | (500,000.00) |
|     Gross profit | n/a | $163,200.00 |

**Table 5-4** Income Statement: with Exchange Rate Fluctuation

|  | UK Pound | USD |
| --- | --- | --- |
| Revenue |  |  |
| 50% advance on June 10 | £200,000.00 | $331,600.00 |
| 50% payment on December 20 | 200,000.00 | 300,000.00 |
| Total | 400,000.00 | 631,600.00 |
| Total expenses | n/a | (500,000.00) |
| Gross profit | n/a | $131,600.00 |

amount of foreign currency earned. To attain the same level of profitability, the organization should start charging more for its service event, hence becomes less competitive. Alternatively, when the U.S. dollar depreciates, services provided by U.S. event management organizations overseas become less expensive, hence more competitive.

# Typical Event Budgets

Your budget is a general guide to the income and expense projected for your event. It may be adjusted as necessary provided that you can justify these changes and receive approval from the stakeholders. For example, if your revenue projections are way ahead of schedule, your variable costs will also increase proportionately. Use the budget as a valuable tool that may be sharpened as needed to improve your percentage of retained earnings.

The following sample budgets will serve as a guide as you develop your financial plans for various events. Each budget has the same structure; however, you will note that in the case of not-for-profit organizations, the term *retained earnings* has been substituted for the term *profit*. Use these budgets as a model as you endeavor to create consistently effective financial management systems for your organization.

## AWARDS BANQUET

| Income |  |  |
| --- | --- | --- |
| 100 | Registrations |  |
| 101 | Preregistrations | $ 25,000 |
| 102 | Regular registrations | 50,000 |
| 103 | Door sales | 5,000 |
| | Subtotal | $ 80,000 |
| 200 | Marketing |  |
| 201 | Sponsorships | $ 15,000 |
| 202 | Advertising | 10,000 |

| | | |
|---|---|---:|
| 203 | Merchandise | 5,000 |
| | Subtotal | $ 30,000 |
| 300 | Investments | |
| 301 | Interest income | 1,000 |
| | Subtotal | $ 1,000 |
| 400 | Donations | |
| 401 | Grants | $ 5,000 |
| 402 | Individual gifts | 10,000 |
| 403 | Corporate gifts | 25,000 |
| | Subtotal | $ 40,000 |
| | Total income | $151,000 |

Expenses

| | | |
|---|---|---:|
| 500 | Administration (fixed expense) | |
| 501 | Site office furniture rental | $ 1,000 |
| 502 | Site office supplies | 1,000 |
| 503 | Site rental | 3,000 |
| 504 | Site telephone expense | 1,000 |
| | Subtotal | $ 6,000 |
| 600 | Printing (fixed expense) | |
| 601 | Design | $ 3,000 |
| 602 | Printing | 5,000 |
| 603 | Binding | 1,000 |
| | Subtotal | $ 9,000 |
| 700 | Entertainment (fixed expense) | |
| 701 | Talent fees | $ 10,000 |
| 702 | Travel and accommodations | 1,000 |
| 703 | Sound | 2,000 |
| 704 | Lights | 2,000 |
| | Subtotal | $ 15,000 |
| 800 | Food and beverages (variable expense) | |
| 801 | 300 dinners @ $50 | $ 15,000* |
| 802 | Open bar for one hour | 3,000* |
| 803 | Ice sculpture | 500 |
| | Subtotal | $ 18,500 |

*Include taxes and gratuities.

| | | |
|---|---|---:|
| 900 | Transportation (variable expense) | |
| 901 | Staff travel | $ 1,000 |
| 902 | Valet parking | 750 |
| | Subtotal | $ 1,750 |
| 1000 | Insurance (fixed expense) | |
| 1001 | Cancellation | $ 1,000 |
| 1002 | Host liability | 500 |
| | Subtotal | $ 1,500 |

| | |
|---|---|
| Total expenses | $ 51,750 |
| Total variable expense | $ 29,250 |
| Total projected income | $151,000 |
| Total projected expense | 51,750 |
| Gross retained earnings | $ 99,250 |
| Percentage of fixed overhead | 25,000 |
| Net retained earnings (reinvestment) | $ 74,250 |

## MUSIC FESTIVAL

Income
| | | | |
|---|---|---|---|
| 100 | Ticket sales | | |
| 101 | Regular advance | $ 50,000 | |
| 102 | Student advance | 25,000 | |
| 103 | Regular door sales | 100,000 | |
| 104 | Student door sales | 50,000 | |
| 103 | Group sales | 25,000 | |
| | Subtotal | $250,000 | |
| 200 | Marketing | | |
| 201 | Sponsorships | $ 50,000 | |
| 202 | Advertising | 25,000 | |
| 203 | Merchandise | 30,000 | |
| | Subtotal | $105,000 | |
| 300 | Investments | | |
| 301 | Interest income | 3,000 | |
| | Subtotal | $ 3,000 | |
| 400 | Donations | | |
| 401 | Grants | $ 10,000 | |
| 402 | Individual gifts | 0 | |
| 403 | Corporate gifts | 25,000 | |
| | Subtotal | $ 35,000 | |
| | Total income | $393,000 | |

Expenses
| | | | |
|---|---|---|---|
| 500 | Administration (fixed expense) | | |
| 501 | Site office furniture rental | $ 500 | |
| 502 | Site office supplies | 500 | |
| 503 | Site rental | 10,000 | |
| 504 | Site telephone expense | 1,500 | |
| | Subtotal | $ 12,500 | |
| 600 | Printing (fixed expense) | | |
| 601 | Design | $ 1,000 | |
| 602 | Printing | 5,000 | |
| | Subtotal | $ 6,000 | |
| 700 | Entertainment (fixed expense) | | |

| | | |
|---|---|---|
| 701 | Talent fees | $ 50,000 |
| 702 | Travel and accommodations | 5,000 |
| 703 | Sound | 5,000 |
| 704 | Lights | 5,000 |
| | Subtotal | $ 65,000 |
| 800 | Transportation and parking (variable expense) | |
| 801 | Staff travel | $    500 |
| 802 | Parking lot rental | 3,000 |
| | Subtotal | $  3,500 |
| 900 | Insurance (fixed expense) | |
| 901 | Cancellation | $  1,000 |
| 902 | Host liability | 500 |
| 903 | Comprehensive general liability | 2,000 |
| 904 | Pyrotechnics rider | 1,000 |
| | Subtotal | $  4,500 |
| | Total expenses | $ 51,750 |
| | Total variable expense | $ 29,250 |
| | Total projected income | $393,000 |
| | Total projected expense | 91,500 |
| | Gross retained earnings | $301,500 |
| | Percentage of fixed overhead | 150,000 |
| | Net retained earnings (reinvestment) | $151,500 |

## CONFERENCE AND EXPOSITION

Income

| | | |
|---|---|---|
| 100 | Registration | |
| 101 | Early bird discount | $100,000 |
| 102 | Regular | 50,000 |
| 103 | On site | 25,000 |
| 104 | Spouse/partner | 10,000 |
| 105 | Special events | 15,000 |
| | Subtotal | $200,000 |
| 200 | Marketing | |
| 201 | Sponsorships | 10,000 |
| 202 | Advertising | 15,000 |
| 203 | Merchandise | 10,000 |
| | Subtotal | $ 35,000 |
| 300 | Investments | |
| 301 | Interest income | $  1,000 |
| | Subtotal | $  1,000 |
| 400 | Donations | |
| 401 | Grants | $  5,000 |
| | Subtotal | $  5,000 |

| 500 | Exposition | |
|-----|------------|--|
| 501 | 200 booths @ $1,500 | $300,000 |
| 502 | 50 tabletops @ $500 | 25,000 |
| | Subtotal | $325,000 |
| | Total income | $566,000 |

Expenses

| 600 | Administration (fixed expense) | |
|-----|-------------------------------|--|
| 601 | Site office furniture rental | $ 1,500 |
| 602 | Site office supplies | 500 |
| 603 | Site rental | 30,000 |
| 604 | Site telephone expense | 1,500 |
| | Subtotal | $ 33,500 |
| 700 | Printing (fixed expense) | |
| 701 | Design | $ 2,000 |
| 702 | Printing | 10,000 |
| | Subtotal | $ 12,000 |
| 800 | Postage (fixed expense) | |
| 801 | Hold this date | $ 1,000 |
| 802 | Brochure | 5,000 |
| 803 | Miscellaneous | 500 |
| | Subtotal | $ 6,500 |
| 900 | Entertainment (fixed expense) | |
| 901 | Talent fees | $ 5,000 |
| 902 | Travel and accommodations | 500 |
| 903 | Sound | 0 |
| 904 | Lights | 0 |
| | Subtotal | $ 5,500 |
| 1000 | Transportation and accommodations | |
| 1001 | Staff travel | $ 1,500 |
| 1002 | Staff accommodations | 1,500 |
| | Subtotal | $ 3,000 |
| 1100 | Insurance (fixed expense) | |
| 1101 | Cancellation | $ 3,000 |
| 1103 | Comprehensive general liability | 2,000 |
| | Subtotal | $ 5,000 |
| 1200 | Speakers (variable expense) | |
| 1201 | Honoraria | $ 10,000 |
| 1202 | Travel | 3,000 |
| 1203 | Accommodations | 1,000 |
| 1204 | Complimentary registrations | 3,000 |
| 1205 | Per diem | 1,000 |
| | Subtotal | $ 18,000 |
| 1300 | Audiovisual (variable expense) | |

| | | |
|---|---|---:|
| 1301 | Rentals (general sessions) | $ 25,000 |
| 1302 | Labor (general sessions) | 10,000 |
| 1303 | Rentals (breakouts) | 2,000 |
| 1304 | Labor (breakouts) | 1,000 |
| 1305 | Prerecorded modules | 5,000 |
| | Subtotal | $ 43,000 |
| 1400 | Exposition (variable expense) | |
| 1401 | Pipe and drape | $ 10,000 |
| 1402 | Aisle carpet | 20,000 |
| 1403 | Signs | 5,000 |
| | Subtotal | $ 35,000 |
| | Total projected income | $566,000 |
| | Total projected expense | 161,500 |
| | Gross retained earnings | $404,500 |
| | Percentage of fixed overhead | 199,000 |
| | Net retained earnings (reinvestment) | $205,500 |

Although most event managers find that financial matters are the least interesting aspect of their role and scope of their jobs, you now understand that to sustain long-term success it is critical that you firmly control this important management area. The better you become at watching the bottom line the more resources that will become available to you for other more creative activities.

# Career Advancement Connections

## GLOBAL CONNECTION

The role that international finance plays in event management industry was highlighted by the changes that occurred within the industry from the moment the North American Free Trade Agreement (NAFTA) was implemented. The entire economy of the United States, including the event management industry, has undergone major changes. Major labor-intensive industries were moved to Mexico because of saving on the labor force. At the same time, more knowledge-intensive industries were concentrated in the United States and Canada.

## TECHNOLOGY CONNECTION

To learn more about financial management and financial markets, I encourage you to become proficient in Microsoft Excel. The following Web sites are also beneficial:

- *www.ft.com*     *Financial Times*

- *www.wsj.com*    *Wall Street Journal*
- *www.sec.gov*    Securities and Exchange Commission
- *www.freedgar.com*    EDGAR (Electronic Data Gathering, Analysis, and Retrieval) database that contains information about financial performance of all companies, including event management, whose stocks are traded publicly
- *www.rubicon.com/passport/currency/currency.html*    for easy, fast currency exchange rate data

## RESOURCE CONNECTION

The best strategy for understanding event financial management is practice. The following are excellent textbooks to assist you further: *Analysis for Financial Management,* 6th ed., by Robert C. Higgins, (2000); *Financial Management: Theory and Practice,* by Eugene F. Brigham and Louis C. Gapenski (1998); *Financial Analysis with Microsoft Excel* by Timothy Mayes (1996).

## LEARNING CONNECTION

Your event management organization is seeking a contract with a large corporation. It is a promotional event that will be organized to promote a new service. In order to make a final decision on whether you want to accept the project, you have to conduct financial calculations and a break-even analysis. Your event management organization is willing to accept the project if the total gross profit for the event is more than $5000. Your client estimates that there will be somewhere between 100 and 300 guests. The company pays $100 per person with a minimum of $10,000. You know that your variable costs (food and beverage) total $30 per person. The total fixed costs are $4000. Now calculate the maximum and the minimum gross profit that you can achieve for this event.

# CHAPTER 6

# Event Leadership

**IN THIS CHAPTER YOU WILL LEARN HOW TO:**

- Identify leadership characteristics in an event manager and in yourself
- Make critical decisions and act decisively
- Solve problems
- Overcome communication challenges
- Use five critical factors to improve your leadership ability

Professional event management is truly a leadership process. Linda Higgison, chairman and CEO of the TCI Companies and instructor of Event Administration at the George Washington University Event Management Certificate Program describes the leadership process this way. "The global event manager must be a leader and he or she must wear many hats in their various leadership roles. One role is the creator, the communicator, another is the visionary, and still another is the problem solver. The successful event manager must not only wear these hats and many more but must also become adept at continually changing hats (roles) to achieve the goals and objectives of the event." Higgison is correct in her assumption that the event manager must indeed play many roles. However, historically management has been a command and control approach rather than a collaborative process. How much command and control should the event manager relinquish if he or she is to become an effective event leader?

Julia Rutherford-Silvers, educational consultant and industry editor for the George Washington University Event Management Certificate Program states: "Leadership requires trust, and trust depends on integrity, competence, and confidence. *Managers* analyze information, make inferences, and make decisions. They allocate resources to solve problems, assign tasks, and make schedules. Leaders influence and inspire others to achieve a goal. Leaders motivate. Leaders evaluate decisions, imagine consequences, and build contingencies."

# Leadership Styles

In class I often use a leadership exercise to dramatically convey the three different leadership styles found among event managers. I divide the class into three groups and give each team a set of popsicle sticks. I then instruct each group to construct an event site using the popsicle sticks. One group will do this using a democratic approach, the other with autocratic principles, and the third from a laissez-faire approach.

The *democratic group* arranges the popsicle sticks easily and efficiently in a pleasing formation, and their conversations, discussions, and decision making flows smoothly. The arrangement of the popsicle sticks is a dramatic representation of the effectiveness of their process.

The *autocratic group* can barely decide how to place their Popsicle sticks, due to dissension and arguments regarding turf. This group is too busy battling among themselves to accomplish the goals required by the event.

The *laissez-faire group* constantly arranges and rearranges their popsicle sticks, as without clear direction or facilitation they have trouble achieving consensus and their popsicle sticks demonstrate this confusion.

Each of these event leadership styles has an important role to play in the event management process. Your ability to navigate among these styles and use the one that is appropriate at the right time is essential to achieving success.

## DEMOCRATIC STYLE

Typically, this leadership style is used during the early stages of the event process. It is an excellent approach for facilitating discussions, conducting focus groups, and building consensus as you assemble your stakeholders. It is also effective as you move from the design phase into the coordination phase. Before you can coordinate your team members' efforts, you must demonstrate that you are willing to listen and that you are able to function as a good facilitator. These two skills—listening and facilitation—are hallmarks of democratic event leadership.

## AUTOCRATIC STYLE

When the fire marshal tells you to evacuate an event site, you should not use the democratic approach. The democratic event leadership style has one major drawback: It takes time to reach consensus. When an emergency evacuation is required, there is no time or any reason to try and reach consensus. Instead, you must use the autocratic approach and give the order to evacuate. Then you must supervise carefully to make certain that your instructions are being followed. The autocratic approach should be used sparingly. It is impossible, for example, to force volunteers and increasing staff members to do things they do not wish to do. Therefore, the autocratic approach should be used only when time is of the essence.

## LAISSEZ-FAIRE STYLE

This approach is least used in event management because it requires a team with skills equal in level, and therefore the event manager does not have to facilitate to ensure that goals are being achieved. It is rare that an event organization has a team with skills at a similar level. Most event organizations are comprised of many people with a variety of different skills and even commitment levels. Therefore, it is impossible for the event manager to site back and let the group decide for themselves how to proceed. Beware the laissez-faire event manager. He or she may be unskilled and is trying to transfer his or her incompetence to the entire event team.

When you are faced with this scenario, move quickly to empower others on the team to assist this person with facilitation decision making to ensure that the event goals and objectives are being met. The most common way to reduce large amounts of complex information about an event to a manageable communications process is through published policies and procedures. All events of substance have such a document and it helps drive the decision making of the event.

# Leadership Characteristics

Throughout ancient and modern human history a number of people have been identified by historians as effective leaders. Some of these people became leaders due to a defining moment or event in their lives, while others sought leadership opportunities to cause positive change. In Table 6-1 the general traits associated with effective leaders are compared to those specialized characteristics that Higgison and Rutherford-Silvers have identified within successful event managers. Although some will argue with this list and ranking, I am firmly convinced, based on my observation of literally thousands of event managers throughout the world, that the six characteristics listed in the right column of Table 6-1 generally define the qualities of the top event management leaders. These qualities or characteristics are ranked in this order for a specific purpose. It is important for event managers to understand that not all leadership characteristics are equal; however, integrity is paramount. Integrity is the value that determines the external perception by others.

**Table 6-1**  Leadership Characteristics

| Traditional Leaders | Event Leaders |
|---|---|
| 1. Communication skills | 1. Integrity |
| 2. Confidence | 2. Confidence and persistence |
| 3. Courage | 3. Collaboration |
| 4. Decision making | 4. Problem solving |
| 5. Enthusiasm | 5. Communication skills |
| 6. Integrity | 6. Vision |
| 7. Persistence | |
| 8. Planning | |
| 9. Problem solving | |
| 10. Vision | |

## INTEGRITY

The event leader must set the standard for integrity. If he or she does not exemplify integrity in performance and decision making, event stakeholders will soon lose faith and trust not only in the event leader but also in the event organization. For example, if an event manager reminds his or her staff that it is inappropriate to accept gifts from vendors and then is seen by his or her subordinates receiving a substantial gift from a vendor, the credibility of the person as well as that of the organization may be shattered. The event manager who exhibits high integrity will not only refuse the gift but will effectively communicate to his or her colleagues that the gift has been refused and why it would be inappropriate to accept this gift. Table 6-2 demonstrates perceptions of high and low integrity by event stakeholders.

## CONFIDENCE AND PERSISTENCE

When your back is against the wall, will you have the confidence and persistence to forge ahead? Typically, most events have a reality check where funds are low, morale is even lower, and impending disaster seems just around the corner. During these times of trial and tribulation, all eyes will be on the event manager. Your ability to stay the course, maintain the original vision, and triumph is what is expected by your event stakeholders.

Let us suppose that you are responsible for acquiring sponsors for your event. Only a few weeks before the event, your biggest sponsor backs out. There is no time to replace the sponsor. In addition, the neighbors whose houses are near your event venue are starting to make rumblings in the media about noise, traffic, and other disruptions that they believe will result from your event. A traditional manager would collect all the necessary information and perhaps assign each problem to an appropriate subordinate after making a decision as to the best course of action. An event leader, however, will use these challenges as opportunities for the event organization to learn and grow. The event leader may ask members of the board as well as staff for recommendations on how to replace or at least mitigate the damage that could be caused by the missing sponsor. Furthermore, the event leader will meet with

**Table 6-2**  Integrity Quotient

| Perception of High Integrity | Evidence | Low Integrity | Evidence |
|---|---|---|---|
| Consistency | Punctuality | Tardiness | Communications |
| Inclusiveness | Participation | Absenteeism | Intolerance |
| Participation | Consistency | Inconsistency | Participation |
| Tolerance | Inclusiveness | Exclusiveness/favoritism | Exclusiveness |
| Punctuality | Tolerance | Intolerance | Inconsistency |

the neighbors or their association and work collaboratively with his or her staff to provide the assurances they need to provide new and long-term support for the event. Event leaders use their confidence and persistence as teaching tools to influence other event stakeholders.

## COLLABORATIVE DECISION MAKING

Since Taylor created the management methods used to propel industrialized America, most management theory has focused on achieving efficiency to maximize profits. As workers began to organize into labor unions, they challenged this approach and sought an equal share in the decision-making process regarding not only the type of work they do but how they do it. Event organizations are not linear organizations such as factories. Instead, they are pulsating organizations that may start with a small staff, swell to a large part-time and volunteer organization as an event grows near, and then rapidly deflate to the original small staff as the event winds down. This type of organization requires close collaboration between the event leaders and those who will actually deliver the services that provide the final perception of the event by the guests.

Collaborative organizations or quality teams have been used for the past three decades by numerous for-profit and not-for-profit organizations to achieve high quality and consequently, better financial results. Event leaders should always perceive their associates (permanent and part-time staff), volunteers, and others as collaborators who share a mutual goal of producing a successful event. Therefore, all decisions should be preceded by close collaboration among the stakeholders. However, there are also times when the event manager must lead by making timely decisions without consulting all affected stakeholders. For example, when the event manager is notified of an unsafe or illegal or unethical activity taking place, he or she must intercede swiftly. Following the decision to act, the event manager must make certain that he or she has used this action as a teachable moment to explain why it is was important. They must notify the affected stakeholders that he or she has taken an action. He or she should then seek their input in case a similar decision would have to be made in the future.

## PROBLEM SOLVING

A colleague of mine once said that she counted thousands of potential problems during the development of an event and therefore concluded that events consist of a series of problems whose solution determines the level of success achieved by event stakeholders. I prefer to see a problem as a challenge that is temporarily testing the skills of the event leader and his or her stakeholders. Few event managers continue in the field unless they are comfortable with their ability to solve problems. Therefore, it is understood that event managers who are experienced and trained possess the skills not only to analyze problems but also to provide a solution or solutions that will improve the outcome of the event. The following list provides the event leader with a framework for understanding, analyzing, and solving event problems.

1. Make certain that you thoroughly understand the size, scope, and time sensitivity of the problem.
2. Identify the key informants and stakeholders affected by the problem.
3. Determine if there is a model or comparable problem whose solution could be used for this problem.
4. Test the potential solution by seeking the collaborative input of those affected by the problem. If the problem is urgent and requires an immediate response, use a precedent or other model to frame your response.
5. Once a decision has been made, monitor the impact to determine if anything further must be done to mitigate future problems resulting from your decision.

Here is an example of how this model would work during an actual event. A Texas university had a tradition of allowing students to construct a giant bonfire before the major football game of the year. This tradition stretched back several decades and had become a hallowed ritual/rite for students and alumni. Unfortunately, the bonfire materials collapsed and killed several students while critically injuring many others. University officials then had to decide whether or not to allow the bonfire to be rebuilt the following year. The framework above may be applied to this problem to produce an outcome that can be accepted by a majority of stakeholders.

First, the president of the university and other administrators had to hold a thorough investigation to make certain that they had all the facts concerning the scope, size, and time sensitivity of the problem. Next, they had to make certain that their empirical information represented input from key stakeholders (those most seriously affected by the problem). Then the president and administrators had to conduct further research to determine if there is a similar problem and solution that may be used as a model for this incident. By researching academic journals, conducting interviews with administrators at other schools, and seeking anecdotal information from other institutions, the administrators may identify responses that may guide them to an appropriate solution.

The institution must first test the potential solutions with key informants and other critical stakeholders to make certain that their response is accurate, thorough, and appropriate. The input that will be received from other stakeholders will further refine not only the strategic solution but also the implementation tactics. Due to the gravity of this problem, university administrators decided immediately to cancel further bonfire structures for the next twelve months pending an official investigation and analysis of the problem. This decision was made to prevent other groups, including off-campus organizations, from continuing the tradition.

Finally, the solution to the problem (canceling the bonfire for a period of years) must be monitored to determine if other challenges occur as a result of the solution. Indeed, as soon as the cancellation was announced, an off-campus alumni organization announced that it wanted to build a bonfire to continue the tradition. University administrators strongly discouraged this activity and promoted their concern to media to go on record opposing this activity.

Most event problems are not of the magnitude of the university bonfire tragedy. However, unless problems are solved efficiently and appropriately, they can easily escalate to a level that may threaten the reputation of the event. Once the reputation is injured or ruined, it may be difficult to sustain the future of the event.

## COMMUNICATION SKILLS

Although communication is a critical component of the entire event process, it is also the single largest culprit when it comes to problems that may arise. How many times has a lack of communication or, more often, miscommunication resulted in a missed opportunity, an error, an oversight, or even a dangerous situation? Although an event manager need not be particularly articulate or even eloquent, he or she must be an excellent communicator. Communication is a continuous process that involves both sending (transmitting) and receiving information. This information may be verbal, written, or even abstract symbols such as body language. The event leader must be able to receive and transmit complex information to multiple stakeholders throughout the event process. The glue that literally binds the various disparate components of the event plan together is the communications process. Therefore, the event manager must lead through excellent communications from research through evaluation. Following are the most common communications problems that may affect the planning process in event management and how to correct them.

- *Communication is not received by stakeholders:* Confirm receipt.
- *Communication is misunderstood by stakeholders:* Ask questions.
- *Communication is blocked among stakeholders:* Promote open communications.

Without open and continuous communication, event stakeholders cannot form the collaborative team needed to achieve common objectives. To promote open communications the event manager must listen, analyze, and act. To listen effectively an event manager must be intuitive, set specific criteria for the analysis of facts, and when necessary, act quickly and decisively to unblock communications among stakeholders.

## VISION

The professional event manager must clearly demonstrate he or she has a vision of the outcome of the event. During the early meetings with the stakeholders the event management leader must describe in a visual manner the outcome that will result from the event. For example, the event manager may state that "on the opening day thousands of guests will line up to buy tickets and once inside they will smile, participate, and have a good time all due to your efforts." Furthermore, the event manager must "lead" the stakeholders toward that vision of the event by asking leading questions such as "Can you see this happening? Are you prepared to help me make it happen? What will you do to help us achieve this goal?"

## THE EVENT LEADERSHIP FACTOR

These six leadership factors ultimately result in an event manager who has the skills, experience, and intuition to form the best judgment and act appropriately to advance the goals of the event organization. This is no small task. It requires continuous monitoring by stakeholders to ensure that the event manager is doing his or her best to lead the team. Event leadership requires constant vigilance and continuing education to ensure that the power that is entrusted to the event manager is used wisely, judiciously, and thoughtfully.

Finally, it is important to note that event leadership is neither charisma nor control, the ability to command nor the talent to inspire. Rather, it is that rare commodity, like good taste, that one recognizes when one sees it. Every event manager should aspire to become the kind of event leader that others will not only recognize but also follow to see where they lead them. Ultimately, the best event managers become leaders that other event stakeholders not only admire but also emulate as they seek to develop their own leadership potential. Through this admiration and emulation, these event stakeholders will soon become leaders themselves, producing even greater events in the twenty-first century.

# Career Advancement Connections

## GLOBAL CONNECTION

The late Speaker of the U.S. House of Representatives, the honorable Tip O'Neill, reportedly said, "All politics are local." In fact, all events are local; however, increasingly many local events are attracting global recognition. For example, events that began as small local festivals now attract international guests who are interested in the specific theme or subject showcased at the event. The modern portal known as the Internet has rapidly globalized many local events. Even a local arts and crafts show may now promote and sell products worldwide using electronic commerce. Therefore, twenty-first-century event leaders should seize these new technologies to establish global connections for their local events. Here are some ideas to help you lead in the global marketplace:

- Use the Web and other research sources to determine if your local event has a global counterpart. Perhaps your event can partner with another event or events to cross-promote and share other critical resources, such as entertainment or speakers.
- Form global consortiums of similar event management organizations to share critical resources and education.
- Brand your event globally through creative partnering with other organizations, such as not-for-profit international charitable causes.

## TECHNOLOGY CONNECTION

The most effective way to expand globally is by leading with a strong technology strategy. The following suggestions will help you develop this strategy.

- Determine who your target audience is and how lists, list servers, and groups can help you reach them most efficiently through the Internet.
- Create virtual Internet events to expand the life cycle for your real events.
- Explore new technologies (lighting, sound) that are emerging in other parts of the world and use them to improve the quality and memorability of your event.
- Use the Internet to improve communications among all stakeholders through real-time online conversations.
- Maintain the vision of your event by designing a Web site for your event staff and volunteers that is password protected.
- Provide your staff and volunteers with a downloadable screen saver of your event logo to remind them constantly of the mission, vision, and goals and objectives that you share as an event organization.

## RESOURCE CONNECTION

There are innumerable resources to assist you in leading through technology. One of the best books I have reviewed is *Technotrends* by Daniel Burrus (1993, Harper Business). This book is written in a novel format and reveals exciting possibilities for the future of technology. In addition to this resource, you should act in the following areas:

- Use online Web site development tools from major software providers such as Microsoft.
- Contact college and university computing departments which may assist you in establishing list service and other technological communications systems at a nominal fee.
- Improve your personal leadership skills through training and actual practice offered through organizations such as the International Special Events Society *(www.ises.com)* and Meeting Professionals International *(www.mpiweb.org)*.

## LEARNING CONNECTION

Complete these activities to advance your growth in the area of event leadership.

1. What are the five most important qualities of twenty-first-century event management leaders?
2. How do these qualities differ from those in other fields, such as politics, education, and others?
3. What are the best methods for improving communications among event stakeholders?
4. How do you solve the following event-related problem using the leadership skills you have learned in this chapter?

    A small event organization has an annual music festival and each year for the past five years the number of volunteers has decreased. This decrease can be attributed to a perception by new volunteers that the organization is too exclusive and does not really value new ideas and opinions. How will you increase the number of volunteers for the next festival without seriously jeopardizing the relationship that you have with other volunteers who have been with the organization for many years?
5. Write a one-page description of the type of leader you believe your staff and volunteers perceive you to be, and then describe the type of leader you can become with proper training and practice (experience).

# PART THREE

# Event Coordination

# CHAPTER 7

# Managing Vendor Contracts

**IN THIS CHAPTER YOU WILL LEARN HOW TO:**

- Develop and implement the design for your event
- Develop appropriate resources
- Coordinate catering operations
- Use trends in event catering
- Coordinate technical resources, including lighting, sound, and special effects
- Conduct and analyze the site inspection
- Develop and construct the production schedule
- Anticipate and resolve operational conflicts

The International Special Events Society annually awards several Esprit prizes for excellence in the spirit (esprit) of teamwork. This is the only awards program that I am aware of in the hospitality, meeting planning, and related industries that salutes achievement through high-quality team work. No single person is honored; rather, the awards are bestowed to teams that are responsible for innovative, excellent event production. ISES members understand that great events are the result of great people working together to achieve a common goal.

# Challenges of Teamwork

If you have ever served on a committee, marched in a band, sung in a choir, or played on a team, you know the challenges of developing successful teams. The most frequent problems that event managers face when developing teams are (1) communications, (2) self-interest, (3) dependability, (4) trust, and (5) collaboration.

### COMMUNICATIONS

Excellent event coordination is the result of continuous, consistent, high-quality communications between the event stakeholders. The event manager is responsible for developing and sustaining the event communications to ensure that all stakeholders are informed, in touch, and involved in each of the phases of managing the event. The following are several methods that you may use to establish and/or improve a high-quality communications network for your event.

1. Conduct a communications audit and find out how your event stakeholders best send and receive information.

2. Avoid communications that are blocked by noise, visual distraction, or other interference.
3. Include an "Action Required" statement on all written communications to confirm that communications have been received and understood.
4. Use nontraditional communications such as audio and video tapes to increase impact, retention, and action.
4. Use written change orders to record changes during your event. Make certain the client or other responsible person signs the change order to authorize the addition, deletion, or substitution of services or products.

## SELF-INTEREST

Many committees are comprised of people who essentially bring their personal views, bias, and agendas to the event planning process. It is the responsibility of the event manager to persuade each person to forgo personal interest for the sake of group interest. Only through a strong group effort can an event achieve a successful outcome. You may wish to invite an expert in team building or conduct team building exercises yourself to develop trust, congeniality, and a common purpose among the team members. One way to begin this process is through an informal series of events such as social functions where the event stakeholders get to know, like, and trust one another before they sit down to deliberate (plan) an event. During this social period the event manager may observe the participants to begin to identify those who naturally work best in teams and those who will need more coaching or persuasion to feel comfortable working in a group project.

## DEPENDABILITY

One of the biggest management problems in working with volunteers is time and attendance. Because volunteers are not compensated for their efforts, many do not feel the obligation to arrive on time or even to show up at all. This is why many event managers actually schedule between 25 and 50 percent more volunteers than will be needed, to compensate for the serious problem of attrition at events.

The Sydney Organizing Committee for the Olympic Games (SOCOG) developed a unique passport system for the 60,000 volunteers who helped coordinate the 2000 Summer Olympic Games. Each volunteer was issued a personal passport and asked to have it stamped each day by their supervisor. When the passport was completely stamped, the volunteer would be entered in a drawing to win a wide range of valuable prizes.

Jason Quinn, a professional stage manager, states that most vendors do not want to be late when purveying an event. Therefore, for the first infraction he waits for a calm moment and inquires "What happened?" Later he may state: "Let me know if there is anything I can do to help you with your scheduling because we are depending on you being on time to ensure a successful event."

Of course, the easiest way to ensure dependability is to recruit dependable people. Keep accurate records of time and attendance and use the records to determine who to engage for future events. During the interviewing or recruiting process, check references carefully to make sure that your stakeholders have a pattern of punctuality that can be shared with your event.

In the event management profession, the definition of punctuality is "early." Because of the numerous variables that can occur before, during, and after an event, it is essential that all event stakeholders arrive at an event site early enough to be able to spot potential challenges and overcome them before the guests or other vendors arrive. When interviewing potential event coordination staff, I often ask: "If the event setup time is at 8 A.M., what time do you believe is the best time for you to arrive at the venue?" Those who answer between 7 and 7:30 A.M. are most likely to receive final consideration for employment. This is because I have often arrived at an event venue to coordinate the setup only to find that it takes up to one hour to open the locked parking lot, contact security to gain entrance to the building, and locate engineering to turn on the lights in order to be ready for the vendors' arrival.

## TRUST

Trust must be earned by the event manager. Trust is the result of the sustained effort by the event manager to develop an atmosphere and environment wherein the event stakeholders invest their trust in his or her behavior and judgments. Trust, in fact, is the net result of a pattern of positive behaviors exhibited by the event manager. When these behaviors are erratic or quixotic, the trust factor begins to diminish. To develop, establish, and sustain trust, the event manager must earn it and ask for it from his or her stakeholders.

Event stakeholders cannot blindly trust every event manager. Rather, they must use their best judgment to determine when and how to invest their trust. Trust should not be invested without question or careful analysis by the stakeholders. However, an event organization that is not firmly rooted in trust between the event manager and his or her stakeholders is one that is precarious and cannot achieve the level of success required to meet the expectations of all the stakeholders.

## COLLABORATION

The final quality of effective event coordinators is the ability to develop close collaboration between all the stakeholders. This is extremely difficult, due to the disparity between the personalities, skills, and experiences of each stakeholder. Imagine a preevent conference with all the stakeholders. You may have at the same table persons with a wide variety of formal education, an even wider range of skill and experience level, diverse ethnic backgrounds, and completely different technical abilities. How does the event manager inspire and encourage close collaboration between such a varied group of stakeholders? The key to collaboration is purpose. The event manager must clearly articulate the purpose of the event and convince each stakeholder that they must work with others to achieve or exceed the expectations of the guests. The distinguished anthropologist Margaret Mead once wrote: "Never underestimate that a small group of people committed to a common goal can change the world. In fact, it is the only way the world can be changed." Your world or universe is the event you are responsible for managing. Therefore, you must firmly remind the stakeholders that self-interest must be left outside the event environment. The purpose of the event team is to cooperate and collaborate to achieve the goals and objectives of the event, and the event manager is the leader of this effort.

# Developing and Implementing the Design for Your Event

Once the design has been developed and the plan finalized, the two must be merged to begin the implementation process. During the coordination phase we arrive at the intersection of research, design, and planning and through the convergence of these three places begin to operationalize the event itself. The coordination phase provides us with the opportunity to see the results of our early labors in research, design, and planning. It is also the opportunity to ensure that we preserve the integrity of our early efforts. Too often, changes are made during the coordination phase that affect the outcome of the event negatively because they do not preserve the integrity of the design and planning process. One technique for ensuring that you continually preserve the integrity of your event design is to appoint one person to monitor the coordination and make certain that there is a obvious relationship between the design, plan, and the final version of the event. Another method is to develop a series of written or graphic cues, such as design renderings or goals and objectives to make certain the stakeholders hold fast to the early vision of the event.

# Developing Appropriate Resources

Event resources generally include people, time, finances, technology, and physical assets. Although each is important, each is also extremely scarce. Occasionally, someone will tell me that they have unlimited resources for their event. I am skeptic about this because of the economic theory which states that you must learn to allocate scarce resources to achieve maximum benefit. No matter how many resources you have, the fact is that they are always limited. The way you stretch your resources is through careful and creative allocation.

The event manager must first identify appropriate resources for his or her event during the proposal stage. It is not unlikely that you will receive a telephone call one morning at 9 A.M. and be told that you need to deliver a proposal by 12 noon to be eligible to earn the right to produce the event. Given this short time frame, the event manager must be able to identify appropriate resources quickly and accurately. Table 7-1 provides a general guide to where to find these important resources.

The event manager must be able to identify quickly the most appropriate resources for their event. Furthermore, the event manager has to attest that these resources are reliable. This is not always possible, due to time constraints. Therefore, after every effort is made to verify the quality of an event resource such as entertainment or catering or venue, the event manager may wish to include the following statement in the proposal to reduce his or her liability: *"The information contained herein is deemed to be reliable but not guaranteed."* It is impossible to verify and confirm every resource within the brief time constraints imposed by most events. Therefore, the event manager should do what is reasonable and inform the client of the status of the level of reliability of the information that he or she is providing.

The most common method for identifying appropriate resources is:

1. Conduct a needs assessment.
2. Determine the budget.
3. Develop the request for proposal document and evaluation criteria.
4. Identify appropriate firms or individuals to submit proposals.
5. Distribute a request for proposal.
6. Review the proposals.
7. Select the suppliers.
8. Negotiate with the suppliers.
9. Develop contracts with the suppliers.
10. Execute and monitor contract performance.

**Table 7-1**  Event Rosources and Where to Find Them

| Category | Examples | Sources |
| --- | --- | --- |
| Money | Starting capital, emergency funds | Investors, credit, vendors, sponsors |
| People | Volunteers, staff, vendors | Convention and visitors' bureaus, destination management companies, schools, colleges, organizations, public relations, event alumni, advertising |
| Physical assets | Transportation, venue, catering | Destination management companies, school districts, caterers, convention and visitors' bureaus |
| Technology | Software, hardware | Internet, industry organizations |
| Time | Scheduling, organization, management, expanded time bands | Scheduling software, delegation strategies and tactics, cloning yourself |

Steps 1 and 2 are critical in order to proceed to develop a effective request for proposal (RFP). They may be conducted during the research phase and will include using historical as well as comparable data. The RFP must include the history of the event and/or the goals and objectives as well as the budget parameters. Step 3 requires that you establish a broad list of qualified organizations or individuals to receive the RFP. These lists can come from the resources shown in Table 7-1 or through historical or comparable information. Regardless of how you acquire this list, it is wise to qualify them further by calling each potential proposer to ask if he or she would like to receive the RFP. The initial list of proposers may be lengthy; however, the final list should not include more than five organizations or individuals. Typically, the average number of proposers to receive the RFP is no more than three.

The average event manager responsible for a large event such as the one described in Figure 7-1 may have as many as 50 or 60 proposals to receive and review. Therefore, it is important that you develop a methodology or system for receiving, reviewing, and responding to these proposals. Table 7-2 provides an example of how to manage this process. Coordinating the flow of documents is the first step in this phase in managing a successful event. Table 7-2 will not only help you track these important documents but also evaluate the qualifications and value of each proposer. Finally, this system will also help you develop a historical profile for each vendor so you can plan more efficiently in the future.

## WORKING WITH SUPPLIERS AND VENDORS

The ability to work with your vendors to satisfy the needs of your guests will ultimately help determine the level of success you achieve as a event manager. There are inumerable vendors; for example:

- Advertising agencies
- Advertising specialty providers
- Amusement games providers
- Animal providers
- Audiovisual providers
- Balloons
- Caterers
- Clowns
- Decor specialists
- Destination management companies
- Entertainment providers
- Envelope addressers
- First-aid providers
- Flag providers
- Florists
- Government agencies
- Hotels
- Insurance brokers and underwriters
- Invitation designers
- Legal counsel
- Lighting providers
- Magicians
- Printers
- Public relations counselors
- Puppeteers
- Pyrotechnic designers
- Security providers
- Special-effects providers
- Translation providers
- Valet parking providers
- Venue lessors

In this chapter we explore two of the most frequently used resources: caterers and technical production specialists.

| | |
|---|---|
| Event title: | Med-Eth Conference and Exposition |
| Sponsoring organization: | International Medical Ethics Society |
| Description of organization: | Med-Eth is the world's largest professional society in the field of medical ethics |
| Tax status: | Med-Eth is a 501.c3 U.S. tax-exempt membership organization |
| Description of attendees: | Medical doctors, medical administrators, suppliers to the medical ethics profession |
| Event date(s): | June 6–11, 2002 |
| Event location: | Washington, DC Convention Center |
| Service(s)/product(s) to be proposed: | Audio-visual equipment and labor |
| Total budget not to exceed: | $5000 |

Technical specifications:

1. Equipment and labor for video magnification and sound for two general sessions with 1000 persons using rear projection.
2. Equipment and labor for seven breakout sessions with an assortment of equipment, including slide projectors, video projectors, personal computers with Power Point, front projection screens, microphones, flipcharts (pads and markers), and laser pointers. Average audience size is 55 persons. Audience size will range from 30 to 75 persons.

Submission requirements:    All proposers must follow these guidelines to be considered for this assignment

1. Company/organization profile and history, including names of owners or principals as well as persons assigned to coordinate the event.
2. Itemized list of equipment and labor that will be provided, including redundant (backup) equipment.
3. Complete listing of all costs, including taxes if applicable.
4. Evidence of insurance company and evidence of commercial general liability with minimum limits of $2 million per occurrence.

| | |
|---|---|
| Deadline for submission: | 5 P.M. EST May 30, 2001 |
| Submission instructions: | Proposals may be submitted electronically to Ms. Jane Doe via e-mail to: |

idoe@med-eth.com

or by mail to:

Attn: Jane Doe
Med-Eth
6000 Massachusetts Avenue, N.W.
Washington, DC 20039

**Figure 7-1**
Typical Request for Proposal

**Table 7-2** Proposal Tracking System[a]

Event name: Med-Eth Conference and Exposition
Service(s)/product(s) required: audiovisual products and labor
Proposal due date: May 30, 2001

| Ranking | Proposer | Date and Time Received | Qualifications | Value | Total Score |
|---|---|---|---|---|---|
| 3 | Sound and Pictures, Inc. | May 15, 2001, 4 P.M. | 4 | 2 | 6 |
| 1 | Techno Services | May 17, 2001, 10 A.M. | 5 | 4 | 9 |
| 2 | Light and Sound, Inc. | May 25, 2001, 2 P.M. | 5 | 2 | 7 |
| 4 | Microphones, etc. | May 27, 2001, 5 P.M. | 3 | 2 | 5 |
| 5 | Video, Inc. | May 29, 2001, 4 P.M. | 2 | 2 | 4 |

[a]Scoring matrix: 1, poor; 2, fair; 3, acceptable; 4, good; 5, excellent.

# Coordinating Catering Operations

As caterers assume increased responsibilities in the event management profession, other members of the professional team will need to adjust their marketing and operations strategies to cope with this new phenomenon. "Can and will caterers charge for event management services beyond the cost of food and service?" and "Will all future catered events place significant emphasis on food and beverage at the risk of ignoring other elements and producing a more balanced event?" are but two of numerous questions that will be raised.

Earlier, I stated that historically, caterers have provided event management services. Now, the question becomes: "Will caterers develop these services further to reflect full depth and breadth of resources available within the event management industry?" If they choose to broaden their education, their force within the industry can have substantial implications. The future of event management may include both good food and beverages as well as equally excellent services managed by the caterer. This consolidation will be welcomed by some clients who desire one-stop shopping and rejected by others who may for a variety of reasons prefer to entrust their event to another event manager. Regardless, the future force in catering will include offering many diversified services carefully combined into a nutritious, filling, and satisfying buffet. At the center of this diversified services bountiful buffet may be event management.

Global event managers must also recognize that trends are typically regional and then national in scope. For example, the trend of reduced alcohol consumption in North America may not be as prevalent in some parts of the United States. For example, recently I have noticed a trend in California toward the design and construction of full-scale ice martini bars. These bars are constructed entirely of ice and even use fiber optic lights to illuminate them internally. The bartenders dispense hundreds of martinis, which are well received by the baby boomers, who want to relive the classic moments from the

1930s and 1940s enjoyed by their parents. The same is true of cigars, which are very popular in many parts of the United States. In other countries a cigar and martini is usual and customary, whereas in North America they are often reserved for special occasions.

To best utilize the trends in event catering, I recommend that you first review all event literature to be sure that you are incorporating a trend that is on an upward trajectory. Next, make certain that you test the trend idea with a focus panel of your event guests and others to make certain that it is appropriate and can be implemented with high quality. Finally, remember the difference between fads and trends. Fads are often short lived. You may purchase 1 million Pet Rocks only to discover that they were in vogue for only six months. Cautiously incorporate trends into your event design to enhance your plan.

## CATERING IDEAS

### The Living Buffet

**Effect**   As guests browse along a seemingly normal buffet table, they are startled as the head of lettuce suddenly starts talking to the cauliflower and the cauliflower turns to the guest for advice on how to handle the unruly lettuce.

**Method**   Using a standard buffet table, cut two 24-inch holes in the top. The holes should be located approximately 12 to 18 inches apart and away from the front edge of the table. Place two actors, in head pieces that resemble lettuce and cauliflower, under the table with their heads penetrating the hole. It is best if the head piece covers the eyes or they keep their heads slightly bowed until time to speak. Elaborately garnish all the area around the fake lettuce and cauliflower. Use theatrical lighting to soften the light on this area of the buffet.

**Reaction**   Guests will shriek with delight and the talking lettuce and cauliflower will become one of the best memories of your catered event.

**Bonus**   Write a brief script between the lettuce and cauliflower in which they engage in a heated discussion about the health and nutrition. Have the actors turn to the guests to ask their opinions.

### The Human Buffet Table

**Effect**   A beautiful woman or man supports an entire buffet upon his or her garment.

**Method**   Place a male or female actor in the center of two buffet tables. The buffet should be slightly elevated on platforms so that the edge of the table is at eye level. Construct a costume for the female and male that appears to support the entire buffet. The woman may wear a long dress and the skirt may be supported with matching fabric used to skirt swag the front edge of the buffet table (see Figure 7-2), or the male may wear a colorful tailcoat with the tails extended with matching fabric to drape the tables. Place bright light on the actors in colors to complement their costumes and slightly softer light on the buffet tables. Match the lighting for the actors' wardrobe with softer lighting in matching colors on the buffet skirting.

**Reaction**   Guests will ooh and ahhh as your elegant actors wave and invite them to dine.

**Bonus**   Direct the actors to freeze and come to life periodically. This will create an ongoing activity for the guests to observe and enjoy.

## Old Black Magic

**Effect**   Thirty servers enter once the guests are seated. Each server is carrying a silver tray with two tophats. Suddenly the entire room begins to glow in the dark.

**Method**   Purchase 60 black plastic tophats. Fill each top hat with 20 glow-in-the-dark bracelets and sticks. Line the waiters up outside the function room service entrance. Upon a cue from yourself instruct the servers to enter as you play music such as "Old Black Magic" or "Magic to Do." As the servers arrive at the tables and place their hats in the center, quickly turn off the lights. Instruct the servers to place their trays under their arms, clap their hands, and distribute the glow-in-the-dark pieces from inside the hats to the guests.

**Reaction**   Your guests may first wonder why there are no centerpieces for this elaborate catered event. However, once the glow-in-the-dark gifts are distributed the guests will applaud as they become the room decor and you produce magic at a fraction of the cost of traditional decor.

**Bonus**   Purchase white gloves for the servers and color them with glow-in-the-dark dye. As the lights go to black, have the servers wave their hands above their heads and then clap them before producing the glow-in-the-dark gifts.

## Dessert Parade

**Effect**   Your guests receive that a unique dessert that has been created for them as your team of servers parades the dessert to their tables.

**Figure 7-2**
Living Buffet

**Method** Use glow-in-the-dark swizzle sticks or other items to decorate the dessert trays. Play a lively march or theme music that reflects the style of the catered event as the servers march forward. Stage the servers so that they enter at the rear of the room and march through the tables holding the trays high above their heads. Lower the lights and use follow spotlights to sweep the room to create additional excitement. Prior to their entrance announce: "The chief has prepared a once-in-a-lifetime dessert creation to celebrate this momentous occasion. Please welcome your servers!" The servers march (or dance) to each table and serve dessert.

**Reaction** Your guests will respond with spontaneous applause followed by clapping rhythm to the music as your servers deliver dessert.

**Bonus** At the conclusion of the dessert parade line, the servers up in front of the stage and have them gesture to the left or right as the pastry chef appears for a brief bow. Make certain that the pastry chef is dressed in all

**Figure 7-2**
*(Continued)*

white with a traditional chef's hat so that he or she is easily recognized. This will cause an additional ovation and perhaps a standing one at that!

## Incredible Edible Centerpiece

**Effect**   Your guests will notice that their centerpiece is both beautiful and edible. The guests will see and smell as well as taste this delicious work of art.

**Method**   Engage a chocolatier to carve a centerpiece out of chocolate for your guests to enjoy. The carving may represent the symbol of the event or the logo of the organization sponsoring the program. Use a pin light to illuminate each sculpture independently. Make certain the sculpture is on a raised platform such as a gold or silver epergne. Include fresh fruit in your display to add color to your final design. One excellent subject is a large chocolate cornucopia filled with fresh red strawberries.

**Reaction**   Your guests will soon notice the work of art gracing their table and engage in lively conversation about its origin. Some guests will take photos, and others may try and nibble!

## Ice-Cold Logo

**Effect**   As your guests arrive for the cocktail reception, they observe an ice carver putting the finishing touches on an elaborate sculpture.

**Method**   Your caterer can refer a professional ice carver who will precarve from a large block of ice your organization's logo, image, name, or other important and valued symbol of your group. Place the carver on a raised platform and use rope and stanchion to provide ample working room and keep your guests from being hit by flying chips of ice. Make certain that the ice carver completes his or her work of art at the very moment your main function is to begin. Upon completion stage, several photos of your key leaders with the new work of art and then announce that the main function will begin.

**Reaction**   Your guests will crowd around the carver and begin intense discussions with one another about his or her artwork. At the conclusion of his artistic effort they will erupt into applause and begin taking numerous photos.

**Bonus**   Ask the ice carver to use an electric chain saw, as this creates noise and excitement. In addition, the use of flame (fire and ice) is another dramatic touch that your ice carver may wish to incorporate into the final design (such as a dragon breathing fire).

## SELECTING THE BEST CATERER

The best caterer is the organization best equipped with experience, knowledge, creativity, personnel, and resources (human and actual equipment) to achieve your goals and objectives. In each community there may be several full-service off-premise caterers with excellent reputations. However, the list will rapidly be narrowed to one, two, or hopefully three by using the following criteria:

1. Find out how many years the company has been in business and the size of events they have catered.
2. Ensure that caterer has health and occupancy permits (and all other necessary permits).
3. If serving alcohol, make sure that caterer has on- and off-premises alcohol beverage permits.
4. If permits are in order, make sure that caterer has liquor liability insurance.
5. Ask to see references and/or client letters.

6. Ask to see pictures of past events—look for professionalism and setup of kitchen/staging area.
7. Identify past and present events that caterer has handled and find out maximum and minimum sizes.
8. Check to see if site meets Americans with Disabilities Act requirements and complies with laws.
9. Find out policies on client tastings.
10. Review printed materials—menu descriptions will tell about level of professionalism.
11. Ask to see design equipment and/or in-house rentals—look for innovation and cleanliness.
12. Leave messages with company receptionist—see how long it takes to return calls.
13. If on-premises, make sure that any electronic or live music complies with Broadcast Music Inc. (BMI) or American Society of Composers, Authors and Publishers (ASCAP) regulations.
14. Check for membership in professional organizations (i.e., National Association of Catering Executives (NACE) and ISES).
15. Find out where executive chef received training.
16. Find out how wait staff is attired for different levels of services.
17. Find out if servers are proficient in French service, modified French service, or plated service.
18. Find out deposit requirements and terms.
19. Review and analyze contracts and cancellation agreements.
20. Call the local party equipment rental company and find out about their working relationship with the caterer.

Event manager Paul Broughton of Raleigh, North Carolina, suggests that these criteria are also important considerations for selecting the best caterer for your event. Broughton, a former catering professional who now plans and produces complete events, believes that selecting the best caterer is one of the most important decisions the event manager must make.

## Catering Coordination

The event manager must closely coordinate all event activities with the director of catering or other catering team leader. Within the catering team, each member has particular responsibilities:

- *Director of catering:* senior catering official who coordinates sales and operations.
- *Catering manager:* coordinates individual catered events, including sales and operations.
- *Banquet manager:* manages specific catered functions; servers report to banquet manager.
- *Server:* person responsible for serving the guests.
- *Bartender:* person responsible for mixing, pouring, and serving alcoholic and nonalcoholic beverages.

To ensure that you are effectively coordinating each element with your catering team, make certain that you hold a series of telephone or in-person meetings to review the various elements that will be included in your event. The first meeting should be used to review the proposal and answer any questions you may have about the food, beverage, equipment, or service and terms of payment. The next meeting will be held prior to signing the contract to negotiate any final terms, such as the inclusion of a complimentary food tasting. Some caterers prefer that you attend a comparable event and taste similar items that will be served at your event. However, if your event is introducing new cuisine, it is essential that you insist on a separate food tasting to ensure the quality of each item prior to serving your guests. In some instances there will be a charge for this service and you should confirm this prior to signing the contract. The final meeting should include a thorough review of all elements, including the schedule, equipment, service levels, and to answer any final questions the caterer may have regarding delivery, utilities, or other important issues.

## Reviewing Proposals

Most caterers will provide a complete proposal, including the type of cuisine, number of servers, schedule, equipment rentals, payment terms, and other pertinent information. Using the following checklist will ensure that all important information is included in the catering proposal.

1. History of the catering organization, including other clients of similar size and scope they have served.
2. Letters of reference from other clients of similar size and scope.
3. Complete description of cuisine.
4. Complete description of style of service, including the number of servers/bartenders that will be provided.
5. Complete description of equipment that will be provided by the caterer. Equipment may include tables, chairs, and serving utensils as well as other items. Make certain that each is described and that quantity is included.
6. List of additional services to be provided by the caterer, such as floral, entertainment, or other special requirements.
7. Complete description of payment terms, including date of guarantee, taxes, gratuities, deposits, balance payments, and percentage of overage provided by the caterer.
8. All schedule information concerning deliveries, setup, service, and removal of equipment through load-out.
9. Insurance, bonding, and other information pertinent to managing the risk of your event.
10. Any additional requirements, including utilities such as water, electric power, and so on.

Negotiating with the caterer is an important step in the process of selecting the best caterer. In smaller event management markets where competition is not as great as larger markets, negotiation may be more difficult. Still, regardless of size, there are traditional areas that may be negotiated:

1. Ask to pay the lowest deposit in advance or to pay a series of smaller deposits spread evenly over a period of months. Even better, if your organization has a good credit record, ask to pay net 30 days after your event.
2. Ask for a discount for prepayment. You may receive up to a 5 percent discount if you prepay your entire bill in advance.
3. Ask for a discount if you are a not-for-profit organization. Although all not-for-profit organizations ask for this concession, you may be successful if you can convince the caterer that your guests may bring him or her additional new business. Offer to actively promote the presence of the caterer at the event to ensure high visibility.
4. Ask for a complimentary service. Some caterers will provide services ranging from a complimentary ice sculpture to a pre- or postevent reception.
5. Ask for a complimentary food tasting for yourself and your key decision makers. This should no take the form of an additional event; rather, it is a business activity for the purpose of inspecting the food presentation, taste, and other important elements of the event.

## The Final Step

The final meeting should be held in person. Often, it is held in conjunction with the food tasting or final walkthrough. This important meeting is your final opportunity to review the critical details regarding the caterer's contribution to your event. The following major points must be covered during this meeting:

1. Confirm the day, date, time, location, parking, and other critical information with the caterer.
2. Carefully coordinate all catering deliveries and access to the loading entrance with other vendors.
3. Review the times for the service and instruct the caterer regarding the other elements of the program and how he or she will interface with these aspects.
4. Review the caterer's alcohol management program. Ask the caterer if his or her staff has received training and how they will handle guests who are obviously inebriated.
5. Review all payment terms and any elements you are required to provide as part of your agreement.

## Cost-Saving Measures

Increasingly, both clients and their event managers are concerned with cost. In some corporate circles it is not the actual cost but the perception of a high-priced event that is of greater concern. To avoid these concerns and lower your overall catering costs, use the following checklist.

1. Carefully analyze the meals that must be provided. Some meals may be taken by guests on their own, such as at networking dinners, where all guests pay for their individual bills. You may also wish to substitute concessions for some meal functions. An individually priced buffet line may be a good alternative for some meal functions.

2. Use buffets and boxed lunches instead of seated banquet service. Reducing labor cost may reduce expense.

3. Price food items by the lowest possible unit (cup, piece, or dozen) rather than by the tray or gallon. Order only the amount of food you will require based on the history of your event.

4. Secure sponsors for meal functions. In a recent study we identified a major interest by sponsors in providing funding for meals that are related to educational programs.

5. Secure in-kind sponsorships from bottlers and others in the food and beverage industry.

6. Reduce or eliminate alcohol from your event. Many events are becoming beer and wine functions in place of full open bar affairs. This change is happening due to concerns about health but also because of the perception associated with heavy drinking and drunk driving.

7. Serve a signature drink to everyone. A signature drink is an original drink that your bar manager creates for consumption by the entire group. The first need of most guests at a catered function is to place a drink in their hands. Offer your signature drink at the entrance to your event and solve this need while reducing your budget by controlling consumption.

8. Allow the guests to serve themselves. This is especially popular with the children's events. Make Your Own Sundae bars and the making of 5-foot-long submarine sandwichs are not only entertaining but may also result in cost savings.

## CATERING TRENDS

A trend is a pattern of behavior that is likely to be sustained over time. Although the event catering profession is susceptible to shifting tastes and is certainly affected by the state of the economy, several trends are emerging. These trends are well worth noting, as they will certainly influence many of the decisions you will make.

Use of nutritious food and beverages is a trend that will affect both perception and reality in the catering field. As the world's population ages (especially in the United States), guests will be more and more concerned with good health and will turn to nutritious foods as a primary means of promoting this lifestyle. Not only must the food perception be that of healthy presentation, but the ingredients must also be carefully considered. Increasingly, more and more people and their hosts will want to know the ingredients in their food and beverages to make wise decisions regarding menu items. Therefore, caterers will want to make available the ingredients and may even wish to list these items in a menu of signs posted near the food items. Furthermore, caterers will also wish to continue the practice of promoting heart-healthy menu items, as offering these items will provide a popular alternative but also differentiate the caterer from competitors because of this attention to low cholesterol.

A second trend is the shift from open full liquor bars to increased emphasis on beer, wine, and nonalcoholic beverages. The changes in lifestyles have, along with concern for responsible drinking, driven this important shift. Even more important, caterers are more cognizant than ever before of initiating and sustaining a thorough alcohol management program. Designated driver programs, along with systems to prevent underage drinking, are admirable initiatives that will grow in the future. As a result of this trend, caterers have had to search for new revenue streams to replace the loss of alcohol sales.

The third trend relates to the second trend in that, increasingly, caterers are seeking additional revenue streams and some are even moving from strictly food and beverage operations into full event management services. This change comes with great challenge as well as potentially great opportunity. Historically, caterers have been involved in all aspects of event management. Caterers, especially in the social life-cycle event market, have been responsible for providing or recommending the services of florists, musicians, decorators, invitation designers, and other allied professionals. Today's trend merely quantifies this historic business opportunity and repositions the caterer as an event manager who specializes in catering services. However, to take full advantage of this trend, the catering professional must be willing to round out his or her education with a rigorous course of study in event management. In every profession, eventually, superior quality combined with good value can conquer fierce competition. Event management is no different from other professions in this regard. If catering professionals are to expand their services to include those of event management, they must be willing to acquire the new skills that will complement their existing talents to improve their quality and provide them with the tools to compete effectively in the event marketplace.

Therefore, these three trends—nutritious and healthy menus, reduction in alcohol service, and the expansion of the caterer's services to include those of an event manager—may be viewed as economic opportunities provided that education and commitment to quality is implemented consistently.

# Coordinating Technical Resources

The event management profession has seen perhaps the greatest paradigm shift in the live production sector of this industry. Live production is also what differentiates events from other entertainment or creative products. Although one may argue that television specials are billed as "special events," in most instances these live events were filmed or taped before a live audience.

Productions ranging from the National Football League Super Bowl halftime show to the Three Tenors concert combine live production with various audiovisual, lighting, sound, special effects, and video resources to produce a well-crafted event that is ultimately viewed by millions via television. The modern event manager cannot ignore this major shift and must understand as well as implement these resources when appropriate.

## WHY = WHAT

Earlier I described that prior to selecting the most effective resources for your event, you must establish clear goals and objectives by asking why this event is necessary. Due to the myriad of new technology now offered, this is more important than ever before. The inexperienced event manager may decide to mix and match a wide array of new technology to impress his or her guests during the event. In fact, this mixture becomes a collage of inappropriate resources that results in confusion to the guests. An award-winning designer reportedly cautioned his young apprentices that "less is indeed more." The event manager must also use caution when selecting appropriate resources to support or enhance his or her event to make certain that each device is well integrated rather than extraneous. The following list may be used as a primary coordination tool for selecting and engaging these resources:

1. Identify the purpose of event technology for your program. Will the event technology be used to attract attention, guests, or to improve communications?
2. Determine the size of the live audience. The technology you select for the audience will be determined by the number of guests.
3. Identify the age, culture, and learning style of your guests. Some guests are visual learners, while others are more attuned to audio influences. Still other audiences, due to their age, may prefer the sound level larger or smaller.
4. Inspect the venue and inventory preexisting light (natural and artificial), in-house audiovisual equipment, utilities, the experience of local technical labor, and any other elements that will interact with your event.
5. Sit in a guest's chair or stand in the guest's place and try to envision the event through his or her eyes and ears. Check for obstructed views and other distractions. Identify potential solutions to develop optimum enjoyment through the entire event.

## PURPOSES OF EVENT TECHNOLOGY

Whether the purpose of your event is to educate or entertain or perhaps both, the technology that you select will help you best achieve your goals and objectives. In the conference event field you may select slide projectors, overhead projectors, a TelePrompter, or perhaps one microphone to improve communications between the presenter and the participant. The entertainment field may require theatrical lighting and special effects such as fog, laser, or strobe lights. Other fields will require different technology, however, ultimately the purpose of the event will determine the final selection and coordination of the event technology. Table 7-3 provides a guide for general use in selecting equipment for the event style and purpose.

## AUDIOVISUAL EFFECTS

The term *audiovisual* was probably coined in the 1950s, when schools, and later businesses and then associations, used slide and overhead projectors for instructional purposes. During the 1970s this technology expanded rapidly with more sophisticated audio tools as well as video enhancement due to the invention of video projection systems. Indeed, today dozens of audiovisual tools are available for use by event managers. However, I concentrate on those 10 tools used most often in the production of civic, entertainment, expositions, festival, and conference events. These tools are readily available in most event markets or may be obtained from nearby larger markets.

Audiovisual projection is divided primarily into two projection fields: visual and audio. The tool and its power depend on the factors described in the checklist above. Audience size, distance, the age, and type of attendee are critical considerations when selecting a tool. The right tool will make your task easier and more enjoyable for your guests, and the improper tool will cause you frustration and irritate your guests. Therefore, when selecting audiovisual tools for an event, refer to the checklist to check and balance your decision.

Digital images are rapidly replacing traditional photography in the event management production industry. Today's slide projector is rapidly being replaced by the notebook computer loaded with hundreds of slides and entire educational programs, including music and video. Monitor industry publications such as *Event World* and *Special Events* magazine to stay current with the latest technological advancements in the audiovisual field.

**Table 7-3**  Matching Technology to Style and Purpose

| Style | Purpose | Technology |
|---|---|---|
| Civic | Attract attention | Special effect: pyrotechnics |
| Conference | Communicate | Audiovisual: video magnification |
|  | Focus | Lighting: key lighting of lectern |
| Education | Build retention | Audiovisual: interactive CD |
| Entertainment | Attract | Sound and lights: announce and chase |
| Exposition | Educate | Video: product description |
| Festival | Communicate | Sound: public address |
| Reunion | Excite | Audiovisual: slide show of guests |

# Conducting and Analyzing the Site Inspection

Site inspection occurs during both the planning and coordination phase. During the planning phase, potential sites are inspected to identify those that should receive request for proposals. Increasingly, this task is conducted using the Internet. However, I caution you whenever possible to visit the site yourself or send a representative to inspect the physical assets. Event using three-dimensional technology on the Internet will not allow you to view every nook and cranny of the venue. Therefore, a physical inspection is essential to confirm and verify the quality of the physical space.

It is particularly important that you schedule a site inspection during the coordination phase to reconfirm that there have been no changes to the site since the planning period. I recommend that you visit the site no less than 30 days prior to the event to reinspect and make certain that you will be able to conduct the event effectively within the venue. If there have been dramatic changes, this type and lead time will give you sufficient time to rework your event design or even, if necessary, change venues. Table 7-4 is a good beginning for you to be able to develop a customized site inspection checklist.

## THE SITE INSPECTION

Perhaps the most important activity involving space is the site inspection. Using a comprehensive, customized checklist will make this task efficient and thorough. It will also allow you to delegate this task to others if you are not able to travel to the site yourself. Always carry a retractable tape measure, instant camera, notepad, and pencil on such an inspection.

Upon arrival, note the ingress to the parking facilities for up to 1 mile away. What will be the estimated travel time in heavy to moderate traffic, and are there alternative routes if the main artery is blocked by an accident or construction? Determine where the parking area will be for your official and VIP vehicles. Find out if special identification is required for those vehicles to park in these preapproved areas. Measure the height of the loading dock (if available) from the driveway to make certain that your vehicles can deliver directly onto the dock. This knowledge alone may save you thousands of dollars in additional labor charges.

Ask the venue officials to show you the entrance door for your personnel and the walking route to the preevent waiting area (dressing rooms, green rooms, and briefing rooms). Write these instructions down and read them back to the official. Note who supplied these instructions, as they will later be given to your personnel, and should there be a problem, you must be able to refer back to your original source for clarification.

Measure the square footage of the waiting area and determine how many persons can be accommodated when official furnishings are included. Locate

**Table 7-4**  Event Site Inspection Checklist Criteria

Amenities
1. Ability to display banner in prominent location
2. Limousines for Very Important Persons (VIPs)
3. Upgrades to suites available
4. Concierge or VIP floors
5. Room deliveries for entire group upon request
6. In-room television service for special announcements
7. Personal letter from venue manager delivered to room
8. Complimentary parking for staff or VIPs
9. Complimentary coffee in lobby
10. Complimentary office services for staff such as photocopying

Americans with Disabilities Act
1. Venue has been modified and is in compliance
2. New venue built in compliance with act
3. Modifications are publicized and well communicated

Capacity
1. Fire marshal approved capacity of venue for seating
2. Capacity of venue for parking
3. Capacity for exposition booths
4. Capacity for storage
5. Capacity for truck and vehicle marshaling
6. Capacity for preevent functions such as receptions
7. Capacity for other functions
8. Capacity for public areas of venue such as lobbies
9. Size and number of men's and women's rest rooms

Catering
1. Full-service, venue-specific catering operation
2. Twenty-four-hour room service
3. Variety of food outlets
4. Concession capability
5. Creative, tasteful food presentation

Equipment
1. Amount of rope (running feet) and stanchions available
2. Height, width, and colors available for inventory of pipe and drape
3. Height, width, and skitting colors available for platforms for staging
4. Regulations for use and lift availability for aerial work
5. Adequate number of tables, chairs, stairs, and other equipment

Financial considerations
1. Complimentary room ratio
2. Guarantee policy
3. Daily review of folio
4. Complimentary reception or other services to increase value
5. Function room complimentary rental policy

Location/proximity
1. Location of venue from nearest airport
2. Distance to nearest trauma facility
3. Distance to nearest fire/rescue facility

**Table 7-4**  *(Continued)*

4. Distance to shopping
5. Distance to recreational activities

Medical assistance/first aid
1. Number of staff trained in CPR, Heimlich maneuver, and other first aid
2. Designated first-aid area
3. Ambulance service

Portals
1. Size and number of exterior portals
2. Size and number of interior portals, including elevators
3. Ingress and egress to portals

Registration
1. Sufficient well-trained personnel for check in
2. Ability to provide express check-in for VIPs
3. Ability to distribute event materials at check-in
4. Ability to display group event name on badges or buttons to promote recognition
5. Effective directory or other signs for easy recognition

Regulations
1. Designation of a civil defense venue to be used in emergencies
2. Preexisting prohibitive substance regulations
3. Other regulations that impede your ability to do business
4. Fire code requirements with regard to material composition for scenery and other decoration
5. Local fire officials' requirements for permission to use open flame or pyrotechnic devices
6. Requirement regarding the use of live gasoline-powered motors
7. Policy regarding live-trained animals

Safety and security
1. Well-lit exterior and interior walkways
2. Venue has full-time security team
3. Communications system in elevators in working order
4. Positive relationship between venue and law enforcement agencies
5. Positive relationship between venue and private security agencies
6. Fire sprinklers controlled per zone or building-wide; individual zone can be shut off, with a fire marshal in attendance, for a brief effect such as pyrotechnics
7. Alarm system initially silent or announces a fire emergency immediately
8. Condition of all floors (including the dance floors)

Sleeping rooms
1. Sufficient number of singles, doubles, suites, and other required inventory
2. Rooms in safe, clean, working order
3. Amenities such as coffeemakers and hair dryers available upon request
4. Well-publicized fire emergency plan
5. Balcony or exterior doors secured properly

Utilities
1. Electrical power capacity
2. Power distribution

**Table 7-4**  *(Continued)*

3. Working on-site reserve generator (and a backup) for use in the event of a power failure
4. Responsible person for operation of electrical apparatus
5. Sources for water
6. Alternative water source in case of disruption of service
7. Separate billing for electricity or water

Weight

1. Pounds per square foot (meter) for which venue is rated
2. Elevator weight capacity
3. Stress weight for items that are suspended, such as lighting, scenic, projection, and audio devices

the rest rooms and note if they are adequate or require upgrading, for example, bringing in nicer amenities, such as specialty soaps, toilettes, perfumes, full-length mirrors, and fresh flowers.

Ask the venue official to lead you from the waiting area to the location of the actual event. Thoroughly examine the event site from the perspective of the spectator or participant. Most important, can the spectator see and hear comfortably? Sit in the seat of the spectator farthest from the staging area. Determine how the person with the most obstructed view can best see and hear.

When possible, ask the venue official to supply you with a floor plan or diagram of the site. Use this site diagram as a general blueprint and then confirm and verify by using your measuring device to measure random locations. Note any variances for later adjustment on the final diagram.

Finally, before you leave the venue sit for a minimum of 15 minutes in one of the chairs your spectator will occupy. Determine if it is comfortable for your guests. If not, ask if alternate seating is available and at what cost.

## DEVELOPING THE DIAGRAM

Transferring the results of the site inspection to a final, carefully produced diagram at one time was a major labor-consuming operation. Today, however, using modern computer tools such as computer-assisted design and drafting Computer Assisted Design and Drawing (CADD) systems, this task has been simplified. For those event managers who are uncomfortable with computers, a manual system has been developed involving scale cutouts of magnets that correspond to the typical inventory of most venues (chairs, tables, platforms, pianos, etc.), and once assembled, the final product may be photocopied for distribution.

Before beginning the process of developing the diagram, audit all internal and external stakeholders and create a list of every element that must be depicted on the diagram. These elements may range from decor to catering tents and from first-aid centers to parking locations. You will later use this checklist to cross-check the diagram and make certain that every elements has been included.

After the first draft diagram has been developed, it must be distributed to stakeholders for a first review. Ask the stakeholders to review the diagram for accuracy and return it within a fixed amount of time with any additions, deletions, or changes.

Finally, after you have received comprehensive input from the stakeholders, prepare a final copy for review by officials who must grant final approval for the event. These officials may include the fire marshal, transportation authorities, or others responsible for enforcing laws and regulations.

Once you have constructed a final, approved diagram, you have made the giant step forward from dream to idea to final plan. The third and final law of event management planning ensures that you implement your plan effectively.

# Determining the Production Schedule

The production schedule is the primary instrument (other than the event diagram) that is used during the coordination phase. During this phase the event manager must implement a minute-by-minute plan and monitor the tasks that lead to the ultimate conclusion of the event itself. The production schedule ensures that you will be able to achieve this goal efficiently. Table 7-5 is an example of a typical production schedule. Note how it is different from the timeline (Table 3-3).

As Table 7-5 suggests, the production schedule begins with load-in and concludes with load-out. The first line in the production schedule generally is "inspect venue" and the last line is "reinspect venue" to review and return the venue to the best condition. You will note that the production schedule is much more precise than the timeline (Table 3-3) and includes minute-by-minute precision. Typically, the event manager will include the production schedule in the time line in the coordination phase and then provide a full version on site at the event for the event coordination staff to manage the minute-by-minute operations.

## ANTICIPATING AND RESOLVING OPERATIONAL CONFLICTS

During the coordination phase numerous operational conflicts will develop. The key is for the event manager to anticipate and resolve these problems quickly by practicing what is often referred to as *damage control*. Following are some of the typical operational conflicts and how you can resolve them quickly:

- *Late-arriving vendors.* Maintain cell phone numbers and contact late-arriving vendors to determine their location.
- *Multiple vendors arriving simultaneously.* Sequence arrivals in logical order of installation.

**Table 7-5** Typical Production Schedule

| Task | Start Time | Stop Time | Details | Person(s) Responsible | Notes |
|---|---|---|---|---|---|
| Inspect venue | 7 A.M. | 7:45 A.M. | Check for preexisting damages, problems | Event manager | |
| Lighting and sound company loads-in | 8 A.M. | 9 A.M. | Arrivals and load-in | Event coordinator | |
| Lighting and sound company installs | 9 A.M. | 12 noon | Set up, hang, focus, test | Event coordinator | |
| Lunch break | 12 noon | 1 P.M. | Lunch for 10 stage hands | Caterer | |
| Florist loads-in and installs | 1 P.M. | 3 P.M. | Decorate stage and prepare centerpieces | Florist | |
| Rental company loads-in and sets tables, chairs, and cloths | 1 P.M. | 3 P.M. | Place tables and chairs and clothe the tables | Rental company | |
| Place centerpieces on table | 3 P.M. | 4 P.M. | Position centerpieces | Volunteers | |
| Caterer loads-in and sets up preparation area | 3 P.M. | 4 P.M. | Setup staging area for food preparation | Caterer | |
| Caterer sets tables | 4 P.M. | 5 P.M. | Final setting of tables | Caterer | |
| Inspection of tables, decor, lighting, sound by event manager | 5 P.M. | 5:30 P.M. | Final review | Event manager | |
| Sound check and rehearsal with band | 5:30 P.M. | 6:30 P.M. | Final sound check | Event manager and talent and technicians | |
| Waiters in position to open doors | 6:45 P.M. | 7 P.M. | Workers ready to open doors for guests | Event coordinator | |
| Open doors | 7 P.M. | 7:15 P.M. | Guests enter and are seated by waiters | Event coordinator | Doors opened early (7:10 pm) |
| Invocation | 7:15 P.M. | 7:17 P.M. | Minister delivers invocation | Stage manager | |
| Salad course | 7:17 P.M. | 7:30 P.M. | Salad served | Caterer | |
| Salad removed, entrée served | 7:30 P.M. | 7:50 P.M. | Entrée served | Caterer | |
| Entrée removed, dessert served | 7:50 P.M. | 8:10 P.M. | Dessert served | Caterer | |
| Coffee and candies served | 8:10 P.M. | 8:20 P.M. | Coffee and candies passed | Caterer | |
| Welcome speech and introduction of entertainment | 8:20 P.M. | 8:30 P.M. | All waiters out of room: speeches | Stage manager | |

**Table 7-5** *(Continued)*

| Task | Start Time | Stop Time | Details | Person(s) Responsible | Notes |
|---|---|---|---|---|---|
| Entertainment | 8:30 P.M. | 9:00 P.M. | Band | Stage manager | Entertainment started late (8:40 pm) |
| Dancing | 9:00 P.M. | 12 midnight | Dancing | Stage manager | |
| Close bars | 11:45 P.M. | 12 midnight | Stop serving | Caterer | |
| End of event | 12 midnight | 12 midnight | Lights up full | Event manager | |
| Dismantle and load-out | 12:30 A.M. | 6 A.M. | All equipment dismantled and removed from venue | Event coordinator | |
| Reinspect venue | 7 A.M. | 8 A.M. | Venue checked for any damages or losses caused by event | Event manager, event coordinator, venue official | |

- *Caterer running late in food delivery.* Monitor service carefully and use distractions such as dancing to cover long delays.
- *Speaker or entertainer cancels.* Use taped music or a pretaped video to cover.
- *Guests arrive too early.* Prepare for this and have appropriate staff greet and serve them.
- *Medical emergency.* Use standard operating procedures and work closely with venue to resolve.

As you can see, that wise event manager Murphy was provident when he wrote: "What can go wrong will go wrong." His cousin, O'Goldblatt, however, was perhaps even more prophetic when some years later he wrote: "Murphy is an optimist."

As a professional event manager the coordination phase is the most exciting and often grueling time during the event process. However, because you care deeply to achieve a high-quality outcome for the event, your ability to research, design, plan, and lead your team will smooth even the roughest edges during coordination of the event. The intersection of coordination can be crossed easily and safely because you are prepared, programmed, and ultimately polished in your ability to make the most difficult and intricate tasks appear easy and seamless.

Finally, during those maddening moments before guests arrive, you may wish to add one additional ritual to your arsenal of coordination tools. A colleague once told me that she closes her eyes for a few seconds before she opens the doors to receive her guests and silently repeats three times: "This event is going to be easy, fun, and successful." Although events are rarely easy, and the fun comes after the guests leave, in fact your event may be more successful if you are relaxed in your approach to receiving the guests. Now relax and let's go on site to begin coordinating the details that will produce your next successful event.

# Career Advancement Connections

## GLOBAL CONNECTION

Moving events around domestically and especially, internationally is a complicated task with a number of challenges. One of the most important parts is transportation. Although a large number of professionals are available to assist you in accommodating transportation needs, it is important for event professionals to have some basic knowledge of the issue. Transportation within one country involves mostly negotiations with a transport agency. A transportation agency usually provides services such as packing, loading, moving, unloading, and sometimes even unpacking as part of a contract. Event professionals should also remember about insurance. Usually, transportation companies provide basic insurance on their services; however, it is important to confirm that the amount of insurance is sufficient not only to cover physical damage or/and loss of equipment but also potential losses that may occur due to event cancellation.

International transportation is more complicated than domestic. Conducting business internationally, event professionals should work with a much larger number of government and private institutions than for local events. Moving equipment to or from overseas venues often involve payment of import or export duties, various excise duties, various fees, and other payments. Before planning any international event activity, event professionals are strongly encouraged to consult international trade and tax professionals, who often will be affiliated with your international transport agency.

## TECHNOLOGY CONNECTION

Use a Microsoft Excel spreadsheet to track all vendor agreements. Utilize event planning software such as Meeting Pro, Event Manager, Day to Day Event Manager, EVENTS, Special Event Management, and other products to efficiently organize and document your event planning operations. For a more extensive list of event software, see Appendix 7. Using software such as Microsoft Outlook E-Mail application will allow you to use the calendar function to set up appointments, send you reminders, and other date- and time-specific operations to ensure more accurate planning.

## RESOURCES CONNECTION

Contact industry associations and local convention and visitors' bureaus or www.ises.com to identify appropriately qualified vendors to support your event. Interview prospective and current vendors and determine what systems they are using to manage your event. This will help you ensure that your systems are congruent.

## LEARNING CONNECTION

Use the Microsoft Excel spreadsheet to establish a list of all vendors supporting your event. The spreadsheet should include contact information, emergency contacts, date of contract issuance, dates of payments, contract due date, and any other relevant notes. Obtain a demonstration copy of event planning software and determine what system is best for your event operations.

---

**Facing Page**

This preevent briefing for the servers is a critical meeting designed to review the menu, timing, service, and other important details prior to arrival of the guests. *Photograph courtesy of Monica Vidal.*

# CHAPTER 8

# On-Site Management

---

**IN THIS CHAPTER YOU WILL LEARN HOW TO:**

- Develop and implement event contingency plans
- Monitor each element of an event during event operations
- Establish and manage efficient registration operations
- Coordinate industry and professional speakers
- Identify and utilize appropriate amenities
- Identify, create, and post informative signs

---

If policies and procedures provide a rationale and regulation for day-to-day event decision making, the timeline and production schedule serve as the map that ensures that you will arrive safely at your destination. The policies, procedures, and practices comprise the rules of the road, but without the production schedule you may never find the right road or navigate so poorly that your event is hopelessly lost before you even begin.

The production schedule is sometimes referred to as the *résumé* or *event order* by event managers. It has also been referred to as the *itinerary* by travel and tourism event managers. In fact, it is the *schedule* that logically and completely describes all the elements that will be *produced* for the event, and therefore it is best termed a *timeline–production schedule*. The *timeline* is a sequential list of tasks that take place before and following an event. The *production schedule* is a detailed list of tasks with specific start and stop times from setup through load-out of an event.

# Improving Event Performance

Hundreds or perhaps thousands of elements must be coordinated to produce a foolproof event. Just as a coach writes down his or her plays and shares these plans with the team, the event manager must reduce his or her plans to writing and communicate these details with the event stakeholders. Using the timeline–production schedule will improve your event performance in many ways. A few of these are listed below to enable you to better understand the benefits of this planning tool:

1. A timeline–production schedule requires the event manager to schedule every element involved in an event systematically and logically.
2. It provides a unique comprehensive communications tool for the use of other team members.
3. It enables external stakeholders such as police, fire, security, and medical to stay informed regarding event operations.

4. It is easily distributed to internal and external stakeholders via a computer modem for quick updates.
5. It provides an accurate historical accounting of the entire event.

Many of the competencies we have discussed in previous chapters, including history, communication, and logical and reasonable thinking, are incorporated in the production schedule process. However, the most important reason for implementing the timeline–production schedule into your planning process is that it absolutely improves event performance. This is accomplished through improved communications. Every member of your event team is able to refer to the timeline–production schedule and determine quickly and efficiently what is supposed to happen at what time. For this reason alone, it is a most valuable tool and should be used from the research period through the final evaluation.

# Improving Financial Effectiveness

One area that governs all other areas of an event is financial management. The production schedule allows you, in spreadsheet fashion, to see how you are allocating your scarce event resources in the most efficient manner. Once you have assembled all the details in logical sequence, you can review carefully to see if there are any duplications or ways in which resources may be reallocated for greater coast savings. For example, if you notice that the installation is scheduled for Sunday at 7:00 A.M. and that will result in paying time and one-half to your crews, you can try and rearrange your Friday activities to schedule the setup within the straight-time rate.

Every element on the production schedule affects your event financially. Therefore, when using this schedule you should look constantly for ways to best allocate your event resources in the most cost-effective manner.

# The Production Schedule

## CREATING THE SCHEDULE

There are three important resources to incorporate when creating your draft document. First, you must check with key informants to make certain that you have incorporated all critical information. Second, you will want to explain the production schedule at an upcoming group meeting to receive feedback from the entire group. Finally, you must recheck the timing, function, and assignment to check for gaps and make certain that your production schedule is logical.

### Key Informants

Ask the senior members of your team to assist you with constructing the draft production schedule. Instruct each team member to create an individualized production schedule reflecting the operations of the individual departments. After you have received all the schedules, combine them into one integrated instrument. Then distribute the draft document to the same key informants and ask them to check your work for accuracy and see if there are additions, deletions, or changes. Typical key informants assisting you in preparing and reviewing the production schedule are:

- Admissions coordinator
- Advertising coordinator
- Assistant event manager
- Audiovisual coordinator
- Caterer
- Decorator
- Entertainment coordinator
- Exposition coordinator
- Facility management
- Fire department
- Food and beverage coordinator

- Legal advisor
- Lighting coordinator
- Medical coordinator
- Police
- Public relations
- Registration coordinator
- Risk management coordinator
- Safety coordinator
- Security coordinator
- Transportation coordinator
- Ushering coordinator

### Group Meetings

Transfer the production schedule to an overhead transparency and use the next team meeting as an opportunity to explain this document. Walk through each step of the schedule slowly and carefully, pausing occasionally to ask if there are any questions. Solicit feedback from the group on how best to depict the schedule as well as ways to consolidate operations and improve efficiency.

### Testing, Timing, Function, and Assignment

The production schedule is a table comprised of six columns. These columns allow you to enter the various key components or elements of the event in logical sequence. It is critical that you test your production schedule by seeking input from critical friends who have produced similar events of the same size and scope. Similar to a budget, the timeline–production schedule is a projection of how things should happen based on the knowledge available to you at this time. Table 7-5 shows a typical event production schedule table. You may adapt this model for your own needs. Make certain that timeline–production schedule includes the five phases of event management: research, design, planning, coordination, and evaluation.

## IMPLEMENTING THE SCHEDULE

After you have completed the production schedule you must circulate a series of drafts to key constituents to ensure that approvals are received before issuing the final document. Always attach a cover memorandum instruction for each reader on how to analyze the production schedule and describe the kind of input you are seeking. For example, you may ask one reader to proof for typographical errors while another is to concentrate on validating the timing for the various activities. Each key constituent should have a specific role to play relevant to their level of expertise. However, each constituent should review the entire plan to check for overall gaps as well as their own particular area of expertise.

## MONITORING THE SCHEDULE

Appoint several capable people to serve as monitors and oversee various stages of implementation of the production schedule. They should have a copy of the schedule and in the notes section list any variances from the schedule published. If, for example, the event is late in starting, this should be noted with the actual start time. If the event runs overtime, this should also be noted with the actual stop time. This kind of information is extremely important when planning future events and budgeting adequate time to the various elements you will use.

The monitor should turn in his or her copy of the production schedule with the notes included immediately after completing his or her assignment. Table 7-5 demonstrates typical notes that your monitor may insert.

## HANDLING CHANGES

About the only thing you can count on today is that things will change and sometimes far too rapidly to update the production schedule. When a change must be made quickly, use a printed bulletin headlined "CHANGE NOTICE" to ensure that every member of your team is aware and able to adjust their schedule to accept this change. Figure 8-1 depicts a typical change notice.

### Using the Timeline–Production Schedule to Manage Change

One of the most useful aspects of the production schedule is its ability to assist you in managing change. As literally hundreds of decisions must be made on a daily basis, the production schedule provides a solid framework for decision making.

Perhaps your celebrity has been delayed in another city and will be arriving late for your function. A quick glance at the production schedule allows you to make the necessary adjustments and see how these adjustments are affecting other elements of the event. In addition, sharing a common document

---

CHANGE NOTICE
Distribution: All event staff and volunteers.

Change: The opening ceremony previously scheduled to start at 10:00 A.M. on May 15, 1996, has been changed. **The new start time is 10:15 A.M.** The reason for this change is that the television feed has been moved and the new time is the actual start of the broadcast.

Summary: Note time changes for opening ceremony.

Previous time: May 15, 10:00 A.M.

New time: May 15, 10:15 A.M.

---

**Figure 8-1**
Typical Change Notice

with your team members you can solicit their input before making the adjustments to ensure that you are in concert with one another.

Using integrated system design network (ISDN) technology you will be able to send the most complex production schedule using fiber optics and involve as many people as necessary in your review and decision-making process. As each of you sits in front of a computer terminal sharing the same document, you will be able to make minute or major changes and immediately see and discuss the ramifications of your decisions. In a world fraught with accelerated change, this will be a major advancement in the event management process.

## THE RÉSUMÉ VERSUS THE PRODUCTION SCHEDULE

Meeting event managers traditionally use the term *résumé* rather than *production schedule*. The résumé comprises not only the time, venue, task, and person responsible but also detailed information regarding room setups, audiovisual, and other components of the meeting. A typical résumé is shown in Table 8-1.

**Table 8-1**    Typical Résumé

| Date | Time | Function | Location | Setup | Attendance | Catering | A/V |
|------|------|----------|----------|-------|------------|----------|-----|
| Friday | 10:00 A.M.–12 M, (noon) | Board meeting | Room 102 | Hollow square | 20 | Coffee, juice | Overhead |

The deficiencies in the résumé shown in Table 8-1 include the absence of a contact person or person responsible for this function and a cell for notes regarding the actual start and stop times for the event. Although the résumé is widely used in the meeting event management field, it has some gaps you must be aware of. When deciding which tool to use for your event, first share your template or model with the venue that will be responsible for handling most of the meeting event logistics. Confirm and verify that the tool you propose to use will be accepted and used by the venue's staff prior to implementation.

## EVALUATING THE SCHEDULE

The best way to evaluate the use of the production schedule is to ask the key stakeholders if the process was effective: "Did the schedule help you understand the big and little picture of the event? Was the production schedule useful in keeping track of start and stop times? Were there any deficiencies in the timeline–production schedule? How could the schedule be improved next time?"

A quantitative way to monitor the use of the schedule is to review the notes section and look for wide gaps between the scheduled start and stop times and the actual times. Carefully study those elements of the event where the gaps were inordinately wide, and seek solutions in planning your next event.

Remember that the production schedule is similar to a budget in that it is a broad project management tool with a history that may be used to improve the overall planning process. Make certain you are diligent about reviewing the final schedule and comparing your projected elements with the final event. From this process improvements will be made and your production scheduling process will become more scientific in the future.

# Catering Management

Historically, events have been associated with food and beverage. Next, we examine how to ensure that the catering elements of an event are well coordinated.

Event caterers are usually one of three business types, and each is defined by location. First is the *institutional caterer,* commonly described as an in-house or on-premises caterer who may or may not have permanent kitchens and offices at the event venue. This caterer may limit the choices for the event manager but can provide greater security by being familiar with the idiosyncrasies of the venue.

The second business type is the traditional *off-premises caterer,* whose clients engage him or her to cater meals at a temporary location. The location or venue may or may not have permanent kitchen facilities. However, the off-premises caterer is responsible for providing the necessary equipment and services to create an atmosphere of permanence in this temporary locale.

The third and final type of event caterer is the *concessionaire.* This person may use a mobile kitchen or concession trailer to dispense his or her product or may work in a fixed venue from a permanent or temporary concession area. In some venues the in-house catering operation operates all concession activities simultaneously as well.

Obviously, there is significant variation in these event-catering business operations. Generally, however, when contracting caterers, the three types will be on-premises, off-premises, and concessions. A growing trend in an effort to boost revenues is for on-premises caterers to begin catering off-premises in private homes and even other venues.

Although the on-premises caterer provides the lion's share of major event-catering operations, the off-premises caterer may actually feed the broadest possible constituency. The off-premises caterer must have the ability to establish a temporary kitchen in a tent, an aircraft hangar, or even in a jewelry store. This type of caterer works closely with party rental specialists to ensure that he or she can provide the appropriate equipment on a moment's notice. Furthermore, the off-premises caterer must establish adequate resources for utilities, deliveries, waste disposal, and other critical elements of any catering operation. Finally, the off-premises caterer must stay abreast of local health and sanitation regulations to ensure that he or she is in compliance regardless of an event's location.

In actuality, although many off-premises caterers may boast of their ability to provide their services uniformly in any location in most major metropolitan areas, this is limited to relatively few in number. When you add multiple events on the same date, this number shrinks dramatically.

As the on-premises caterer continues to expand off-premises, he or she is learning that the rigor of the temporary location is much greater than the fixed or permanent venue. Some on-premises caterers have ceased off-premises operations for this very purpose. They quickly discover that on- and off-premises are two very different catering skills and that when trying to conquer both worlds, one inevitably suffers.

## LOCATION, LOCATION, LOCATION

Of the five W's in event management, "where" is perhaps most critical to the on- and off-premises caterer for a variety of reasons. First, the caterer must comply with specific health department codes and regulations that will govern where he or she may operate. Second, food and beverage preparation is time dependent and the distance between the food preparation area and the serving location can determine an entire range of quality and service issues. What happens if hot food becomes cool or even cold during transit? How will the guests feel about slow food delivery? Finally, what utilities, equipment, and other resources are available to the caterer to prepare, serve, remove, and clean up successfully?

The location of the event is therefore a critical consideration for the off-premises caterer. However, the on-premises caterer must also be sensitive to these issues, as even the most routine event can suffer from logistical problems. As one example, what happens in the convention center when the caterer must serve 1000 guests on the ground floor, the kitchen is located on the second floor, and the elevator stops working? Or perhaps the event manager has asked the caterer to serve the meal in an unusual location such as in a tent in the parking lot. Does the caterer have the necessary equipment and additional labor to accomplish this task successfully? These questions and many more must be considered well in advance of establishing the location for the catered meal.

## EQUIPMENT

Obviously, tables, chairs, china, silver, and other standard equipment will be required to serve a high-quality meal. However, the event manager must ensure that the caterer has access to the appropriate style and quantity to match the needs of the event. Some caterers own a sufficient inventory of rental equipment, while others have close relationships with party and general rental dealers to provide these items. The event manager must inspect the equipment to ensure that the caterer has not only sufficient quantity but that the quality is appropriate for the event.

When considering quantity, remember that the caterer may have multiple events on the same date. Make certain that additional inventory is available in case your guest list increases suddenly at the last moment. Furthermore, make certain that if the quantity of items is increased, the inventory will remain high quality.

Beyond china and silver, some caterers also maintain a healthy inventory of tables, chairs, linens, and other serving utensils, such as chafing dishes, props, and other elements that will provide you with a cohesive look. Some caterers stock unusual items from a specific historic period or feature items that reflect their style of catering. A caterer who primarily services the social life-cycle market may provide latticework props and gingham linens, while the caterer who works in the corporate event market may provide white linens and more traditional china and silver. The event manager must select a caterer who has existing equipment and experience that matches the goals and objectives of the specific event.

## UTILITIES

As the caterer plugs in the coffee urn, the music from the band suddenly comes to a screeching halt. The puzzled guests look confused while standing on the dance floor, but both the event manager and catering director know that what has happened is an overloaded circuit caused by the coffee urn. The event manager must audit the caterer's utility needs as well as those of the other vendors to determine if the venue can support these requirements.

In addition to electricity, the caterer will require water. The proximity of the water will also be an important factor, as costs may increase if water must be transported from a great distance. The third and final requirement for all catering operations is waste management. The caterer must have a system for disposing of waste materials. The event manager must ensure that the caterer has the necessary resources to perform professionally.

## TIME CONSTRAINTS

Time is of the essence in most catering operations, for a variety of reasons. First, the caterer must prepare and deliver his or her product within a reasonable amount of time to ensure freshness and quality. Second, the caterer must carefully orchestrate the delivery of his or her product within a complex setting in which multiple activities are being staged. For example, a dinner dance may require that the caterer serve various courses between dance sets. At some events the caterer must provide his or her entire service within a short time frame to ensure that all servers are out of the function room in time for speeches or other aspects of the program.

## SERVICE STYLES

The term *service* refers to the method used for serving a catered meal. In the United States the three most popular forms of service are the seated banquet, the standing or seated buffet, and the standing reception, where food items are passed by servers to guests. Each of these service types helps satisfy specific goals and objectives. Table 8-2 provides a simple guide on when to employ a specific type of service.

In addition to these service styles, the exposition is an important venue for effective catering. Exposition managers know that food and beverages serve as a strong attraction and increase traffic multifold in an exposition hall. One of the more popular methods is to provide guests with an apron (usually donated by a sponsor and imprinted with their logo) and then distribute pocket sandwiches. With this technique the guests can walk, talk, shop, and eat. It is a very efficient way to provide food service for guests at an exposition and resembles a giant walking picnic.

Picnic style is also a popular technique for corporate and reunion events. Although this style is difficult in terms of service, it is extremely popular

**Table 8-2**  Event Catering Service Styles and When to Use Them

| Event | Service Style |
| --- | --- |
| Brief networking breakfast | Standing buffet |
| Breakfast with speaker | Seated buffet |
| Breakfast with speaker, program | Seated banquet |
| Brief networking luncheon | Standing buffet |
| Luncheon with speaker | Seated buffet |
| Luncheon with speaker, program | Seated banquet |
| Brief cocktail reception | Passed items |
| Extended cocktail reception | Standing buffet or individual stations |
| Brief dinner | Standing buffet or individual stations |
| Dinner with speaker, program | Seated banquet |
| Formal dinner | French service |

among guests who want to sit together as one large group. This style is also popular with Octoberfest events, as it resembles a German beer hall.

English and Russian services, although not very popular in the United States, are two styles that may be implemented for the right occasion. English style involves serving each table from a moving cart. In Russian service the server uses silver platters from which he or she places each course onto a guest's plate. Both styles of service may be requested, but the caterer must be equipped and schooled properly to produce an effective result.

## LOGISTICAL CONSIDERATIONS

Proper and efficient guest flow as well as effective methods for ensuring timely delivery of food and beverages are essential considerations for a catered event. The event caterer may have substantial experience working in a permanent venue, but when asked to provide services off-premises he or she may not be aware of the additional rigor required to survive in the jungle. To survive and thrive one must know the basic laws of the event jungle.

1. Determine in advance the goals and objectives of the catered event and match the logistical requirements to these objectives. For example, a brief networking event should use fewer chairs and tables, to allow guests time to mix and mingle.
2. Determine the ages and types of guests and match the requirements to their needs. For example, for older guests, more chairs may be needed to provide additional comfort during an extended reception.
3. Identify the food preparation and other staging areas and ensure that there is a clear passageway to the consumption area. Check the floors to make sure that they are free of debris and allow the service staff to move quickly.

4. Whenever possible, use a double buffet style for this type of service. The double buffet not only serves twice as many guests but allows guests to further interact with one another as they receive their food.

5. Do not place food stations in areas that are difficult to replenish. Large crowds of guests may prevent service personnel from replenishing food stations efficiently.

6. When passing food items, place a few servers at the entryway so that guests notice that food is available. This technique ensures that most guests will see and consume at least one of the food items being offered.

7. Use lighting to highlight buffets, carving, and other stations. Soft, well-focused lighting directs guests' eyes to the food and makes it easier to find as well as more appetizing.

8. Use servers at the entryway to pass drinks rapidly to guests as they enter, or open the bars farthest from the entrance first. For smaller events with ample time, passing drinks may be preferable; however, for larger events where the guests must be served quickly, staggering bar opening may be beneficial. Once the distant bars begin to experience lines of 10 or more persons, succeeding bars are opened, working back toward the entryway.

9. Instruct the bar captain to close all bars promptly at the appointed time. Use servers to line up at the entryway to assist in directing guests into the main function room.

10. Provide return tables to accept glassware as guests go to the next event. Staff these areas to avoid too many glasses accumulating.

11. Request that servers distribute welcome gifts or programs during the setup period and be staged in each dining station to assist with seating. Servers should be requested to offer chairs to guests without hesitation, to expedite seating.

12. Use an invocation, moment of silence, or a simple "bon appetit" to begin the meal.

13. The following service times should typically be used for catered events.
    - *Cocktail reception:* 30 minutes to 1 hour.
    - *Seated banquet:* 1 to 2 hours.
    - *Preset salad consumption and clearing:* 15 to 20 minutes.
    - *Entree delivery, consumption, and clearing:* 20 to 40 minutes.
    - *Dessert delivery, consumption, and clearing:* 15 to 20 minutes.
    - *Coffee and tea service:* 10 to 15 minutes.

14. Make certain that all service personnel have exited the function room prior to the program or speeches. If this is not possible, make certain that front tables have been served and that servers continue service as quietly as possible in back of the function area.

15. Request that servers stand at exit doors and bid guests goodbye and distribute any parting gifts from the host or hostess.

Your catering event professional will suggest other ideas to help you accomplish your goals and objectives. However, remember that you must prioritize the event's goals and objectives, and catering may or may not be high on the list. Therefore, it is important to maintain balance as you decide where to focus your emphasis during specific periods of the event.

Once you have identified the event's goals and objectives, you choose the service style to make certain that your guests' needs are satisfied. After basic needs are satisfied, it is time to add some magic to turn an ordinary catered affair into an extraordinary special event.

# Audiovisual Effects Management

Audiovisual, lighting, sound, special effects, and video are growing in importance with emerging techniques, lower costs, and improved quantity.

## STANDARD AUDIOVISUAL EQUIPMENT

### Liquid Crystal Display Projector

**Technology**   The liquid crystal display (LCD) projector is used in conjunction with a computer to project graphic text onto a screen. This technology, which allows a presenter to have maximum flexibility when preparing and showing slides, is rapidly replacing traditional overhead transparencies.

**Use**   An LCD panel may be used to present complex charts and graphs, text, graphics, and other images in a lively format similar to that of television production incorporating wipes, crawls, rolls, and other moving images. Make certain that you have the proper cabling for the LCD panel, as the Macintosh and PC use different attachments. With additional technology, it is possible to incorporate video and audio into your presentations to create an attention-grabbing program and liven up even the most tedious lectures. Be careful not to allow your content to become buried under too much technological wizardry. Content must supersede presentation to maintain the integrity of your message.

### Microphone

**Technology**   The lectern microphone is perhaps the most common technology in use in conference events. Two primary types of microphones are available for use by event managers. The *unidirectional microphone* is ideal for the individual speaker, and the *omnidirectional microphone* is designed for occasions when several people share the lectern. In addition to the lectern microphone, the *lavaliere* or *clip-on microphone* (sometimes the names are used interchangeably) allows a presenter to be mobile and move around the stage or room. Although more expensive, the wireless handheld or lavaliere microphone provides even greater freedom, as no cable is attached. Using an FM transmitter and receiver, the audio signal is patched directly into the audio system and produces high-quality sound.

**Use**    When using a clip-on microphone, placement of the microphone head is extremely important. The head should be as close to the mouth as possible. Therefore, it should be placed on the upper part of a man's necktie or coat lapel. Women should wear it high on the blouse or in the upper part of a jacket lapel. It is wise to provide redundant wired microphones for wireless systems. I usually place a wired microphone with 50 feet of cable in the lectern to provide security for the speaker and make the transition from wireless to wired as smooth as possible.

### Overhead Projector

**Technology**    If the slide projector is the workhorse of the conference industry, the overhead projector is the most often requested projection device for smaller meetings. One major benefit of the overhead projector is its ability to project slides in a fully illuminated venue. Due to distance, a slide projector requires that the area immediately surrounding the projection surface be darkened to provide a bright image. However, the overhead projector is typically only a few feet from the projection surface and the image is much brighter for most media. One advantage of the overhead projector is the ability to use markers to illustrate and underscore the comments of the lecturer.

**Use**    One of the more unusual ways I have used the overhead projector was to provide suspense and excitement for an awards program. In advance of the program I retained a caricaturist to sketch portraits of the award recipients. The artist was given photographs of each winner and the rough sketches were approved by a family member or close friend of the honoree. The overhead projector was placed behind the stage and projected on a rear projection screen. The front of the screen was decorated to appear as a white canvas surrounded by a gold-gilded frame. As the award presenter described each recipient's accomplishments, the artist began quickly to sketch the portrait. The audience, both hearing and seeing the life of the person, began to recognize the identity of the person being honored. When the name was finally announced, the audience immediately responded with gasps of recognition, followed by sustained applause for both the recipient and the artist.

## Projection Screens

**Technology**  Event managers use both rear and front projection screens for different reasons and different venues. A front projection screen generally provides brighter illumination; however, a rear projection screen makes it possible to hide the projection equipment from audience view. Typically, two types of screens are used. A *tripod screen* is supported by a metal tripod, and a *fast-fold screen* is supported by a metal frame and may be either supported on legs or hung from above. Projection screens generally range in size from 6 feet high by 8 feet wide to 15 feet high by 20 feet wide. These screens accept slides produced in horizontal formats. In addition to the screen, most audiovisual suppliers will provide a dress kit for the fast-fold screen. This kit consists of a skirt, valance, and perhaps side drapes for masking. You may also wish to use other pipe and drape to run off to the side of the room to further mask the backstage area.

**Use**  Screens may be used for laser, overhead, slide, or video projection. Typically, screens are underutilized at conferences. Consider using the screen surface to project the names of your event's sponsor or other information in addition to the educational content of the conference. Avoid leaving screens blank by using a title slide to cover periods when no video or slides are required. In case of an emergency, to create an instant title slide without the expense of a slide projector, use the video camera to shoot the lectern sign that usually features the organization's logo or name. This shot will then be projected onto the screens as if it were a title slide.

## Slide Projector

**Technology**  The 35-millimeter slide projector may be the most basic visual tool for the conference event field. Either used singly for lectures or in combination with dozens of others to create a dramatic and emotionally moving image, this technology is truly the workhorse of the conference field. This equipment will require the correct lens for proper focus as well as a wired or remote control device to advance the slides. When used in combination with other projectors, a dissolve unit is required to network all the units and produce smooth transitions. The term *35-millimeter* specifies the size of the slide that is projected by this equipment. Obviously, one of the major considerations and perhaps the most common problem is the burned-out lamp. Therefore, having a spare lamp or two is important. Newer slide projectors have a spare lamp included. A powerful unit is the *xenon slide projector,* whose xenon lamp is much brighter than the standard 35-millimeter slide projector and with proper lensing allows the projector to be placed many more feet away from a projection surface.

**Use**   In the conference event field the slide projector is used to illustrate lectures and to provide other visual enhancements. One of the most effective uses is to project a slide on the front of a curtain or surface other than a screen. For the fiftieth anniversary of an association I projected a slide of the original founders of the organization signing the first articles of incorporation. This slide was front projected onto a translucent curtain known as a *scrim*. After the guests settled into their seats and the venue lights dimmed, the voices of the founders were heard. A few moments later lights from behind the scrim rose to reveal the original founders seated in the same pose as in the slide. The men, now in their 90s, rose to greet the audience, and thunderous applause was heard throughout the room.

Another effective technique for slide projection involves using a slide to create a backdrop for a speaker or stage set. During a patriotic program I used a slide of the American flag rear projected onto a curtain to create a 30-foot-long by 10-foot-high image at a fraction of the cost of renting, installing, and removing an actual flag.

### Video Projector

**Technology**   Video projector technology first enjoyed widespread use in the 1970s and has expanded rapidly to become a staple of many conferences and other events. The video projector may be used to show close-up video images of the speaker or entertainers or others at a program or event. In addition, it can be used to project slide media or a prerecorded program such as a videotape of a new product or future destination that is being introduced. Increasingly, it is used to project computer data and graphics. Miniaturization has changed this technology from larger cumbersome devices to manageable small-carton-size equipment. The video projector may be used for either front or rear projection. Using two projectors (layered on top of one another) provides a brighter image and also provides a redundant unit in case of trouble. The projection distance will vary based on the size of the screen. However, for a 15- by 20-foot screen, plan on approximately 20 feet between the projector and the screen. For greater distances, high-powered projectors are available.

**Use**   Use the video projector to show a welcome videotape describing the destination where the event is being held or to magnify the image of the speaker or other presenter. During one event I used a combination of pretaped and live video to create the impression of a live television production. A local newscaster was hired to pretape a "breaking news story" about our association president. Next, the tape cut to the president giving a "live" interview across town near a prominent monument. Then the tape cut to the president running to the meeting, and seconds later, the door to the ballroom opened as the president walked briskly into the room in person, followed by the press corps, and as she ascended the stage, the now-live video followed her movements. Upon her arrival on stage, she made an announcement to the assembled media and the program officially began.

## Cost-Saving Measures

When renting audiovisual equipment, remember that this business, like many in the meetings and conference field, is seasonal. Therefore, the prices for the equipment may be negotiable. The price for labor is typically not negotiable. When bidding audiovisual equipment, make certain that you list every possible application and time required for labor so that the bidders may evaluate the total value of your event. Many (if not most) audiovisual rental firms will offer a 25 percent producer's discount. You may be able to receive greater discounts on equipment by adjusting the dates of your event to reflect periods when equipment is more readily available.

Still another way to save money is to find multiple uses for your audiovisual equipment during the same 24-hour period. Too often, event managers use a video projector for one hour when in actuality the rental is factored on a 24-hour period. Preplan the use of this equipment to maximize the value. For example, can the projector be moved to a different room instead of renting a separate piece of equipment?

Finally, look for ways to share costs on audiovisual equipment with other groups. Perhaps there is another organization meeting in the same venue at the same time as your organization. Can you co-rent equipment with them to save costs?

## LIGHTING

When God said, "Let there be light," it may have been the first time in recorded history that a lighting cue was called. Since that fateful day lighting has come to symbolize safety, mood, atmosphere, and transition as well as time of day and location. In almost every event environment, lighting improves the atmosphere. It may be used to focus attention on the speaker and to enhance the look of decor and food as well as to change the mood dramatically from one scene to another.

Miniaturization has affected the lighting field in major ways. Only a few years ago, a lighting control system would require enough space to fill a small bedroom. Today, the same system fits compactly on a card table. This major reduction in size has made lighting more flexible and available than ever before.

Table 8-3 demonstrates how lighting may be used in a variety of event situations. These applications are only the tip of the iceberg, because many event managers combine different lighting effects, much as a visual artist combines color and texture to create the desired effect. The following lighting technology is commonly used by event managers to achieve these desired effects.

**Table 8-3** Applications for Lighting

| Activity | Lighting Application |
|---|---|
| 1960s or space age | Ultraviolet light |
| Atmosphere | Lighting projections (gobos) |
| Centerpieces | Pin spots |
| Change of mood | Backdrop colorization |
| Dance floor | Moving lights |
| Entertainer | Follow spotlights |
| High-tech focus | Laser light show |
| Product reveal | Chaser light |
| Space age effect | Fiber optic backdrop |
| Speaker at lectern | Key light for focus |
| Stage set | Set light and back light |

### Chase Lights or Rope Lights

**Technology**   Chase lights or rope lights are miniature lights that may be encased in clear or colored plastic flexible tubing or assembled on a string of electrical wire. They are a low-wattage way to create excitement and direct focus.

**Use**   Chase lights may outline a new product or sign, edge a stage or arch, or be incorporated in ceilings to create a starlight effect.

### Dimmer or Control Board

**Technology**   A dimmer or control board allows the lighting operator to fade, black out, and perform other lighting cues. Many, if not most control boards are computer driven, allowing the operator to store the cues in memory and then at the press of one button, perform dozens of tasks.

**Use**   The control board sends the electronic signal to the individual lighting instrument, instructing it to perform on cue a specific effect. These cues may range from blackouts to slow fades to everything in between. Some control boards have a light organ built in that allows the lights to pulse to the beat of live or recorded music. Also use the control board to cue the house lights or make certain that the control board is placed near the house light control so that you may coordinate these two functions.

### Ellipsoidal Spotlight

**Technology**   The major difference between the ellipsoidal spotlight (also known as *leko*) and the par cam is the ability to focus light selectively and to use a template for projecting specific images.

**Use**   Using shutters, the ellipsoidal spotlight allows the event manager to focus light narrowly to highlight specific areas in either a cylindrical, horizontal, or vertical format. Additionally, this instrument accepts a metal or glass template known as a *gobo*. The gobo uses a design that can be projected on a surface such as a curtain, wall, floor, or other area. These designs may be mixed and matched to create a variety of effects. Using a scrim curtain, you can project an image such as a window, and using a rear light source, an actor may actually appear to raise the window by adding a second gobo of an open window. Gobos may also be used to project text such as sponsor names. This is a quick and inexpensive way to add sponsor recognition to an event.

### Fiber Optic Drop or Curtain

**Technology**   Thousands of microthin fibers carry light from a central source and create changing colors or chase effects.

**Use**   This relatively new technology provides a dramatic backdrop for a stage set and may also be used in a theme event to create the illusion of a galaxy of stars.

### Follow Spotlight

**Technology**   A manually operated, focusable spotlight with the ability to add color through gels, this spotlight can follow speakers, actors, or other persons as they perform.

**Use**   Focus attention on a principal performer or on a prop or other important symbol. This technology is also used to create excitement as the spotlight bally's (rapidly moves left and right) through the audience onto the stage.

### Intelligent Lighting

**Technology**   Robotic lights are able to tilt, pan, turn, change color, change gobo patterns, change focus, and perform other maneuvers at the touch of a switch. One intelligent lighting unit may be able to replace a dozen other units, due to the flexibility it offers. Although significantly more expensive than traditional lighting instruments such as par cams, these units are able to perform many more functions.

**Use**   Intelligent lighting is most appropriate for large-scale productions where high-tech lighting will support or enhance the production. I have used them for theme parties, inserting the client's gobo in the units and then ballying the image throughout the room. I have also used them when I required a flexible system that could change the look of the event environment several times over a short period of time.

### Par Cam Lighting Instrument

**Technology**   If the slide projector is the workhorse of the audiovisual field, the par cam performs that same function among the many instruments in the field of lighting. The par cam provides a broad floodlight and is used to fill a stage with light. This instrument is traditionally used to flood large areas and to provide color to create mood and atmosphere.

**Use**   From lighting the front area of a stage, to providing side fill light for a lectern, to creating dramatic mood lighting for a backdrop, the par cam has many uses. Gels may be inserted to provide color. To create an effect similar to *Star Trek's* "beam me up, Scotty" illusion, I used four par cams placed on the floor of each side of a platform. Adding fog, the lights projected up through the particulate matter and created a low-cost but highly effective impression.

### Pin Spot

**Technology**   A pin spot is used to provide a narrow focused beam of light on a table centerpiece.

**Use**   This low-wattage instrument is extremely effective for lighting a specific area such as a centerpiece.

### Strobe Light

**Technology**   This rapidly flashing light creates the illusion of slow or fast motion when used with movement. It is available in a variety of sizes, including small egg-shaped products that when used in combination with other instruments produce a starlight effect.

**Use**   In a theatrical production, strobe lights may be used to simulate slow motion. I have used strobe lights to create a space age effect in an entrance tunnel as well as egg-shaped strobes to decorate the exterior of a building.

**Caution**   Both chase lights and strobe lights may cause discomfort or even injury to guests with disabilities such as hearing loss or epilepsy. When using these devices, post a sign at the entrance stating: *The following special effects are used during this event: strobe light and chasing lights.*

### Ultraviolet or Black Light

**Technology**   Popular during the 1960s, ultraviolet or black light technology has improved tremendously. Originally available only in tube format, its major drawback was the limited throw distance. In recent years manufacturers have invented new technology that allows longer throw distance and focusable light to create fantastic new effects.

**Use**    This technology may be used to create a dark and haunting atmosphere or a space age thrill. As the light excites the color in a sign, the graphic will suddenly pop out at the audience. I have effectively used this technology to reveal new products by outlining the new item in colors that are sensitive to black light and then at the appointed time illuminating the appropriate instrument.

### Cost-Saving Measures

The easiest way to save money on lighting equipment and labor is to select a venue that has lighting equipment permanently installed in its facility. Sometimes the venue will include in the rental fee the use of some or all lighting equipment. You may also wish to share the costs of equipment rentals with other groups in the same venue.

When required to rent lighting equipment, make certain that you solicit bids. When possible, ask bidders to inspect the venue with you, as they may be able to offer additional ideas that you may not have thought of previously.

Finally, remember that costs escalate rapidly when work is performed outside normal business hours. Find the time frame for straight time and work within this window. Sometimes this will require renting the venue on a weekday to prepare for a weekend event. Compare the labor cost savings to the rental charges and determine which is better. Schedule labor carefully to avoid overtime charges.

## SOUND

The level of complexity and purpose of the event determines the level of audio support that is required. In most event environments, audio is used for simple, noncomplex productions. However, as the size of the audience increases or the complexity of the production rises, simple audio must be replaced by the services provided by a production sound company.

Sound is used for public address, entertainment, to project speakers, and to transmit sound from video or film as well as numerous other applications. Table 8-4 describes some of these applications and the type of equipment that may be required.

### Cassette Player

**Technology**    Cassette players are rapidly being replaced by compact disk or digital audiotape (DAT) machines. However, it is still a staple of many events. This machine accepts a 30-, 60-, 90-, or 120-minute cassette tape. Some machines feature automatic rewind, automatic cueing of sides, and automatic stop.

**Use**    One way to use this machine is to place it near a live tropical bird such as a parrot. Use a voice-over expert to record the sound of a parrot's voice

**Table 8-4**  Applications for Sound Equipment

| Sound Equipment | Application |
| --- | --- |
| Audio console and rack | Full-sound production capability, including playback and recording. |
| Boom attachment | Television, film, recording, specific sound source, and large groups. |
| Cassette player/recorder | Recording live sound. |
| Compact disk player | Playback of instrumental music and other sound, including effects. |
| Delay speaker | Used to project sound to areas that are a greater distance from the original sound source. In a stage setting the delay speakers may be mounted halfway over the audience. The signal received by these speakers is delayed to avoid an echolike quality. |
| Digital audiotape (DAT) machine | Synchronized music. |
| Fill speaker | A speaker used to send sound signals to dead spots such as the front center of an audience |
| Mixer | Used for blending sound sources through one central unit. |
| Omnidirectional microphone | Chorus. |
| Perimeter zone microphone (PZM) | Chorus, singers, and piano. |
| Reel to reel | Slide or audio synchronization. |
| Speaker | Used for projecting sound to either a specific area or a wide distribution. |
| Speaker cluster | A group of speakers clustered together to project a wide distribution of sound. |
| Speaker tripod | A speaker mounted on a tripod. |
| Stage or ear monitor | Playback from other instruments and vocalists. |
| Unidirectional microphone | Solo speaker. |

welcoming the guests to the party. Using an endless loop cassette tape, the bird will repeatedly welcome the startled guests. You may also use this equipment to play walk-in, background, or walk-out music at the event.

### Compact Disk Player

**Technology**   A compact disk (CD) player produces high-quality audio and video signals and provides enduring quality. Unlike the audiocassette player, the compact disk player allows for instant cueing and random access to specific audio or video segments. Stills photos (slides) and data storage are also important uses of this technology.

**Use**   Instrumental music and/or video/slides may be retrieved instantaneously with this technology. Use for background or specific audio musical cues as well as to project photos or video images. Ideal for instrumental music for background music, fanfares, or dancing.

## Equalizer

**Technology**   The range between treble and bass is equalized using this valuable technology.

**Use**   A professional sound engineer is required for this task, and he or she will use either your prerecorded sound source or the live performance to equalize the sound to provide a full range of audio dynamics.

## Mixer

**Technology**   A mixer is used to blend or mix different sound inputs or sources and transmit them into a central output. The number of inputs may vary from four to dozens.

**Use**   Instrumental musicians and multiple vocalists as well as event programs that feature both live and recorded sound sources will require the services of a mixing unit.

## Perimeter Zone Microphone

**Technology**   The perimeter zone microphone (PZM) is a flat microphone that picks up sounds in a 180-degree radius. It is used inside a piano, on the floor of a stage, to record choirs or large musical ensembles, and other applications where sound may originate from more than one point.

**Use**   Place the PZM inside the piano lid, on the center of a table for a group discussion, or on the floor of a stage to record or broadcast sound from multiple sources.

## Sound Console or Rack

**Technology**   A sound console or rack is a multicomponent system that may feature a recorder, player (cassette and/or compact disk), equalizer, mixer, and other important technology.

**Use**   The term *rack* originates from the way the equipment is stacked on racks in a vertical system.

## Stage or Ear Monitor

**Technology**   The stage monitor is used to monitor sounds from other instruments in a musical group, including vocals, as well as to monitor the sound level as the audience experiences it. Increasingly popular among entertainers is the ear monitor. This small hearing-aid type of device is custom fitted to the ear and allows for monitoring of sound as well as cueing and synchronizing when singing or performing to a prerecorded track.

**Use**   Singers and musicians use stage monitors to communicate with one another and to review their sound as the audience hears it. Singers, television performers, and others use ear monitors to receive cues from the director and monitor their vocal performance.

## Wireless Microphone

**Technology**   Both handheld and clip-on wireless microphones are regularly used for conferences, meetings, and live entertainment as well as video production. The speaker may move freely before and among the audience using this equipment.

**Use**   When conducting a presentation featuring audience questions and answers, the wireless microphone is ideal. It is also the instrument of choice for speakers who move randomly on the stage and among the audience. Remember to have redundant equipment in the form of a wired microphone in case the wireless microphone should fail.

## Sound Opportunities

There are generally three periods when sound is utilized for most events. First, sound is utilized prior to the event to prepare certain audio products, such as sound tracks or fanfares, for the live performance. Second, sound is used during the actual event for broadcasting both to the live audience attending the event and to those listening by radio and television. Finally, sound production may include a postproduction session when the live sound recorded during the event is further processed to documentary, marketing, or other use.

**Preproduction**   The preproduction period generally occurs during the design, planning, and coordination phases. Preproduction may include the design and production of specific audio elements for the event. These elements will vary depending on the complexity of the event. Your task could be as simple as selecting appropriate instrumental music tracks or as complex as mixing an entire symphony orchestra to provide recorded accompaniment for a major megaevent such as the Olympic Games opening or closing ceremony. The preproduction period must be planned carefully, as others may need to review the finished product before use in the actual event. Therefore, allow sufficient time to identify the appropriate resources, produce the product, and receive feedback from your important event stakeholders. When budgeting this time, I usually allow 25 to 50 percent more time than estimated to handle last-minute changes and requests.

**Production**   During this period the event manager *coordinates* the live, broadcast, or recording of sound from the actual event. Depending on the size and complexity of the event, the event manager may wish to assign a specific person from his or her staff to monitor the sound production. In most cases a competent and capable sound technician will handle the myriad of details required for this function. However, in those circumstances when the event is new or highly specialized, it is wise to have one person supervise the sound department to ensure that this element of production is consistent with expectations. Too often, event managers assign too low a budget for production sound. Do not fall victim to this error. Make certain that you have budgeted carefully for the level of quality required. One way to do this is to be certain that you have retained a sound console operator as well as a stage sound technician. Speakers, actors, singers, musicians, and others who are using sound equipment will benefit from the knowledge that a qualified sound technician is nearby to help prevent or correct problems. A simple mistake such as failing to turn on the wireless microphone can easily be prevented by investing in a professional sound technician to monitor these important details.

**Postproduction**   Once the event has ended, the sound responsibilities may continue. More and more events are being recorded for both documentary and marketing purposes. Therefore, during the design, planning, and coordination process of the event, careful attention must be paid as to how you may use the sound product after the live event has ended. Although the two most common uses are documentation and recording, it is also possible to use the sound portion of your event for communications as well as risk management purposes. For example, a well-edited sound version of your event may be an effective way to communicate with your volunteers. You may duplicate this program on cassette tapes and distribute them to volunteers to enjoy during their drive time to and from work. Should your organization become involved in a lawsuit resulting from a risk management incident, the sound recording may provide evidence that you practiced a standard of care acceptable in your area. For example, a recording of the evacuation announcement may provide you with evidence that you conducted this important activity with a reasonable degree of care to prevent injury. Throughout the research and design process the event manager must carefully consider how he or she will later use the sound product created during the event.

## Soundscaping

Olympic Games and Super Bowl sound designer Bob Estrin of Creative Event Technology in Orange County, California, may have been the first person of his generation to soundscape a room. The soundscaper works very much like the landscape artist or architect in that he or she designs specific areas of the event venue to reflect the form and function of the event theme. Estrin has used miniature speakers to transform a themed environment into a symphony of sound effects that subtly transport the guest into a total experience.

## Sound Ideas

There are no limits to the possibilities for exciting sound production for your event. However, implementing these ideas requires careful planning and well-executed coordination.

**Famous Voices**    To attract the attention of an audience meeting in Houston, Texas, home of the U.S. space program, I quickly lowered the houselights and played an audiotape of President John F. Kennedy describing the space program. As President Kennedy spoke, we showed a video with sound effects of the launch of the space shuttle. Using surround sound, the entire room felt as though it were preparing to lift off. Carefully and selectively, we added one speaker at a time until the entire room thundered with sound. As the audio program concluded, a burst of fog appeared from stage left and the presiding officer entered the stage to greet the space age delegates.

**Invisible Actors**    The president of a corporation wanted to reward his senior staff with a series of bonuses. To introduce this announcement dramatically, the president agreed to dress as Ebeneezer Scrooge and meet the ghosts of Christmas past, present, and future. However, due to budget constraints, there were no funds to hire or wardrobe actors to play the ghosts. Once again, we solved the problem by prerecording the voice of one actor playing all three ghosts. When the ghosts appeared we used fog and simple lighting effects to create the illusion of a ghost. The president impersonating Scrooge spoke to this area of the stage and the ghost answered him. At the end of the ghostly visit the president agreed to distribute the bonuses to his senior staff.

**Goof-Proof Sound**    Only a few weeks before a major convention, the meeting planner changed the theme of the event to reflect an international program. To open the convention we selected an international children's choir that featured children from over 50 different countries wearing native costumes. The children ranged in age from 5 to 7 years. Concerned that their voices would not be strong enough to fill the event venue, I arranged for them to be prerecorded so that they could sing to tracks and be certain that they were in full voice on the day of the show. As it turned out, nearly half of the children had bad head colds; however, the audience heard only clear, beautiful tones prerecorded in a studio several days prior to the event.

The element of sound will be the technology that is noticed in most events. How many times have you attended an event and winced at the sound of screeching feedback pouring forth from the oversized speakers? I have often said that the only two things that most people have a strong opinion about at events are the temperature and the sound level. In most cases the temperature will be either too hot or too cold and the sound too loud (usually) and too soft (sometimes).

The event manager must recognize that today many people have high-quality stereophonic sound systems in their homes and automobiles. Because of this new sophistication, your guests are extremely discriminating when it comes to the quality of sound used at your event. Make certain that you determine in advance the level of sophistication of your listeners and then allocate your resources effectively to satisfy their needs, wants, and desires.

## Cost-Saving Measures

Wireless products are significantly more expensive than wired ones. Unless the production requires wireless products, avoid this costly equipment. In some cases you will still pay for wired equipment, as you will want to have redundant equipment, as described earlier.

Labor can be a major cost in installing heavy-duty sound equipment. Consult with your sound rental expert and determine if small units may be used to avoid the rental of lifts and riggers required for the larger equipment. Bid sound equipment carefully to make certain that the experience of the operators and condition of the equipment will ensure that you meet the goals and objectives of your event. For example, in the Washington, DC, area there are only three or four sound companies that have the capabilities to handle the large-scale sound requirements for major demonstrations and marches. Using an inferior company can incur much greater costs than selecting the most qualified and perhaps higher bidder.

## SPECIAL EFFECTS

It is interesting that most special effects reflect variations in the weather of the planet. Effects such as fog, rain, thunder, lightning, and even pyrotechnics (fireworks) immediately conjure images of dramatic changes in the climatic conditions. Weather is perhaps the most talked-about subject in the world. As so much depends on it, including one's mood, it is natural that special effects have come to play an important role in the development of event management.

Event managers use special effects to attract attention, generate excitement, and sustain interest as well as startle, shock, and even amuse. The key to proper integration of special effects into an event scheme is to determine during the design process how special effects will support or enhance an event's goal and objectives. The most common error made by event managers when using special effects is to add too many different components and thereby confuse the guests. Instead, special effects should be viewed as a natural and necessary part of the entire event strategy.

Table 8-5 lists the most common special effects used in event management. However, it is important to remember that some event technicians also use the term *special effects* to describe a variety of specialty lighting devices, such as black or strobe lights.

## Balloon Drop

**Technology**   A bag or net suspended above the heads of the audience opens and releases hundreds of balloons.

**Table 8-5**  Applications for Special Effects

| Effect | Application |
| --- | --- |
| Air-propelled confetti cannons | Shower of paper flutters over and on guests as part of finale of entertainment |
| Balloon drop | Hundreds of balloons drop onto the heads of the audience from a net or bag suspended above |
| Dry ice | Low-level fog for ground cover |
| Flash pot/box | Explosion |
| Flying | Aerial effects such as outer space or illusions |
| Fog | Ghost, magic, laser beam projection, explosion, and outer space |
| Hologram | Illusion, attraction, and communications |
| Laser | Communication, entertainment, focus attention, and reveal product |
| Pyrotechnics (indoor) | Reveal new product and finale of production |
| Pyrotechnics (outdoor) | Capture attention and finale of sport or other event |
| Wind machine | Blowing, billowing trees, flags, and other fabric |

**Use**  Traditionally used on New Year's Eve as well as at the conclusion of U.S. political party conventions, this technology is always appropriate as a capstone or finale element for a significant event. In some instances, prizes may be placed in the balloons or slips of paper announcing gifts.

### Confetti Cannon

**Technology**  Air-propelled cannons range from small to huge and can propel large pieces of confetti over 100 feet.

**Use**  A confetti cannon provides a fitting conclusion to an important meeting or conference or an effective way to attract attention through the introduction of a new product.

### Dry Ice

**Technology**  A 50-gallon drum combined with dry ice, heat, and a blower will easily fog a large stage floor surface. Unlike chemical fog, this substance clings to the stage surface and creates the illusion of ground cover.

**Use**  A remote moat, graveyard, or lagoon at a theme party as well as a snowy winter wonderland can be established easily with this effect.

### Flash Pot

**Technology**  A small amount of gun powder and flash paper combined with an electric charge creates a flash followed by a small amount of smoke.

**Use**   The appearance of a genie, ghost, or other magical moment is appropriate for this startling effect.

## Flying

**Technology**   Individuals, props, or both can appear to float effortlessly over the stage and sometimes over the heads of the audience. The most established purveyor of this art form is the firm Flying by Foy based in Las Vegas, Nevada.

**Use**   Flying is appropriate for a space age illusion or theme incorporating magic. May be used to levitate individuals or new props being introduced to the audience.

## Fog

**Technology**   Fog is usually dispensed from a small box using a chemical ingredient and heat. Chemical fog rises and may set off smoke sensors. It is available in a variety of scents or in an odorless form.

**Use**   From creating an eerie graveyard scene at a theme party to establishing a cone shape for a laser beam to highlight in producing a "beam me up, Scotty" effect, fog has become an indispensable part of many events.

## Hologram

**Technology**   A hologram is the result of a film image and light combined to create a three-dimensional image.

**Use**   A hologram may be used to depict a product or spokesperson in a trade show booth or onstage.

## Indoor Pyrotechnics

**Technology**   Indoor pyrotechnics are small devices that emit little smoke and create sparks, flame, or other indoor effects.

**Use**   Over an ice rink at the conclusion of an opening ceremony a shower of sparks falls from the ceiling or on the front of a stage, or flames appear to leap from the footlights.

## Laser

**Technology**   A laser is a high-powered light source cooled by either water or air. The water-cooled laser projects beams many hundreds of feet.

**Use**  From creating a vertical laser cone to introduce the chief executive officer in a "beam me down Scotty" effect to creating a waving canopy over the heads of the audience, lasers can dynamically animate the activities of an event. Using graphics, the laser beams can create logos and animation to tell a story or set the tone for an event.

### Outdoor Pyrotechnics

**Technology**  Outdoor pyrotechnics are large shells ranging in size from three to twelve inches propel up into the night sky and burst creating patterns and other colorful effects.

**Use**  Many professional sport events conclude with an aerial fireworks display and some organizations use fireworks as a way of celebrating the culmination of a historic meeting or holiday, such as Independence Day in the United States.

### Pyrotechnic Set Piece

**Technology**  A pyrotechnic set piece is a large sign that is illuminated with pyrotechnics. Sometimes it includes moveable pieces that spin, rotate, rise, and fall.

**Use**  A pyrotechnic set piece can be used to announce a new idea or product, celebrate a historic occasion or holiday. Sometimes used in combination with indoor or outdoor pyrotechnics.

### Wind Machine

**Technology**  A wind machine is a large high-powered fan mounted on a secure floor base.

**Use**  A wind machine can be used to blow curtains, flags, or other scenery or costumes to create the illusion of movement by wind.

### Cost-Saving Measures

When using special effects there are usually ancillary costs such as site preparation and cleanup as well as additional security. Make certain that you factor in all costs before you blast the confetti cannon and later realize that a cleanup fee of several hundred dollars must be paid to the janitorial staff.

Some lighting and production companies will include special effects devices in the total bid for equipment. Consult with lighting and production vendors to determine what equipment they own and then include these items in your specifications.

Finally, use special effects only if they support the overall goals and objectives of the event. Special effects may be the first areas of a budget that can be trimmed unless the added value is justified.

## VIDEO

Due to the growth of television and the rapid acquisition of videocassette recorders (VCRs), video has become an integral part of many live events. Video is used to enhance the live image of the speaker or performer so that a person seated in the far reaches of a venue may see his or her facial reactions. Video is also used to document the entire event for future use, such as for historical or marketing purposes, or both.

The expansion of this field has placed the video camera in the hands of large numbers of the public, and as a result, guests are more sophisticated with regards to video production. Because of supply and demand, even editing equipment is now available to consumers, allowing them to perform simple editing functions for home video features.

Table 8-6 identifies the most common uses for video at an event and the types of equipment required for these purposes.

### Character Generator

**Technology**   A character generator (CG) is an electronic device used to create titles and project text on the video image.

**Use**   It may be used to identify speakers, project messages to the audience, or create other communications through video production.

### Off-line Editing

**Technology**   Off-line editing is designed primarily for simple edits such as cuts only. During off-line editing the video product is refined further prior to the more expensive online editing session.

**Table 8-6**  Video Uses and Typical Equipment

| Use | Equipment |
| --- | --- |
| Audience interaction event | Multiple cameras and video switcher |
| Complex special effects editing | Online editing equipment |
| Corporate communications | Animated character |
| Image magnification | VHS or four-chip camera and projector |
| Multi-image communications | Video wall system |
| Simple cuts only editing | Off-line editing equipment |
| Video roll | Video player and projector |

**Use**   Simple video products may be prepared during the off-line session or may be used to prepare the product for the online session.

## Online Editing

**Technology**   Sophisticated, complex special effects may be achieved using online editing equipment.

**Use**   During online editing, complex digital effects are included to produce exciting transitions, sweeten the music, and add other technical elements to complete the production.

## Switcher

**Technology**   A switcher enables the video operator to switch electronically between two or more cameras and also cue prerecorded video products.

**Use**   Complex event production that requires two or more cameras and use of prerecorded video products must be programmed through a switching system.

## Video Animation

**Technology**   An operator uses a mechanical device similar to a finger puppet and creates a dancing, talking electronic figure video projected on a screen.

**Use**   Video animation can be used to establish a new image or character, interact with the main presenter at the meeting, improve corporate communications, or improve other communications. When Xerox introduced its new logo—the digitized X—I retained Interactive Personalities of Minneapolis, Minnesota, to create an animated character we named Chip. He immediately brought the new symbol to life for the guests and even endeared himself to them as they literally became friends during this conference.

## Video Camera

**Technology**   Consumer as well as broadcast-quality cameras are available for rental from most audiovisual production firms. The broadcast camera is a four-chip model that may record on Beta videotape, the highest quality available for editing. However, for simple events where editing will not be required, consumer equipment may be acceptable.

**Use**   Either live coverage for video magnification or live and recorded for future use, the video camera is the primary tool in video production. One drawback with regard to video production at live events is the presence of the video camera, tripod, and sometimes a platform to elevate the equipment. This complex setup may interfere with the audience's view of an event's live performance. Bob Johnson of Corporate Video Communications has overcome this challenge with the invention of robotic cameras designed for event production. In the Video Bob system, each four-chip camera is placed on a thin metal rod and is operated electronically by one operator. This saves both labor and space. One experienced operator may be able to control up to eight different cameras simultaneously.

### Video Player/Recorder

**Technology**   Either $\frac{1}{2}$-inch VHS or $\frac{3}{4}$-inch Beta tape may be played or recorded on this machine. Beta $\frac{3}{4}$-inch allows for sophisticated editing techniques.

**Use**   This equipment is used either to record the event activities or to play back prerecorded video products during the live event.

### Video Wall System

**Technology**   A video wall system may include as few as four or up to 10 times that many video monitors which project a video image simultaneously. A separate processor allows the video signal to produce a variety of effects, including geometric images to generate visual excitement.

**Use**   This is a high-tech solution for spreading a corporate message or introducing a new idea or product. May also be used as a background for an event stage set.

### Cost-Saving Measures

Contact a local university or college and determine if its radio, television, or film program can provide you with equipment for preproduction or postproduction. Significant savings may be available through use of these facilities.

When shooting, keep in mind that the better you plan your shots, the less time may be required in postproduction. Shoot with editing firmly in mind. Some video directors shoot in a style that requires very little postproduction by matching shots carefully and maintaining continuity.

Plan your postproduction schedule carefully. The majority of time should be devoted to off-line editing, as this costs less. The more you can accomplish in off-line editing, the greater the overall savings.

Check with the postproduction editing facility to find out if you can use off-peak times to complete your project. Avoiding normal business hours may result in significant savings.

Retain an experienced crew that can handle multiple functions. For example, the shooter or camera person may also be able to coordinate the audio feed, and this will eliminate additional labor costs.

Video crews can range from $750 to over $1500 per day, depending on the type and quantity of equipment and labor required. Always solicit bids for these services and ask to see a demonstration reel of the crews' work.

Use robotic cameras for simple meeting and conference event production and include an option (with the permission of the speakers and entertainers) to sell tapes to the attendees. By selling the tapes you may not only recover all video production costs but also generate additional net proceeds for your sponsoring organization.

### SYNERGY OF AUDIOVISUAL EFFECTS

Carefully integrate audiovisual, lighting, sound, special effects, and video to ensure a smooth and seamless event. Avoid overproducing your event merely to demonstrate the latest high-tech wonders. Most production personnel will state that their work is designed to support and enhance, never to dominate. In fact, these technologies should be so well incorporated into event planning and coordination that they are invisible to guests. However, as a result of their combined power, a positive enduring effect should result.

# Music and Entertainment Management

Deciding whether or not to use music and entertainment at your event can be the difference between captivating your audience and confusing them. Next we discuss the major issues that involve event entertainment.

Although most events benefit from music and entertainment, not every event needs to incur this expense. The event manager must assess the needs of his or her guests carefully and determine whether or not music and entertainment is appropriate for each event. For example, the groundbreaking of a historic battlefield site may require speeches, but it would be inappropriate to engage a Dixieland jazz band. Too often, music and entertainment is engaged based on the personal tastes and desires of the organizers with little regard for the appropriateness of the event or the interests of guests. To avoid making this mistake, use the following checklist to conduct some preliminary research.

1. Research the history of the event to determine if music and/or entertainment was used in the past.
2. Interview the event stakeholders through a formal focus group or informally to ascertain their individual and collective tastes.
3. Determine how music and/or entertainment will be used to further the goals of the event.
4. Analyze the event budget to determine available resources for music and/or entertainment.

**5.** Review the time frame for planning and production to determine if sufficient time is available for incorporating these elements into the event.

## IDENTIFYING THE RESOURCES

Once you have conducted the research to identify the need, the next step is to identify the most appropriate and cost-effective resources for your event. Fortunately, in the postmodern entertainment era there have been more choices.

In most communities literally dozens of resources are available for music and live entertainment. Many resources are available for both professional and amateur music and entertainment (see Table 8-7).

Matching the best music and entertainment resource to the needs, wants, and desires, as well as the goals and objectives of your event, is a complex task. The first step is to comprehend the various musical and entertainment options that are available (see Figure 9-2). Although descriptions of music and entertainment are largely composed of industry jargon and may vary according to location, the terms are considered standard and customary in these fields. See Table 8-8 for a list of music and entertainment terms. For further definitions, refer to *The International Dictionary of Event Management,* by Wiley (2000, Wiley).

## MUSIC FOR MOOD, ATMOSPHERE, ANIMATION, AND TRANSITIONS

According to veteran band leader Gene Donati of Washington, DC, music is used to create the proper mood, sustain the atmosphere, and most important, to "animate" the room. According to Donati, "The music should begin before the doors open, to draw people into the room. Up-tempo songs should be used to energize this segment of the party." Donati and his colleagues not only conduct the musicians but in fact conduct the guests using music to animate their actions.

Alice Conway, a musician and instructor of event coordination at George Washington University (GWU), recommends that event managers first try to identify the proper atmosphere their clients are trying to create and sustain. To do this, she asks clients to close their eyes and describe what they envision their guests doing as they listen to the music. As clients describe guests listening, dancing, applauding, and performing other activities, Conway takes careful notes and then creates a sequence of music and entertainment to accomplish these goals.

Music may be used as a transition to create punctuation marks in the order of a program. One of the best examples is the awards event. Using music associated with the presenters or award recipients helps the audience remain interested and focused on the program. Following are some typical tunes for awards programs:

- Person from California          "California, Here I Come"
- Person from New York City    "New York, New York"

- Sports-related award     Olympic Games fanfare theme
- Championship award     Main theme from the film *Chariots of Fire*
- Chapter of the year     Theme from the film *Rocky*
- Person of the year     "Let a Winner Lead the Way" from the musical *Wildcat*
- Volunteer of the year     "Together" from the musical *Gypsy*
- Leadership award     "The Washington Post March"

**Table 8-7**   36 Resources for Music and Entertainment

1. *Academy Players Directory,* a list of television and film stars (see Appendix 5)
2. Actor's Equity Association, the union of professional stage actors and actresses
3. Agents who represent a variety of acts
4. American Federation of Musicians
5. American Federation of Television and Radio Artists, the union of television and radio artists
6. American Guild of Variety Artists, the union of live entertainment artists, such as circus performers
7. Amusement parks and permanent attractions, such as zoos
8. Arts advocacy societies and commissions
9. Bars, nightclubs, restaurants, and taverns
10. *Cavalcade of Acts and Attractions,* a directory of live entertainment (see Appendix 5)
11. Churches
12. *Circus Report,* a magazine for circus enthusiasts
13. Clubs, including fraternal organizations
14. Dance clubs, groups, and dance advocacy organizations
15. Educational institutions, including public, private, primary, middle, and secondary schools, as well as colleges and universities
16. *Event World,* the official magazine of the International Special Events Society (ISES)
17. Fraternal organizations, such as the Shriners
18. Historical reenactment organizations
19. Institutions, such as museums that may provide lecturers
20. Instrumental music organizations
21. Musical contractors
22. Native American organizations
23. Newspaper critics familiar with local arts organizations
24. Parks and recreation organizations that offer dance, music, and other arts programs
25. Producers of radio, television, or live entertainment programs
26. Radio disc jockeys who are familiar with local bands and who may provide DJ services
27. Religious organizations other than churches and synagogues
28. Schools, colleges, and university music and theater departments
29. Screen Actors Guild, the union of film actors and actresses
30. Shopping centers that feature live music and entertainment
31. *Special Events Magazine* (see Appendix 4)
32. Synagogues
33. Theatrical organizations from professional to community or amateur groups
34. Travel agents familiar with local entertainment resources
35. Very Special Arts, an organzation representing disabled people who are artists
36. Zoological parks

From behind a soundboard an audio technician can mix, balance, and ensure that the sound is perfect for every member of a live events audience. *Photograph courtesy of Monica Vidal.*

A train station is transformed thoroughly to provide a celebrity entertainer with professional lighting, sound, staging, and other technical resources to create a unique and memorable experience for event guests. *Photograph courtesy of Monica Vidal.*

Amateur sport events must provide thorough risk management, safety, security, and other resources to ensure that both spectators and athletes achieve a winning experience every time the starting pistol is fired. *Photograph courtesy of Monica Vidal.*

A proper blend of lighting, sound, decor, and professional entertainment can bring event audiences to their feet time after time. *Photograph courtesy of Monica Vidal.*

Design Cuisine of Washington, DC creates an elegant social event through a seamless blend of rentals, swaged ceiling linens, and candelabra. *Photograph courtesy of Monica Vidal.*

Intimacy is achieved in Washington, DC's International Trade Center's cavernous venue through the use of video projection and a camera boom to pan, tilt, and zoom in for up-close and personal moments. *Photograph courtesy of Monica Vidal.*

Crowd control and management are critical in the planning and coordination of major events such as this dedication of a U.S. memorial to women in the military service. *Photograph courtesy of Monica Vidal.*

Gobo lighting effects transform stately columns into dramatic works of art. A proper blend of color, design, and gobo patterns provides an appropriate atmosphere for an elegant evening and beautiful memories. Event venue: National Building Museum, Washington, DC. *Photograph courtesy of Monica Vidal.*

A NATO meeting in Washington, DC involves attention to numerous aspects of protocol to ensure that the proceedings take place in an orderly and symbolic manner. The central seating for NATO world leaders and ancillary seating for their ministers is typical of a conference featuring global participation. Event venue: U.S. Departmental Auditorium. Event design: Hargrove, Inc. *Photograph courtesy of Monica Vidal.*

The placement of flags, seating of dignitaries, and other protocol considerations rely on the ancient rule of precedent. Global event managers must conduct research to determine proper seating, location of flags, and handling of other symbolic elements. Event venue: International Trade Center, Washington, DC. *Photograph courtesy of Monica Vidal.*

**Table 8-8**  Music and Entertainment Terms

Act: a self-contained, rehearsed performance of one or more persons.

Agent: a person who represents various acts or artists and receives a commission from the buyer for coordinating a booking.

Amateur: a musician or entertainer who does not charge for his or her services, usually due to lack of professional experience.

Arrangements: musical compositions arranged for musicians.

Band: a group of musicians who perform contemporary music, such as rock 'n' roll, jazz, or big band.

Booking: a firm commitment by a buyer of entertainment to hire an act or artist for a specific engagement.

Combo: a musical ensemble featuring combined instruments (usually, piano, base, and drums)

Commission: the percentage received by an agent when booking an act or artist.

Conductor: a person responsible for directing/conducting the rehearsal and performance by musicians.

Contractor: a person or organization that contracts musicians and other entertainers. Handles all the agreements, payroll, taxes, and other employment tasks.

Cover song: a tune popularized by another artist performed by a different artist or group.

Doubler: a musician who plays two or more instruments during a performance.

Downbeat: the cue given by a conductor to musicians to begin playing.

Drum riser: a small platform used to elevate a drummer above the other musicians.

Drum roll: a rolling percussive sound used for announcements and to create a suspenseful atmosphere.

Duo: an act with two persons. Also known as a double.

Fanfare: a musical interlude used to signal announcements of awards or introductions. Usually includes horns but not always.

Fife and drum corp: a small or larger musical ensemble featuring fifes and drums playing music from the eighteenth century.

Horn section: a group of musicians that specializes in wind instruments and is usually part of a larger ensemble.

Leader: a person who organizes and conducts a musical or entertainment group.

Manager: a person who provides management services to an artist, act, or several artists and acts. The manager normally handles all logistics, including travel and negotiates on behalf of the artist or act. The manager is paid by the act or artist from fees that are earned through performing.

Marching band: a musical ensemble of persons who play and march simultaneously usually comprised of percussion, horns, woodwinds, and other instruments.

Minimum: the minimum number of hours musicians must be paid.

Octet: a musical ensemble comprised of eight musicians.

Overture: the music performed before actors or entertainers enter the stage. Also known as preshow music.

Professional: a musician or entertainer paid for his or her services.

Quartet: a musical ensemble comprised of four persons.

Quintet: a musical ensemble comprised of five persons.

Road manager: a person who travels with an act or artist to handle all logistical arrangements.

Sextet: a musical ensemble comprised of six persons.

Sideman/men: musicians within a musical ensemble who accompany an artist.

Single: an act with one person.

Soloist: a single performer.

Stage manager: a person who coordinates the technical elements for the act or artist, cue the performer, and provides other services to support the performance.

**Table 8-8**  *(Continued)*

Stand: the music stand used to hold sheet music.

Top Forty: the top 40 musical compositions/recordings selected by *Billboard* magazine. A top 40 band is able to perform these selections.

Trio: a musical ensemble comprised of three persons.

Walk-in, walk-out music: live or recorded music played at the start and end of an event as guests enter or leave a venue.

Walk music: live or recorded music played as award presenters, speakers, and recipients enter or exit the stage area.

Windjammers: the slang name for circus musicians (mostly horn players).

Use awards music to introduce the presenters by sequencing the music in the following manner. First cue the drummer to perform a drum roll. Next, have your offstage announcer introduce the presenter using the following text: "Ladies and gentlemen, please welcome the president of XYZ corporation, from New Orleans, Louisiana, Ms. Jane Smith!" As the presenter's name is announced, the remainder of the musicians should play a lively Dixieland jazz melody and conclude promptly when Ms. Smith reaches the microphone. This will help accelerate the action for the event and keep things running on time.

As Ms. Smith introduces the award recipient, the musicians should begin to play immediately as the name is called. Because musicians need a warning before they begin to play, I recommend that you give the cue to play as the first name is announced so that as the surname is announced, the tune has begun. Here is an example: Ms. Smith: "And now welcome our award winner, from New York City, Mr. (cue conductor) John Doe (music begins)." The music should continue until Mr. Doe reaches Ms. Smith and then conclude with a brief fanfare as the award is presented. A generic walk-off melody may be played as Mr. Doe exits the stage.

Properly sequenced and timed, music can ensure that your event runs on time. Even Ole Blue Eyes himself, Frank Sinatra, learned at the Grammy Awards that unless you sustain the interest of the audience, the music will abruptly change the mood, ending one segment and cueing another.

### Musical Formulas for Success

Veteran society band leader Lester Lanin of New York City recommends that event managers carefully consider the number and type of guests that will be attending an event prior to the selection of musical performers. Lanin reports that while at one time both opera and classical music were commonly used for social life-cycle events, today it is not uncommon to incorporate contemporary music.

Cantor Arnold Saltzman of Adas Israel Synagogue in Washington, DC, cautions people involved in religious events to work closely with their clergy to select appropriate music that is in accordance with the traditions and customs of the religious denomination. As one example, a bride asked Saltzman for

**Table 8-9** Attendance and Minimum
Musicians Required as Recommended by
Lester Lanin

| Number of Guests | Minimum Number of Musicians |
|---|---|
| 125 | 5–7 |
| 250 | 7 |
| 500 | 12 |
| 750 | 12 plus strings if budget allows |
| 1,000 | 15–20 |

permission to use the theme from *Star Wars* as the processional music. Since the event was a secular occasion, no policies were set by the location. However, Saltzman correctly counseled the bride and groom that if this music was used for the processional, the guests might be distracted by this departure from tradition and the rest of the ceremony could suffer as a result.

Shown in Table 8-9 are the staffing levels that Lanin recommends for musicians at specific events. While a few years ago a thirty-member orchestra might have been standard fare, in today's cost-conscious times, Lanin's formulas are more likely to be used.

### Electronic Music

Miniaturization in lighting and sound has also found its way into the orchestra. Many modern musicians use electronic instruments to perform the sounds of dozens of instruments. It is not unusual today to see four musicians performing music that once required a 100-member symphony orchestra. However, there are liabilities that accompany this progress.

### Managing Musicians

Musicians, as well as other personnel, require careful management to be able to deliver an optimum performance. Musical artists require the event manager to provide support systems that allow them to do what they do best: deliver a quality musical performance. The most common considerations for effectively managing musicians include:

1. Provide clear, written instructions regarding date, time, and location.
2. Communicate a profile of the guests so that appropriate music may be selected.
3. Provide an event schedule, and supply the leader of the musical group with a summary of the musical activities.
4. Arrange for parking for the musicians, and notify them of the locations authorized.
5. Identify and communicate to the musicians where equipment may be loaded into a venue.

6. Select and notify the musicians of a room where their cases may be stored during a performance.
7. Provide adequate dressing room for breaks.
8. Adhere carefully to required breaks.
9. Arrange for and provide food and beverage service if required by contract.
10. Assign a key contact person to serve as principal liaison to the leader of the musical group.
11. Locate adequate electric power.
12. Provide ample performance space as required by contract.
13. Adhere to schedule specified by contract.
14. Warn musicians if overtime is required.
15. Assist musicians with load-out/departure and offer thanks.

## Union Requirements

Whether contracting union musicians or other entertainers affiliated with labor unions, it is important that the event manager study union contracts carefully and comply with the responsibilities that apply to the event sponsor. For example, union musicians must be compensated separately if their performance is audio- or videotaped. Failure to provide additional compensation can result in severe penalties for the event organizer. In addition, union members must be given a certain number of breaks during each performance or be paid additionally for performing continuously without the prescribed number of breaks. Therefore, it is important that the event manager work closely with his or her music contractor when engaging union musicians. Certain union locals have established trust funds that will provide some money for musicians to perform for worthwhile causes at no cost to the sponsor. Check with your local American Federation of Musicians to determine if your event may qualify for this outstanding opportunity.

## Electronic Music

During the 1970s, as recording quality improved, disk jockeys became popular at many events. Indeed, in some situations electronic or recorded music is more appropriate than live music, for several reasons. First, electronic music may be easily controlled. Unlike live music, it may be faded, stopped, started, and refocused through different speakers. Second, it is usually less expensive than the engagement of live musicians. Finally, and perhaps more important, for those events with space restrictions, electronic music solves important logistical problems.

Today, disk jockeys provide not only music but entire party production services, including lights, effects such as fog, and interactive games. In addition to providing music for dancing and background atmosphere, electronic music may serve other purposes as well.

In lieu of using a live orchestra, many professional entertainers and industrial productions use prerecorded tracks to supplement their live performances. When using these systems it is critical that the event manager use redundant equipment in case of failure. In other situations, live musicians actually play along with the recorded tracks, creating a combination of live and recorded sound. In still other situations, the orchestra will perform some music live and pantomime to the prerecorded sound in other numbers.

As discussed earlier, when music is synchronized to video or film, separate rights must be negotiated and obtained. Usually, these rights include a clause limiting use to certain mediums and time periods. Ultimately, someone will pay for the use of privately owned music each time it is used. Therefore, the event manager must budget for this expense.

## Music Licensing

In the early 1990s, the two major music licensing firms in the United States decided to enforce their rights to collect fees from sponsors of meetings, conventions, and expositions as well as other events. Prior to this date the American Society of Composers, Authors, and Publishers (ASCAP) and its competitor, Broadcast Music Inc. (BMI), collected fees from restaurants, nightclubs, hotels, and even roller skating rinks. However, perhaps recognizing the enormous possibility for revenue from the meetings, convention, exposition, and events industry, these organizations made it clear that they planned to require sponsors of these events to pay for the use of live or recorded music they licensed.

The first organization to sign a separate agreement with ASCAP and BMI was the International Association for Exposition Management (IAEM), and soon the American Society of Association Executives (ASAE) convened a task force to study this issue. As a member of this task force I asked both organizations to assign the responsibility for payment to either the musical contractors or the professional producers of these events. Both organizations rejected this request, and today there continues to be acrimony regarding who pays what to whom and why.

The official sponsor or organizer of an event, the entity that bears the financial responsibility for the event, is responsible for obtaining a license for the use of protected music from either or both ASCAP or BMI or other rights-licensing organizations. The only exception to paying these fees is for events that are small gatherings of people who are known to you. This usually means social life-cycle events, such as weddings, bar and bas mitzvahs, birthday parties, and other events attended by family and friends.

ASCAP and BMI each have separate licensing agreements that require careful consideration by event managers. Both electronic and live music is covered in these agreements. According to ASCAP, the majority of popular music is licensed through its organization. However, most event managers obtain on behalf of their sponsors, agreements with both ASCAP and BMI for obvious reasons. Among these reasons is the problem associated with the live dance band and the guest who requests a tune from the band leader only to have the band leader decline because the rights are assigned to BMI and the license is with ASCAP.

For most events, the costs associated with music licensing are minimal, and the filing of the license agreement is merely another part of the long paper trail that is a natural part of event management. However, in the field of expositions, especially the larger ones that attract tens of thousands of persons, the costs can quickly mount. How are these fees assessed?

Both ASCAP and BMI assess fees based on the daily attendance at each event. The fees are, therefore, charged daily and are factored using separate formulas for recorded and live music. If both recorded (electronic) and live music are used, the costs are higher.

To enforce these licenses, both ASCAP and BMI use spotters who visit event venues randomly and investigate organizations that are using their licensed works unlawfully. The penalties for this illegal activity are substantial.

Recent court cases concerning expositions have somewhat weakened the position of ASCAP and BMI to require that sponsors of expositions assume responsibility for their individual exhibitors with regard to the use of music. However, ASAE continues to investigate the entire music licensing issue, with the major concerns relating to potential monopolies by ASCAP and BMI, which control the majority of all musical composition.

What music is covered? Literally any musical work licensed by ASCAP and BMI, and this includes "Happy Birthday." Even classical compositions may be covered if they have recently had a new, authored arrangement.

Alternatives to paying music licensing fees are limited. First, the event manager may, of course, elect to not use music at all. Second, the event manager may commission an original work of music and purchase the song or selections for use at the event. Third, the event manager may purchase commercial music produced by a private firm. Commercial music may be obtained from recording studios or other private organizations and usually includes some sound-alike tunes that are appropriate for use at awards programs and events other than those where popular tunes may be requested. Still larger organizations may negotiate individually with ASCAP, BMI, or other rights-licensing organizations and seek to create a separate agreement. In some cases, licensing fees may be waived. However, this is a rare occurrence.

In order to play, you must pay. Failing to do so may adversely affect your event sponsor and your reputation. Therefore, it is the responsibility of the event organizer to fully comprehend the requirements for music licensing and allow sufficient planning and coordination time to attend to these important details.

## ENTERTAINMENT OPTIONS

Table 8-7 presents a variety of resources for music and entertainment. However, now it is time to consider entertainment as a separate resource. Following are the most commonly used entertainers for live events:

- Acrobats
- Animal acts
- Balloon sculptors
- Ballroom dancers
- Bands
- Cancan dancers
- Caricaturists
- Carnival games
- Carnival rides
- Clowns
- Comedians
- Contortionists
- Dancers
- Disk jockey
- Dixieland band
- Escape artists
- Folk dancers
- Flamenco dancers
- Fortune tellers
- Horseshoes
- Humorists
- Hypnotists
- Illusionist
- Japanese Koto musicians
- Jazz band
- Jugglers
- Limbo dancers
- Magicians
- Marching band
- Marionettes
- Mentalists
- Mimes
- Modern dancers
- Oompah band
- Opera singers
- Organ grinders
- Organists
- Palm readers
- Pep band
- Puppeteers
- Rap artists
- Robots
- Singers
- Spaceship
- Sport games
- Square dancers
- Stilt walkers
- Tap dancers
- Tight-wire walkers
- Trapeze artists
- Ventriloquists

## Inexpensive Options for Live Entertainment

The term *amateur* implies one who has not yet begun to charge for his or her services. However, the term literally means "what one does for love." Every community is filled with hundreds and perhaps thousands of people whose avocational interests include performing. From barbershop and sweet Adeline singing groups to entire community orchestras, with a little detective work you can identify lots of entertainment at low cost.

When using amateur performers, make certain that you supplement their performance with those elements that will achieve the level of sophistication required for your event. This may mean the addition of professional costuming, lighting, or other elements. In some cases you will need to assign a professional producer to develop the amateur performer's act further to fit the needs of your event.

Amateur performers will require more time, in advance, immediately preceding, and during the production. Therefore, although you will save significant dollars by using nonprofessional performers, you must allocate additional resources and allow more time for this opportunity.

Professional performers may be obtained directly by contacting the performer or his or her manager, through agents, or by holding auditions. When contracting professional performers, first identify all the tasks you wish the performers to handle during your event. List these tasks and then prioritize them so that if you find you cannot afford everything you want, you will quickly be able to identify the most important elements that must be preserved.

One way to save lots of money when using professional performers is to *block book* the act or artists with other organizations. Block booking entails contacting other organizations in your city or area that may also be able to use the services of the act or artists. By offering performers a series of engagements closely connected by time and location, you may be able to save as much as 50 percent of the cost.

Another way to save is to work with acts that are routed annually through your area. Major music and entertainment groups that tour frequently may be able to add your date to their tour at nominal expense. To identify the routing for these groups, track them through publications such as *Variety, Billboard, Amusements Business,* and *Performance* magazine.

Often, performers will participate in additional events for the same basic fee. Therefore, determine well in advance what other activities, such as book signings, media conferences, and hospitality events, you want the performer to participate in and incorporate these into the agreement.

Travel expenses can often be a significant part of an act's cost, especially for those that require a large retinue of performers. To save money on travel, first determine if the act will travel coach versus first class. Next, contact the major airlines and seek sponsorships. Finally, although performers like to have flexibility, arrange the travel as far in advance as possible to take advantage of lower fares.

Whether contracting amateur or professional entertainers, the event manager is ultimately responsible for the final performance. To ensure the satisfaction of your client and guests, invite the client to attend the sound check or lighting rehearsal so that he or she can meet the performer in advance of the event. Furthermore, make certain that the performer mentions the name of the sponsoring organization during his or her act. To facilitate this, I write this information in large block letters on an index card and hand it to the performer during rehearsal. A second copy is given to the performer before he or she walks on stage for the final performance, in case the first copy was misplaced or lost.

Sourcing, contracting, and managing live entertainment carefully will further ensure the financial and artistic success of your event. When you make the decision to include live entertainment as an important element of your event, you have assumed a considerable and complex responsibility. Make certain that you devote the proper time and resources to fulfill this important responsibility effectively.

## Celebrities and Speakers

The professional speaker is a relatively new phenomenon. Only a few decades ago a speaker was a scholar, clergyman, or entertainer who received an honorarium. Today, the National Speakers Association in Tempe, Arizona, reports that its association represents over 3000 people who earn some or all of their living by giving speeches, conducting seminars, or presenting workshops. Their topics may range from anthropology to zero population growth. However, as members of this association, they are committed to improving their performance on the public platform.

Previously, the professional speaker was an accomplished person whose credits from another field produced demand for public appearances and speeches. Consequently, people such as film and television stars, politicians, and leading religious figures delivered speeches to their devotees. According to most futurists, continuing education will be the major growth industry of the new millennium. As a result, there is greater demand than ever before for sales trainers, motivators, and other experts in both content and performance.

When contracting a professional speaker for an event, first identify the needs, wants, and desires of your audience. Next, identify how you will use the speaker from a marketing perspective. Will the speaker's name or subject matter help increase attendance? Finally, and perhaps most important, determine what you expect to happen as a result of the speaker's appearance. The outcome of the event is paramount to every other decision.

Matching the speaker type to the outcome is the most important task facing the event manager who has decided to use a professional speaker. Although speaking fees may range from a few hundred dollars to tens of thousands of dollars, the most important consideration is what value will be derived from this investment. For example, if the sales trainer's fee is $10,000 and there is the potential of generating $100,000 in sales as a result of his or her appearance, the outcome is well worth the investment.

Table 8-10 lists the most popular types of speakers and the audience locations that may benefit from their content.

In addition to professional speakers, most organizations can provide you with outstanding lay speakers whose industry expertise qualifies them to speak to your audience. However, it is important to consider that the failure rate for lay speakers is extremely high. Therefore, plan to provide them with coaching or support equal to their stature on the program. For example, if the lay speaker is your plenary keynoter, you may wish to provide a speech coach to assist the speaker with his or her talk. However, if the speaker is presenting a workshop,

**Table 8-10**  Speakers and Their Audiences

| Speaker | Plenary or General Session | Luncheon | Spouse or Partner Program | Evening Banquet |
|---|---|---|---|---|
| Author | ✕ | ✕ | ✕ | ✕ |
| Celebrity | ✕ | | | |
| Futurist | ✕ | | | ✕ |
| News person | ✕ | ✕ | | ✕ |
| Humorist | | ✕ | ✕ | ✕ |
| Hypnotist | | | | ✕ |
| Magician | | ✕ | | ✕ |
| Motivational speaker | ✕ | ✕ | ✕ | ✕ |
| Psychologist | ✕ | ✕ | ✕ | |
| Sales trainer | ✕ | ✕ | | |
| Seminar leader | | ✕ | ✕ | |
| Workship leader | | ✕ | ✕ | |

it may be sufficient to work with him or her via telephone to fine tune his or her content and presentation techniques.

All speakers require an investment of time and time is money. To maximize your investment, communicate clearly and often to the speakers what you want them to accomplish. Determine if they can perform other functions at your event (such as serving as emcee for the banquet) and perhaps author an article in advance for your newsletter or magazine. Finally, ask if there is a discount for multiple engagements in one day or week. You may be able to save substantial dollars by block booking your speaker as you would an entertainer.

Finding the appropriate speaker involves finding the right resources, auditioning the speaker either in person or using videotape, and then confirming your assumption by speaking directly with the speaker. The following are possible resources for locating the appropriate speaker for your event.

- Agents and bureaus that represent professional speakers
- Churches
- Colleges and universities
- Corporate speakers bureaus
- Industry speakers
- National Speakers Association "Who's Who in Professional Speaking" (see Appendix 5)
- Synagogues
- Volunteer speakers bureaus

**Negotiating with Celebrities and Speakers**    Most personal appearances require some degree of negotiation prior to signing a contract. The success of the negotiation will ultimately depend on both parties' desire to complete the deal. The greater the desire from both parties, the more quickly the deal will come to fruition.

Remember that you are in search of a win–win–win outcome. In this scenario, the guest, the celebrity or speaker, and the event manager win because of hard work and persistence. Do your homework to determine the history of fees for celebrities or speakers. Also find out what other income they have generated from the sale of books, tapes, and other products. Next, explain to the celebrity, speaker, or their representative your desire to book the person. Describe in detail the role the celebrity or speaker will play at your event. Explain the outcome you desire from his or her involvement. Then, and only then, ask him or her to quote a fee. Tell the person that you would like to have a few days to consider this fee and then thank the person for his or her time. At this point two things may happen. First, the celebrity or speaker or representative may call you back and offer a better deal, or the person may accept another engagement.

To prevent the latter, you can ask the person to put a tentative hold on this date for a specified period of time. A tentative hold implies that the person will contact you prior to accepting another engagement on the same date as your engagement. If another client calls the celebrity or speaker, he or she will tell the other client that he or she is tentatively holding the date for you and then will check with you first before accepting the other engagement.

After a few days, call the speaker, celebrity, or representative back, and ask him or her to reserve a time to discuss the engagement with you when he or she will not be interrupted. During the discussion/negotiation, offer other incentives in lieu of the full fee. For example, if you are providing video magnification, you could offer to provide the speaker with a professional video of his or her speech (estimated value of $3,000) or you could allow the speaker to sell books, tapes, and other products in advance, during, and after the engagement. Another valuable concession is to offer the speaker your mailing list or offer to promote his or her services to your guests. After determining the value of these concessions, ask the speaker to work with you on the fee so that you may complete the contract. Once you make your request, ask for his or her reaction. Tell the speaker to take his or her time to think about your offer but set up a time frame to complete the agreement. When the person calls you back within the specified period of time, ask for his or her answer. Now you have the first news. It may not be the best news, but it is sufficient for you to provide a counteroffer. Make certain that you are prepared to make a counteroffer, such as shifting the date, shortening the responsibilities, or increasing the fee. When you use these techniques, step by step, you and your negotiating partners will move closer to closure.

If for any reason you fail to reach closure, always thank your negotiating partners for their time and interest and tell them you will recommend their services to others but are not able to work with them at this time. Do not be surprised if the other party calls you in a few days with a very attractive offer to use his or her services.

**Contracting with Celebrities and Speakers**  A letter of agreement, a contract, or a contract with rider must be prepared and/or executed by the event manager to engage a celebrity or speaker. In some cases, the celebrity or speaker will provide his or her own contract, and in others the event manager will be responsible for drafting the agreement.

The *rider* is the attachment on the contract that spells out the special conditions under which the celebrity or speaker will perform. The rider may specify lighting, sound, transportation, food, beverage, and other conditions. To make certain that you are providing only necessary items in the rider, contact previous clients and find out what they provided. In some instances, the rider may be used to incorporate everything, including the kitchen sink. You cannot allow the celebrity or entertainers to use the rider as a tool to abuse your limited resources.

## Trends in Music and Entertainment

The music and entertainment field has undergone tremendous change during the past several decades since Howard Lanin and Jack Morton first organized their orchestras. However, changes in the last decade of the twentieth century have far surpassed all of the previous changes.

During this decade many musicians have been replaced by electronic instruments. The electronic synthesizer, the musical instrument digital interface (MIDI), and the development of additional computer software for composing have revolutionized the music field. Entertainment too has experienced great change. Perhaps the most significant change is the incorporation of technology such as video and computers within the context of a live performance. This blend of live and electronic media is known as *interactive media*.

**Interactive Media**     The interactivity inherent in interactive media is supplied by online users, who provide both proactive and reactive techniques for event purposes. For example, a general session at an association meeting may require that a vote be taken by hundreds of delegates to settle an important issue. Instead of requiring a manual show of hands, a large screen flashes the command "Vote Now" and each delegate presses green for yes, red for no, or yellow for abstain. Their votes are recorded and tallied electronically, and in seconds the results are shown on the screen both numerically and graphically.

Another example of interactive media involves live performers interacting with electronic media. This engagement may be live action combined with pretape. In one such occasion I produced a film of a car racing down a track, and suddenly the car came to a screeching halt. The film was shown using rear production on the back of a screen. The screen had a small door cut into the exact location where the driver would later emerge. When the car stopped, the door opened and the president of the corporation walked right through the screen. This is but one of many examples of live and electronic media interacting with one another.

Perhaps in event management's education field, the potential for interactive media is greatest. Using technologies such as CD-ROM, modems, and powerful personal computers, tomorrow's event may look something like this. First, the guest enters the venue and is greeted by a robotic registrar who requests that the guest insert his or her credit card in the "Welcome" station. Upon reading the card the machine welcomes the guest to the meeting and issues a smart card that contains all critical information about the guest, including medical data, to ensure a safe and productive visit. The same card may be used to gain access to his or her sleeping room.

Next, the guest reports to his or her first meeting and uses his or her smart card to receive a complimentary computer disk from the Communications Center, a multistation machine that provides workspaces for telecommuting with the home office. The computer disk will be used to record the lecture to be delivered by the keynote speaker.

Finally, the guest is seated in an ergonomically correct chair, fastens his or her seat belt, and "experiences" the opening ceremony. His or her experience includes not only a visual and auditory presentation, but also such olfactory experiences as smell, taste, and touch. The visual images are delivered three-dimensionally as the guest wears glasses provided by a commercial sponsor. His or her chair moves hydraulically, controlled by dozens of levers and pumps as the visual images unfold on the 10-foot high-definition screen.

The audio portion of the program is enhanced with over 100 miniature speakers positioned throughout the venue to create a total surround-sound effect. At the conclusion of the opening ceremony the guest is invited to vote using his or her smart card to gain access to the ballot box. He or she will vote to select the topics the electronic speaker will address. Instead of merely receiving what the motivation speaker delivers, the guest will become an interactive learner, selecting those topics that are most useful at this time. Once the selection has been made, the prerecorded speaker will instantly process the choices and provide state-of-the-industry knowledge that the guest most requires.

Have no fear. All of this new technology will not decrease the demand for in-person events. Instead, it will create even greater demand as people meet online and seek other opportunities and venues within which to interact in person. For example, asynchronous discussion groups such as one offered by the George Washington University Event Management Distance Learning Program encourage electronic discussants to meet in person for further inquiry. People who participate in list servers or other bulletin board–type communications technologies will discover new organizations and new groups where they want to affiliate in person to improve their skills or simply enhance their lives. These new technologies will serve as the catalyst for bigger and better events.

**Virtual Reality**   Perhaps one of the most startling and certainly most effective interactive media innovations is virtual reality. Since the early 1990s it has been used for entertainment and education as well as sales. As an entertainment device, it can be used to engage the guest in navigating through a virtual game. Wearing a large helmet the guest sees a virtual environment. Using movements from his or her hand, the guest can run, jump, and even fly through outer space. In education, virtual reality may be used to train pilots (for whom the technology was first developed) and other technicians such as surgeons to perform complicated maneuvers without risking human life. In sales, virtual expositions are fast becoming effective methods for introducing buyers to the concept of virtual shopping.

**Teleconferencing: Up-Link, Down-Link, and Fiber Optic**   Increasingly, meetings and conferences as well as other event fields are being linked using both satellite and fiber optic technologies. In the case of video, the satellite technology is less expensive and more reliable. However, data transmission is more cost-effective via fiber optic technology. This may change as economies of scale prevail in the telecommunications industry.

When assessing the need for a teleconferencing or data transmission component for your event, first determine what resources currently exist and then review the added value of using these technologies. If the added value provides significant advantages, the added cost will be relative to the investment. However, some event managers succumb to these technologies as the latest bells and whistles to use without careful thought regarding the need, the added value, and the return on the investment.

To select a firm to assist you with teleconferencing, first discuss your needs with the venue directors to find out what vendors they recommend. The venue is usually your best reference because the recommended vendors have probably transmitted or received communications successfully for a previous organization. In some instances, modern conference and congress centers have this technology in place and can purvey this service directly through their staff audiovisual or communications personnel.

Next, meet with those who will provide this service or those who will submit bids. Provide them with a list of transmission dates, times, content, purpose, locations, and other pertinent data. Seek their recommendations for reducing costs and improving quality.

Finally, put a contingency plan in place. Weather, power blackouts, and other unforeseen problems can affect your transmission or reception. Determine in advance how you will cover for an interruption in the signal. In some instances, it may be appropriate to ask the audience to adjourn and reconvene. In other cases, you may wish to have a local moderator lead a discussion and generate additional questions to be used when the teleconference continues. Regardless of what you decide, it is important to have an alternative plan or program firmly in place.

**That's Edutainment!**    The term *edutainment* may have been coined during the early 1970s when a large number of corporations began to combine entertainment with education to motivate their human resources. Edutainment is simply the use of live or recorded entertainment to promote learning.

Edutainment productions may range from a group of actors that present short skits about sales, customer service, or negotiation to an elaborate interactive multimedia program involving video, slides, teleconference, and live entertainment to motivate customers to invest in a new product. When designing edutainment programs for your event, start with behavioral objectives in mind. Focus carefully on what you want to happen as a result of your edutainment activities.

Perhaps the best example of edutainment is the murder mystery phenomenon, which became very popular during the mid-1980s. During this period, largely due to popular television programs such as *Murder She Wrote,* murder mystery companies began popping up all over the United States as well as in other countries. In Harrogate, England, the Royal Swan Hotel (where Agatha Christie was found mysteriously after having been missing for several days) stages a popular murder mystery weekend. During the opening reception the guests witness a murder. The next morning a real coroner/medical examiner delivers the autopsy results as the "detectives" take exhaustive notes. By Sunday evening the mystery is solved and everyone goes home satisfied that they participated in finding the murderer.

Corporations and associations in the United States as well as other organizations may use the murder mystery premise as a way of delivering important messages about sales, customer relations, membership development, ethics, and other principles. To use this medium as your message, first interview several murder mystery directors and select the one who will carefully customize his or her script to meet your goals and objectives. Next, make certain that you see his or her troupe in performance before you make engagement plans. While a videotape is a convenient audition device, it is far better to see them in person and determine how they handle the important audience-participation segments of their production.

Whether you use a murder mystery, a musical production, or a tightly scripted three-act play, it is critical that the message be simple, repeated, and well produced. Too often, event managers develop a complex message that requires too much explanation to make sense to the guests. In other instances, the message is used once and never repeated. This denies the guests the opportunity to review and have the message reinforced. Retention requires repetition. Finally, regardless of what budget is assigned to this production, make certain that it is produced with high-quality ingredients. The message will suffer if the packaging is not of sufficient quality.

# The Event Manager as Producer

The modern event manager is both consultant and producer. He or she not only must research, design, and plan, but also must coordinate all the event elements, as a producer does with a play, film, television show, or other theatrical presentation. While the music and entertainment will ultimately reflect the tastes of your clients and their guests, you must never allow your own taste to be compromised. Remember that your signature is part and parcel of every production. Your next opportunity to produce an event is tied directly to the one you produce today. Quality, and only quality, must prevail if you are to have the opportunity to produce future events. Therefore, see every event management opportunity as your personal and professional challenge to produce the very finest music and entertainment with the time and logistical and financial resources that may be allocated.

# Career Advancement Connections

## GLOBAL CONNECTION

Do your homework to be certain that you are aware of the subtle but important language and cultural differences with conducting on-site management. For example, in the United States, if you request shag, the vendor will deliver carpeting. However, in Great Britain, the vendor may give you a curious look because the term *shag* refers to sexual favors. Furthermore, body language had significant cultural implications. In North America the index finger curled to join the thumb signifies that everything at your event is "OK." However, in Brazil, this gesture is an insult that could erupt into a fistfight. Therefore, it is important that you review books such as *Gestures: The Do's and Taboos of Body Language Around the World,* by Roger E. Axtell (New York: Wiley, 1990).

## TECHNOLOGY CONNECTION

Invest in radios (walkie-talkies), cell phones, pagers, clear-com headsets, and other forms of communication to ensure that you are connected to all critical stakeholders during an event. Assign appropriate codes for emergencies such as first aid, evacuation, criminal activity, and other issues that may develop during the event. Test all communications equipment carefully prior to the start of the event to ensure stability. If you are using simultaneous interpretation systems, rehearse with speakers and interpreters to ensure that the rate, language ability, and other critical factors are synchronized to provide consistently excellent communications for your participants.

## RESOURCE CONNECTION

Read the *Complete Guide to Meeting and Event Coordination* by Catherine Price (1998, The George Washington University) see also the *CIC Manual and Glossary of Terms* (2000, Connection Industry Council) for additional techniques to improve on-site operations.

## LEARNING CONNECTION

Create a sample production schedule for your event. Once you have completed the production schedule, adjust the times by 15 minutes to a lot for last-minute changes. How will this affect the financial, operational, and other outcomes of your event. Now you must also teleconference or videoconference this event to another country. How will the production schedule be affected by the different time zones?

---

**Facing Page**
Sport events such as the East Coast Invitational must accommodate a wide range of particpants and spectators with special needs. *Photograph courtesy of Monica Vidal.*

# CHAPTER 9

# Accommodating
# Special Needs

**IN THIS CHAPTER YOU WILL LEARN HOW TO:**

- Arrange and organize tours
- Develop special events within events
- Organize and conduct accompanying persons programs
- Comply with the Americans with Disabilities Act

A good host is sensitive to the needs of *all* of his or her guests. This sensitivity includes the need to anticipate and recognize special needs. Some guests require greater accommodation than others, however, the professional event manager provides equal accommodation to all guests when they arrange and organize tours.

# Arranging and Organizing Tours

Many events use tours and other off-site visits to expand the educational value of the program. Other events regularly incorporate tours of the destination and its attractions to provide guests with added value. Finally, some event organizers incorporate tours to offer diversions for accompanying persons such as spouses, partners, friends, or young people attending with their parents. Regardless of the reason, increasingly, the arrangement and organization of tours is a critical component of most conferences, conventions, reunions, and even weddings.

There are three steps to consider when planning and coordinating tours for your event:

1. You must conduct an audit of the destination to determine if there are attractions or activities that are of interest to your guests. You can obtain this information from the local convention and visitors' association or from the chamber of commerce. Make certain that you ask the providers of this information what programs are most appropriate for specific market segments (females, males, children, mature guests, etc.).

2. Use this research to begin to assess the interest levels of your prospective guests with a brief survey of their interests. If you can match their strong interests with the best attractions and activities in the destination, you are well on your way to finding a winning combination guaranteed to increase attendance and produce excellent quality reviews.

3. Find a price point that will be acceptable to your guests and perhaps provide excess revenues for your organization. To do this you will need to obtain bids from local providers. In many destinations a for-profit or-

ganization known as a *destination management company* (DMC) provides tour services. These services are generally priced on a per person basis and require a minimum number of participants to operate the program successfully.

In addition to tours, the DMC can provide services such as planning and coordinating local transportation, receptions, parties, and other events within your large event, as well as a wide range of other services. The DMC field has grown in sophistication during the last decade. Production Group International (PGI) is the largest operator of destination management companies in the United States, with offices in most major U.S. convention cities. In addition to PGI, there are dozens of independent DMC companies in both large and midsized cities in the United States and other countries.

Outside the United States, the term *professional congress organizer* (PCO) is often used to refer to destination management companies (DMCs). The PCO generally provides an even greater range of services than the DMC. In addition to tours and events, the PCO may provide travel bookings, marketing of the event, and registration services, among many other services.

Two organizations represent the top DMCs and PCO organizations. In the United States, the Association of Destination Management Executives (ADME) represents the leading destination management companies, and in Europe, the International Association of Professional Congress Organizers (IAPCO) represents the most respected PCO firms. Both organizations are listed in Appendix 1.

# Developing Special Events within Events

The event management professional is often required to organize numerous individual events with a larger special event. In fact, this is so prevalent that the certified special events professional programs requires that candidates understand and be able to coordinate accompanying person events, tours, and other auxiliary programs related to special event management. The following are typical events that often help the form overall the context of a larger special event.

- Accompanying person programs
- Arts and crafts displays and/or sales
- Auctions (live and silent)
- Book signings
- Carnivals
- Children's activities
- Coffeehouse
- Cyber café areas
- Dance lessons or parties

- Educational programs
- Etiquette seminars
- Exhibitions
- Fashion shows
- Festivals
- Films
- Formal dinners
- Golf tournaments
- Hospitality rooms
- Hot-air ballooning

- Museum tours
- Sport activities or programs
- Team-building activities
- Tennis tournaments
- Tours (city, scenic, historic, cultural)
- Youth programs
- Zoological programs and tours

The event management professional must assess through research how the internal or external events will support the overall goals and objectives of the total event. These events should be seen as the frame of a large umbrella. Each spoke or event must carefully support the individual objectives of the overall event. If any one event is poorly planned or weakly coordinated, the entire structure may weaken. Therefore, the event manager should conduct an audit of typical event guests, as well as those who are atypical and nonattendees, to determine the interest, needs, wants, and desires. These data can be very helpful in determining which events to offer and during which times they will be most popular.

Once the audit is completed, the event manager will usually contact a third party, such as an entertainment, production, or other professional to obtain proposals to present the type of event or attraction that is required. Make certain that you encourage the proposers to use their creativity to develop your event ideas further. For example, a game show requested by a major corporation became an "event" when the game company supplier suggested a hostess who was a Vanna White lookalike and a set that reflected the popular game show, *Wheel of Fortune*. The creativity of others can quickly embellish your event design and bring added value without additional cost.

The final consideration when selecting the events that will comprise your larger event is to confirm the reliability of the vendors. Too often, event organizations driven by committees will develop extraordinary ideas with ordinary budgets and resources. It is much better to select those event elements that will bring high quality and consistent excellence to your event than to stretch the event to the breaking point. To confirm the reliability of individual vendors it is best to inspect the event during operation before a similar group of guests or to seek references from organizers of events that are similar to the one you are producing.

# Organizing and Conducting Spouse and Partner Programs

One of the key competencies in the coordination knowledge domain of the certified special events professional program is the organization and coordination of spouse and partner programs. The term *spouse* is actually somewhat antiquated and has been replaced with the term *accompanying person* to reflect the broader spectrum of persons who are attending an event with the invited guest. The actual taxonomy of the guest list is as follows:

1. Delegate or principal invitee or guest
2. Guest of principal invitee or accompanying person
3. Observer

The accompanying person may have a wide range of interests that must be satisfied during the overall event experience. Typically, the accompanying person will be invited to all social events with the principal invitee, delegate, or guest. In addition, special programming as discussed above may be organized to provide diversions while the delegate, principal invitee, or guest is involved in official functions such as education, governance (debate, discussion, elections), or other similar activities that generally are not of interest to the accompanying person.

The event manager must strike a balance between diverting the accompanying person and totally disengaging him or her from the basic goals and objectives of the overall event. To ensure that the accompanying person is fully engaged and recognized, the person should be identified through credentials as a guest, accompanying person, or observer. In addition, an orientation program should be organized at the beginning of a conference or other multiday event to help accompanying persons to understand the opportunities available during the larger event as well as to make them feel welcome and answer any pertinent questions.

The accompanying person very often influences the principal guest or delegate to return to an event year after year, so it is critically important that the person has an excellent experience that is equal although different from that of the person he or she is accompanying. To monitor the experience it is important that accompanying persons be surveyed or monitored through a focus group to thoroughly analyze their event experience, to allow you to improve your practice continually in the future.

# Complying with the Americans with Disabilities Act

It is projected that the number of persons in North America with disabilities will grow exponentially in the next two dozen years as the baby boomers begin to show the natural signs of the aging process. As a result, the large number of persons with visual, auditory, and physical disabilities will significantly affect the research, planning, design, and coordination phases of twenty-first-century event management.

During the research phase the event manager must assess the types of disabilities that are most likely to be reflected by event participants. These important data may be obtained through historical information or through a survey of potential guests. Research will include learning about individual disabilities in order to best prepare and serve the population that will be attending your event.

The design phase enables the event manager to work closely with the disabled community to determine the services and accommodations that must be implemented to ensure the comfort and satisfaction of all guests. During the design phase many creative solutions may be suggested by members of the disabled population to help the event organizer satisfy their needs with little or no additional investment.

During the planning and coordination phases the event manager fine tunes the recommendations proposed by the disabled community and works with event vendors and staff to implement the best ideas to achieve the best outcomes for the overall event. These two phases should include the identification of contingency plans for serving disabled individuals who were not identified previously but must be accommodated once they arrive at the event.

# Providing for Special Needs of Your Guests

Once you have gathered all the quantitative data from the site inspection, it is time to analyze your findings and determine what implications emerge for your event environment design. Most important considerations include the legal, regulatory, and risk management issues that are uncovered during site inspection.

If the venue is not in full compliance with the Americans with Disabilities Act, you may need to make certain modifications in your design. For example, a large quasi-government corporation asked me to create a tropical theme, including a small bridge at the entrance where guests would stroll over a pond containing live goldfish. In creating this design, we factored in the need to provide full and equal access for disabled guests and ramped both ends of the bridge to satisfy this need.

According to Ross Weiland, writing in the January 1995 issue of *Successful Meetings* magazine, the event industry must be more sensitive to the rights of the disabled. It is not only the moral and ethical importance that must be considered—it is a matter of federal law.

The statute states:

> *Title III-Sec. 302 a) General rule. No individual shall be discriminated against on the basis of disability in the full and equal enjoyment of the goods, services, facilities, privileges, advantages, or accommodations of any place of public accommodation.*

As a result of this historic legislation, wheelchair ramps, braille menus and signs, sign language interpreters, and other elements have become commonplace at events. Event managers are responsible for complying with this law.

Following is a comprehensive checklist for incorporating the Americans with Disabilities Act into an event environmental design.

1. Survey your guests in advance of the event to determine what accommodations will be required.
2. Include the following language on all brochures or other offerings: "If you require special accommodations, please describe below."
3. Survey the venue to determine what gaps must be closed prior to your event.
4. Establish wheelchair seating positions.
5. Maintain a clear line of sight for guests who will be using sign language interpreters.
6. Work with disabled speakers to provide access to the podium.
7. Provide audiotranscription services of the stage action for the visually disabled.
8. Select venues with, or provide handrails for, guests with physical infirmities.
9. Provide tables with appropriate height for wheelchair users.
10. Contact the U.S. Department of Justice if you have additional questions about designing an event environment that meets compliance regulations. Telephone the Americans with Disabilities Act information line at (800) 514-0301.
11. Train your staff to better meet the needs of people with disabilities.

After seeking written feedback from your prospective guests regarding their special needs, it is important to take one additional step to meet their expectations fully. You may wish to invite people with special needs to conduct their own site inspection of your proposed venue and become part of the planning team. People in wheelchairs, older guests with limited mobility, and the visually and hearing impaired can provide you with important information to improve a total event environment. Local organizations such as Easter Seals or the Muscular Dystrophy Association can refer you to people who will volunteer to offer their advice and counsel during the planning stage. Listen carefully to their suggestions and incorporate where feasible. Your goal is to produce an event environment that is accessible and effective for everyone.

Every guest has special needs. Abraham Maslow recognized these needs with his hierarchy of needs, which ranged from basic needs to ephemeral requirements, including the need to be loved. The professional event manager may not be able to forecast or satisfy every need their guests bring to an event. However, guests must sense that the event manager or host is genuinely concerned with their welfare and will work diligently to attempt to anticipate, identify, and satisfy their needs to provide them with a total high-quality event experience. When this occurs, the guest experience rises to a heightened level, as defined by Maslow. When guests begin to feel appreciated or even loved, this ultimately defines in an intangible but powerful way their enduring memories or experiences from your event.

# Career Advancement Connections

### GLOBAL CONNECTION

Working with multicultural organizations can be challenging unless the event management professional does his or her homework. For example, many events held outside the United States suggest that guests wear formal attire or national dress or costume to a formal dinner. It is appropriate to further define national costume as "that which reflects the culture, ethnicity, or national pride of the country where the guest has sworn national allegiance."

### TECHNOLOGY CONNECTION

The Internet has numerous sites that provide valuable information concerning disabilities as well as the Americans with Disabilities Act. The U.S. Department of Justice administers the act and may be contacted at *www.usdoj.gov*.

### RESOURCE CONNECTION

Numerous resources are available to assist event managers with organizing events within events. The Resort and Commercial Recreation Association is listed in Appendix 1 and provides courses and instructional materials for the organization of leisure and recreation activities. In addition, organizations such as the American Society of Association Executives (see Appendix 1) information central provide numerous educational programs and resources regarding programs for accompanying persons.

### LEARNING CONNECTION

To improve your professional event management, practice completing the following exercise. Describe how you will provide relevant and appropriate programming for each of the following groups who will be accompanying your guests to a three-day medical conference: youth, young children, heterosexual, and gay and lesbian partners. Twenty-five percent of your delegates have visual, auditory, or physical mobility disabilities. Describe how you will accommodate these delegates. Finally, describe how you will evaluate your performance for serving each of these populations to ensure continual quality improvement at your event.

# Event Marketing

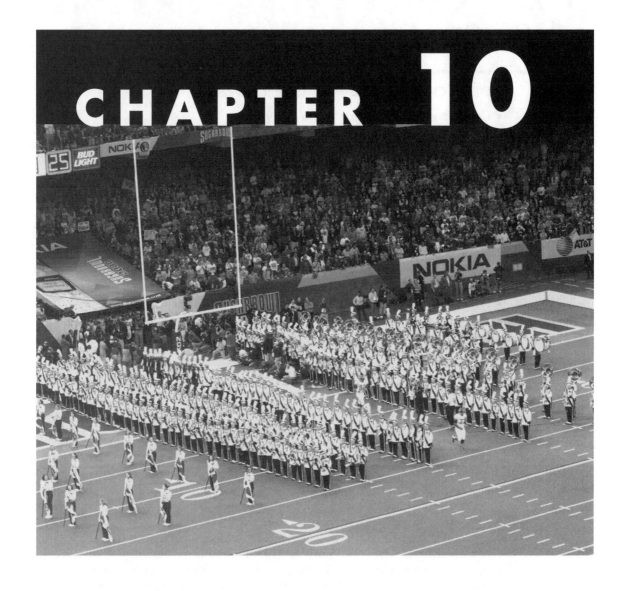

# CHAPTER 10

# Advertising, Public Relations, Promotions, and Sponsorship

**IN THIS CHAPTER YOU WILL LEARN HOW TO:**

- Conduct event marketing research
- Develop an integrated marketing program
- Use the five P's of event marketing
- Incorporate both internal and external marketing programs
- Develop retail marketing events
- Promote fairs and festivals
- Launch new products
- Develop, design, and execute print, electronic, and other advertising programs
- Develop comprehensive public relations programs
- Organize street promotions and creative stunts
- Develop and manage effective sponsorship programs
- Create and conduct successful cause event-related marketing programs
- Integrate the Internet into the event marketing strategy
- Comprehensively evaluate event marketing programs and measure return on event (ROE)

The international television program, *Who Wants to Be a Millionaire* was described in the media as *event television* and the Broadway musical version of *Saturday Night Fever* was labeled *event theater* by the *Wall Street Journal* because the audience is encouraged to dance in the aisles at the conclusion of each show. It seems that everywhere you look someone is marketing events or events are being used to market products and services.

The first step in the event management process, research, is mirrored in the marketing process. Without valid and reliable research, you may waste scarce time and resources. Therefore, the first step in the event marketing process must be careful, thoughtful, and comprehensive research. The outcome of this research must result in the identification of measurable goals and objectives for your event marketing campaign or program.

A campaign is usually an extended series of marketing activities designed to market an event, cause, product, or service, whereas a program may include many campaigns targeted at a wide variety of different market segments. For example, regional shopping centers design and implement annual marketing programs that may include a separate campaign for each of the four seasons or for specific events such as the expansion of the center or introduction of a new major anchor store.

Regardless of whether you are designing a campaign or an entire program of marketing activities, the resources and channels available to you are expanding rapidly. However, with this expansion there is also greater competition than ever before. This growth and competition are well documented.

*Advertising Age,* the weekly tabloid that many in advertising consider the bible of their profession, has added a new feature to its editorial section in addition to the traditional mix of advertising, public relations, and promotions. The new section is entitled "Events and Promotions." According to an editorial in *Advertising Age,* the editors have determined that events are a critical component of marketing.

Traditionally, marketing students have recognized that product, promotion, price, public relations, and location, or place, are critical components in the marketing process. Each of these five P's of marketing is a catalyst for sales. Although marketing has become more sophisticated in the twentieth century, savvy event marketers recognize that ultimately marketing is only a three-syllable word for sales.

The founder of *Parade* magazine, Red Motley, once wrote: "Nothing really happens until someone sells something." According to some marketing experts, the most efficient and cost-effective way to make sales is through events. Whether you are selling a product, service, idea, or cause, an event allows you to use all of the senses to persuade the prospect to make an investment. The components of product, promotion, price, public relations, and place directly influence the desire and decision to make this investment. However, it is important to remember that a festival, fair, wedding, meeting, exposition, or other event is a legitimate product that also must be developed and sold.

# Product

Successful salespeople have both expert product knowledge and effective sales skills. Expert product knowledge is essential in today's competitive environment. The expertise the salesperson demonstrates regarding the sponsorship package or other event component will differentiate this person from the competition. More important than sales skills, demonstrated product expertise shows the client that he or she is making a purchase that has added value and helps to develop confidence as well as long-term loyalty.

Every event product combines history, quality, and value to produce a unique program. Even new events may draw from the experience or history of the organizers. This demonstration of consistent capability to produce similar events will influence prospective clients to recognize the overall quality of the event organization. Finally, every event product must convey not only perceived value, such as dollar-for-dollar worth but also added value. The concept of added value is perhaps best described with the Cajun word *lagniappe.* This term literally means "everything one deserves and a little bit more." The little bit more may mean providing the client with the home telephone number of the key contact person, developing a unique approach to achieving the event objectives, or perhaps simply spending additional time with the client to better understand his or her needs.

# Promotion

You may have the best-quality event product, but unless you have a strategic plan for promoting this product, it will remain the best kept secret in the world. Even large, well-known megaevents such as the Super Bowl, Rose Parade, and Olympic Games require well-developed promotion strategies to achieve the success they require.

Following is a systematic checklist to assist you with identifying and budgeting for your event promotion.

1. Identify all event elements that require promotion from the proposal through the final evaluation.
2. Develop strategies for allocating scarce event promotion resources with efficient methods.
3. Identify promotion partners to share costs.
4. Target your promotion carefully to those market segments that will support your event.
5. Measure and analyze your promotion efforts throughout the campaign to make corrections as required.

The promotion strategy you identify for your event requires a careful study of past or comparable efforts, expert guidance from people who have specific expertise in this field, and most important, setting benchmarks for specific measurement of your individual promotion activities.

There are a variety of ways to measure promotion efforts. First, you may measure awareness by your target market. Anticipation of the event may be tantamount to ultimate participation. Next, you may measure actual attendance and the resulting investment. Finally, you may measure the postevent attitudes of the event promotional activity. Did the promotions you designed persuade the participants or guests to attend the event?

Promotion is the engine that drives the awareness of your event by others. Throughout event history, legendary promoters such as Bill Veck, Joe Engel, and perhaps most important, P.T. Barnum realized that you must shamelessly promote your event product to attract the attention of the public.

Veck did this in major league baseball by hiring midgets as players. At the time of this stunt, there was no height requirement, and Veck took advantage of this oversight to promote his Chicago team. Engel, a minor league baseball promoter in Chattanooga, Tennessee, staged a fake elephant hunt on the baseball diamond to generate capacity attendance for his losing team. And, of course, P.T. Barnum continually amused the public with his legendary promotions, such as the smallest man (Tom Thumb) and the biggest mammal (Jumbo).

Most event marketers use a variety of media to promote their products. However, it is essential that event managers carefully select those media outlets that will precisely target the market segments that are appropriate for their events. Targeting promotion strategies is essential to ensure the alignment of the event's attributes with the needs, wants, and desires of potential attendees.

# Price

Market research will help you determine price. Part of this market research will include conducting a competitive analysis study of other organizations offering similar event products. You may initially believe that your product is uniquely different from every other event. However, when you interview potential ticket buyers or guests you may be surprised to learn that they consider your event similar to many others. Therefore, you must carefully list all competing events and the prices being charged to help you determine the appropriate price for your event.

Typically, two factors determine price. First, the event manager must determine the financial philosophy of the event. If the event is a not-for-profit venture, the organization may not be concerned with a large commercial yield from the event. Instead, the philosophical purpose of the event may be to generate overall awareness and support. However, if the event is a commercial venture, the goal is probably to generate the greatest potential net profit. Once the philosophy is clear, the event manager will be able to determine price. The price must reflect the cost of all goods and services required to produce the event plus a margin of profit or retained earnings.

The second factor is the perceived competition from similar events. If your event ticket costs $100 and does not offer the same *perceived value* as a similar event selling for $50, your prospective guests are more likely to select the latter event. Therefore, you must be price-competitive. Becoming price-competitive does not mean lowering your ticket price. Rather, it may require raising the perception of value (as discussed earlier) to justify the slightly higher price.

These two factors—the cost of doing business and the marketplace competition—certainly influence price. A third area that may also influence price is the general economic conditions, not only in your area, but also the region, your country, and increasingly, the world. During times of recession, some events with lower ticket prices will flourish while other upscale-event products may not be as successful. Keep a close eye on market economic indicators to make certain that your price matches the purchasing power of your target market.

# Public Relations

Advertising is what *you* say about your event, whereas public relations is what *others* (or that perception) are saying about your event. Since many events require a second-party endorsement or even review to encourage people to attend, public relations is significantly more valuable and effective than traditional advertising.

In the 1930s and 1940s public relations consisted primarily of press agents who worked diligently to convince the print media to devote editorial space to their clients. With the influence of leaders such as Edward Bernays, the public relations effort soon became more complex and respected. Bernays recognized the psychological factors that govern a person's decision-making ability. Therefore, he advocated that public relations professionals first engage in research, including focus groups, to determine the values, attitudes, and lifestyles of their target markets and carefully match their messages to these important factors.

Today, in many event marketing campaigns, public relations is at least equal to and in many cases, even more important than traditional advertising. However, public relations involves much more than merely grinding out a short press release.

The effective event public relations campaign will involve research with event consumers as well as the media; the development of collateral materials such as media kits, fact sheets, and other tangibles; the organization and implementation of media conferences; the development of a speaker's bureau; and on-site media relations assistance at the event.

Event public relations helps create the overall impression that others will develop about your event. In that regard it is significantly more valuable than advertising because it implies greater credibility. For that reason the Public Relations Society of America, an organization that includes membership of professionals in the public relations profession, states that public relations exposure is more valuable financially than advertising. For example:

- Half-page newspaper advertisement

$$\text{cost} = \$5000$$

- Editorial about your event in the same space as the advertisement

value = $15,000 to $35,000 (3 to 7 times more) depending upon placement

Use the power of public relations to beat the drum loudly for your event. Carefully select those public relations tools that will most effectively and cost-efficiently help you inform and persuade others to support your event.

# Place

In real estate, location is everything. In event marketing, distribution of your product may be everything as well. The location of your event often determines the channels of distribution.

If your event is located in a rural area, not only may it be difficult to promote the event due to limited media resources, but it may also be difficult for your target market to make the purchase due to logistical restraints. However, in a study I conducted in 1994, I discovered that rural events are growing in number and size in the United States. Therefore, despite these limitations, demand due to lack of competition and need for tourism dollars has overcome these obstacles.

The place where you locate your event ultimately will determine the marketing efforts you must exude to drive sales. For example, it has been shown that those events that are close to inexpensive, safe public transportation or those events that feature closed-in reasonably priced parking will attract more guests than those that do not offer these amenities. Furthermore, those events that are connected to other nearby attractions or infrastructures (such as shopping malls) may also draw more attendees due to the time efficiency of the destination. For upscale events, the addition of valet parking may improve the chances of attracting guests to a new or nontraditional location.

The event manager must seriously consider place when designing the marketing program for the event. Place not only implies the taste or style of the event, it also, in large part, defines the type of person that will be persuaded to invest in the event. In this regard, the event marketer must determine the place in the early stages through research and design. This is the perfect time to convene a focus group or conduct a survey to determine who is likely to attend your event when they are given a variety of location choices. Making certain you have thoughtfully analyzed this important issue will save you time and money throughout the entire event marketing process.

# Internal versus External Event Marketing

Event managers may use an event or a series of events as one of the marketing methods to promote external events, products or services such as shopping malls, tourism destinations, or attractions (such as amusement parks or zoos), or any entity that is appropriately promoted through events.

However, in most cases, event managers use marketing forces such as advertising, public relations, promotion, advertising specialties, stunts, and other techniques to promote individual events. These traditional marketing techniques should be used to inform, attract, persuade, sustain, and retain potential customers for your event.

Increasingly, a blend of internal and external event marketing is being utilized to promote events. In some cases, event managers use miniature events as a means of promoting major events. The Sydney Organizing Committee for the Olympic Games (SOCO) staged a major fireworks display to celebrate the decision by the International Olympic Committee to stage the games in Sydney, Australia. The fireworks spectacular began the marketing process of identifying Sydney as the city of the next Olympic games. Smaller events, such as a torch run, are used throughout the days preceding the opening ceremonies to promote this event.

On a smaller scale, fundraising organizations such as the National Symphony Orchestra use smaller focus-type events (e.g., receptions) to promote larger events (e.g., the Symphony Ball or the annual Designer's Show House). These ancillary events serve to promote the larger event to different market segments and maintain excitement about the overall event product.

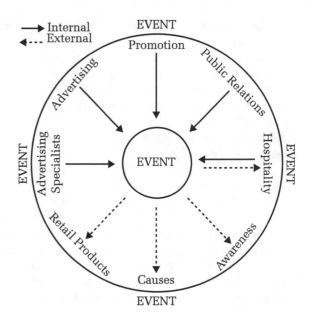

**Figure 10-1**
Internal and External Event
Marketing Model

Therefore, both internal and external event marketing are important strategies for your event. Figure 10-1 depicts how this process is used to market your event product. Since resources are always limited for marketing it is important to select those internal or external elements that will most effectively reach and influence your target market.

# External Event Marketing

Using events to market products and services is increasing. As mentioned earlier, *Advertising Age* has declared that events are now critical in the total marketing effort. Therefore, although using an event marketing strategy may be more costly due to the additional labor required, it must be considered seriously when promoting products and services.

## RETAIL EVENTS

Our firm began by producing fashion shows, petting zoos, Santa Claus appearances, and other retail events. During the mid-to-late 1970s, regional mega-shopping centers opened throughout the United States, and mall developers such as the Rouse Company and Homart recognized that they were the new main streets of America. To attract the appropriate target market, a series of events was developed and implemented to position the shopping mall as an attraction.

Using the fashion show as one example, the shopping mall management cold satisfy the needs of both its internal and external customers. First, the store owners and managers could showcase their goods and services to a highly targeted audience in a cost-effective manner. Second, the external customer—the shopper himself or herself—would be held captive during the 20- to 30-minute production and then directed to visit each store for special discounts during the time immediately following the show. According to the International Council of Shopping Centers, the trade association that educates and promotes the shopping center industry, many marketing directors are earning the Certified Marketing Director (CMD) designation to develop specialized knowledge of this increasingly complex and competitive profession.

Table 10-1 lists several retail events that have proven successful and the market to whom they are best targeted. You will note that most of these events target women, as historically women have comprised the largest customer bases for retail businesses. However, these demographics are shifting as two-income families have emerged in the United States, and now both men and women increasingly share the responsibilities and pleasures of shopping. Therefore, successful event managers will look for events that they may use to develop other markets with disposable income such as men, teenage boys, and even senior citizens.

**Table 10-1**  Retail Events and Their Target Markets

| Event | Target Market |
| --- | --- |
| Arts and crafts shows | Women and senior citizens |
| Children's entertainer | Young children |
| Circus and petting zoo | Young families |
| Computer show | Men |
| Cooking demonstration/ tasting | Women |
| Fashion show | Women and teenage girls |
| Fine art show | Women and men |
| Health fair | Senior citizens |
| Magician | Young boys |
| Model railroad show | Young boys and men |
| Puppeteer | Young children |
| Soap opera star appearance | Women and teenage girls |
| Sport celebrity appearance | Men and boys |
| Sport memorabilia festival | Men and teenage boys |

Timing is everything when developing and producing the retail event. To allow the consumer to devote as much time as possible to spending money, the live event should be brief in duration (under 20 minutes) and offered frequently throughout the day to allow a variety of customers to experience the event activity. Obviously, due to the increase in working adults, the middle-of-the-week-day should be avoided so that the most consumers can witness the event. Finally, many retail events are tied directly to paydays. Find out what the pay period is from large organizations such as factories, government, or other sources of large numbers of consumers and then time your event to coincide with this window of time when there will be a large amount of expendable income available.

## FAIRS AND FESTIVALS

Fairs, festivals, and other public events may also serve as temporary retail locations (TRLs). These events often contract space to vendors, craftspeople, and others to demonstrate and sell their products and services. However, like their permanent retail counterparts, to be successful they must be marketed aggressively through both internal and external event marketing efforts.

A media preview event is an excellent way to inform the media about the size, scope, and excitement being offered at your fair or festival. Designing a ribbon-cutting event featuring prominent local citizens along with celebrities is an important way to announce "open for business." Finally, a series of ongoing ancillary events held at other public venues such as sporting event halftime shows is an important form of external marketing to introduce and remind other market segments of your event's importance.

## LAUNCHING NEW PRODUCTS

Perhaps one of the most important activities within the event marketing area is that of launching new products developed by corporations. Each year in the United States and other countries billions of dollars are invested in advertising to promote new products. Before these products are introduced to the general public, they are usually showcased before retailers or dealers. An event such as the launch of a new automobile serves several constituent groups. First, the trade media may be invited to promote the product to others. Second, the general media (newspapers, radio, and television) may be invited to help make the general public aware of the new product benefits and features. Finally, and perhaps most important, the product launch must target those people who will either sell the item to others or purchase it themselves.

The organization and presentation of the product launch event may be one of the most important steps in the overall marketing effort. Whether introducing software such as Windows '95 or an attraction such as the Trump Taj Mahal Resort and Casino, great thought must be given to the goals, objectives, and desired outcomes to create a successful event.

Following is a checklist for developing and producing consistently successful product launch events.

1. Determine the goals and objectives of the product launch event.
2. Identify the target market(s).
3. Coordinate planning with sales promotion, public relations, human resource development, and other critical departments.
4. Conduct research to refine your general production plans.
5. Use creativity to introduce your product in a nontraditional yet attractive manner.
6. Use creativity to unveil a new product.
7. Identify who will speak, for what length of time, and why.
8. Identify ways to reach those who could not attend the event (such as through a video program or satellite presentation).
9. Measure and analyze your results by how sales are affected.
10. Develop opportunities for added value the next time you produce a similar event.

Sometimes lavish plans for product launch events have been foiled by circumstances beyond the control of the event manager. However, most circumstances can be controlled easily through close communication with other parties. Make certain that you contact the corporate communications or public relations department early in the process to identify their goals and incorporate them into your plans. Next, and equally important, make certain that the vice-president or director of sales is closely involved in your planning, as your activities will directly affect his or her efforts. Finally, ensure that senior management, including the chief executive and operating officers, understands, supports, and is committed to your success. However, despite all this careful interaction with other stakeholders, sometimes old Murphy raises his devilish head.

# Event Promotion Techniques

There are five typical or traditional techniques used to promote events. These techniques include advertising, public relations, cross promotions, street promotions, and stunts. Some events use only one of these techniques; others may use all of them to ensure that their message is received and acted upon by their target market.

## ADVERTISING

Advertising includes print and electronic media, transportation media (such as bus and rail), advertising specialties (calendars, key rings, coffee mugs, and other products), and outdoor media (billboards). Larger events may use many of these media resources, while smaller events may carefully target their message to one or two media.

Print advertising is not limited to magazines and newspapers. It may also include membership directories, inserts in local newspapers, flyers (sometimes called one sheets), posters, church and synagogue newsletters, brochures, and virtually any printed media. When analyzing your print advertising needs, make certain that you test your advertising product in advance with a small distribution to test its effectiveness. Specialists in direct mail recommend that you use a *split test* approach. This requires that you mail one type of advertising printed matter to one group and a different type to another to test the best response from both types. Varying items such as the color of the ink, copy, type and weight of the paper, or other decisions may produce different results. Test your print advertising using focus groups to make certain that your event product is well positioned for success.

Classic advertising terms such as *free, discount, now, sale,* and *new* may help you influence the consumer to invest in your event. Clever graphics, endorsements, testimonials, and other credibility-building devices will help differentiate your event product from others.

Electronic media include radio, television, the Internet, and any form of advertising that involves electronic delivery. Radio advertising is typically used to remind the listener about the event, whereas television is used to build excitement. The Internet is an excellent means with which to reach upscale consumers and those who are interested in science, technology, and travel. Before you select electronic media as a means to advertise your event, examine all potential media outlets.

Within television media you may elect to cast your event broadly through major networks or narrowly cast by selecting a finely targeted cable station. For example, if you are promoting an arts-related event, you may select a cable station with arts programming. These decisions may require the assistance of experts in media buying or from an advertising agency specializing in radio or television media.

Transportation media require that you place your message on buses, subways, and other forms of transportation. Usually, these media are aimed at a very wide market but has proven effective for circuses, fairs, festivals, and other events that require large attendance from diverse groups.

Advertising specialties are those items that are usually given away or offered as a premium, as an incentive to purchase a product or service. Advertising specialties include thousands of products; however, the most typical are calendars, refrigerator magnets, coffee mugs, writing instruments, and key chains. In recent years clothing has become popular as advertising specialties, and some event organizers give away clothing to the media and other key constituent groups and sell the rest at souvenir stands. Once again, research this purchase carefully to ensure that the recipient values the item and will use it. Prolonged use will serve as reminders of your event.

Outdoor advertising was, at one time, one of the major forms of advertising in the United States. However, during the late 1960s many billboards were banned in a "beautify America" campaign. Still, the outdoor billboard is an excellent way to reach large numbers of potential event participants for an extended period of time.

Regardless of the type of advertising media you select, make certain that you first conduct market research followed by tests to determine actual response. Once you have found a medium that effectively reaches your target market, use repetition to build reinforcement and retention. Finally, measure all responses to develop history and determine where your advertising dollar will pull best for each event.

## PUBLIC RELATIONS

Public relations involves informing the media and your target market about your event and persuading them to support your programs. Public relations activities for your event may include designing, printing, and distributing media kits, producing public service announcements for radio and television, producing and distributing audio and video news releases, or even producing events. In fact, according to many public relations professions, events are the fastest-growing segment of the public relations strategy.

The media kit is typically a presentation-type folder that contains a fact sheet, request for coverage notice, media releases, and even a public service announcement (either written or recorded). This kit is distributed well in advance of the event to the print and electronic media to inform them of opportunities for coverage. In smaller markets, some media outlets may print your media releases word for word, whereas in larger, more sophisticated markets, members of the media may use the kit for background information alone.

A *public service announcement* (PSA) is a written or prerecorded audio or video announcement about your event. Broadcasters in the United States are required by federal law to provide a certain allotment of time for public service announcements. In some cases, the broadcaster may provide help, as a further public service, in producing these announcements. Often, a local celebrity or nationally prominent person will participate at no charge, to add credibility to your announcement.

The audio or video news release, while a relatively new phenomenon, is one of the most effective ways to distribute your event message. Audio news releases (ANRs) and video news releases (VNRs) require that you pretape a news story about your event and then by overnight mail or use of satellite transmission send the story to local stations that you would like to have air the story as part of their news programming. Since news programs are often the most watched segments of television programming, this type of public relations has the potential of reaching a large, well-targeted audience in a credible and cost-effective manner.

Finally, events themselves often become major public relations vehicles. To promote the opening of a new shopping center, movie actress Teri Garr starred in a public service announcement to benefit the National Center for Missing and Exploited Children. Garr filmed the announcement in the mall.

Later she appeared on *The Tonight Show* with Johnny Carson and described in detail her activities on behalf of the national center, including the filming of the public service announcement in the mall. This *event-within-an-event* serves to further position you firmly in the minds of those in the target audience.

Remember that the two chief goals of public relations are to inform and persuade. Therefore, using collateral materials, public service announcements, and audio and video news releases as well as smaller events are excellent ways to accomplish these two important goals of an overall marketing campaign.

## CROSS PROMOTIONS

To allocate market resources in the most efficient manner, you must identify and incorporate marketing partners into your campaign. These organizations may actually contribute marketing dollars or may provide in-kind services, such as providing celebrities, tagging their ads with your event date and time, or contributing other valuable components to your campaign.

When seeking marketing partners to develop a cross-promotional strategy, study the advertising and marketing activities of compatible businesses in your area. Determine which of these activities will benefit your event. Next, develop a proposal that clearly describes the resources that you can bring to the event. Finally, present the proposal to your prospective marketing partners and answer any questions they may pose.

*Tagging advertising* involves your marketing partner adding a line of copy to his or her regular advertising placements that promote your event. It may read, "Official supporter of XYZ event" or "Meet us at XYZ event, date and time." Tag lines may appear in both print and electronic advertising.

Make certain that you chronicle all marketing activities so that you can report to your partners after the event and describe in intricate detail those placements that were successful. Cross promotions and tie-in activities are sensational ways to reach a much larger market in a cost-effective manner.

## STREET PROMOTIONS

This marketing activity requires that you literally take your message to the street. Street promotions may include the handing out of flyers by a clown in a high-traffic area, the appearance of a celebrity at a local mall, contests, or other promotional activities designed to draw high visibility to your event. Before leafleting (handing out flyers), make certain that this is allowed by local code. You certainly don't want to generate negative publicity by having the clown arrested for causing a disturbance. A celebrity appearance can help generate significant publicity if it is handled properly. Schedule the celebrity to include radio and television interviews, appearances at a local children's hospital or other public facility, and ceremonial events with local, state, provincial, or federal leaders. At each appearance make certain that the celebrity is well informed about the event and articulates your event message in a consistent manner. Contests and other promotional events also require analysis to ensure that they are within the bounds of the local code and that they are appropriate for your event. For instance, selling raffle tickets at a nonprofit event may require that you file legal forms.

## STUNTS

During the early 1950s in the United States, advertising agencies used stunts as an important method of breaking through the clutter of traditional print and electronic advertising. Today, stunts continue to be effective but must be crafted carefully to ensure that the integrity of the event is preserved.

A stunt involves an activity designed to generate media coverage and attendance by spectators to promote a specific event or series of events. Radio stations continue to rely heavily on stunts and will often provide remote broadcasts to cover stunts involving their on-air personalities. Stunts can be tied to charitable endeavors such as locking up prominent officials until enough donations are raised to cover their release. Other stunts may involve creating the world's largest pizza, cake, sandwich, or other product. Before you incorporate a stunt in an event marketing program, it is important to analyze how the stunt will further your marketing objectives and to determine all associated costs. Finally, make certain that you chronicle all media coverage that results from the stunt, distribute bounce-back coupons to attendees, and track all responses resulting from the stunt.

## THE INVITATION

Whether your invitation is a print or electronic advertisement, a flyer, or a formal engraved document, the copy that is composed, art that is created or selected, and paper that is chosen will greatly influence the response. The central components of all effective invitations are:

1. Name of host or event organizer
2. Date, time, and location
3. Dress requirements
4. Parking
5. RSVP

Additional components may include:

1. Purpose of the event
2. Names of honorary board or committee
3. Names of prominent speakers
4. Frequency or historic nature of the event (first annual, 100th anniversary celebration, or biannual event)

**5.** Limited supply of tickets

**6.** VIP status

Remember that an invitation is an official offer to the consumer or guest to participate in your event. Therefore, from a legal perspective it is important that you choose your words carefully to reflect the actual event you are promoting.

Each of these components is designed to generate a specific response from the recipient. The most important response is to build anticipation toward acceptance followed by actual attendance.

# Marketing Thrust

Noted corporate marketing expert Ira Westreich described the word *event* as an acronym that represents "extract value with every new thrust." The purpose of your event marketing campaign is to ensure that every decision you make provides greater value for the overall event outcome. To do this you must carefully match the objectives to the strategies, test all ideas using feedback from actual event consumers, and perhaps most important, use creativity and innovation to differentiate your event product as a unique and valuable investment. By integrating marketing activities such as advertising, public relations, cross promotions, street promotions, and stunts you will be able to build a strong campaign that will effectively promote your event to your target audience.

# Event Sponsorship

According to the International Events Group (IEG) of Chicago, sponsorship investment grew from $6.5 billion to over $9 billion in a period of two years (1996–1998). IEG is a recognized leader in the field of sponsorship research and education. Although the vast majority of sponsorship dollars are invested in sports-related events, there is a trend to diversify funding into festivals, fairs, and cultural events. The primary reason for this diversification of investment is due to the need by advertisers to reach more targeted demographics. Sports have generally attracted broad demographics, whereas cultural events are able to target high-income and well-educated consumers.

Sponsorship becomes more valuable if the event organization is able to offer precise targeting that matches the marketing objectives of the prospective sponsor. The growth in sponsorship is due primarily to the need by advertisers to find alternative marketing channels to inform, persuade, promote, and sell their products and services. However, the number of events that require sponsorship has also grown in recent years.

Without sponsorship, many events would not be financially feasible. Other events would not be able to provide the quality expected by event participants. Still other events would not be able to achieve their specified goals and objectives. Suffice it to say that more often than not, sponsorship provides the grease that allows the event wheel to function smoothly.

Historically, sponsorship has its earliest modern origin in professional sporting events. These events have always appealed to the widest demographics and were therefore perfect event products for sponsorship. Sponsorship is a uniquely American invention brought forth from the need of advertisers to reach certain markets and the need of event organizers to identify additional funding to offset costs not covered by normal revenue streams, such as ticket sales.

In recent times there has been a noticeable shift in sponsor dollars away from sporting events and toward arts events. The reason for this shift is that sponsors are seeking more highly targeted upscale demographics and the arts' audience delivers that market segment. Therefore, those events that deliver the higher-income demographics are predicted to benefit most from sponsorship dollars in the future.

Perhaps the best example of sport sponsorship is the 1984 Summer Olympic Games in Los Angeles, California. For the first time in the history of the modern Olympic Games movement, sponsors were aggressively solicited as marketing partners for this unprecedented event. Offers were made, deals were cut, and the Los Angeles Olympic Organizing Committee received a net earnings of over $200 million.

From fairs to festivals to hallmark events such as a world's fair, the role of the sponsor has earned a permanent place in the marketing lexicon of events. Following are typical types of sponsors for a variety of events.

- *Fair:* bottler, grocer, automotive, and bank
- *Festival:* department store and record store
- *Sport:* athletic wear manufacturer, bottler, brewery, and hospital or health care facility
- *School program:* children's toy stores, children's clothing stores, and amusement park
- *Meeting/conference:* printer, bank, insurance broker, and associate member firms

Use this list as a guide to begin to identify sponsors for your event.

## SPONSORSHIP NEEDS ASSESSMENT

Although most events may benefit from sponsorship, not every event is appropriate for this component. Sponsorship is a commercial endeavor and is extremely time consuming. Therefore, unless you are prepared to enter into a commercial relationship with other parties and have the time resources to devote to this activity, you may instead wish to solicit donations.

Many event managers confuse sponsorship with benevolence. A fundraising event where donors contribute without any expectation of commercial benefit is a benevolent activity. Sponsorship, on the other hand, is a commercial transaction in which two parties agree by way of an offer and acceptance. The offer generally involves marketing services provided by the event organizer in exchange for the sponsor's cash or in-kind contribution to the event. The marketing services may range from advertising to banner displays to hospitality to a full-blown marketing plan involving public relations, advertising, and promotion.

As you can begin to see, these marketing services place new demands on the event organizer. Therefore, the event resources may need to be reallocated to handle this new demand. Not every event is able to do this.

Before you give the green light to soliciting sponsorships, use the following checklist to determine if your event is appropriate for this activity.

1. Does the event require an infusion of sponsor dollars to achieve the quality required?
2. Are there sufficient internal and external resources to support this activity?
3. Is commercial sponsorship appropriate for the nature of the event?
4. Are there sufficient prospects for sponsorship sales, and is the timing appropriate to approach them?
5. Is this activity legal, ethical, and appropriate for the spirit of the event organization?

These questions can save many event organizations much wasted time, energy, and heartache. Examining the internal and external resources may be one of the most important aspects of this process.

Although sponsors may provide much needed funding for your event, to help you achieve the quality that is required, sponsors also require that your own financial resources meet their objectives. They may, for example, require that you commit a certain amount of marketing dollars. Second, they may require minimal or substantial hospitality services that may amount to hundreds or thousands of dollars per day. Finally, if you are going to retain these sponsors assign one or more people to monitor the activities, service these accounts, and develop long-term relationships. Yes, sponsors can provide needed funding; however, as in any commercial transaction they must also receive a fair return on their investment. You are responsible for orchestrating this return.

Your event may benefit from additional exposure through sponsorships. Earlier we discussed using tag lines in advertising as one way to increase your exposure inexpensively. Sponsors may also provide you with *shelf space* in their retail stores to promote your event through coupons. Your sponsors can also help you with the development of a public relations campaign or can supplement their own public relations efforts with your message. Some sponsors have celebrity athletes, television stars, and movie personalities on contract who they may wish to involve with your event.

Perhaps one of the most important reasons event organizers align themselves with commercial sponsors is the opportunity to achieve greater credibility for the event. Securing the sponsorship of AT&T, IBM, Coca-Cola, or other Fortune 500 firms immediately positions your event as a major player and may help your event organization secure additional funding from other sources.

## DEVELOPING SPONSORS

The competition by event organizers for sponsors is keen at every level. Whether your event is a local event or a national one, you must first conduct a competitive analysis to identify all competing events and study their sponsorship history and present activities. Following are several suggestions on how to identify appropriate sponsors for your event.

1. Determine the financial level of sponsorship you require. Not every sponsor can make a five- or six-figure decision.
2. Review trade journals such as *Advertising Age* and *Sponsorship Report* to track sponsor activities.
3. Review the local business tabloid in your area to search for prospective sponsors.
4. Network with advertising and public relations agency officials to find out if their clients have an interest in your event.
5. Conduct a focus group with prospective sponsors to solicit and later analyze their opinions and attitudes toward your event.

Once you have developed a list of prospective sponsors, the next step is to qualify them for solicitation. Do not waste your valuable resources by making endless presentations to sponsors who do not have the interest or resources to support your event financially. Instead, qualify your sponsors by contacting local organizations such as the chamber of commerce, board of trade, banks, and other centers of commerce to inquire about the financial viability of the prospective sponsor. Next, thoroughly review the sponsor's past marketing efforts to determine if the sponsor's overall marketing plans are conducive to sponsoring your event. Finally, talk to advertising and public relations executives and attempt to forecast where your prospective sponsor may put his or her marketing dollars in the future. Perhaps the logical place for investment is your event.

## SELLING SPONSORSHIPS

Always do your homework regarding the sponsor's needs, wants, and desires prior to attempting to sell a sponsorship. To make the sale, the sponsorship offer must be an exact fit with the needs, expectations, goals, and objectives of the commercial sponsor. Customize the offer to achieve these goals and objectives prior to your presentation.

Constructing a successful proposal is equal parts of art and science. As an artist, you must design an attractive, enticing, and aesthetically pleasing product that the sponsor will want to purchase. Therefore, describe the capability of your organization and past sponsors (if any), incorporate testimonials and references from leading individuals, and package the proposal in a professional design. Avoid being clever. Remember that the sponsor will be making a business decision and will prefer a serious business plan over hokeyness. The science part involves carefully identifying your target market and linking all sponsorship activities to sales or recognition that will benefit the sponsor. List the benefits and activities the sponsor will enjoy as a sponsor of your event. For example, the sponsor may be able to provide free samples of his or her product or service and conduct marketing research. He or she may be able to offer his or her product or service for sale and measure the results. Or the sponsor may benefit from public relations exposure. Regardless of the benefit or feature, detail each potential activity that may result from the sponsorship.

Include in the proposal sponsorship terms for payment and any requirements the sponsor may have in addition to these payments. In some events, the sponsor is allowed to provide an exhibit at his or her own cost. In other events, the exhibit is provided as part of the sponsorship costs. Describe any additional costs or services the sponsor is required to contribute to avoid any future surprises. The following list summarizes the key elements in a winning sponsorship proposal.

1. Describe the history of the event.
2. Include a capability statement about your organization's resources.
3. Incorporate testimonials and references from other sponsors.
4. Describe the benefits and features that the sponsor will receive.
5. List all financial responsibilities that the sponsor must accept.
6. Describe any additional responsibilities that the sponsor must accept.
7. Describe how you will chronicle the sponsorship activity.
8. Include a time and a date for acceptance of the offer.
9. Include a provision for renewal of the sponsorship.
10. Include an arbitration clause in case you and the sponsor disagree regarding the sponsorship activities.

One of the most effective ways to persuade sponsors to participate in an event is to organize a prospective sponsor preview program. During this program you and your staff describe the benefits and features of your sponsorship activities to a large number of prospective sponsors. You may wish to invite a couple of previous sponsors to provide in-person testimonials about the benefits of the sponsorship. You may also wish to presell one or two sponsors so that when you ask for a reaction from those in attendance, at least two from the group will respond favorably. Their favorable response may, and usually does, influence others. Avoid trying to hard sell during this program. Use this program to plant seeds that will be further cultivated during meetings with individual sponsors.

## OVERCOMING SPONSOR OBJECTIONS

Most sponsors will want their sponsorship activities customized to achieve their specific goals and objectives. Therefore, they may have some preliminary objections after receiving your initial offer. Once you have presented the offer, ask them for their reaction on each benefit and feature. Listen carefully and list these comments. Make two lists. One list is for approvals, those items that they see the value in sponsoring. The second list is for objections, those items that they cannot see the value of at this time. Your goal is to move all the items from list 2 into list 1. To do this, ask sponsors what is required by their organization to overcome their objections on each point. In some cases it may be additional exposure. In other cases it may be the price of the sponsorship. To overcome these objections, be prepared to provide them with the tools they need to make a positive decision. For example, if their objection is cost, you may be able to combine their sponsorship with others and lower their contribution. If their objection is limited exposure, you may be able to reposition their involvement inexpensively to provide them with greater and more sustained visibility. Handling objections is an integral part of the sponsorship sales process. Rehearse these discussions with your internal stakeholders to identify other common objections and be prepared to provide the solution your sponsors need to remove these barriers.

## NEGOTIATING YOUR SPONSORSHIP

Almost every sponsorship will require intense negotiations to move it into fruition. Whenever possible, conduct these negotiations in person with the decision maker. Assign a specific date and time for these negotiations and confirm that the sponsor is a feasible prospect before entering into a serious negotiation. In most negotiations both parties desire a win–win–win outcome. In this type of negotiation you win as the event organizer, the sponsor wins as the event funding agent, and the stakeholders of your event win from your mutual efforts to secure these dollars.

Carefully analyze what your sponsor expects from the sponsorship prior to your negotiating session. Determine in advance what additional components you may be able to offer if required. Also, list those concessions that you cannot make. Finally, list these items that may require further approval from your board or others before you agree to them. Begin the negotiation by asking the prospective sponsor to list all items that are acceptable, bundle them, and have the sponsor approve them. Now you are prepared to focus on those items that require further resolution. Ask the sponsor to describe his or her concerns about each negotiation point and take careful notes. Look at your list of concessions and decide if any item you have listed will help resolve these concerns. If it is appropriate to offer a concession, do so and ask the sponsor for his or her approval. Once the sponsor has approved, ask him or her to provide you with an additional service, usually at modest additional cost to the sponsor, to balance his or her end of the negotiation. If the sponsor is unable to provide you with an additional service or product, determine if you are able to proceed to the next point.

Do not be afraid to walk away. In some cases the concession that the sponsor will ask for may sacrifice the credibility or reputation of an event. In other cases, the sponsor will want a concession that may undermine the financial wealth of your event. Do not concede your reputation or the financial success of the event. Instead, thank the sponsor for his or her time, offer to work with him or her in the future under different circumstances, and leave the room as quickly as possible. In some instances, event organizers have reported that this approach has forced the prospective sponsor to reexamine his or her position. It is not unusual to have the sponsor call the event organizer the next day and offer a greater concession to save the sponsorship.

## CLOSING THE SPONSORSHIP SALE

You must always *ask for the order* when presenting your sponsorship proposal. State at least three times that you want to develop a positive relationship with the sponsor. Start your discussions by stating that your desired outcome is to ensure that the sponsor understands all the benefits and features of your event and will desire to become a sponsor.

Throughout your presentation ask for feedback from the sponsor and build on the sponsor's positive reactions by telling him or her that you are pleased that he or she recognizes the value of your event product. Finally, at the conclusion of your presentation, ask the sponsor for his or her overall impression and state once again that you would like his or her business.

Unfortunately, these techniques may not be enough to get a clear answer. In some cases you may have to say something like, "So, can we count on you to sponsor our event?" Sometimes you need to secure the answer to this question in order to plan your next step in sponsorship negotiations or to decide to move forward with the next sponsor. The word *ask* is the most powerful three-letter word in sponsorship sales. Unless you ask, you will never know. Remember to ask early, often, and before leaving to confirm the sponsorship sale.

## SERVICING SPONSORSHIP SALES

Once the sponsor has accepted your offer, the next task is to service the sale in order to retain his or her support in the future. One of the most common reasons that sponsors fail to renew their sponsorship is due to poor communications. In Part One of this book we discussed in great detail the importance of open and continuous communications. Make certain that you develop methods for implementing positive communications with your sponsors. Some event organizers use newsletters to update their sponsors, others provide regular briefings, and still others offer their sponsors marketing seminars to help them design a booth or target their product or service to event guests. It is wise to assign one or more persons on your staff to service all sponsorships and communicate regularly with sponsors to make certain they remain informed, excited, and committed to the event activities.

Another reason that some sponsorships go sour is due to the inability of the event organizers to deliver what they promise. If you promise that the sponsor's banner will be suspended on the main stage above the head of the performing artist, you must first confirm with the artist that this is acceptable. It is unacceptable to renege later on your commitment to the sponsor. It is always best to underpromise and overdeliver when stating the benefits of sponsorship. Exceeding the sponsor's expectations is how you turn a one-year sponsorship into a five-year plan with options to renew forever.

Every sponsor has a hidden agenda. It can be as simple as the chairman of the board wanting to meet his or her favorite celebrity or as complex as the sales manager's bonus and promotion decision resting on this particular sponsorship activity. Ask the sponsor's representative what else you need to know about the needs of his or her organization as you design the sponsorship measurement system. For example, if the sponsor's representative is in the public relations department, his or her interest may be in seeing lots of ink and television time devoted to the name of the sponsor. Therefore, you will want to measure these outcomes carefully to assist your sponsor. Remember that you may sign a sponsorship agreement with a large corporation or organization, but the day-to-day management of this agreement is between people. Find out what these people desire and try to provide them with these outcomes.

Although communications between you and your sponsors is critical to your success, perhaps even more important are the internal communications between the event manager and his or her operations personnel. You must first confirm that your personnel will be able to support sponsorship activities at the level required by the individual sponsors. Determine if you have sufficient internal resources to satisfy the requirements both in contract as well as implied to ensure the well-being of your sponsor's investment. For example, if your sponsor wants a hospitality setup arranged at the last minute, do you have a catering operation that can handle this request? One way to ensure that the sponsors' needs are handled expeditiously is to create a written system of orders, changes, and other instructions that clearly communicate those activities required by your sponsors. Prior to distribution of these forms, have the sponsor's representative sign one copy. Then have the event's representative initial approval before forwarding it to the appropriate department or team leader.

## EVALUATING SPONSORSHIPS

To secure multiple-year sponsorships it is important that you develop and implement a system for measuring the sponsor's activities. First, decide what needs to be evaluated and why. The answers to these questions typically may be found in the goals and objectives of the sponsorship agreement.

To collect these data, conduct sponsorship evaluations that are comprehensive in scope. You may wish to interview the sponsors, your own staff, the sponsor's target market, and others to solicit a wide range of opinions regarding the effectiveness of the sponsorship. Furthermore, you may wish to include in the event survey-specific questions about the sponsor's participation. Finally, ask the sponsor for tracking information regarding sales that have resulted from the sponsor's participation in your event.

You may measure the sponsor's public relations benefits by measuring the number of minutes of television and/or radio time as well as the number of inches and columns of print media that was devoted to the sponsor's products or name. List the comparable value using the 3:1 ratio provided by the Public Relations Society of America.

Ask the sponsor how he or she would like to see the data you have measured presented. Some may prefer an elaborate in-person presentation using video clips and slides; others will prefer a simple summary of the goals, objectives, and outcomes that were achieved. Make certain that you present this information in a manner that is useful to the sponsor and that you take the time to prepare this presentation professionally to address the sponsor's needs. All future sponsorship activities will come from this important activity.

## TIMING IS EVERYTHING

The process for identifying, soliciting, negotiating, securing, servicing, and evaluating sponsorships is a complex one. However, as is true with most things, timing is everything. Allow a minimum of 12 to 18 months to formulate and consummate a successful sponsorship program. Following is a typical timeline for the various stages described above.

| | |
|---|---|
| 18 months in advance | Conduct needs assessment and research. |
| 16 months in advance | Identify prospective sponsors. |
| 14 months in advance | Develop and present proposals. |
| 12 months in advance | Negotiate proposals and sign agreements. |
| 9 months in advance | Implement sponsorship operations plan. |
| 6 months in advance | Audit sponsor's changes and additions. |
| 4 months in advance | Review changes and additions with staff. |
| 2 months in advance | Meet with sponsor to provide update on event progress. |
| 1 month in advance | Begin sponsor public relations campaign. |
| 1 month after event | Meet with sponsor to provide analysis of results. |

Some event organizers have come to see sponsorship as the goose with the golden egg. However, while specific benefits come from individual sponsorships, an event manager must audit for each event the needs, resources available, and benefits offered, prior to engaging in this time-consuming and expense-laden activity. When developing sponsorship activities always start small and build a base of sponsors year by year or event by event from your ability to deliver high-quality and successful events consistently. This is the best way to make sure that your goose lays a golden egg, not a rotten one, for your event organization.

# Internet Event Marketing

Not since the invention of the printing press has advertising been changed as dramatically as with the introduction of the Internet. For example, the number of Internet users in the events industry grew from 50 percent to over 80 percent between 1996 and 1998. Event marketing has now fully embraced the electronic marketplace. Reggie Aggarwal, CEO of Cvent.com, a leading Internet event marketing firm, told the Convention Industry Council Forum attendees that "the fastest, most precise, easiest, and most cost affordable way to reach prospective event attendees is through e-mail." According to Aggarwal, the penetration of the Internet will soon be 100 percent and will soon be equal to or even replace traditional television and radio in some segments as an electronic source for daily information and communications.

Cvent.com is one example of how the technological revolution is driving the event management industry. Aggarwal started the firm after he used e-mail invitations and reminders to promote registration for a local association that he directed. He soon discovered that he could increase the response rate significantly and better target his prospects using e-mail communications. For example, Cvent.com technology enables meeting planners and event managers not only to send e-mail messages but also to note whether or not they have been read. Direct-mail marketers cannot monitor whether or not their communications are read, as they can only note when a purchase or inquiry has been received. This innovation gives Cvent a competitive edge in event market because they can determine quickly whether or not the e-mail event invitation has been opened and read. If it has been opened, the event marketer can assume that there is interest and build upon that interest with follow-up communications. This customized marketing approach is one of the many benefits of the new technologies that are being developed to assist event marketers.

When developing event marketing, Internet marketing must be considered as a central part of any strategy. For example, regardless of size, all events should have a Web presence through either a dedicated Web home page, banner on an existing Web home page, or link to a separate page. Following are points to consider when developing a comprehensive e-marketing event strategy:

- Identify your event market segments and targets.
- Design your web strategy to reach your target market quickly, efficiently, and precisely.

- Use a focus panel of prospective event attendees to review your plans and suggest modifications to your overall design.
- Audit and evaluate the competition to determine how your Web presence can be more effective.
- Match the color scheme and design components to your printed matter.
- Determine whether or not you require a separate home page for your event or a link from an existing home page to a unique page.
- Identify and establish links with all marketing partners.
- Determine whether you will need a transaction page and ensure security for your ticket buyers.
- Determine whether you, your staff, or others can build the pages and/or make changes should they be needed.
- If consultants are contracted to build your site or pages, determine how they will be maintained (frequency, speed, and reliability).
- Use viral marketing (e-mails copied to prospective attendees) to promote your event.
- Use search engines to promote your event, with careful selection and registration of your URL.
- Use e-mail reminders to increase attendance during the last two weeks of an event.
- Use online registration systems.
- Use online evaluation systems to collect survey information before, during, and after an event.
- Use online chat rooms to create discussion areas for preregistered attendees and to generate follow-up discussion postevent.
- Carefully monitor all online activity for potential data mining to determine future needs, wants, and desires of your target audience.

The Internet will continue to drive the development of the global event management industry. You must use this dynamic technology quickly and accurately to ensure that your event remains competitive throughout the twenty-first century.

# Event Marketing Evaluation

Reggie Aggarwal and I coined the term *return on event* or (ROE) to identify the percentage of earnings returned to an event organization sponsoring the event based on marketing efforts. The ROE is an important concept for all event marketers, regardless of event size. For example, if you are marketing a small event for 100 persons and you increase attendance by 25 percent due to your new e-marketing strategies, you may in fact not only have saved a significant amount of money but also generated a sizable net profit that may be directly attributable to this marketing activity. Table 10-2 outlines how this formula may be used to identify the ROE.

**Table 10-2** Measuring Return on Event:
Income Statement for Family Festival of Fun

|  | Year 1 | Year 2 |
|---|---|---|
| Expenses |  |  |
| Advertising |  |  |
| Newspaper | $25,000 | $35,000 |
| Radio | 15,000 | 20,000 |
| Television | 50,000 | 60,000 |
| Direct mail |  |  |
| Design and Printing | 10,000 | 10,000 |
| Postage | 5,000 | 5,000 |
| Internet | 10,000 | 15,000 |
| Promotions | 5,000 | 5,000 |
| Public relations | 5,000 | 10,000 |
| Subtotal | $120,000 | $160,000 |
| Income |  |  |
| Ticket sales | $100,000 | $125,000 |
| Sponsorships | 25,000 | 45,000 |
| Subtotal | $125,000 | $170,000 |

The income statement shows a significant increase in total revenues in year 2 as well as a slight increase in net income. Now we measure the increase in return on marketing and see how the marketing function performed as part of the overall financial analysis (Table 10-3). By careful monitoring, tracking, and measuring of each marketing activity you are able to identify that in year 2 your event generated a 160 percent return on marketing investment as compared to year 1, with only 39 percent. To monitor, track, and measure each of these separate marketing functions you need to use a variety of simple but effective systems.

**Table 10-3** Evaluating the Return on Event

| Expenses | Year 1 | Year 2 | Penetration (%) | Response (%) |
|---|---|---|---|---|
| Advertising |  |  |  |  |
| Newspaper | $25,000 | $35,000 | 25–40 | 5–10 |
| Radio | 15,000 | 20,000 | 10–15 | 1–5 |
| Television | 50,000 | 60,000 | 5–7 | 20–25 |
| Direct mail |  |  |  |  |
| Design and Printing | 10,000 | 10,000 |  |  |
| Postage | 5,000 | 5,000 | 75–85 | 5–10 |
| Internet |  | 15,000 | 0–55 | 1–90 |
| Promotions | 5,000 | 5,000 | 1–2 | 3–10 |
| Public relations | 5,000 | 10,000 | 5–7 | 5–10 |
| Subtotal | $120,000 | $160,000 |  | 39–160 |

## CODING

Make certain that you assign a unique code to each marketing response item. For example, if you allow your attendees to register by mail, phone, newspaper, radio, and Internet, each marketing channel should have a separate code. Table 10-4 demonstrates how to code and track each response. By identifying the response ratios from each marketing channel, you are better able to adjust your marketing efforts during the promotional period prior to the event and evaluate where to place your marketing dollars in the future.

Determining the return on your event accomplishes several fundamental purposes that are critical to your future marketing success. First, you are able to track where your responses are being generated. Second, you are able to compare investment versus actual marketing performance by each channel. Third, you are able to compare return on marketing with other economic performance indicators, such as risk management, labor, and utilities, on an annual basis and determine whether or not you need to increase or reduce the budget accordingly to achieve your revenue targets in future years.

## OTHER MARKETING EVALUATION TOOLS

The ROE is a quantitative system for evaluating marketing response. However, in addition to quantifying your responses, you must also qualify them as well. Using a focus panel to review marketing promotional campaigns, including ink colors, logo design, and copy, will help you fine tune your visual impressions to match the tastes of your prospective event attendees.

You may also wish to use personal interviews to determine why nonattendees refuse to accept your invitation to participate in your event offer. These telephonic interviews can reveal important information that will help you in marketing your event in the future. For example, a nonattendee may reveal that they have trouble finding a babysitter. If this comment is replicated

**Table 10-4**  Coding and Tracking Event Marketing Responses

| Response Method | Code | Total Year 1 | Year 2 | Response (%) |
|---|---|---|---|---|
| Direct mail | DM99 | 100 | 200 | <100 |
| Internet | IN99 | 1000 | 3000 | <200 |
| Newspaper | | | | |
|    *Daily Courier* | DC99 | 1000 | 1200 | <20 |
|    *Weekly Standard* | WS99 | 500 | 750 | <25 |
| Radio | | | | |
|    WLAC | R-WLAC | 15 | 25 | <10 |
|    WPIR | R-WPIR | 10 | 15 | <5 |
| Television | WNEW | 150 | 300 | <100 |

with a large enough sample you may wish to consider offering on site child care to increase attendance by families with young children or add more children's activities to your event programming.

The overall benefits associated with marketing should not be focused solely on the economic performance of an event. Remember, even if someone did not attend your event, he or she may have recommended it to others. Furthermore, he or she may be positively influenced to attend in the future. Following are some of the qualitative areas you may wish to measure in your marketing analysis and measuring techniques for each.

- *Image improvement:* survey, interviews, focus panel
- *Recall of event name:* interviews, focus panel
- *Recall of event slogan:* interviews, focus panel
- *Increase in number of volunteers:* survey, focus panel
- *Increase in sponsorship:* focus panel, survey
- *Increase in gifts (philanthropy):* interviews, survey
- *Improved political relations:* interviews
- *Improved media relations:* interviews, clipping and clip monitoring
- *Improved community relations:* interviews, focus panel
- *Increased Internet traffic:* monitoring the event Web site
- *Increased Internet discussion:* monitoring chat rooms related to your event

The overall purpose of marketing analysis and evaluation is to provide you with the essential information you need to make better decisions in the future. Whether your event is one that recurs year after year or is a one-time affair, the data you collect from your marketing analysis will help you in the development of many different types of future events. Make certain that you assign a line item in the event budget for marketing evaluation. Some of the typical costs include survey development and printing, focus panel facilitation, interviewer fees, data collection, tabulation, analysis, and report writing. In addition, you may wish to contract with third parties, such as a clipping services firm, to track the media generated about your event. Your ability to measure the return on marketing for your event comprehensively will provide you with dividends for many years to come. Do not miss this opportunity to improve your competitiveness, your event's image, and your profitability now and in the years to come.

# Career Advancement Connections

## GLOBAL CONNECTION

When marketing to two or more cultures, make certain that you use focus group research to review all marketing communications. Simply translating a marketing slogan into a language other than English will not always achieve the meaning or intent you require. Furthermore, some cultures are sensitive to certain colors and may not respond favorably to your design. Convene a focus panel comprised of people from various cultures to review your marketing plan and designs prior to implementation.

## TECHNOLOGY CONNECTION

Use desktop publishing software to create simple advertisements, flyers, brochures, and other print matter. Use the Internet to distribute your media releases to targeted media. Use audio and video news releases (ANRs and VNRs) to broadcast your event news item to television and radio stations worldwide.

## RESOURCE CONNECTION

The Public Relations Society of America *(www.PRSA.org)* publishes the informative *PR Journal,* which documents the latest trends in public relations research and methodology. The American Advertising Federation *(www.AAF.org)* offers extensive research information at the World Advertising Research Center. The International Events Group *(www.sponsorship.com)* offers an annual sponsorship seminar that includes informative seminars concerning how to find, recruit, and keep sponsors. The American Marketing Association *(www.ama.org) Journal of Marketing* offers an online journal that includes marketing research and many other resources. The most comprehensive book on the subject of event marketing, *Event Marketing* by Leonard Hoyle (New York: Wiley, to be published in late 2002), is part of the John Wiley & Sons Event Management series.

## LEARNING CONNECTION

Develop a marketing plan for your event that identifies the competitive advantages, target market(s), strategies, tactics, budgets, schedule, and evaluation methodologies. Describe how you will increase your marketing performance through creative and innovative tactics despite a significant reduction in the marketing budget.

---

**Facing Page**
The future of event marketing is through the Internet. Use this powerful tool for weddings, conventions, expositions, and hallmark events such as the Olympic Games. *Photograph courtesy of Monica Vidal.*

# CHAPTER 11

# Online Marketing

**IN THIS CHAPTER YOU WILL LEARN HOW TO:**

- Understand the role and scope of the emerging Internet marketplace
- Differentiate the major advantages in online marketing
- Maximize your Web marketing opportunities
- Determine the major types of Web sites and their characteristics
- Identify, prevent, and correct common mistakes in Web site management
- Include security and confidentiality for your Web site
- Incorporate special features for your Web site
- Measure and evaluate the data collected through your online marketing activities

There is no question that the development of the Internet has become the most important communication and marketing media breakthrough since the printing press in the mid-fifteenth century. It has fundamentally reshaped understating of sales and marketing. However, since so few years have passed since the Internet has become available for widespread public use, the marketing tools used in cyberspace are still "works in progress." You can take an active role developing Internet marketing rules and standards for event management.

# Internet Marketing for Events

The Internet can be a highly efficient tool in overall event management organizations' marketing program. At the same time, it can be a major financial burden if an event management organization does not formulate specific goals for its Internet marketing policy. The objectives for each event management organization may vary depending on company size, dynamics of operations, financial and staff resources, location, overall development strategy, and client base. The Web site for a small event management startup will differ from that of a large multinational event management conglomerate. Major marketing concepts enhanced by online tools include brand building, direct marketing, online sales and online commerce, customer support, market research, and product or service development and testing.

## BRAND BUILDING

Online marketing combined with television, media, and print is a major brand-building tool. The biggest advantage the Internet has over television and old-fashioned media is the favorable cost/benefit ratio. Event management organizations can achieve a much higher return on their marketing investments in Internet promotions than in a traditional campaign. The research conducted by Millward Brown Interactive, a 20-year-old international advertising research group, found that an organization can achieve significant progress in brand recognition simply by placing its logo on banners of search engines or online databases. One great place for an event management organization to put its logo is the DOME database (Data on Meeting and Events at *www.domeresearch.org*). It is important for an event management organization to secure the presence of its logo on the Web. You can start simply by trading space on the banner section of your Web site with a partner organization. You place your logo on your partner's Web site and create a hyperlink from his or her Web site to yours, in exchange for placing your partner's information on your Web site. It is very important to submit your company's profile to all major search engines. Five years ago, when students were conducting a search on Yahoo using the key words *event management,* they obtained only a few matches, whereas now there are hundreds. Submitting your company's profile to most search engines is free, so there is no reason not to do it.

To register your Web site with a search engine:

1. Enter a search engine (Altavista, Yahoo, etc.).
2. Go to "register your site."
3. Carefully describe your site's profile.
4. Try it, after submission.

## DIRECT MARKETING

According to Bruce Ryan, vice-president and general manager of Media Metrix, a research firm that studies Web users' characteristics and profiles, more than 80 percent of personal computer (PC) owners have at least one college degree. Their average household income is about $50,000 per year, well above the $35,000 U.S. household average. These consumers could be a prime market niche for event management organizations. Customers with household income of less than $40,000 per year often cannot afford to contract a professional event manager. By placing well-designed information and ads about your event management services on the Internet, you gain immediate direct contact with your target market group. In addition, larger competitors have no significant advantage over smaller organizations on the Internet.

## ONLINE SALES

An online sales concept is more applicable to companies that sell consumer goods, not services. However, event management organizations can still benefit greatly from Internet electronic commerce features. Event management organizations conduct registration, ticket sales, and distribution of materials over the Internet. All of these are segments of event sales. By putting them online, event management companies achieve financial savings and preserve resources that can now be reallocated.

Among the most important problems of online commerce is a problem of security. If an event management organization conducts financial transactions over the Internet, security of clients' personal financial information is the top priority. Data that contain such information as credit card and social security numbers are very sensitive. It is important to ensure that these data be protected. Since this is a critical point, it is highly recommended that you involve security professionals in this aspect of your Web site development.

## CUSTOMER SUPPORT

Event customer support is one of the areas where the Internet can prove truly indispensable. To date, few event management companies have realized the full potential of this opportunity. Industry analysts predict that in coming years, many event management companies will shift their telephone customer support services to the Web. This does not mean that telephone-based services will disappear but will become a secondary source that customers will use if they need to get a more detailed response or resolve a problem. The primary source will be the Internet.

The first step in shifting at least part of their customer support services online is to start a frequently asked questions (FAQ) Web section. Simply by adding this section to an event management organization Web site an organization can achieve better customer service and improve efficiency. The Event Management Certificate Program at George Washington University started an FAQ Web section in 1998. Before that happened, a large portion of all questions that the program received from students were about the same issues: location of classes, directions, and registration process. By posting answers to these frequently asked questions on the Web at *www.gwu.edu/emp,* the program was able to direct a majority of telephone questions to online answers. This move contributed greatly to customer satisfaction and enhanced the positive image of the program. The next step after posting an FAQ page is to personalize online customer service. This can be accomplished by adding the following interactive feature to a customer support site. A customer is asked to type his or her question and submit an e-mail address. Then the customer receives an answer within a certain time frame via either e-mail or telephone. By adding this feature an event organization can achieve much more personalized customer service and can also collect very valuable data about its clients.

## MARKET RESEARCH

Increasingly, event management organizations are recognizing the Internet potential for market research. Burke Inc., a leading international market research firm with a history of over 65 years, conducts online focus group meetings for its client in addition to face-to-face interviews and telephone surveys. Using Internet technology, the company was able to bring together participants from different parts of the world for small, real-time chat sessions. Clients can observe these chat sessions from anywhere in the world. Software such as Aptex, Autonomy, Adforce, and Accrue can monitor user's behavior constantly. This information can then be used to improve the site or services or to personalize content for users.

Web sites can be used to conduct market research by surveying visitors. This information can be effective if the process is well planned. Unfortunately, many Web sites require users to complete online registration forms without providing incentives. As a result, users often submit incorrect information or simply ignore the forms. This behavior can be explained by the desire of users to guard their privacy online and fear that their e-mail addresses will be sold to third parties. The best way to overcome this constraint is to build a sense of trust between event organization and clients or to compensate users for submitting their data.

## PRODUCT OR SERVICE DEVELOPMENT AND TESTING

The Internet is an ideal place for event companies to test new products/services before they are launched. An event organization can post information about a conference that it is planning to organize online and monitor the interest that users express toward the conference. By doing this the organization can see a market's reaction to the conference before they invest large amounts in actual planning. This refers to the first stage of successful event management event research. One of the biggest advantages that the Internet has over other marketing tools is real-time contact. Marketing professionals use a number of special technical features to leverage this point. Chat rooms, live broadcasting, and time-sensitive promotions are only a small part. The Internet allows marketing professionals to change and update content in almost no time, hence to ensure that customers have the most recent information.

# Web Design and Management

Today, after experiencing five consistent years of cyber growth, event marketing specialists are speaking about second and third generations of Web sites. The best definition I have heard of all three stages of online marketing development comes from Jupiter Communication, a leading Internet research firm based in New York. The company's analysts describe three types of Web sites, from least to most effective from the Internet marketing point of view:

1. The first and least developed type of Web site is *brochureware*. This type of Internet event marketing material has long been recognized as

the most primitive and boring type of marketing material. Web sites of this type are static and contain basic information about an organization, including its address and services. The site reflects a paper brochure placed on the Web. These kinds of sites miss the entire idea of marketing on the Web, and their effectiveness today is not very high.

2.  The second group of Web sites is known as *show-biz*. These sites try to amuse visitors through interactive features, flashing pictures, news reports, or press reviews. Although these features can serve the purpose of making an event management organization's Web site more attractive, the features are often not appropriate for the content and only distract the viewer's attention.

3.  The last and most developed type of Web sites are called *unilitarian*. These sites offer viewers a unique and balanced interactive service that is both highly informative and helpful in building brand recognition and loyalty. A classic example mentioned by Rick E. Bruner in *Net Results: Web Marketing That Works* (Hayden Books, 1998) is FedEx online services. The company's Web site does not contain a lot of flashy effects, is easy to navigate, and contains useful features such as shipment tracking and customer address books. The result of such well-performed online marketing strategy is that today about two-thirds of all FedEx customer contacts are conducted electronically. In addition to offering great customer service via the Internet, the company's Web site saves millions of dollars a year in regular customer support costs and marketing expenses.

The examples and models described above are applicable to most professional services, including event management. You can visit Web sites of various event management organizations and observe how lack of proper planning or understanding of online marketing concepts results in boring Web sites, useless online questionnaires, and annoying e-mail list servers. At the same time, those event organizations that carefully plan their online activities and balance design and content succeed in achieving their Internet marketing goals.

# Career Advancement Connections

## GLOBAL CONNECTION

Carefully evaluate the type of coding and bandwidth required for your data transmission. Remember that your ability to reach prospective event customers through the Internet depends largely on their communication infrastructure. Therefore, you must first determine if your target market can download your event e-marketing message easily and quickly. Also be very careful to ensure that the design, color, and language are appropriate and effective for the market you are trying to influence.

## TECHNOLOGY CONNECTION

Familiarize yourself with the following software applications:

- Microsoft FrontPage
- Netscape Composer

Familiarize yourself with the George Washington University Event Management Program's Web page at *www.gwu.edu/~emp* and learn how technology has been used to promote the program online.

## RESOURCE CONNECTION

Visit the following Web sites to learn more about online marketing and successful Internet marketing campaigns. You are also encouraged to read the following books about Internet marketing: *Net Results: Web Marketing That Works,* by USWeb and Rick E. Bruner (Hayden Books, 1998); *Creating Killer Web sites,* by David Siegel (Hayden Books, 1998).

## LEARNING CONNECTION

Locate 15 event organizations randomly on the Internet using any search engines. Visit their Web sites and try to divide the sites into the three major categories described in this chapter.

# PART FIVE

# Legal, Ethical, and Risk Management

**Facing Page**
Modern events incur high risks and require comprehensive risk assessment, planning, management, and control. *Photograph courtesy of Monica Vidal.*

# CHAPTER 12

# Risk Management: Legal and Financial Safeguards

## IN THIS CHAPTER YOU WILL LEARN HOW TO:

- Recognize and comply with standard and customary event regulations and procedures
- Read, understand, and evaluate legal event documents
- Access, plan, manage, and control potential event liabilities
- Obtain necessary permits and licenses to operate events
- Develop and manage risk management procedures

Most modern events have a potential for negligent activity that can lead to long and costly litigation. As the number of professionally managed events has increased, so has the concern for risk management and other legal and ethical issues. During the mid-1970s in the United States, many events were held to celebrate the 200th anniversary of American independence. During this period most events were organized by amateurs. As a result of a lack of understanding or training in risk management, there was a corresponding interest by the legal profession in bringing litigation against negligent event managers. This relationship continues today with one notable difference. Event managers are becoming smarter with regard to legal, ethical, and risk management issues.

The Convention Liaison Council publishes a newsletter edited by attorney Jeffrey King that addresses legal issues in the meetings and conference field. The International Events Group has published an entire volume, entitled *The Legal Guide to Sponsorship* (Chicago: IEG), that covers most legal issues related to this complex subject. Seminars, workshops, and courses are being offered throughout the United States covering recent developments in the areas of legal, ethical, and risk management issues relating to event management. Perhaps the best evidence of this change has been the development of alternative dispute resolution (ADR) programs to avoid lengthy and expensive litigation. Indeed, the paradigm has dramatically shifted from an environment governed by ignorance to one where education and proactive measures may reduce the level of risk and the resulting cost to event organizers.

# Contracts, Permits, and Licenses

Most public events in the United States as well as other countries require some type of official permission to be held. The larger the event in terms of attendance or technical complexity, the more official oversight that is usually required. Official review may come from local (town, city, county), state or province, or federal agencies. There are numerous reasons why an event must comply with existing laws and regulations. The four primary reasons are to protect your legal interests, to abide by ethical practices, to ensure the safety and security of your event stakeholders, and to protect your financial investment.

## PROTECTING YOUR LEGAL INTERESTS

Preparing proper contracts, researching the permits and licenses that are required, and complying with other legal requirements helps ensure that your event may proceed without undue interruption. Contracts or agreements may range from a simple letter or memorandum of understanding to complex multipage documents with lengthy riders (attachments). The event manager should utilize the services of competent legal counsel to review all standard agreements, such as hotel contracts, to ensure validity prior to execution. Furthermore, when writing new agreements, local legal counsel must make certain that the contract conforms to the code of the jurisdiction where it is written and executed (usually, where the event takes place). Lawyers are admitted to the state bar in the United States and must be experts on the state code (laws). Therefore, it is important to use an attorney who is admitted to the state bar where your event is being held or where, in the case of litigation, the case may be tried.

The majority of permits and licenses will be issued by local agencies. However, some state, provincial, or federal authorities may also issue licenses for your event. Therefore it is wise for the event manager to audit past and similar events carefully to identify the customary permits and licenses that are required for an event.

The permitting and licensing process may require weeks or even months to accomplish, so the event manager must carefully research each jurisdiction where he or she will produce an event and meet these time requirements. The cost for permits and licenses is typically nominal. However, some larger events or events that pose high risk (such as grand prix auto racing) may require the posting of expensive bonds.

Listed below are the major reasons why you must convince your event stakeholders of the importance of legal compliance and the need to obtain all necessary permits and licenses.

1. Event managers are legally required to obtain certain permits and licenses to conduct many events. Failure to do so may result in fines, penalties, interest, or cancellation of an event.
2. You have a fiduciary responsibility to event stakeholders to plan, prepare, and provide evidence of compliance. Avoiding compliance can have dire economic consequences.
3. You have an ethical responsibility (as stated by various industry code of ethics) to comply with all official regulations and to provide written agreements.
4. Although an oral agreement may be binding, the written agreement usually takes precedence. Written agreements provide all parties with

a clear understanding of the terms, conditions, and other important factors governing the event.
5. One of the primary ultimate responsibilities of an event manager is to provide a safe environment in which to conduct an event.

Although North American countries have many more regulations and compliance requirements, other countries are rapidly developing controls to ensure the safe and legal operating of events.

## HONORING ETHICAL PRACTICES

One of the primary definitions of a profession is adherence to a code of ethical conduct. As event management has emerged as a modern profession, a code of ethics has been developed by the International Special Events Society (ISES) (see Appendix 1), and many related industry organizations, such as Meeting Professionals International, have separate but similar codes. The code of ethics is different from biblical moral laws and from legal codes voted by governing bodies.

A code of ethics reflects what is standard and customary in both a profession and a geographic area. In that sense it is somewhat elastic in that it is applied in various degrees as needed for different circumstances. For example, when a hotelier offers an event manager a complimentary lunch at the first meeting, should this be construed as a bribe by the event manager and, therefore, refused? Attorney Jeffrey King, an expert in the field of event legal procedures, states that he advises his event manager clients always to pay for their lunch when meeting with a hotelier for the first time. "This immediately lets the hotelier know that the relationship is equal and represents a business transaction," according to King. It also sets an ethical standard for future discussions and the building of a relationship.

Although many professional societies, including ISES, enforce their code of ethics with a grievance procedure, in most cases it is up to the event manager to determine using the code of ethics as a guide for what is and is not appropriate ethical behavior. Robert Sivek of The Meeting House Companies, Inc., suggests that event managers use the "front page of the newspaper" rule. "Ask yourself if you would like to wake up and see your decision or action plastered across the front page of the newspaper," says Sivek. This may quickly determine whether or not your proposed action is one that is acceptable, not only to you but to others in your events community. Ethics are covered in detail in Chapter 13.

## ENSURING THE SAFETY AND SECURITY OF EVENT STAKEHOLDERS

A *safe event environment* implies that it is free from hazards. A *secure environment* is one that is protected from future harm. The event manager is responsible for constructing a safe, secure environment and sustaining it during the course of an event. Do not transfer this responsibility to others. The event manager either extends the invitation or coordinates the event at the invitation of others. You have both a legal and an ethical responsibility to event stakeholders to design and maintain a safe and secure event environment.

## PROTECTING YOUR FINANCIAL INVESTMENT

The legal, ethical, and safety-security aspects of an event can affect the bottom line dramatically. Therefore, every decision you make that is proactive may reduce your risk of unforeseen financial impacts. Practicing thorough legal, ethical, and risk management proactive measures may actually help your event produce greater revenues.

Although not every contingency can be anticipated, the more adept you are at strategically planning preemptive measures to prevent contingencies, the better your balance sheet may look at the end of the event. Lapses in legal, ethical, and risk management judgment may cause not only loss of property, life, and money, but loss of your event's good name as well.

# Key Components of an Event Management Agreement or Contract

The event management contract reflects the understanding and agreement between two or more parties regarding their mutual interests as specified in the agreement. A binding contract must contain the key components described below.

## PARTIES

The names of the parties must be clearly identified. The agreement must be described as being between these parties, and the names that are used in the agreement must be defined. Typical event management agreements are between the event manager and his or her client or the event manager and his or her vendor. Other contracts may be between an event professional and an insurance company, an entertainment company, or a bank or other lending institution.

## OFFER

The offer is the service or product tendered by one party to another. The event manager may offer consulting services to a client or a vendor may offer products to an event manager. The offer should list all services that an event professional offers to provide. Any miscommunications here may lead to costly litigation in the future.

## CONSIDERATION

The consideration clause defines what one party will provide the other upon acceptance of an offer.

## ACCEPTANCE

When both parties accept an offer, they execute (sign) the agreement confirming that they understand and agree to comply with the terms and conditions of the agreement.

## OTHER COMPONENTS

Although the key components are the parties, the offer, consideration, and acceptance, usually event management agreements include many other clauses or components. The most typical clauses are listed next.

### Terms

The terms clause defines how and when the funds will be paid to the person extending the offer. If the event manager offers consulting services, he or she may request a deposit in the amount of the first and last month's retainer and then require that the client submit monthly payments of a certain amount on a certain date each month. These terms define the financial conditions under which the agreement is valid.

For some large events, payments are made during a specified period. In this case, or in case of another complicated payment arrangement, a separate *payment schedule* should be attached to a contract. This schedule should be treated as an essential part of the contract and signed and dated by both parties. In case an advance payment is mentioned in the payment term section, special attention should be paid to the provisions of how the deposit is returned in the case of event cancellation. For example, is the deposit credited toward future transactions within a specific time period or is a cash refund offered?

Within the event management industry, event professionals are increasingly concerned with reducing internal or operational risk in order to improve profitability of their enterprise. Internal risk issues include theft, slippage, and intellectual property safeguarding. Event professionals must work closely with colleagues to put in place procedures aimed to reduce internal risks.

### Cancellation

Events are always subject to cancellation. Therefore, it is important to provide for this contingency legally with a detailed cancellation clause. Usually, the cancellation clause defines under what circumstances either party may cancel, how notification must be provided (usually in writing), and what penalties may be required in the event of cancellation.

## Force Majeure (Act of God)

In the force majeure clause, both parties agree on which circumstances, deemed to be beyond their control, will permit an event to be canceled without penalty to either party. The force majeure clause must always be specified to reflect the most common or predictable occurrences. These may include hurricanes, earthquakes, floods, volcanic eruption, tornadoes, famine, war, or other disasters.

## Arbitration

It is common practice to include in event management agreements a clause that allows both parties to use arbitration in place of a legal judgment when they fail to agree. The use of arbitration may save the parties substantial costs over traditional litigation.

## Billing

Because many events involve entertainers or are theatrical events in and of themselves, the agreement must define how entertainers will be listed in advertising and in the program. Generally, a percentage, such as 100 percent, is used to describe the size of their name in relation to other text.

## Time Is of the Essence

The time-is-of-the-essence clause instructs both parties that the agreement is valid only if it is signed within a prescribed period of time. Usually, this clause is inserted to protect the offerer from loss of income due to late execution by the purchaser.

## Assignment

As employees have shorter and shorter tenures with organizations it is more important than ever that agreements contain clauses indicating that the contract may not be assigned to other parties. For example, if Mary Smith leaves XYZ company, the agreement is between XYZ company and the offerer and may not be transferred to Smith's successor, who may or may not honor the agreement as an individual. Therefore, Mary Smith has executed the agreement on behalf of XYZ company.

## Insurance

Often, agreements will detail the type and limits of insurance that must be in force by both parties as well as a requirement that each party coinsure the other. Some agreements will require copies of certificates of insurance that name the other party as additional insured in advance of the event date.

## Hold Harmless and Indemnification

In the event of negligence by either party, the negligent party agrees to hold the other party harmless and to defend them (indemnify) against harm.

### Reputation

The production of an event is a reflection of the personal tastes of the event organization and sponsors. Therefore, some event managers include a specific clause that recognizes the importance of the purchaser's reputation and states that the event manager will use his or her best efforts to protect and preserve the reputation during management of the event.

### The Complete Agreement

Typically, the complete agreement is the final clause and states that the agreement constitutes the full understanding of both parties. Figure 12-1 demonstrates how these clauses are used in a typical event management consulting agreement.

## RIDER

A rider is an attachment to a main agreement and usually lists the important ingredients that support the main contract. These may include sound equipment and labor, lighting equipment and labor, food and beverages, transportation, housing for artists/entertainers, or other important financial considerations other than the artist's fee (e.g., a payment schedule). The rider should be attached to the main agreement and the rider should be initialed or signed separately to signify acceptance by both parties.

## CHANGES TO THE AGREEMENT

Most agreements will require negotiation prior to execution, and the result of these executions will be changes. If only two or three nonsubstantial changes are made, you may choose to initial and date each change prior to returning the agreement for execution by the other party. Your initial and date signify your acceptance of the change but do not obligate you to fulfill the entire agreement until you have affixed your signature. If there are substantial changes (such as in the date, time, venue, or fees) or more than three changes, it is best to draw up a new agreement.

## TERMS AND SEQUENCE OF EXECUTION

First and foremost, always require that the purchaser sign the agreement prior to affixing your signature. Once both signatures are affixed, the agreement becomes official. If you sign the agreement and forward it to the other party, and they make changes and sign it, you may be somewhat obligated for those changes. It is always wise to request the purchaser's signature before affixing your own.

Second, never use facsimiles. Should you be forced to litigate the agreement, the court will seek the "best copy" and that is usually an original. You may use a facsimile for an interim memorandum of understanding, but binding, official agreements must be originals.

*Agreement*

This agreement is between Jane Smith Productions (otherwise known as Event Manager) and ABC Corporation (otherwise known as Purchaser).

Event Manager agrees to provide the following services:

1. 50 hours of research regarding XYZ festival.

2. 40 hours of design regarding XYZ festival.

3. 30 hours of planning regarding XYZ festival.

4. 20 hours of coordination regarding XYZ festival.

5. 10 hours of evaluation regarding XYZ festival.

A total of 150 hours of consulting time will be provided by Event Manager.

Purchaser agrees to provide:

1. A total fee in the amount of $7500.

Terms:
The Purchaser agrees to provide a nonrefundable deposit in the amount of seven hundred and fifty dollars (U.S.) ($750.00) to officially retain the services of Event Manager. The Purchaser furthermore agrees to provide monthly payments in the amount of seven hundred and fifty dollars (U.S.) ($750.00) on or before the fifteenth day of each month commencing August 15, 2002, until the balance has been paid in full.

Cancellation:
In the event of cancellation, notice must be received in writing. Should Purchaser cancel 90 days or more prior to event, Event Manager shall be entitled to retain all funds paid as of this date. Should Purchaser cancel less than 90 days prior to event, Event Manager shall receive full payment as specified in the agreement above.

Force Majeure:
This agreement is automatically null and void if event is canceled due to an act of God, including hurricane, earthquake, flood, volcanic eruption, tornado, famine, or war. In the event of cancellation due to an act of God, neither party shall be liable for any further payments.

Insurance:
Both parties shall maintain in full force one million dollars ($1 million) per occurrence comprehensive general liability insurance. Each party shall name the other as additional insured for the duration of the event. Both parties shall provide a certificate of insurance demonstrating evidence of additional insured status prior to the start of the event.

Hold Harmless and Indemnification:
Both parties agree that if either party is negligent, they will defend the nonnegligent party and hold them harmless against future action.

**Figure 12-1**
Event Management Sample Consulting Agreement

Arbitration:
Both parties agree that if a dispute arises concerning this agreement, a professional arbitrator certified by the American Arbitration Association or the alternative dispute resolution process through the Conventional Liaison Council will be used in place of normal litigation.

Reputation:
Both parties agree to use their best efforts to preserve and protect each other's reputation during the conduct of this event. The Event Manager recognizes that the Purchaser has over time developed good standing in the business and general community and will use the best efforts available to protect and preserve this reputation from harm.

Billing:
The Event Manager shall be listed in the official program of the event with the following text in type the same size and style as the body copy.

*This event managed by Jane Smith Production.*

The Event Manager shall be listed in the official program with other staff in the following manner with text in type of the same size and style as the body copy.

*Jane Smith, Event Manager*

Time Is of the Essence:
This agreement must be executed by July 15, 1996. After this date this agreement must be considered null and void and a new agreement must be created.

Assignment:
This agreement may not be assigned to others. The persons executing this agreement have the full authority to sign this agreement on behalf of the organizations they represent.

The Full Agreement:
The agreement and any riders attached represent the full understanding between both parties. Any amendments to this agreement must be approved in writing and separately attached to this agreement.

Execution:
The signatures below confirm complete understanding and compliance with the terms and conditions described in this agreement.

_____          _____
ABC Corporation, Purchaser                        Date


_____          _____
Jane Smith, Event Manager                         Date

**Figure 12-1**
*(Continued)*

Third, take the time to sign the agreement in person. Explain to the purchaser that the terms implied in the agreement are only as valid as the integrity of the persons signing the document. Offer your hand in friendship as you jointly execute this agreement.

# Other Agreements

In addition to the main event consulting agreement, the event manager may be required to prepare and execute other types of agreements. Samples of these agreements may be found in Appendixes 8 and 9. Following are typical event management agreements.

- *Consulting agreement:* an agreement whereby one party (usually the event manager) agrees to provide consulting services for another party
- *Employment agreement:* an agreement whereby an employee agrees to specific terms for employment
- *Exhibitor contract:* an agreement between an individual exhibitor and the sponsor of an exposition to lease space for a specific booth at the exposition
- *Hotel contract:* an agreement between a hotel and the organization holding an event to provide rooms and function space as well as other services (food and beverages) for a specific event or series of events
- *Noncompete agreement:* an agreement whereby an employee agrees not to compete within a specific jurisdiction or marketplace for a specified period of time following termination of employment
- *Purchase order:* an order to a vendor to provide services or products
- *Sponsorship agreement:* a contract between a sponsor and an event organizer in which the organizer agrees to provide specific marketing services to the sponsor for a prescribed fee and/or other consideration
- *Vendor agreement:* an agreement between a vendor and an event manager or client to provide specific services or products for an event

These agreements, along with many others, may be required to ensure the professional operation of an event. To identify all the agreements that may be required, check with other event organizers and local officials as well as your vendors to determine the critical documents that must be executed prior to start of the event.

## PERMITS

Permits are issued by local, state, provincial, or federal governmental agencies and allow you to conduct certain activities at your event. Table 12-1 details the typical permits that may be required. Allow sufficient time to obtain the permits. A permit may be issued only after you have submitted the appropriate

**Table 12-1**  Typical Event Management Permits and Where to Obtain Them

| Permit | Source |
| --- | --- |
| Bingo | Lottery or gaming department |
| Food handling | Health department |
| Lottery | Lottery or gaming department |
| Occupancy | Fire department |
| Parking | Transportation and parking department |
| Park use | Park department |
| Public assembly | Public safety and police department |
| Pyrotechnics | Fire department |
| Sales tax | Revenue or tax collector's office |
| Sign and banners | Zoning department |
| Street closing | Transportation and parking department |

documentation and have paid a fee. Determine well in advance what type of documentation is required by the issuing agency and how funds are accepted.

Remember that permits are not issued automatically. A permit reflects that an agency is permitting your event organization to conduct certain activities provided that you conform to the regulations established. Make certain that you are able to comply with these regulations prior to applying for the permit. If you are denied a permit, you may consider appealing your case. In some cases, event managers have sued an agency to obtain permission to conduct an event. However, since most event managers rely on the goodwill of local agencies to conduct an event successfully, litigation should be the absolute final resort.

## LICENSING

A license is granted by a governmental institution, a private organization (as in music licensing) or a public entity to allow you to conduct a specific activity. The difference between a permit and a license may be slight in some jurisdictions. Usually, the requirements for obtaining a license are much more stringent and require due diligence (evidence of worthiness) prior to issuance.

Table 12-2 lists the most common licenses required for events and their sources. Additional licenses may be required for your event. To determine what licenses are required, make certain that you examine the event's history, check with organizers of similar events, and confirm and verify with the appropriate agencies that issue these licenses.

**Table 12-2**  Typical Event Management Licenses and Where to Obtain Them

| Permit | Source |
| --- | --- |
| Alcohol | Alcohol beverage control boards |
| Business | Economic development agency; recorder |
| Food | Health department |
| Music | American Society of Composers, Authors, and Publishers or Broadcast Music Inc. |
| Pyrotechnics | Bureau of Alcohol, Tobacco, and Firearms; fire department |

One of the best sources of information will be your vendors. Audit your vendors, especially in the technology field, and determine if licenses are required (as in the case of laser projection) or if the event manager must obtain a license.

For many events both permits and licenses must be secured. The larger the event, the more likely the number of permits and licenses will increase. Remember that licenses and permits are the government's way of establishing a barrier to entry to protect their interests. Work closely with these agencies to understand their procedures, time frames, and inspection policies. A close working relationship with the agencies that issue licenses and permits will help ensure the success of your overall event operation.

## CONTRACTS, PERMITS, AND LICENSES: A SYNERGISTIC RELATIONSHIP

Professional event managers understand, and use to their advantage, the synergy between a well-written and executed contract and the acquisition of proper permits and licenses. All three instruments are essential for the professional operation of modern events. When developing an agreement determine in advance who is responsible for obtaining and paying for specific permits and licenses and incorporate this language into the agreement. Unless you have specified who is responsible for obtaining and paying for permits and licenses, this can lead to an interruption of your event and conflicts among the various stakeholders.

Therefore, conduct research carefully during the planning stage to identify all necessary permits and licenses and determine who will be responsible for coordinating this process. Include this information in your master event consulting agreement as well as your vendor agreements. Since permits and licenses are unavoidable in most event situations, it behooves the event manager to practice the maxim that an ounce of prevention (or risk management) is worth a pound of cure. Use the planning phase to examine potential permit processes and then use the coordination stage to link these two important steps within the event management process.

Contracts, permits, and licenses have legal, ethical, and risk management ramifications. To ensure that these impacts are positive, event managers must understand their importance and work diligently to communicate with the required agencies as well as to prepare and execute valid agreements.

# Risk Management Procedures

"Hundreds of people burned to death in tent during graduation ceremony in India," shouted the headlines. Whenever human beings assemble for the purposes of celebration, education, marketing, or reunion, there is an increased risk of loss of life or property. This has been proven many times, as similar newspaper headlines have reported accidents that have occurred at events.

With increased injuries, thefts, and other misfortunes, comes, of course, increased expense. This may stem from two sources: the loss of revenue resulting directly from the occurrence, and increased insurance premiums when underwriters are forced to pay large settlements as a result of negligence. Perhaps the most profound loss is the loss of business opportunity that results from the bad publicity attached to such tragedies. After all, who wants to visit an event where a tent might collapse and injure people or where there is a risk of food poisoning?

Alexander Berlonghi, an expert in the field of risk assessment and risk management, has devised a method for attempting to identify and contain the many risks associated with events. Berlonghi describes the first step in the risk assessment process as that of holding a risk assessment meeting. Following is a step-by-step guide to holding such a meeting. I suggest that you use it for each of your events—it could be a lifesaver.

## ORGANIZING A RISK ASSESSMENT MEETING

The first question to ask when organizing a risk assessment meeting is: Who should attend? Ideally, all key event stakeholders should be involved in this meeting, and you may wish to use a written survey to audit their opinions regarding risks associated with an event. However, for practical purposes you must first identify those event team leaders who can bring you the best information from which to manage present and future risks associated with your events. The following event team leaders should be included in the risk assessment meeting.

- Admissions manager
- Advertising manager
- Animal handler
- Box office manager
- Broadcast manager
- Catering manager

- Comptroller
- Computer or data processing manager
- Electrician
- Entertainment specialist
- Fire department liaison

- Food and beverage manager
- Hotel security director
- Insurance broker
- Laser specialist
- Lighting specialist
- Office manager
- Parking specialist

- Police liaison for event
- Public relations manager
- Pyrotechnic specialist
- Security director for event
- Sound specialist
- Special effects specialist
- Transportation specialist

## Before the Meeting

Once you have identified the participants for a risk assessment meeting, it is time to put them to work. Assigning prework helps meeting participants focus on the seriousness of the meeting and will probably improve the efficiency of the meeting. Figure 12-2 demonstrates a typical risk assessment meeting announcement that you may customize for your own use.

Make sure that you follow up with the meeting participants to ensure that all lists have been returned and that you understand the risks they have identified as important to their area. Once you have received responses it is time to compile a master list of all risks that have been identified. You may either list these risks in alphabetical order or subdivide them by event area.

The final step in preparing for a risk assessment meeting is to prepare a detailed agenda that may be used to conduct the meeting. Prior to the meeting, circulate the agenda and seek feedback from the participants. Figure 12-3 provides a sample agenda and premeeting announcement that you may customize for a risk assessment meeting.

---

| TO: | Event Risk Assessment Team |
|---|---|
| FROM: | Event Manager |
| SUBJECT: | Meeting Announcement and Instructions |
| DATE: | August 15, 2002 |
| ACTION REQUIRED: | Return your list of potential risks by July 15, 2002. |

A risk assessment meeting will be held on July 20, 2002 at 1 P.M. for the purpose of identifying and managing the major risks associated with this event. Prior to this meeting you should audit your area and prepare a comprehensive list of risks associated with your event responsibilities.

Interview the team members in your area and ask them to assist you in this important task. Risks may involve potential injuries, loss of life or property, or other risks.

Submit this list to me by the close of business on July 15, 2002. Thank you for your contribution to this important process.

---

**Figure 12-2**

Risk Assessment Meeting Announcement

```
TO:                    Event Team Leaders
FROM:                  Event Manager
SUBJECT:               Event Risk Assessment Meeting Agenda
DATE:                  July 15, 2002
ACTION REQUIRED:       Return the enclosed agenda and return to me with
                       your comments by July 18, 2002.


                       Tentative Agenda


   I. Welcome and introduction
  II. Explanation of purposes, event manager
 III. Comprehensive risk review, all participants
  IV. Additional risks not covered in listing, all participants
   V. Recommendations for risk management, all participants
  VI. Economic impacts of risk management, all participants, comptroller
 VII. Postmeeting work assignment, event manager
VIII. Adjournment
```

**Figure 12-3**
Event Risk Assessment Meeting Sample Agenda/Announcement

## Conducting the Meeting

After the agenda has been distributed, corrected, and approved, it is time to convene the risk assessment meeting. Use a hollow square seating design and prepare tent cards for each participant, listing his or her name and event area of responsibility. A flipchart displayed on an easel stand should list the agenda for the meeting, and subsequent pages should list the risks previously identified by meeting participants. In addition, participants should receive a typed copy of the agenda and the comprehensive list of risks, along with any other collateral material that will help them make the important decisions that will be required during the meeting.

As the event manager, you are also the meeting facilitator. To facilitate the participation of all, first welcome the participants and explain that the meeting will be successful only if they participate actively by offering their expert opinions and engaging in a lively discussion concerning recommendations for reducing or alleviating the risks that have been identified.

After you have set the tone for the meeting, review the list of risks and ask the meeting participants to study them for a few moments and identify any gaps. What risks have been overlooked?

The next stage of the meeting is to begin discussions on how to reduce, control, transfer, or eliminate the risks that have been identified. This is a good time to ask the participants to form small groups that represent cross-disciplinary task forces. For example, you may ask the admissions, box office, and comptroller team members to work on reducing the risk of theft from the box office or eliminating the risk of gate crashing. Allow 15 to 30 minutes for this activity.

When you reconvene the group, ask them to communicate their recommendations to the entire group and try to seek consensus from group members. Do not rush this process. During these discussions important concerns may be expressed and you must make sure that you address and attempt to satisfy these concerns before moving on to the next stage.

Every risk decision will have corresponding financial impacts. This is a good time to use a Likert scale to rate the importance of each risk in terms of the overall event. For example, to identify risks that should receive the greatest consideration when considering the financial impact on your event, ask each participant to assign a number to each risk, with 1 representing least concern and 5 representing most concern. Theft from the box office might rate a 5 while rain might receive a 1. Once you have reached consensus on the level of importance of each risk, you may concentrate the discussion on risks that the group deems most important.

### Documenting the Meeting's Recommendations

The final stage of a risk assessment meeting is to document your recommendations and assign postmeeting work groups to continue to address the important issues covered in the meeting. Assign one person as a scribe during the meeting and ask them to prepare review notes from the meeting to be circulated within three business days. The notes should reflect the substance and content of the discussion and list the recommendations the group has agreed to pursue.

The work groups are responsible for conducting additional research to identify ways in which to better manage the risks that were discussed at perhaps lower the cost of the event. Their work may include interviewing external experts or brainstorming with their fellow event stakeholders to seek better solutions.

The review notes also serve the important purpose of preserving the history of the meeting. Should there be an incident at your event that requires evidence that you conducted risk assessment and management procedures to attempt to prevent this occurrence, the review notes may serve as valuable proof documenting your proactive stance.

## SAFETY MEETING AND OTHER CONSIDERATIONS

Before you allow vendors to install the various event elements, you must conduct a brief safety meeting to alert all event stakeholders to the standards your organization has established with regard to safety. Notify the event stakeholders in writing and explain that this meeting is required for participation in the event. Usually, the meeting is held prior to installation and is conducted by the event manager. Survey the event stakeholders to determine if they have particular expertise in event safety. You may wish to call upon this expertise during the safety meeting.

Use a checklist or written agenda distributed to each participant at the meeting to remain focused on the goals and objectives of the meeting. Detail your expectations of minimum safety requirements for the event. These may include taping or ramping of exposed cables, grounding of all electric power, keeping the work areas cleared of debris, nonsmoking policies, and other important issues.

Ask those assembled if they have been trained in the Heimlich (choking) maneuver or CPR (cardiopulmonary resuscitation) during the past three years. Ask those who have been trained to serve as first responders for the event if someone requires this level of response. The event manager should be trained in both the Heilmich maneuver and CPR and be prepared to use these techniques to sustain or save lives if required.

Make certain that you ask each person to sign in when they attend the meeting. This will provide you with a record of those who participated and may be helpful if there is a later claim against the event. Conclude the meeting by reminding all participants that the overall goal of this event is zero percent tolerance of unsafe working conditions.

## INSPECTIONS

Prior to opening the doors to admit guests to your event, conduct a final inspection. Walk the entire event site and note any last-minute corrections that must be made to ensure the safety of guests. Walk-throughs are best conducted by a team that includes your client, key vendors, key event team leaders, and when possible, police, fire, and other officials.

During the walk-through, use an instant camera and/or video to record corrections you have made and post caution signs where appropriate to notify guests of possible risks.

The following areas must be reviewed when conducting a walk-through prior to admitting guests to your event:

1. Accreditation systems are in working order.
2. Admissions personnel are in place.
3. Air walls are in working order in case of evacuation.
4. Bar personnel have received alcohol management training.
5. Doors are unlocked from inside the venue in case of evacuation.
6. Edge of stage is marked with safety tape.
7. Electric boxes are labeled with caution signs.
8. Electric cables are grounded.
9. Electric cables traversing public areas are taped or ramped.
10. Elevators are working.
11. Light level is sufficient for safe ingress and egress.
12. Lighting has been properly secured with safety chains.
13. Metal detectors are in place and operational for VIP appearances.
14. Ramps are in place for the disabled.

15. Security personnel are posted.
16. Signs are visible and well secured.
17. Staging has chair and handrails.
18. Stairs have handrails, and individual steps are marked with safety tape to highlight edge.
19. Ushering personnel are in place.

These are but a few of the areas that must be inspected prior to admitting guests. You may wish to prepare a checklist to inspect each area systematically or simply use a small pad of paper and note areas that must be corrected prior to the event. The walk-through should be conducted one to two hours prior to the official start time of an event. This will give you time to make any minor corrections that are required.

## DOCUMENTATION AND DUE DILIGENCE

Each of the steps included in the walk-through demonstrates to officials, and perhaps one day to a jury, that you have attempted to do what a reasonable person would be expected to do under these circumstances to ensure the safety of guests. Documenting your risk assessment, management, and prevention steps may assist you in demonstrating that you have practiced due diligence for your event. The goal is to achieve or exceed the standard of care normally associated with an event of this size and type. The steps listed above will help you move rapidly toward this goal.

## OBTAINING INSURANCE

Insurance is used by event managers to transfer the risk to a third party, the insurance underwriter. Many venues require that the event manager or event organization maintain in full force a minimum of $1 million per occurrence of comprehensive general liability insurance. Some municipalities require similar limits of insurance for events to be held in their jurisdiction. Events that are more complex and pose greater risks may be required to have higher limits of insurance.

Identifying a properly qualified insurance broker is an important first step in receiving expert advice regarding the types of insurance that may be required for your event. After checking with the venue and municipality to determine the level of insurance required, you will need a well-trained specialty insurance broker to advise you further on coverage available.

A specialty insurance broker has insurance products and services specifically relevant for the event management profession. For example, large firms such as Marsh and McLennan or K & K provide products for clients ranging from the Super Bowl to local parades and festivals. They are experienced experts in providing advice and counsel for the unique risks associated with events.

## Identifying the Appropriate Premium

After you have contacted two or more specialty insurance brokers and determine the type of insurance products that may be required for your event, you will request quotes from each broker. The brokers will ask you to complete a detailed form listing the history of the event, specific hazards that may be involved (e.g., pyrotechnics), and other critical information. The broker will submit this information to several underwriters and present you with a quote for coverage.

The most cost-effective premium is an annual policy known as comprehensive general liability insurance. Some event managers pay as little as $2000 annually to provide coverage for a variety of risks for which the event manager may be liable. Other event managers pay their premiums on a per event basis. Your insurance broker will help you decide what the best system is for you.

The following insurance products are typically associated with events:

- Automotive liability
- Board of directors' liability
- Business interruption
- Cancellation
- Comprehensive general liability
- Disability
- Earthquake
- Errors and omissions
- Fire
- Flood
- Health
- Hurricane
- Key person
- Life
- Nonappearance
- Office contents
- Officers
- Rain
- Worker's compensation

Your client or others involved with your event may ask that they be named as an additional insured on your policy. The term *additional insured* means that if for any reason there is an incident, your insurance policy will cover claims against those listed as additionally insured. Before agreeing to name the other party or parties as additional insured, check with your insurance broker to find out if there is an additional charge or if this is appropriate. You may also want to ask the other parties to name you as additional insured on their policies.

## Exclusions

Every insurance policy will list certain hazards that are excluded from coverage. Make certain that you check with your broker and review your policy carefully to make sure that there are no gaps in coverage for your event. For example, if your event is using pyrotechnics and they are excluded specifically from your current coverage, you may wish to purchase additional coverage to protect your event.

## Preexisting Coverage

Before purchasing any coverage, audit your existing coverage to check for gaps regarding your event. Your event organization may already have in force specific coverage related to the risks associated with your event. Once you have conducted this audit, your specialty insurance broker can advise you with regard to additional coverage for your event.

## RISK CONTROL

### Theft Prevention

The best strategy for theft prevention is segregation of duties. All transactions that involve cash handling, returns, and deposits should have at least two employees performing that transaction.

### Cash

Cash must be handled accurately. I encourage you to establish a special cash log where all cash transactions should be recorded. Even small petty cash numbers add up to a substantial amount, so if you think that $20 cash expense is not worth recording, you are wrong; $20 dollars per week turns into $1080 per year. Anyone who handles cash should be given occasional unscheduled vacation days to check this employee's cash-handling practice. A replacement employee is in a very good position while an employee is away to catch all illegal activities set up by the employee.

### Inventory

One of the most important tools in preventing theft of inventory is incorporation of special procedures for inventory management. Storage facilities should be monitored; two people should be involved in storage operations. All records of inventory disbursement should be stored and checked on a random basis. In a real-time computer system inventory should have bar codes that have to be entered into the system as soon as inventory is disbursed.

As an event manager and supervisor, you should approve all equipment breakdowns and/or replacements. Management of event management organizations should analyze the level of breakage that is typical for their operations. Any constant abnormalities should be investigated in more depth. Physical inventory counts should be taken regularly. Shortages should be reviewed, comparing them to acceptable loss levels.

### Copyright

Some event management organizations have their brand names listed separately in their assets. This is an important part of their goodwill. Any event management organizations should protect its brand. Event professionals should consult copyright and intellectual property specialists to evaluate copyright areas where an organization can have potential problems. All brand names and logos of event organizations should contain clear copyright marks and warning statements.

## MANAGING RISK: EVERYONE'S RESPONSIBILITY

The field of event risk management has grown so rapidly that there is emerging a specialization within the profession for risk experts such as Berlonghi and others. Larger events such as the Pope's visit to Colorado may require the expertise of a risk manager such as Berlonghi to manage this complex event from a risk perspective. However, for most events, the event manager is also the risk manager.

As the risk manager, you must assemble a risk management team that will assist you in identifying and managing the risks to improve your event operations. You must communicate to all event stakeholders that event risk management is everyone's responsibility.

# Career Advancement Connections

## GLOBAL CONNECTION

Once you have created a list of written ethical policies, procedures, and practices, ask a colleague in another country to examine these statements to determine if they are acceptable in their culture. To avoid committing an offense, use advisors in other countries to guide you in your ethical practices.

## TECHNOLOGY CONNECTION

Use appropriate etiquette when using the Internet. Avoid spamming (marketing without permission), flaming (using all capital letters, exclamation points, and harsh language), or inappropriate language that may offend a reader. Visit the ISES Web site *(www.ises.com)* and other industry sites to review their codes of ethics.

## RESOURCE CONNECTION

The American Society for Individual Security *(www.asisonline.org)* provides a wide range of books, articles, and videos to help you understand the many issues regarding safety, security, and risk management. The most comprehensive book in this field is entitled "Event Risk Management" and will be published by Wiley in late 2002.

## LEARNING CONNECTION

Design a risk management plan for your event. Describe how the plan will change based on changing weather conditions. Explain how you will conduct, if necessary, a mass evacuation due to a catastrophic condition such as fire or violence. List the types of insurance that must be purchased to reduce your financial exposure.

**Facing Page**
This small parade has moral, legal, and ethical implications for the organizers and participants. *Photograph courtesy of Monica Vidal.*

# CHAPTER **13**

# Morality, Law, and Ethics in Event Management

**IN THIS CHAPTER YOU WILL LEARN HOW TO:**

- Understand the difference between morals, laws, and ethics
- Identify common ethical problems in the special events industry
- Avoid some ethical problems
- Establish policies and procedures for ethical issues
- Identify and use industry ethical guidelines
- Appoint an "ethical brain trust" to guide your ethical decision making

This could be the longest chapter in this volume, but instead, it is the briefest. One decade ago this chapter would probably have not appeared in this book or any business book, for that matter. However, as businesses have grown and the event management industry in particular has expanded rapidly, more and more ethical issues have appeared. Only a few years ago when I introduced a required unit on ethics in my master's degree courses, several students told me that the other business professors found this to be ironic in a business school curriculum. I have persevered and continue to include this unit, and slowly but surely more and more business schools are now requiring not only units but also entire courses in business ethics. Largely prompted by their corporate supporters who ultimately employ their graduates, business schools have come to realize that a discussion of business ethics may be the first and last time students are exposed to this important issue. Indeed, the majority of the population may never earn an advanced degree, so providing this discussion at the baccalaureate or graduate level could fill in a gap left by parents and teachers. I often tell my colleagues that we must teach ethical decision making because it may ultimately affect and influence students' actions at the university as well as beyond. As faculty and mentors we have a responsibility to help students make the personal and professional decisions that ethical behavior requires. I suggest that event managers also have a responsibility to themselves and those they mentor to understand the requirements for making sound ethical decisions.

# Differences between Morals, Laws, and Ethics

Historically, the term *moral* is related to the Mosaic code as received by Moses at Mount Sinai during the biblical period. When Moses received the original 613 commandments he also realized that if he or his followers disobeyed, there would be penalties. Morals are personal decisions that have personal consequences. The legal system is a series of laws (many based on the Mosaic code) that are linked to specific punishments. Laws are enacted by groups, and punishment is imposed by peers (juries) or judges. Unlike morals, laws use third parties to enforce them and issue the punishment based on the degree of the violation. Ethics are, however, neither morals nor laws. Some argue that ethics incorporate both law and morals, but in actuality, ethics are the actions by individuals or groups based on the business culture that is accepted at the time of the action. Although ethics are personal decisions, they are guided by group behavior and group acceptance.

To better understand the difference between morals, laws, and ethics, ask yourself a series of questions. Let us start with a moral question: "Would you commit murder?" A moral person would immediately answer "No, never." However, what if your children were being attacked by a violent person and the only way to stop the attack would be to murder the assailant?

"Would you steal?" Once again most people would answer, "No." However, let us suppose that your children are starving and their very lives are threatened unless they receive some food to nourish them. Now what would you do?

"Would you attack someone?" Most of us would answer negatively. However, if your country were attacked and you were part of the army that must defend your nation, you would answer in the affirmative or face serious punishment.

As you can see, many ethical questions also have moral and legal repercussions. Most of us will not be confronted on a daily basis with serious moral or legal decisions; however, many members of this profession regularly face serious ethical dilemmas.

# Common Ethical Problems in the Special Events Industry

Ethical problems often vary according to type of industry and geographic location. In the special events industry, some ethical problems faced by hoteliers may or may not affect those in the party rental industry. The same may be said about the event manager in the country of Brazil versus the event manager in the United States. For example, in Chapter 12 you examined some risk management and legal issues associated with the consumption of alcohol. In the United States the person who pours the alcohol may be legally responsible if a person being served overindulges and causes injury to others. In Brazil, just the opposite is true. The legal system of Brazil places the responsibility on the drinker rather than on the server. This has important ethical ramifications. If you are serving alcohol in Brazil, is it ethical to allow your guests to drink until they are inebriated and capable of causing injury to others? As you can see, the type of industry (or industry segment) and the geographic location often dictate the customs, practices, and values that are practiced by the members of that community. These customs, practices, and values of the industry and local culture often drive the ethical decision making within the event organization.

Numerous typical ethical issues are addressed on a regular basis by members of the event management industry. Table 13-1 lists some of the ethical issues that you will encounter most often.

# Avoiding or Addressing Ethical Problems

The proactive methods described in Table 13-1 illustrate some of the simple and practical steps that you can take to avoid the pitfalls of unethical behavior. Realistically, you cannot predict every ethical dilemma that may arise. You can however, be prepared to resolve these problems with a proven three-step process: admission, remorse, and correction.

Despite your best efforts to avoid ethical misconduct, you can always recognize the mistake and notify the person or persons who may have been affected and tell them, "I made a mistake. I'm sorry. I will try not to let it happen again." Too often, individuals and organizations attempt to avoid confronting the problem of ethical misconduct, and the misdeed festers like a wound that never heals. From the highest office in the land to the local church or synagogue, most of us know far too many examples of ethical violations that are swept under the rug with the supposition that they will go unnoticed.

**Table 13-1** Typical Event Industry Ethical Issues

| Issue | Those Affected | Proactive Measures |
|---|---|---|
| Breach of confidentiality | Staff members | Include a confidentiality clause in employment agreements and policies and procedures. |
| Gifts versus bribes | Buyer and seller | Define gifts, set limits for receipt of gifts, and establish policies and procedures. |
| Sexual harassment | Staff members, supervisors, clients, guests | Establish written policies and procedures in accordance with federal laws, conduct training for new staff, and notify clients of policies and procedures. |
| Staff members soliciting clients from previous employment at new place of employment | Staff members | Establish employment agreements that limit this exposure. |
| Taking credit for others' work | Staff member and organization | Clearly identify who is responsible for work produced. |
| Theft of ideas by clients and competitors | Clients, competitors | Insert a copyright statement on proposals, and notify others of infringement. |
| Vendors accepting work directly from clients | Vendors and clients | Establish written policies. |

Despite the rug, these ethical infractions continue to smell, and the small lump under the rug may grow and trip others in the future unless you address the problem promptly.

There are numerous successful examples of the three-step process for handling the problem of ethical violations. This is why it is important that you and your organization develop policies, procedures, and practices to address ethical issues when they arise. One of the best examples of professional handling of a major ethical situation is the 1982 Tylenol tampering incident. Johnson & Johnson, the maker of Tylenol, immediately withdrew the product from all shelves worldwide and issued a statement describing their plans for researching the problem and improving the safety measures for their products. As a result of their response, Johnson & Johnson received plaudits from the media and customers, and sales remain strong today.

How did Johnson & Johnson know how to respond to this ethical issue? The Johnson & Johnson credo states in the first paragraph that their company exists for the purpose of providing safe products and services: "We believe that our first responsibility is to the doctors, nurses, and patients. To mothers and fathers and all others who use our products and services." You can create your own credo to guide you as you face the many ethical decisions you will encounter in your career. One of the important facets of the Johnson & Johnson credo is the statement "We must strive to reduce costs . . . we must be good citizens." These statements not only reflect the credo of the organization but also address the operational aspects to enable managers and other employees to make decision on a daily basis that are congruent with the values of Johnson & Johnson. When you draft your credo, make certain that it is more than cold type on a page; instead, it should burn like a branding iron into the hearts and minds of all persons who are responsible for serving as the stewards of your organization's good name.

Nearly 50 years ago my father opened his small hardware store in Dallas, Texas. Instead of hanging a grand opening banner or blowing up balloons, he sat down and composed a simple but profound message to his customers. The message was then transformed into elegant calligraphy and displayed just inside the front door of his store, where it greeted customers for almost 50 years. As I write these lines, that message faces me, and it reads:

> *Once upon a time, I met a stranger . . . not so many years ago . . . in a distant city. When he learned that he knew my grandfather, the stranger looked at me and said, "You have a good name." He went on to explain that my grandfather held the respect and esteem of his fellow businessmen, his customer bestowed their confidence upon him, and his compassion and service for others was an inspiration to all. It is the hope of this business that we will so conduct our affairs that someday, somewhere one of our descendants will meet a stranger who will say, "You have a good name."*
>
> —MAX B. GOLDBLATT (1911–1995)

## ESTABLISHING POLICIES AND PROCEDURES FOR ETHICAL ISSUES

In Appendix 15 you will find the ISES Code of Ethics. This is one example of how an industry establishes standards for ethical behavior. Some ways to avoid or resolve many of the issues within the code of ethics are:

- *Do not accept expensive gifts.* Ban or set a limit on gifts.
- *Avoid confusion regarding a change in an agreement.* Put all agreements (and changes) in writing and have both parties initial acceptance.
- *Avoid improper promotion of your services.* Seek written authority while working for another event manager.
- *Avoid claiming credit for an event you produced while working for another firm.* Clearly disclose the circumstances concerning the production of the event.
- *Avoid submitting photos of an event as an example of your work.* Clearly disclose that you helped produce your specific contributions to this event.

## IDENTIFYING AND USING INDUSTRY ETHICAL GUIDELINES

In addition to the International Special Event Society, many related industry organizations use guidelines for professional practice or ethical beliefs to guide decision making. One criterion that you may wish to use for joining a professional organization is whether or not they have established a strong code of ethics along with appropriate enforcement procedures. Although these guidelines are at best guideposts rather than firm edicts, they will not only be useful to you but also to your clients as they raise the image of your profession.

## APPOINTING AN ETHICAL BRAIN TRUST TO GUIDE YOUR ETHICAL DECISION MAKING

I have always relied upon wise counselors and advisors to help me when faced with making a difficult ethical decision. Rather than assembling this brain trust at the last minute or on a case-by-case basis, I recommend that you identify people who know you well enough to provide you with critical input during times of ethical decision making.

A colleague of mine was faced with a tough ethical decision when he discovered some papers that contained highly personal information in a file left by a recently deceased relative. The papers included letters describing the circumstances of a death that took place 60 years earlier. After consulting with his immediate family members, he decided to contact his minister, who had been a friend of the family for nearly 60 years. The minister listened to the dilemma and asked a few questions relating to the medical consequences of the case. Finally, the minister offered simple but important advice that would spare much future pain to the survivors of the person who had died. "There is a reason the letters were hidden for 60 years. Burn the letters and do not discuss this with anyone." Obviously, the minister had faced this dilemma many times before and knew the framework for reaching this critical decision.

In another instance, someone's will granted lifetime use of a house for a long-time friend of the family. When told of the gift, the friend declined to live in the house and authorized sale of the property. The heirs wanted to share with the friend some of the proceeds from the sale, but a question arose as to how much would be appropriate. Once again a brain trust was contacted. This time three wise and experienced persons were consulted: a minister (and long-time family friend), an attorney, and a peer of the same chronological age who had recently had a similar experience. The consensus of the advisors was to use the rule of tithing and provide a gift of 10 percent of the net proceeds to the friend but to forward the funds in the form of a specific gift for past services rather than an arbitrary amount.

These are the types of complex and difficult decisions that require the collective wisdom of the community to reach an appropriate ethical conclusion. Once you reach this conclusion, you can feel confident that your judgment has not only been tested but also strengthened by the counsel of others, who in many instances are more experienced than yourself. Therefore, once you make the decision, do not look back. Instead, look forward to the next ethical decision you will face because you will use the experience of all of your past decisions to make future ones.

According to the *Washington Post,* the Washington, DC Millennium–Bicentennial Celebration resulted in $290,500 in unpaid bills. The *Post* also reported that there were questions of ethics violations. The District of Columbia established a not-for-profit organization for the purpose of raising funds to plan and coordinate the millennium and bicentennial celebrations for the District of Columbia. However, there were questions about whether or not the organization used District of Columbia government employees to raise money for the event.

Polly A. Rich, the ethics counselor in the District of Columbia corporation counsel's office wrote in a memo that city employees should not raise money for nonprofits or solicit contributions from companies and individuals who do business in the District. Anthony W. Williams, Mayor of the District of Columbia, responded to the criticism by stating: "Clearly, the lesson from the millennium–bicentennial events and the loss of a substantial amount of money from a lot of this nonprofit fundraising is: 'What is the proper mechanism to do it?'" The question of appropriateness is not solely moral or legal but also an ethical dilemma that every event manager must address.

# Career Advancement Connections

## GLOBAL CONNECTION

Once you have created a list of written ethical policies, procedures, and practices, ask a colleague in another country to examine these statements to determine if they are acceptable in their culture. To avoid committing an offense, use advisors in other countries to guide you in your ethical practices.

## TECHNOLOGY CONNECTION

Use appropriate etiquette when using the Internet. Avoid spamming (marketing without permission), flaming (using all capital letters, exclamation points, and harsh language), or inappropriate language that may offend the reader. Visit the ISES Web site *(www.ises.com)* and other industry sites to review their codes of ethics.

## RESOURCE CONNECTION

The Ethics Resource Center *(www.ethics.org)* in Washington, DC provides a wide range of books, articles, and videos to help you understand the many issues affecting ethical decision making.

## LEARNING CONNECTION

- You have been offered an expensive gift from a vendor in exchange for your business. Is there any situation or circumstance where it would be acceptable to accept this gift? How do you know this? Where will you get the information? How will you make the decision? How could the decision be different if this occurred in another culture, where the giving and receiving of expensive gifts is accepted, usual, and customary?
- One of your event guests complains to you about inappropriate behavior from one of your vendors. Although the vendor is not your employee, do you have an ethical responsibility to intervene on behalf of your event guest? How do you know what to do? Where will you get the information? What steps will you take to make the decision?
- You have been asked to bid on a future event. You are asked by your prospective client to show examples of your past work. Some of the work you have completed was when you were in the employ of others. Do you explain to your prospective client that some of this work was completed while you worked for another firm, or do you simply ignore this fact and present the work to the client as though you were responsible as an individual? How do you know what to do? Where will you get the information to make the proper ethical judgment? How do you know that this judgment is correct?

---

**Facing Page**

The explosion of technology resources for event managers has increased efficiency and improved quality. *Photograph courtesy of Monica Vidal.*

# PART SIX

# Technology and Career Advancement

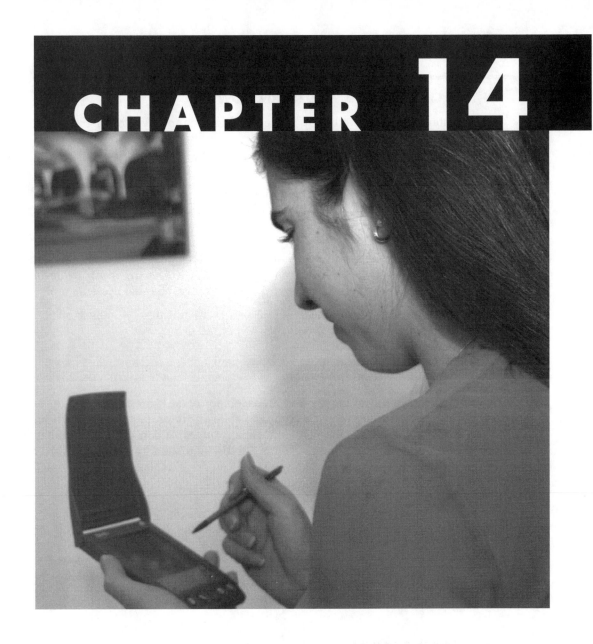

# CHAPTER 14

# Technology for Modern Event Management

## IN THIS CHAPTER YOU WILL LEARN HOW TO:

- Understand the role and scope of emerging technology within the event industry
- Find resources for efficient technological solutions
- Differentiate data processing systems
- Apply technological solutions to solve problems

The major task of the technology and information system in modern event management is to collect, store, and provide data to the different levels of users. The comparative advantages of technology over manual systems are:

- Opportunities to use data in a more efficient and timely manner
- Greater reliability; less possibility of human error
- Consistency of operations
- Better data security
- Real-time analysis and review

The current trend of most event management organizations is to move toward a paperless office, where a company relies fully on software collection, storage, and retrieval of data. There are many types of computer technology systems currently in use. These systems are distinguished by the method they use to process information, by the type of filing systems used for data storage and retrieving, and by hardware configuration.

# Data Processing Systems

There are three major types of event data processing systems: (1) batch processing, (2) online real-time processing, and (3) time sharing and service bureaus.

## BATCH DATA PROCESSING

In batch processing systems, event transactions are accumulated and processed in groups. All revenues and invoices for a day are viewed as batch transactions, to be processed as a group. For example, sales divisions of an event management company sees all sales for a single day as one "day sale" and are entered into a computer system as one batch. Simplicity and reliability distinguish this system. The general rule in technology is that the more complicated the system, the more areas it contains for mistakes. The biggest advantage of batch processing systems is their cost. Since the systems do not require networks, instant backup, and training of the entire staff, they are relatively cheap. However, a batch processing system does not allow the quick processing of transactions, and therefore, event managers don't always have the potential to retrieve current information. Because of their characteristics, batch processing systems are rarely used in large event management companies. They are more common for small and middle-sized event management companies.

## REAL-TIME DATA PROCESSING

In a real-time processing system, transactions are entered as they occur. Given the continuous updating of the database as transactions are entered, the status of all major accounts, such as admission revenue, sales revenue, and inventory, can be determined at any moment. Data processing systems of several event management subsidiaries can be connected to the main office's processing unit. The main office can process the data either in real time or using the batch processing principle. Event managers may have different levels of access to the central data processing unit. Middle-level management can be authorized to retrieve all the data from all units or may be limited in its ability to browse through the data.

The system tracks all activities through an event management company. It allows event managers to set their activities schedule in the most beneficial manner. The system provides event managers with a great tool for inventory control and for control over collection of revenue and of comparison data. Since this system requires real-time transactions and networking, it is more expensive than batch processing. Real-time systems are common for middle-sized event management companies with diverse operations or/and for large event management companies.

## TIME SHARING AND SERVICE BUREAUS

Time sharing occurs when a system services more than one branch of an event management company at the same time. A service bureau is a company that processes transactions for other entities. Many small and middle-sized event management companies often hire bureau companies to handle small operations (e.g., payroll and collection of receivables). In this case the event company internal data processing system can be either linked or not linked to the bureau company data processing system.

# Hardware Configuration

Several basic types of hardware configuration are common in the event management industry: (1) online systems, (2) PC systems, and (3) distributed data processing.

**Figure 14-1**
Direct Method

## ONLINE SYSTEMS

Online systems are unique in that each transaction is entered via a communication device connected to a computer. Magnetic cards are a good example of such systems. Online systems may or may not be real-time systems, depending on whether transactions are processed and updated immediately as they happened.

*Electronic data interchange* (EDI) is currently being adopted by an increasing number of large event management companies. EDI is a computer-to-computer exchange of intercompany information and data in a *public standard form*. In an EDI system, documents such as purchase orders, invoices, attendance projections, and checks are converted into standard form, permitting other companies to read and accept them. There are two methods available for implementing EDI: direct and indirect. The direct method links the computer system of an event management company with major client or a supplier, such as a major beverage supplier (see Figure 14-1). When an event management company makes adjustments to its attendance numbers, the system informs the supplier, which helps to eliminate inventory shortages.

The indirect method utilizes a network of various companies' computers and companies, provides a "mailbox" for use by all (see Figure 14-2). The network transforms senders' messages into the format preferred by receivers. The advantage of this method is that the sender can transmit documents to several

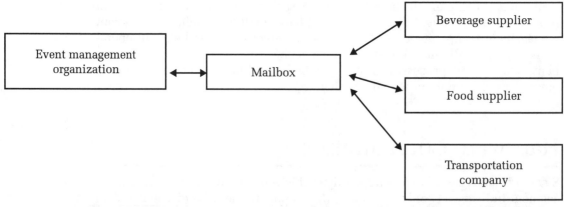

**Figure 14-2**
Indirect Method

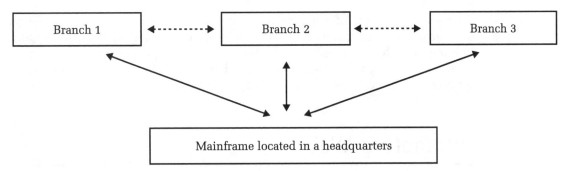

**Figure 14-3**
Distributed Data Processing System

receivers without changing the format each time. For example, an event management company submits all information about a forthcoming event (e.g., attendance, menu, list of beverages, setup requirements) to the mailbox. Then suppliers visit the mailbox and submit offers matching the requirements.

## PC SYSTEMS

PC systems may consist of stand-alone computers used by a single event manager, or they may be connected to one another and/or to mainframe computers through a form of networking.

## DISTRIBUTED DATA PROCESSING

Many large event management companies use PCs extensively for both data processing and analysis. Event management companies with branches in various locations frequently use networks to process each branch's transactions and transmit them to the major office via communications links. At the same time, local event managers can use a PC for various kinds of analyses. Distributed data processing systems are usually connected to a mainframe computer located at the headquarters office of an event management company (see Figure 14-3). Additionally, they can be linked to one another through a networking system such as a local area network (LAN) or a wide area network (WAN). Networks are used to enable PCs to communicate with one another and share workloads.

# Access Control

To prevent unauthorized use and alteration of files and data, access must be limited to authorized individuals. In an online, integrated file system and EDI, access limitation is archived through control over *passwords,* codes used to access various parts of a database. Some passwords allow only examination and retrieval of data; others allow data alteration. Database control includes voiding and changing passwords. However, it is important to ensure that at least two people have master access to a database so that if a person with master access is unavailable, company's operations will not suffer.

# Interactive Web

Development of the Internet was one of the most significant events of the last decade. At first it was available only to academia and the military, but very soon it became an integrated part of the business environment. As the technology becomes more affordable, more companies are entering the departing cyberspace. As a starting point, companies set up Web sites. At the beginning sites may be viewed as simply an informative tool. Small event management companies usually start Web sites to post basic information about their services, employees, history, and information on how to contact them. However, the effect of posting the information is similar to listing your company in the Yellow Pages. The moment an event management company develops a Web site, it starts to create ways to attract potential customers to the site. All the information becomes immediately available to the general public, and if presented correctly, can serve as a great marketing tool.

There are several ways that companies attract potential customers using their Web sites. As a starting point, new sites should create general visitor traffic. This can be accomplished by registering the site with various search programs, such as Altavista, Yahoo, and HotBot. Once a Web site is registered with all major search engines, you can be reasonably sure that it will be available to a potential client who is conducting a search. Usually, a search is conducted using *key words,* such as "event management," "event management New York," or just "event." The more general the key words, the more potential matches that a search program generates.

A Web site is an excellent marketing tool that can be either used or misused. There are certain advantages that a site can provide to an event management company:

- Wide market reach
- Ability to update information in a very difficult manner
- Ability to track and collect data about potential clients
- Ability to cut marketing expenses

The Internet is a great equalizer. Small and middle-sized event management companies have the same opportunities as industry giants to reach potential customers. Although larger companies have more technical resources to invest in the development of Web sites, the difference usually comes down to having more "cookies," or action. Web sites that are too complicated and contain much flashier but unnecessary effects may be annoying and make the information difficult to read. In my experience, user-friendly, well-developed, well-designed Web sites are often those of smaller and middle-sized event management companies or even individual event professionals. At the end of the day, all companies have the same opportunity to reach clients.

If you think that one must be a programmer to operate a Web site, you are wrong. In the early days you had to know one or even several programming languages (e.g., HTML, Java) to make simple changes in a Web site. Today, many computer applications, including Microsoft FrontPage and Netscape Composer, allow users to change sites without learning the coding. Working with your site using these software applications is similar to writing a letter using Microsoft Word. The program automatically transforms the changes you want to make into HTML format. The most difficult part is posting the contents you have created to the World Wide Web, but this can be learned in a one-time professional consultation. After your site is designed and launched (which usually requires professional assistance), you can maintain the site yourself.

A Web site can be an excellent tool for collecting information about existing and potential clients. Often, event management companies ask their site visitors to register. Usually, visitors are asked to provide their e-mail address, area of interest, basic geographic data, and other material. This information turns into a customized database of clients that you can use later. If a person visited your site and registered, it means that this person is interested in your services or at least potentially interested. By collecting and analyzing these data, you can optimize your marketing expenses. You can use your Web site as a tool for customizing services. Major site development software applications provide the owner of the site with an opportunity to monitor not only traffic in general but also to obtain more detailed information about what parts of the site generate the most *clicks* and who is doing the clicking. If, for example, your site contains information about two major services that your company offers—private banquet services and corporate events—and the corporate event service generates much more traffic, this should send you a strong signal about current and future market needs.

# Event Management Databases

The event management industry is growing rapidly. Although there are several large event management companies in the market, new players come in every day. A major database-related challenge that companies face in every fast-growing industry is the problem of keeping a database up to date. How often do you dial a number that you found in a catalog only to find that the company or person has changed the number? It happens to me all the time. Almost every catalog is outdated the moment it leaves the print shop. The accuracy of documents decreases dramatically over time. Getting online is one way of ameliorating this problem. Internet databases are the most reliable in the event industry. One event association executive told me that within a few days of allowing members to update their online records, over 200 persons made changes to electronic directory.

Two major criteria distinguish a database. The first is its resources. The more resources that a database has, the more valuable it is. Because resources are collected over time, young databases usually contain fewer data than older ones. The second criterion relates to search features. You can search a database in a number of ways: alphabetically, by region, by service offered, by price, and by age. The more criteria a database has, the more valuable it is. Search criteria should be user friendly and easy to customize. Even users with moderate database search experience should be able to find necessary data quickly. Some databases make their search engines overly complicated and the search process becomes very confusing.

Development of the Internet has provided new opportunities for event management, such as real-time information databases, interactive databases, and commercial databases. Content can be updated online and users have access at any time. You can receive catering quotes immediately after answering required questions and can book event facilities all over the world. Search criteria can be customized and changed much easier than in a paper version. The search itself can be customized to an unbelievable extent. In electronic databases users can enter key words and the database will conduct a global search based on these words. I encourage you to visit DOME, one of the best available event management industry databases to familiarize yourself with the vast online event management resources. You can find this database by visiting *www.domeresearch.org*.

# Technology Trends

Twenty years ago technology was a luxury for small and middle-sized companies. The situation is different now. It is hard to imagine any event management office without a computer, Internet, and e-mail. Although it is hard to predict what will happen with technology in 10 years, there are recognizable trends. The technology will become more customized. Several years ago, small and middle-sized event management companies did not have a lot of options when choosing software applications, as the number of major software packages was limited. Software programming services were not very affordable. But the situation has changed. We have much more technology and software development companies today than we had even a few years ago. Development of the Internet has allowed software development startups to sell their products directly to customers. As a result, the software development market has become more competitive, services more user-friendly, and prices more affordable. People who a short time ago did not know how to create a document are now getting more and more comfortable with computers. With this in mind, we can talk about the growth of virtual offices and the amount of online business overall globalization of event management services.

One of the most important innovations in the global high-technology revolution is the development of the wireless application protocol (WAP). WAP was developed within the wireless industry, from companies such as Phone.com, Nokia, and Ericsson. The WAP standard is to serve Internet contents and services to wireless clients using WAP devices such as mobile phones and terminals. The opportunities for use of WAP-driven products in the event management field is significant. According to *The Profile of Event Management* (Indianapolis, IN: International Special Events Society, 1999) over 90 percent of event professionals regularly use cellular technology. Due to the mobility of the event management field, the cell phone is an indispensable tool. However, what about the potential use for event guests?

In Japan, firms are testing the use of WAP technologies to improve networking among guests attending events. By preprogramming the cell phones of guests with vital demographic information, WAP technology enables event guests quickly to identify others with similar interests within a few feet of the venue space. Imagine walking into a reception, and as you approach a guest, your cell phone vibrates. You glance quickly at the cell phone screen and see the message "buyer" and can connect instantaneously as seller and buyer. Furthermore, all critical buying information is downloaded via the Internet to the expanded computer memory within your cell phone.

Indeed, WAP technology is going to make it easier, faster, more cost-efficient, and ultimately more profitable to connect with others locally and globally. One excellent source for WAP information is *www.wapforum.org.*

# Career Advancement Connections

## GLOBAL CONNECTION

Developments in technology are rapidly erasing geographical borders in the global event industry. Event management companies conduct registration, planning, control, and supervision of events over the Internet. An event management company located in the United States can produce an event in Germany, and vice versa, without physically relocating its staff and/or setting up an office. As the event management industry becomes more competitive, the development of technology will further amplify and accelerate competitive factors.

## TECHNOLOGY CONNECTION

In using technology, especially the Internet and other networks, it is important to remember that all processes should be available for all participants. If one of your partners has a very slow Internet connection, the entire network should be designed around this limitation to ensure that the user with the slow connection can receive the same services as others can.

## RESOURCE CONNECTION

The George Washington University Event Management Certificate Program offers courses entitled "Event Information Systems" and "Internet Event Marketing" *(www.gwu.edu/emp)*. Cvent.com provides online event marketing, regulations, and data analysis services *(www.cevent.com)*. Other online event service providers, including Event411.com *(www.event411.com)* and B-there.com *(www.b-there.com)*, provide excellent online event marketing and registration services. An excellent reference book is *Internet World: Essential Business Tactic for the Net,* by Larry Chase and Eileen Shulock (New York: Wiley, 1998).

## LEARNING CONNECTION

Your event management organization is about to acquire a small event management company with inadequate technology resources. You are assigned to manage the technology transition. Prepare a checklist describing possible high-risk areas in technological integration that your organization may face during and after the acquisition.

---

**Facing Page**
Empire Force Events promotion for Hong Kong, China in New York City confirms the globalization of the industry. *Photograph courtesy of Monica Vidal.*

# CHAPTER 15

# Advancing Your Career in the Twenty-first Century

## IN THIS CHAPTER YOU WILL LEARN HOW TO:

- Advance your event management career through formal and informal education
- Gain more professional experience to build your résumé
- Become a certified special event professional (CSEP)
- Earn the credentials you need for employment, promotion, and long-term success
- Build both a life and a career

An event management employer telephoned me recently and asked: "What am I doing wrong? I can't find the people I need and once I hire them, I can't keep them!" Regrettably, this call was typical of the complaints I have heard recently from employers of event management professionals. Part of this predicament may be attributed to the growing global economy, which has provided unprecedented growth in North America and increasingly in other regions of the world as well. This new and rapid growth has resulted in the lowest unemployment in modern history in the United States and provides enormous opportunities for those entering the event management field while presenting troubling concerns for employers of event management professionals.

Economists know that this period of sustained growth will probably begin to subside at some point. Therefore, it is important for event management professionals to prepare and position themselves to succeed despite the macroeconomic influences that affect the general economy.

# Education

Only a few years ago, education was considered to be a minor requirement for employment as an event management professional. I remember participating in the first meeting designed to develop questions for the Certified Special Events Professional (CSEP) examination. I argued that the questions should be more rigorous. The professional educators attending this meeting reminded me that because there was so little formal education in the field at that time, it might be difficult for even experienced event managers to pass the test.

A few months later a brave group of industry veterans sat for the first CSEP examination. They literally trembled as they walked into the examination room. Although combined they represented hundreds of years of professional experience, none had the benefit of formal education in the special events field. Today, the landscape is dramatically different. According to studies conducted by George Washington University, more than 150 colleges and universities throughout the world offer curriculum, certificates, and/or degrees in the event management–related studies field. These courses include the following:

- Advertising
- Anthropology
- Art
- Beverage management
- Business administration
- Catering
- Communications
- Culinary
- Design
- Floral
- Folklore
- Hospitality
- Hotel
- Law
- Museum studies
- Music
- Political science
- Public relations
- Recreation
- Sport management
- Television
- Theater
- Tourism
- Travel

In addition to these related fields of studies, many colleges and universities offer specific programs in the field of event management. While the George Washington University Event Management Program is the largest and most comprehensive, it is not alone in focusing on this new, emerging specialized field of study. The University of Nevada at Las Vegas offers concentrations in special events, entertainment, and meetings and expositions. Northeastern State University in Tahlequah, Oklahoma may have been the first college in the United States to offer specialization in the field of meeting planning and destination management. In addition, 14 colleges and universities throughout the world have adopted the George Washington University Certificate Program, so it is now possible to receive standardized training in this field in Spain, Morocco, Puerto Rico, and the Philippines as well as the United States.

This growth in formal education for event managers may be compared to the related field of information technology. In both areas of expertise, specific skills are required to ensure that high-quality performance is achieved consistently over time. However, unlike information technology, event managers must also master the critical human resource skills essential for working effectively in teams. This dimension adds challenge and opportunity for educators as they work to develop a standardized field of study similar to that of medicine, law, accounting, or public relations.

Since over 60 percent of event professionals have earned a bachelor's degree and nearly 10 percent have a postgraduate degree, it may be assumed that professionals in this field are highly educated compared to the general working population in the United States. This means that those entering this competitive profession should expect to have a formal education plus experience in order to succeed. Increasingly, a major part of this formal education is specialized in the area of event management studies.

## A BODY OF KNOWLEDGE

Organizations such as the Convention Industry Council, the International Association for Exhibition Management, and the International Special Events Industry have identified specific bodies of knowledge within their industry sector. This knowledge is encapsulated in the certification programs that each organization has developed. While the body of knowledge varies according to the organization, generally each of these fields includes knowledge in the following domains:

- Administration
  - Communications
  - Financial planning, management, and analysis
  - Information technology
  - Organizational development
  - Scheduling
  - Tax liabilities and regulations
  - Time management
- Coordination
  - Amenities
  - Audiovisual
  - Awards
  - Catering
  - Decor
  - Entertainment
  - Etiquette
  - Human resource management
    - Conflict resolution
    - Staff recruiting, training, supervision, and reward
    - Volunteer recruiting, training, supervision, and reward
  - International customs
  - Lighting
  - Parking
  - Prizes
  - Protocol
  - Sound
  - Speakers
- Transportation
  - Venues
- Marketing
  - Advertising
  - Analysis
  - Assessment
  - Conflict resolution
  - Evaluation
  - Negotiation
  - Planning
  - Promotion
  - Proposal development and writing
  - Public relations
  - Sales
  - Sponsorship
  - Stunts
- Risk management
  - Assessment
  - Compliance
  - Contracts
  - Financial Impacts
  - Insurance
  - Licensing
  - Management
  - Permits
  - Planning
  - Safety
  - Security

In addition to these broad categories, each specialized field emphasizes additional requirements, such as exhibit planning and management, hotel and convention center negotiation, and catering. However, through consolidation, perhaps there will soon be an era of unprecedented collaboration among the various industry subfields. Event management should, in my opinion, adopt the model generated by medicine many years ago. Event managers should be trained as general practitioners (such as the CSEP program), then earn additional certifications as specialists in individual fields. With this model, clients and employers worldwide will be able to use a global standard for event management training and identify specialists who have advanced training in certain areas.

## EDUCATION AND YOUR EVENT MANAGEMENT CAREER

Obviously, it is important for you to obtain a strong general studies education at the undergraduate and perhaps graduate levels. In addition to general studies, you may wish to focus your education in areas where the majority of event managers have earned degrees (business administration, education, and tourism, in that order).

Increasingly, event management professionals are earning advanced credentials, such as professional certificates in event, meetings, expositions, and related fields. The professional certificate is often more valued by industry employers because it represents a specialized body of knowledge that is immediately useful to organizations that employ event professionals. Therefore, to be successful, it is important for event managers to understand both the theory and practice of event management. To sustain your career, you should carefully design an educational blueprint from which to construct your future career. This blueprint should include a thorough understanding of the history and theory of the profession, skill training, and practical observation and application. Following is a model blueprint for developing your event management education.

1. *General studies education:* arts and sciences, business administration (observation/internship)
2. *Postgraduate education:* business administration, tourism, event management (practical training/externship)
3. *Executive development:* certificate in event management, meetings, expositions, or related field (observation/externship)
4. *Certification:* CSEP, Certified Meeting Professional, or other respected industry certification program (practical training)
5. *Continuing industry education:* through professional associations, such as ISES, Meeting Professionals International, and others (observation/practice)

In addition to this formal education, successful event managers combine classroom experience with extensive practical training. Our students at GWU have benefited from internships and externships ranging from small event management consulting organizations to the Olympic Games. They have coordinated expositions for up to 40,000 people and have observed small social events. Every opportunity has provided a rich learning opportunity for these professionals. I strongly suggest that you invest a minimum of 15 to 30 hours per year observing or practicing under the aegis of another event organization. By observing the best (and sometimes worst) practices of others, you will find that the educational theory and skills you studied previously will synthesize into a new foundation for future success.

# Professional Experience

Finding a worthwhile internship or externship can be a daunting task, especially for a newcomer to the industry. First, it is important to understand the difference between internship and externship. Generally, *internship* is used to describe a supervised experience that an undergraduate or graduate student affiliated with a college or university receives while earning academic credit. *Externship* refers to the practical experience that a senior professional employed in the event management industry receives in an organization other than his or her own.

The internship and externship should both include a blend of observation and practice. One of the earliest descriptions of formal education is that provided by the philosopher Socrates, who described the educational process as including observation and questioning. Using the Socratic method, you should find outstanding organizations or individuals or both, observe them, ask lots of questions, and then draw your own conclusions from this experience. In the best scenario, your industry teachers or mentors will simultaneously question and challenge you (just as Socrates did with his protégés in ancient Greece).

### FINDING AN INTERNSHIP OR EXTERNSHIP

One of the easiest ways to identify a high-quality practical training opportunity is through a formal institution of learning such as a college or university. Another way is through professional networking in an industry organization. Using the auspices of a college or university may provide you with additional credibility for obtaining a high-quality practicum experience. In fact, a professor of event management studies can help you open doors that were closed to you heretofore. Many event management employers may even be suspicious of persons who wish to engage in a practicum for fear that this is merely a ploy to steal ideas for use in their own companies. Therefore, the intervention of a college professor or mentor can provide an employer with reassurance that the practicum experience is required for graduation and that students will be supervised to ensure proper ethical behavior.

Once you have identified an appropriate practical experience, you should send the potential supervisor a one-page brief description of the observations, experiences, and outcomes you desire from this experience. Figure 15-1 is an example of such a document.

Date

Dear Employer, Supervisor, etc.

Your organization is one of the most respected in the special events industry, and therefore I am requesting the opportunity to receive a practical training experience under your auspices. The training will require the following commitment from your organization:

1. Five to ten hours per week on site at your place of business, observing your operations

2. Participation in practical experiences you design for me to enhance my learning experience

3. Your supervision of my practical training

4. Completion of a brief form evaluating my performance at the end of my practical training

5. Submission by your firm of a letter of recommendation (if appropriate) for me to assist me in career development

I will be contacting you in a few days to discuss this opportunity and I thank you in advance for your consideration of this request.

Sincerely,


Jane Event Manager

cc: Dr. Joe Goldblatt, CSEP, Dean and Professor Alan Shawn Feinstein Graduate School of Johnson & Wales University

**Figure 15-1**
Proposal for Practical Experience Opportunity

    Some internships are paid, others include a small stipend, a few provide living expenses, and still others provide no compensation or expenses. You must determine the best setting for your needs and whether or not compensation is required. If you are an event manager who is providing a practical training opportunity, it is important to remember that U.S. labor laws prohibit displacing a paid employee with an unpaid intern. Therefore, event management and other employers may use interns to support staff but should not utilize them as a means of displacing current employees to reduce expenses.

    During the internship or externship you should exhibit good work habits (e.g., attendance, punctuality, dress) and conduct yourself in a highly ethical manner. For example, it is important to ask your supervisor about proprietary information and then to abide absolutely by their requests for confidentiality. Finally, remember that you are there primarily to learn from these people, who are more experienced than you. Therefore, refrain from offering unsolicited advice. Instead, carefully write down instructions, observations, and other notes in a journal to help you document what you are learning. At the same time, note any questions and then ask for time with your supervisor to probe him or her with questions concerning any areas of the practicum where you need further clarification.

At the end of the practicum experience, both you and your supervisor should have a debriefing session to evaluate the practicum. Forms should be completed by the supervisor describing your attendance, punctuality, performance, and learning capacity as well as a letter of recommendation for use with future employers. You should promptly write a thank-you letter to the supervisor expressing your appreciation for this unique opportunity.

A good practicum experience requires the commitment of both a generous supervisor and a curious and loyal student. When you plan this experience carefully, you will find that you have not only established a rich learning opportunity but have built a life-long connection with mentors who will encourage your success.

# Certification

Professional certification is the sign of professions who have matured and seek a uniform standard to ensure consistent levels of excellence. Most professional certification programs, such as Certified Public Accountant, were developed early in the twentieth century. One of the reasons for the development of industry standards and certification was to limit the role of government in licensing emerging professions. The event management industry has followed this historic pattern.

The International Special Events Society established the Certified Special Events Professional (CSEP) certification program based on the empirical studies conducted by the Canadian government. ISES elected to consolidate the Event Management Event Coordinator into one comprehensive vocation entitled Event Manager or Special Event Professional.

According to the Canadian government and the ISES certification committee, the vocation of event management requires competence in four knowledge domains. These represent the body of knowledge in the field of event management and therefore require a high degree of competence in administration, coordination, marketing, and risk management. ISES further ratified the findings of the Canadians by stating that the critical path for the production of a professional event required administration, followed by coordination, succeeded by marketing, and then finally, reduction of exposure through well-developed risk management.

Today, there are over 100 persons in the world who hold the title of Certified Special Events Professional (CSEP). To obtain this difficult and challenging designation, they must exhibit a high degree of professional experience, formal education, and service to the industry and pass a three-part examination process. The CSEP is the most rigorous examination in the event management industry, and those who earn this designation are considered to be the preeminent practitioners in the industry. You should aspire to join their growing ranks. I often point to the example of doctors as one reason why it is so important to ensure that professional event managers function at a consistently high level. Doctors have the ability to save lives, but also lose lives one person at a time. Event managers, by contrast, can save or lose hundreds or thousands of lives at one event, depending on their level of training, experience, and that illusive quality called judgment. Therefore, the event manager, in my opinion, has an even higher degree of responsibility than doctors. In addition, event managers often organize seminars or educational programs that train current and future doctors, so our responsibility extends into their profession as well.

## HOW TO BECOME A CSEP

The CSEP affirms that you have achieved the highest level of training, experience, and recognition by your peers in the event management industry. This recognition is achieved as follows:

1. Enroll in the CSEP program through ISES [1 (800) 688-ISES or *www.ises.com*].
2. Obtain 35 points through service to the industry, education, and experience.
3. Pass the CSEP exam.

ISES provides a form to assist you in documenting your points to submit to ISES staff for review and approval. ISES also provides study materials (including this textbook) to help you prepare for the CSEP examination. The CSEP exam consists of three parts. Part 1 comprises 100 multiple-choice questions drawn directly from the *International Dictionary of Event Management* by (2nd ed., 2000, Wiley). These terms represent the vocabulary of the profession. Two hours is allowed for this exam. Part 2 is an essay-style exam in which you are given a choice of two case studies and are required to use the CSEP blueprint of administration, coordination, marketing, and risk management to develop a theoretical event. The exam may be completed by hand or using a personal computer. The time allowed for part 2 is four hours. Part 3 of the examination process is the submission of a professional portfolio documenting that you have produced a professional event during the previous two years. Extensive guidelines are provided to aid in the development and preparation of the portfolio.

The exams are reviewed by academics in the field of event management studies as well as other certified special event professionals. Using a blind review process, each exam is marked by a panel of three industry professionals and/or academics and the results are forwarded to the certification committee for validation. Successful certification candidates are notified by ISES by certified mail that they have now joined the ranks of the preeminent leaders in the special events industry. Many new CSEPs remark that when they receive the envelope with their name listed "Jane Event Manager, CSEP," it is one of the proudest moments of their professional lives.

## RECERTIFICATION

Many certification programs require that certified managers be recertified every few years to ensure that they are currently engaged in the industry and that they remain knowledgeable about developments in the field. The process for recertification typically requires documentation of education, experience, and service to the industry. The CSEP program requires recertification every five years after the initial certification has been granted.

# Credentials

I am often asked by prospective students to quantify the value of a master's degree versus a certificate. Typically, the questioner asks: "What do I need to be successful in event management, a certificate or a master's degree?" The question automatically assumes that credentials or third-party validation is important to success in the special events industry. This is a correct assumption. Although it has not always been the case, the facts clearly indicate that in the U.S. economy, those who have credentials earn more, are promoted more often, and enjoy more economic and career opportunities than those who do not have appropriate credentials.

The type of credential you earn depends largely on which sector of the events industry you decide to enter. For example, in the government and education sectors, it is generally known that the education you attain affects the promotion or appointment by salary grade, whereas in the association sector, although education is important, it is also acceptable to obtain certification to demonstrate your training, competence, and experience level. However, in the corporate sector, increasingly, it is not unusual to find MBAs who are responsible for coordinating major events.

Bill Morton, chairman and chief executive officer of Jack Morton Worldwide, the world's largest event management firm, once told me that his firm actively recruited MBA students from leading business schools for senior management positions. He explained that the blend of strategic thinking skills, marketing analysis and execution, and financial management training and experience helped his firm ensure that strong management leaders would sustain and advance the mission of the 60-year-old firm.

It is interesting that Morton did not mention the need for experience in event management as a prerequisite for appointment as a leader in his firm. In fact, event management experience, although important, is not essential to succeed in many organizations today. What is essential is proof or evidence that you are competent to advance the goals and objectives of your employer. Increasingly, employers are turning to third-party organizations such as colleges, universities, and certification organizations to vouch for this competence.

When I give references for graduates of the George Washington University Event Management Program, potential employers ask the typical questions about persistence, punctuality, and intellectual capacity. However, ever more frequently, they ask questions about the ability of the candidate to work in a team, to communicate, and to lead an organization to accomplish specific goals and objectives. Although it is difficult to quantify, much less rate these abilities, employers count on them to determine if the person they will hire will succeed quickly after he or she is appointed. This is another reason why it is important to obtain a credential. Behind every credential are people who tested, assessed, and can vouch for the integrity, persistence, communications, and leadership abilities of the person holding the credential. Whether they are former professors, industry certifiers, or even internship supervisors, each one has had a prolonged, intimate, and objective opportunity to evaluate the candidate. For this reason alone, it is important to earn a credential, for with it comes references and contacts that will help you gain employment and promotion.

So you may ask what credential is most valuable. The simple answer is: all of them. I recommend that you determine what your industry sector demands in terms of a credential, and as soon as you earn it you begin exploring how you can earn the next credential. In today's competitive global business environment you must demonstrate your competence continually. Whether you are in Asia, the Americas, Europe, Africa, or other parts of the world, governments as well as nongovernmental organizations are developing higher standards for event managers. For example, the governments of Great Britain, South Africa, and Australia have joined Canada in developing standards for event management professionals. These standards require high levels of professional education as well as experience. Therefore, to compete in the global event management industry you must continually seek the credentials that future employers demand to ensure your long-term success in this growing field.

# Power Tools

Once you have mapped your journey, you need transportation tools to ensure that you arrive speedily at your destination. Historically, the most powerful tools have been the résumé and cover letter. I recommend that you use the following techniques to best apply these tools:

1. Create a preliminary list of employers who have (or are likely to have) open positions in your field.

2. From this short list of 25 to 50 people, create a computer database using Access, Filemaker Pro, or a similar contact program.

3. Send a cover letter to each contact as shown in Figure 15-2. Customize the letter for each organization based on the homework you have completed to learn about the person and the organization's strengths.

4. Wait two weeks after the letter has been mailed, and then call each contact between 7 and 9 A.M. or between 5 and 7 P.M. These are the best times to reach your contact directly without interception by an administrative assistant.

5. When you reach the contact, reintroduce yourself and assume that the person has received your letter. ("I am calling about the letter I sent you requesting a personal interview.")

6. Ask for an interview at one or two specific times. ("Could we meet in person or by telephone on Tuesday at 10 A.M. or Thursday at 4 P.M.?")

7. If the contact agrees to meet with you in person or by telephone, thank the person immediately and reconfirm in writing via e-mail or other correspondence.

8. If the person refuses to see you, ask if there are others who you should see or other organizations that could benefit from your skills to which the person can refer you. Get at least three to five referrals. Add these names to your database.

9. If you confirmed the meeting in person or by telephone, conduct further research about the organization so that you are prepared to ask pertinent questions.

10. During the personal interview session, do not offer your résumé unless requested. Instead, show your portfolio of an event or events that you have produced. Conclude the session by asking directly: "What would be necessary for me to earn the opportunity to work for your outstanding organization?" Do not speak again until the contact tells you specifically what is necessary to earn the job.

Finding a great job in this field is a combination of timing, persistence, and talent. Timing is the most illusive part of the equation because rarely is a job created specifically for you. Instead, you have to wait until a position needs to be filled. This is why persistence is important. You may wish to create a postcard that has your photograph and a few lines about your experience, skills, and credentials and mail this to your contact list on the same date each month as a reminder of your interest in working for them. You should personalize the card with a handwritten note that says "I am writing further to indicate my interest in working for your outstanding organization. Please let me know if there is an opportunity to work with you in the near future."

The postcard technique has been highly effective with my students for the last decade, as the tenure of employees in an organization has shrunk from two and one-half years to less than one year. Employers during a period of full employment are constantly on the lookout for capable people able to start work immediately. Instead of conducting a formal search for candidates, your postcard may arrive at just the right moment and the employer may pick up the phone and telephone you to interview for the job. You have already shown interest, enthusiasm, organization, and persistence, and these are qualities that employers value. You have also made the company's job easier by helping them find you quickly. The two critical tools, the résumé and the cover letter, must be consistent with the standards used traditionally in the event management field. Figures 15-2 and 15-3 provide models for you to use in the future.

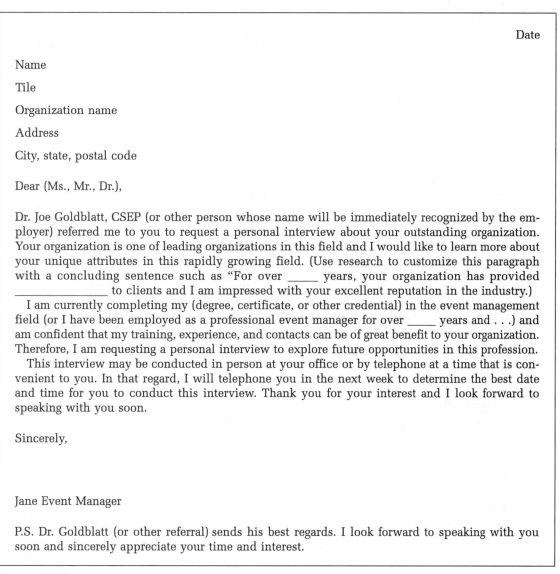

**Figure 15-2**
Model Cover Letter

**Résumé**
**Jane Event Manager, CSEP**
**1234 Main Street**
**Celebration, Florida**
**Telephone: 304-544-1234**
**E-mail: jem@eventsrus.net**

***Career Objective***

To assist a leading event organization to achieve high quality and rapid growth through my contributions as a event management professional.

***Professional Experience***

- Managed a 2000-person health care exposition with a budget of $150,000 in March 2000
- Coordinated a 500-person legal conference with a budget of $50,000 in September 1999
- Developed and managed a 50-person executive education retreat with a budget of $19,000 in July 1999

***Related Experience***

- Conceived and coordinated a 1000-person community festival with a budget (including in-kind contributions) of $50,000 in spring 1999
- Led a 25-person event planning workshop/retreat with a budget of $1000 for the purpose of organizing a annual conference for a community services organization

***Volunteer Experience***

- Founded a 500-person bazaar with 50 exhibitors and a budget of $500 for Holy Name Church
- Created and managed a 250-person banquet for Cub Scout Awards with a budget of $1200
- Organized and managed a 100-person fundraising walking event for AIDS prevention with a budget of $3000

***Education and Training***

- Candidate to receive the *George Washington University Professional Certificate in Event Management (May 2001)*
- Recipient of the *George Washington University Master of Tourism Administration, Concentration in Event Management, degree (May 2000)*
- *Certified Special Event Professional (1995, recertified 2000)*

***Awards and Recognition***

- International Special Events Society Volunteer of the Year, 2000
- Dean's List, Johnson Wales University, 2001
- Employee of the Month, Regent Hotel, May 1997

***Technology Skills***

Access, computer-assisted drawing, Excel, Word, World Wide Web, Web design (HTML)

***Languages***

Spanish (high verbal and written)
Portuguese (moderate verbal and written)
French (low to moderate verbal)

***References***

Available upon request

**Figure 15-3**
Model Résumé. (*Note:* Résumé should not exceed one page.)

The purpose of the résumé and the cover letter is to reduce to writing the impression you will make in person. These important tools rarely result in helping you obtain a job unless they are supported by a good reference, your homework about the organization, and most important, your impression in person. I strongly suggest that you work with a career coach through a local university or college or someone in private practice to help you optimize your abilities when you are ready to make that all-important first impression.

# Life and Career

Too often, event management professionals build a successful career and at the same time risk ruining their personal lives. Although mental and physical stress are not unique to the events industry, the constant demand for creativity, innovation, and the increasing speed of delivery has the potential of causing event management professionals to literally burn the candle at both ends until exhaustion and illness cause some intervention by professionals.

Recently, a leader in the festival industry grew irritated with me when I explained that many of the generation described by demographers as cuspers or busters do not want to work a traditional workweek of five eight-hour days. Instead, according to research, many prefer to work a shorter workweek with longer workdays. The reason for this major paradigm shift is in recognition of the preceding generations seven-day workweek that ultimately led to rapid burnout. The cuspers and busters in protest choose to work a shorter number of days and a longer number of hours per day. This schedule permits them to separate work and leisure activity and grants them longer weekends (three days as opposed to one). Furthermore, they prefer to separate work from leisure in order to fully enjoy recreation, culture, and other activities.

Perhaps there is a lesson to be learned here. Or several lessons. In an age often defined by technology, it is often difficult to escape from the world of work. Therefore, to find a life in addition to a career, one must be ever vigilant about understanding the difference between these two values. Experts in leisure study define work as the absence of leisure. However, for work to be enjoyable, it must be rewarding and fulfilling. Therefore, to sustain life and career it is important to understand the nuances that define the difference between each of these two similar but different states of being.

Because the special events industry is perceived by guests as "a fun business," practioners often forget that, in fact, this is the business of fun. As a business it requires hard work, persistence, and talent. Each of these tasks is bound to deplete your energy. You must replenish this expenditure of energy with a healthy lifestyle that includes proper exercise, nutrition, and spiritual nourishment. This replenishment is essential if you are going to experience both the joy of work and the *joi de vivre* (joy of life).

## THE OLD YELLOW CABINET

The joy of life is something many of us too often take for granted. I was reminded of this when I was recently invited to give a commencement address. As I pondered what I might say to this group of students, faculty, and friends, I suddenly remembered an event that was not joyful but fraught with meaning. When my mother died, my sister generously and ably took the responsibility of cleaning out my parents' home of over 50 years. One night while doing this difficult and emotional task, she called me and said, "Guess what I found?"

Before I could inquire she described an old yellow cabinet in our parents' home. The cabinet stood outside my bedroom door but I had long since forgotten about it. "That cabinet is filled with so many memories," she said, as she described how our mother had meticulously collected and preserved our school papers, report cards, photographs, locks of hair, and even baby teeth. My sister added, "That cabinet was filled with her love, pride . . ." and I added, "her dreams."

Mama dreamed and hoped that her children would one day find happiness and success just as all parents wish for their offspring. The old yellow cabinet was her way of reminding us of the importance of memories, milestones, and the celebrations that mark them. That cabinet contained locks from first haircuts, first visits by the Tooth Fairy, birthdays, graduation parties, weddings, and many other very special events recorded, remembered, and celebrated by mama then and by my sister and me today.

As we enter the twenty-first century it is important that we record, remember, and celebrate the triumphs, joys, and even sorrows of our lives. You are responsible for leading this effort. You are a modern pioneer destined to explore, expand, and improve the global event management industry in the twenty-first century. The global technological revolution we have created can hollow us, or hallow us, depending on how we embrace it. I prefer to use the metaphor that the twentieth-century scientist Albert Einstein envisioned when describing his theory of relativity. Einstein wrote that "science without religion is lame and religion without science is blind." He envisioned that one day he would be able to ride a laser beam of light into the twenty-first century and indeed, his theories and ideas continue to challenge and illuminate us today. Einstein continues to ride into the future taking us along with him, as our dreams become realities just as his theories became scientific fact.

The lamplighters in our industry come from many different parts of the globe, however, few will have had the influence of Francisco G. Sicilia of Madrid, Spain. He was truly one of the pioneers of this profession and less than a century ago began to plant the early seeds that would soon grow into a modern profession.

In 1935 an International Congress was to be held in Madrid, Spain. The International Congress of the History of Medicine, chaired by Prof. Gregorio Mara'non and promoted by Dr. Cortezo would require the organizational skills of what one day would be entitled a professional congress organizer.

In 1932 a young man named Francisco G. Sicilia was asked to start working in the organization of this major meeting. Professors from all over the world were to be contacted in order that Spanish Royal Academy of Medicine could highlight the extraordinary new developments of medicine in the 19th and 20th century.

In the early part of the twentieth century only mail was used to promote and organize the congress. Telephones were available but considered devices to be used on only special occasions. Electronic data, as known today, did not exist. Through event research and contacting foreign medical universities and journals and talking to the Spanish Doctors, an extensive list of participants was developed by Francisco Sicilia. Doctors from all over the world but mainly from North & South America, Europe and the Mediterranean countries were contacted, invited to attend and to contribute with their discoveries.

Over 600 doctors attended this important congress from both Americas. A large contingent of doctors arrived from Latin America by ship as no other way of transportation existed in 1935.

Continuous translation was provided although the technical devices for simultaneous translations were still in the process of being invented. The major conferences were held in the Senate's Amphitheater as no other venue in Madrid could hold them. A theater would not have been considered because the doctor's would have considered it too frivolous for their serious profession.

The congress was a enormous success and changed the way events were organized in Europe and throughout the world. Two leather books of proceedings containing the 150 Abstracts, printed either in, English, French, German, Italian or Spanish, with some reproductions in latin and greek, can still be found today in the Library of the Royal Academy of Medicine.

Young Francisco G. Sicilia fell in love with the profession of event management and he created in 1940 a publisher and publicity agency for medical journals, which during his lifetime published about 50 different journals, a Professional Congress Organization (PCO) which managed more than 200 meetings and was designated the official secretariat of over a dozen medical associations.

He gave them all his enthusiastic support and know how, and loved them and event management from his heart. He received the esteem and friendship of many prominent professionals, and the satisfaction of organizing major international events with outstanding success. He prided himself in the perfect managing of logistics, information dissemination, protocol, press and the thousands of details that come into the making of a successful event. His goal was to provide his clients with the peace of mind and infrastructure, essential to put together the seamless event.

While coordinating each individual detail he always kept in mind the whole picture. The Spanish National Association of Clinical Pathology and the Spanish National Association of Othorrinolaringology gave him the Gold Medal of their respective Associations presented at their Gala Dinner at Congresses he himself had organized for them.

His daughter, and successor Carolina Sicilia recalls that both associations had kept this surprise and important detail from him therefore he was very uneasy, not knowing who was to receive the Gold Medal, and not being able to brief him/her on the logistic proceedings.

According to Señora Sicilia events and congresses have been a tradition in her family since her firm was founded by her father. Today one of her sons, the third generation of Sicilias is already as committed as was his grandfather. However, events and congresses, have changed dramatically since 1935.

During the 2nd part of the 20th century meetings became necessary and regular. Wars had created the awareness, as well as the infrastructure, of feasible, safe, and relatively inexpensive traveling. In a world that was beginning the process of globalization, professionals of diverse areas tried to envisage how to create world wide ways of communication between themselves, professional guidelines to be followed by their members: medical doctor, engineers, physics, lawyers, and even event managers. The ultimate goal would be through events to establish and continually raise strong global standards.

Those who achieved these standards whether they be doctors or event managers could ultimately become recognized by local and federal governments as leaders in their fields. Simultaneously, technology rapidly developed as electricity, radio, television, audio-visual, equipment for simultaneous translation of multiple languages, airplanes, computers, the world wide web, modern venues, hotels, roads, facilities, and staff of all types continued to improve creating a global environment destined to make events easier and more successful.

As a result of this growth and demand for quality standards professional congress organizers and event managers (PCO's and EM's) were immediately in demand as more professionalism was required, more knowledge needed, technical, legal, technological, languages, marketing, logistics because clients wanted to profit, to obtain the maximum value for their time, their career, for their personal cultural enrichment and for their investment.

Today event managers throughout the world are working effectively together to improve this growing profession. Virtual events, once seen as a menace to face to face meetings, have resulted in enhancing and stimulating the development of event more events. People meeting virtually wish to do so face to face, video conferencing and similar devices have helped to lower organizational costs and to transfer real time, (and mostly inside company) knowledge, better and more quickly.

The past 70 years have seen a tremendous growth of the meetings, incentives, convention, and exposition-events (MICE) industry. If the environment continues to support the growth of the event industry and transportation, venue, and housing costs do not inflate then PCOs and EM's will become more professional and service oriented and the industry will thrive in good health.

Change is to be expected in any industry that is growing and Carolina Sicilia believes that independent PCOs may be fewer in number while in-house event managers and PCO's may increase as congress and convention centers may develop in-house PCOs, as an important asset for their clients. According to Senora Sicilia, a second generation professional event manager, good professionals, either as independent companies or integrated into larger structures will always be in demand, because somebody has to do the actual work of event management.

She forecasts a strong recognition of the MICE professionals including PCOs and Destination Management Companies (DMC's) who will be considered for what they are, "forgers of the infrastructure that allows all types of professionals to meet, exchange ideas, reach conclusions, perform duties, choose and vote their boards and councils, to present proposals of international value for their sector, to the different country governments, and have the capacity to ensure that their aspirations are taken into account."

As the field of event management rapidly hurdles into the twenty-first century Francisco G. Sicilia must be smiling in gratitude, appreciation, and pride as his daughter and grandson continue to build upon his rich and precious legacy. In less than a century the Sicilias have joined thousands of other event management professionals throughout the world in developing from ancient traditions a modern profession. One source of pride for Señor Sicilia must be the knowledge that his daughter served recently as the international president of the world's most prominent organization of Professional Congress Organizers, the International Association of Professional Congress Organizers (IAAPCO). This honor bestowed by her peers continues to demonstrate why the legacy Francisco G. Sicilia leaves our profession is so well regarded even today.

Only two centuries earlier lamplighters would stroll at dusk from lamppost to lamppost kindling the wicks that would light the way for future travelers. Only one century later, twentieth-century laser light designers use their infinite illumination technology to attract thousands to enjoy outdoor special events. Today, as we boldly walk through doorway of the twenty-first century, all of us have the greatest opportunity in the brief history of this profession. Together we can build successful and sustainable events and just as important, through these events improve the quality of life for all humankind. I am confident that you understand the rare opportunity that lays before us as we ride this beam of light to see where it leads us. Just as my mother and aunt rejoiced in the joie de vivre in their era, you must create memories and milestones for future generations to celebrate. As you begin your journey, I lift my glass in a toast to those who have brought us to this magical moment and to you who will take us farther than anyone ever dreamed. Cheers! Salud! Prosit! Chin Chin! L'chaim!

# Career Advancement Connections

## GLOBAL CONNECTION

There are infinite opportunities for global event careers. From multinational corporations to international associations the opportunities are rich for travel, transnational experiences, and multicultural stimulation. To identify international career opportunities, you need to network through international organizations such as MPI Europe or the International Congress and Convention Association (ICCA). ICCA represents professionals in the meetings and events industry in over 100 different countries around the world. The ICCA membership list is available at *www.icca.nl*. Click on "membership" and then search in the category "Professional congress organizers."

## TECHNOLOGY CONNECTION

The breadth and depth of online education has grown dramatically in the past decade. This growth reflects the overall growth of the Internet itself. Leading providers of distance learning programs in event management–related studies include The George Washington University Event Management Program *(www.gwu.edu/emp)*, the University of Nevada at Las Vegas *(www.unlv.edu)*, the American Society of Association Executives *(www.asaenet.org)*, and Meeting Professionals International *(www.mpinet.org)*.

## RESOURCE CONNECTION

The American Society of Association Executives publishes a newsletter listing hundreds of jobs in the not-for-profit sector. The newsletter is available by subscription. Contact ASAE at *www.asaenet.org*. The International Special Events Society also lists jobs on their Web page at *www.ises.org*. George Washington University (GWU) also lists dozens of global career opportunities on their password-protected Web page. To obtain access to this page, you must register for one of the certificate courses at GWU. You may also wish to visit *www.monster.com* and use key words such as *special events, event management, meeting planning,* and *exposition management*. When I checked this listing there were over 1000 part- and full-time positions being advertised in the event-related categories listed above.

## LEARNING CONNECTION

Develop and write a new résumé that includes the skills and abilities you have mastered as a result of studying this book. Include in this résumé the related experiences you have experienced in your lifetime that are relevant to the event management profession. Invite an experienced event management professional to review your résumé and provide you with honest feedback. Just as the growth in online programs has been dramatic in the past decade, the same growth has been experienced in the classroom. Over 140 universities and colleges throughout the world offer courses, curriculum, degrees, or certificates in event-related studies. Today, you can obtain a bachelor's degree with a major in meeting planning from Northeastern Oklahoma University, a master's degree with a concentration in event management from George Washington University and certificates in event management–related studies from dozens of universities and colleges throughout the world. Each year institutions of higher education expand their event studies–related course offerings. To identify an educational provider for your continuing education needs, contact the International Congress and Convention Association *(www.icca.nl)* and click on "education" or *www.unlv.edu* and click on "William Harrah School of Hotel Management." Both sites provide comprehensive listings of event management–related courses in numerous universities and colleges throughout the world. The George Washington University has licensed its Event Management Certificate Program to universities in Barcelona, Spain, Toronto, Canada, São Paulo, Brazil, Efrane, Morocco, Bethlehem, Palestine, Amman, Jordan, Manila, the Philippines, San Juan, Puerto Rico, San Diego, California, Ashland, Oregon, and Seoul, Korea. The advantage with the GW program is that the curriculum is standardized and allows you to study the same course material in different cultures throughout the world. In addition, GWU offers annual event-related study tours. GW students have studied the Bastille Day celebration in Paris, France, the Expo 2000 in Hanover, Germany, the Oktoberfest in Munich, Germany, and the Carnival Winners Parade in Rio de Janeiro, Brazil, among others. For more information about these programs, visit GW's Web site at *www.gwu.edu/emp* and click on "consortium" or "study tours." Finally, contact the Alan Shawn Feinstein Graduate School of Johnson & Wales University (*www.jwu.edu*) for the latest research and training programs for advanced professionals in the event management industry.

**Facing Page**

This discussion to clarify flag protocol confirms that behind every event there is a story that illustrates, illuminates, and enumerates the opportunity for improving the next event you organize. *Photograph courtesy of Monica Vidal.*

# CHAPTER 16

# Case Studies in Twenty-first-Century Event Management

A case study of an event problem is an excellent device to compare, contrast, explore, and perhaps expand discussion regarding critical issues in the field of event management. Therefore, Julia Schiptsova challenged 50 Master of Tourism Administration Event Management concentration students at The George Washington University to develop case studies that reflect a wide range of problems and issues in the event management field. The following 15 case studies examine many of the types of problems you have or probably will encounter in the event management field. Through these case studies you may be able to develop an efficient early warning system as well as identify new strategies for managing events efficiently now and in the future.

# Taking a Gamble
## (CORPORATE PRODUCT LAUNCH)

A major casino developer organized a televised launch for his billion-dollar resort and contracted with an independent event manager to research, design, plan, coordinate, and evaluate this important project. The independent event manager also took a huge gamble with his client as he planned and executed this corporate product launch. First, the client did not arrange for the proper permits for a pyrotechnic display, and this required that the event manager had to hold innumerable meetings with the fire department as well as the pyrotechnics operators. In addition, the last pyrotechnics display had caused injuries and left debris all over the event area. Therefore, the event manager needed to work closely with the fire department to provide the necessary assurances that this would not recur.

Next, on the day of the major event, a man who identified himself as the chief steward of the drapery motion addressed the event manager. According to the steward, the event manager had not used union labor to hang a large red grand opening bow, and now he would have to pay exorbitant penalties and fines. After further negotiation the event manager agreed to hire members of the union to observe the bow, and they were paid even though they did not perform any work.

Finally, the independent event manager received a telephone call from a firm that had also bid to produce this corporate product launch. The other firm claimed that the event manager stole their original ideas and demanded compensation or threatened a lawsuit. According to the other firm, the event manager used an Aladdin's lamp as a prop, and this was in the proposal they submitted during the bidding process.

Most of the problems listed in this case study could easily have been avoided. The event manager should have required in their contract with the client that all usual and customary permits be provided by the client no later than three weeks before the event dates. In addition, the event manager should have investigated the union requirements thoroughly and transferred any oversights to the client. Finally, the event manager should have required the client to state in writing that all ideas that were provided for the event (including the Aladdin's lamp) by the client were the sole creation and property of the sponsoring organization (the client's organizations).

## CASE QUESTIONS

- How does the event manager protect the image and corporate brand when producing a corporate product launch?
- What legal and ethical issues are typically present in corporate product launch events that may not be as critical in other types of events, such as social life-cycle events?
- How does the event manager know to whom to report in the corporation and to whom to turn when he or she has a question or needs a decision made?

# Festival Challenge
(FESTIVAL)

The event manager sighed as the festival approached and she had only five crafts vendors who had committed to take part in the marketplace. She and her assistant were frantic. They had been pounding the streets, attending festivals all over the city trying to recruit artists and vendors to sell artwork, crafts, authentic items, and concessions at the event. With only nine days before the event and only a few vendors confirmed, they were afraid that the event would be a failure.

At the end of April, the event manager was asked to plan the festival with only two months to put everything together. In addition, the budget was minimal and was heavily dependent on vendor participation. The festival was supposed to be a positive community event promoting a neighboring shopping center where the event would take place. The opening was promoted in local newspapers as an event that would bring the community together.

The problem was that despite the fact that the shopping mall was located in a unpopular neighborhood, the main stakeholders wanted to have a first-class celebration with upscale vendors and the best entertainers. However, the shopping mall where the event was taking place mainly featured stores that targeted middle- and low-middle-income shoppers. Therefore, the vendors selected could not benefit from people living in the area because they did not have the income to purchase upscale merchandise or simply were not interested. However, all the entertainers and contractors were confirmed and the local shop owners were determined to have a festival and marketplace for the neighborhood. The event manager and her assistant made the decision to reduce the vendor participation fee from $25 to $15. Due to the short time frame, they went to comparable festivals and distributed fliers to prospective vendors. Fortunately, 25 vendors were recruited, close to their goal of 30. However, they both felt that they should have talked with the owners about raising donations and sponsorship money to offset the cost rather than recruiting more vendors for the marketplace.

## CASE QUESTIONS

- What could the event manager and her assistant have done to market their event effectively to vendors?
- What integrative marketing techniques would be most effective for this type of event, given the low budget?
- Do you think the situation would have been the same if the event manager had more time?
- How could the event manager incorporate cause marketing in this event? Would it have been appropriate?
- What types of sponsors would have been appropriate for this event?
- What negotiation strategy would you use to negotiate sponsorship for this event?

# Hot-Headed Hostesses
## (WEDDING/BRIDAL)

It was late December and Jen was becoming more and more excited about the prospect of getting married to David in June of the following year. They had been engaged for almost six months now and planning was in full swing. Just as she was daydreaming about the wedding, the phone range and brought her back to reality. It was her sister Marcy. She wanted to throw Jen a bridal shower but was worried about not having enough time or money to make all the arrangements. After a couple of minutes chatting about some options, Jen suggested involving other people. Perhaps David's sister, Alyson, would be interested in helping with the planning. Jen wanted a bridal shower so badly that she knew she had to overcome Marcy's objection about paying for the event. Marcy had just graduated from medical school and gotten married herself; she was overburdened with debt. Then it hit them: Their aunt, Carol is a single, successful businesswoman with plenty of financial resources at her disposal. Marcy quickly got off the phone and called her aunt. Carol welcomed the idea, but warned that she was too busy to do any of the grunt work. She would pay for the event—that was it. Excitedly, Marcy called Alyson to enlist her help. Alyson accepted readily, despite the fact that she realized that she would be doing much of the research, design, planning, and coordinating.

Alyson knew that the first stage in planning an event is to do research about previous events similar in size and scope. She was anxious to begin discussing possible dates and general locations (i.e., Philadelphia or Wilmington, Delaware) so that she could start gathering data. By early February, Alyson and Marcy had engaged in some initial brainstorming about the design of the event. Together, the three hostesses selected a date: Saturday, May 13, 2000. Both Marcy and Carol gave Alyson permission to proceed in researching specific venues in the Wilmington area. They selected this location because nearly all the guests were located between New York and Washington, DC. There were three essential benefits of having the event in Delaware:

1. The groom's parents live in Wilmington and can accommodate a number of overnight guests in their home.
2. Everything tends to be less expensive in Delaware than in Philadelphia.
3. Alyson is from Wilmington and is very familiar with a number of venues and vendors, whereas none of the three hostesses are from Philadelphia, nor do they have any contacts there.

Alyson spent much of the first two weeks in February collecting costs and specifications about various venues in the Wilmington area. Alyson told Carol that she would fax all the information she had collected by the end of the business day on Friday, February 11. When 5 P.M. rolled around, however, Alyson was still awaiting the response of one very nice hotel, the Hotel duPont. Instead of faxing the incomplete information, she decided to wait until Monday, when she hoped the information would be complete. Quite to Alyson's surprise, Jen called Alyson that Sunday to express her excitement at having the bridal shower in Philadelphia. Confused, Alyson asked Jen who had told her that the shower would be held in Philadelphia. Jen explained that Carol had changed her mind and decided to book a hotel in Philadelphia instead of Wilmington, as the three hostesses had decided previously. Alyson was enraged and hurt. She faxed Carol a letter expressing her disappointment, accompanied by all the information she had collected on possible venues up until that point. In the letter, she "graciously decline[d] the honor of being a hostess," as she felt that she had little value to add to the planning function should it be located in Philadelphia.

The next day, Jen called Alyson again and begged her to rethink her decision. Alyson refused until she received an apology directly from Carol. Just over a week later, Carol e-mailed Alyson an apology and expressed how impressed she had been with the information that Alyson had collected and faxed to her. She had been so impressed, in fact, that she had selected a venue for the event, the Hotel duPont in Wilmington. She asked Alyson to rethink her decision and to rejoin the effort to plan Jen's shower. Alyson knew how much it meant to Jen and agreed. Throughout the remainder of the planning, Alyson and Carol remained very distant and communicated only when it was critical to the success of the event. The event, however, turned out to be an overwhelming success.

## CASE QUESTIONS

- Who was the event manager in this scenario?
- What type of leadership style did Carol use? Was it successful? Why or why not?
- What policies, procedures, or practices could have eliminated this conflict?
- What would have been some effective ways to motivate Alyson to cooperate more fully with Carol?

# Preparation Anyone?
## (SOCIAL)

Ann decided to give her husband a thirtieth birthday party on a Saturday in the fall. The party was not to be a surprise, and the couple's family and friends would all be there. The party was to begin at 3:00 P.M. and would run until everyone felt like going home. Ann wanted everything to be perfect but did not want to be running around refilling cups and cleaning plates all night, so she hired outside staff to coordinate the party.

The two staff, Anthony and Sarah, were hired through referrals from another party they had recently coordinated. Ann was impressed with their professionalism and hired them for her party. Anthony and Sarah do not own any catering equipment, nor do they cook any of the food at the parties they coordinate. The two are only hired as staff. This meant that Ann had to use an outside caterer for the food. Because this was a picnic, a local pork barbecue restaurant was hired for food delivery.

The staff arrived three hours prior to the party. They had been informed previously that they would be responsible for decorating the tables, presenting the food, displaying the birthday gifts, presenting the birthday cake, and keeping the beverages flowing. That Saturday afternoon was warmer than a usual fall day and the two staff arrived to find that they would now be responsible for setting up a 40-foot tent the hosts had rented. Also, 10 tables and 50 chairs had to be set up and guests were to arrive in three hours. Remembering that there were many other duties to be done before guests arrived, Anthony hurried into the kitchen, leaving Sarah to struggle with the tent. The hostess had not bothered to measure the lawn before ordering the tent, and after the entire tent was laid out, it was discovered that the lawn was too small. After two hours of struggling, the tent was set up half on the lawn and half down the hill beside the house. This only left one hour for table setup, decorating, and food.

The food had arrived from the restaurant during the tent fiasco and sat in the kitchen for another hour and a half getting cold. As the last tablecloth was placed on and the beer keg had been tapped, the first guests arrived. Anthony had just begun to warm up the food. Ann told him to use anything he could find. He grabbed a platter from the cabinet, filled it with pork barbecue and threw it in the oven to warm. A few minutes later as Sarah and Anthony stood preparing other food, a loud pop was heard coming from the oven. They threw the oven door open and saw the platter split in three pieces and the pork spilling all over the oven. Quickly the two worked to carefully remove the platter and pork. They than had to go to Ann and tell her what had happened. She did not seem to mind. Fortunately, the rest of the evening flowed smoothly, although there were many children under the age of 5 and they were left to fend for themselves behind the house as the parents partied. Something that had struck Sarah was that one of the guests had a handicapped child. It did not seem to her that the hosts made any efforts to make the child comfortable. There was a step to get into the front entrance to their home and the back was gated off for a dog. There was no possible way to get a wheelchair in the house. Eventually the child was brought inside, but the father and caretaker had to lift the chair up and over the steps. The lawn was also uneven and the child's caretaker had trouble maneuvering the wheelchair around.

As mentioned before, the event did not have an official ending time. As Anthony and Sarah wrapped up the last food in the kitchen, they began wondering when they could leave. Finally, after about 20 minutes, they went to the hostess and asked to be dismissed. Ann paid, provided a tip and wished them well.

## CASE QUESTIONS

- What could have Ann done to better prepare for the party?
- What suggestions would you give Anthony and Sarah to better prepare themselves next time they coordinate an event?
- What accommodations could Ann have provided for the disabled child and other children?
- How would you have handled the problem of erecting the tent?

# Unhappy Tournament
## (SPORT)

Shoot for the Cure: 3-on-3 Basketball Tournament, organized by the American Cancer Society (ACA) and coordinated by Mark, the event manager, was going smoothly. The games were running on schedule and everyone seemed to be enjoying the entertainment. Overall, the event seemed to be a success. Suddenly, the atmosphere of the event changed drastically. Sally, a participant in the next game, reported to the basketball court for the beginning of the last 3-on-3 game. The game began, then all of a sudden there was a loud cry from the courts.

Sally had been struck by a falling basket. The entire apparatus had fallen on Sally as she went to make a basket. The volunteer first-aid squad assigned to monitor the event was on the scene immediately. The injury was severe. Sally lay on the court with the apparatus still sitting across her body. She was not breathing and was losing blood. Her arms were severely torn. Sally was airlifted to the closest trauma center, where she received a high level of treatment.

Sally would survive the incident. After an extended stay at the hospital, Sally was released; however, almost a year after the incident, Sally still did not have full function in her right arm and hand. The prognosis was poor. As full function had not returned by this point, there was little hope that it would ever return. Sally would invest much time and energy in occupational therapy to relearn life skills that she had previously taken for granted.

During Sally's recovery time, the ACA and the event manager were busy gathering all of the paperwork that they would need in the event that after recovery Sally would press charges and demand payment for her injuries. While gathering the paperwork, they noticed that Sally's parents had not signed a release form for her to be cared for or transported by event medical personnel. They also realized that their registration package did not include a form for participants to sign that indicated that they understood that there were risks involved in participation and that they assumed these risks. Because a precedent had already been set in the courts of New Jersey, the location of the event, these missing documents would be extremely detrimental to the society and the event manager. The ACA knew that they would be targeted as the deepest pockets and that the event manager would be accused of negligence.

Sally's parents did bring a lawsuit against Mark and the ACA. They claimed that their daughter did not receive proper medical attention and that they did not consent to having their daughter airlifted to a hospital outside the local community. They claimed that the time spent waiting for the helicopter should have been spent transporting their daughter to the local hospital, where she would have received treatment sooner. They also claimed that they were not informed that such a serious injury could result from their daughter's participation in the event. The complaint ended with the assertion that the ACA and the event manager were negligent in using equipment that could fall on and injure participants.

The ACA and the event manager had no defense in this matter and eventually had to settle even though the incident was an accident and the equipment was inspected prior to use. The ACA agreed to assume a large portion of the financial burden and the event manager agreed to forfeit all profits and pay an additional sum out of his own pocket.

## CASE QUESTIONS

- What should the event manager have done to ensure that both she and the ACA were protected against lawsuits brought by an injured participant?

- What forms should the event manager have included in the registration package?
- What specific details should be included in a medical release form?
- How could the event manager prove that she had inspected the equipment and was it an issue in this case?

# We Are Sold Out!
## (ASSOCIATION CONVENTION)

A professional trade association holds an annual meeting every October for the purpose of education and networking for its 12,000 members. Traditionally, the meeting is held in convention hotels and the site is reserved three years in advance. These plans are made based on past growth of the meeting and the projected increase in membership of the association. In budgeting for the meeting each year, the association carefully considers the break-even point as well as the goal for increased attendance and membership in each progressive year. Since this is a nonprofit organization, the primary goal is to attract enough attendance from its membership base to cover the costs of the meeting and allow the meeting to continue each year.

During the preconference meeting held two days before the annual meeting, the event manager constantly heard herself telling the convention manager to max out every meeting room in theater-style seating. Over the last few weeks of registration, the meetings staff began to worry about the ramifications of allowing too many members to register for the meeting based on the space available in the hotel. Trying to find this balance between earning increased revenues based on more registrations and providing a high-quality event for a smaller number of attendees given the space parameters is an issue facing many event managers. It is critical to plan ahead for these circumstances to ensure a high-quality event that will also fulfill financial expectations.

Three weeks before the meeting was to be held, the director of meetings realized that registration income had more than exceeded the projected level of income for the year, based on the number of registrations in each of three price categories. Since previous meetings had never been sold out, and members had always been able to register on-site, the meetings department decided to keep registration open to all members waiting to register until the last minute. The association did not want to disappoint members who counted on being able to register at the late date.

In the last three weeks of registration, a disproportionately large number of people continued to register for the meeting. The meeting manager did not cut off registration until 5:00 P.M. on the last day of business before the meeting. For convenience, the association had three different ways that members could register. The most traditional way was to send the registration form through the mail with the registration check. The second was to fax the registration form and include a credit card number for payment. Third, the attendee could register online and provide credit card information. Regardless of the method, registrations were tracked and accounted for through an online registration database.

When attendees preregistered they could choose from all the sessions and it was not necessary to provide both first and second choices. The database was not equipped for this type of selection and therefore the registrants were essentially guaranteed that they would be able to attend their first choice of sessions. In reality, preregistration was only for the purpose of reserving meeting room space and attendees could go to any session in a time slot regardless of which they preregistered for. The association does not have the staff to monitor each session room to be sure that everyone preregistered for a specific session.

About one month before the meeting, the director of meetings needed to assign session rooms at the hotel so that these room assignments could be published in the program guide and so that speakers would know ahead of time where they were going to present. When this scheduling of rooms occurred, the director of meetings knew that several sessions were completely full but figured that some people would attend different sessions in the end and that some of the registrations would be canceled. Since registration was much greater in the last month than was expected, many session rooms were overbooked. The registration database was not equipped to close out certain sessions or to alert registrants that a session was full.

Also, after the final room assignments were made, there was no way to change them to make certain rooms larger and others smaller. The managers knew that there would be some unhappy attendees, especially those that preregistered for sessions months in advance, however, they felt that there was no flexibility for the location, and they wanted to try to satisfy the greatest number of members.

After evaluating the results of the 2000 annual meeting, the association directors began to seriously contemplate the goals of the annual meeting. The directors knew that for the meeting in three years, they would be able either to find a hotel with even larger meeting facilities or to use a small convention center. However, the problem lies in the location of the meetings for the next two years, for which the hotel has already been reserved based on smaller attendance numbers.

## CASE QUESTIONS

- Ethically, should the association allow unlimited registration to earn more revenue from increased demand, or should it limit registration and focus on the quality of the event?
- If the association limits registration, how should they alert members about the change in procedure?

- When booking a location for the meeting in three years, how can the meetings department predict how large demand for registration will be?
- What could the association do to allow members to access information from the meeting if they get cut off from registration?

# Trials of the Trade Show
## (EXHIBITION)

The trade show event manager stood on the loading dock with sweat dripping down her brow as she watched dozens of trucks and other vehicles line up for what seemed like miles in the distance. As the sun continued to bear down on the loading dock area, two union workers began to exchange heated words about the jurisdiction of work. Finally, the event manager glanced at her watch and realized that the load-in for the event was running two hours behind schedule, thus incurring thousands of dollars in overtime charges. And this was only the beginning of trials for the trade show event manager.

Once the doors to the exhibition opened, hundreds of buyers streamed in and promptly clogged the aisles on one side of the exhibit floor. For nearly four hours the exhibitors on the other side of the exhibit floor were virtually ignored by the buyers. A few minutes after the start of the exhibit several exhibitors complained to the event manager that other exhibitors were playing loud music and stepping into the aisles to bring people into their booths. The exhibit manager was also reminded by their legal counsel that it was illegal for the exhibitors to play recorded music in their booth without permission from the American Society of Composers, Authors, and Publishers or Broadcast Music International.

These problems could easily have been prevented if the event manager had conducted proper research, design, and planning. For example, the load-in should have been smooth and seamless because of proper advance scheduling and a nearby marshaling facility for the vehicles. The issue of labor jurisdiction should have been clarified immediately and resolved by the union steward or union business manager. The problems with crowding and crowd flow could have been anticipated and rectified in advance by establishing attractions (such as food and beverage), entertainment, or perhaps human traffic directors to route the arriving buyers. Finally, the issue with activities being conducted in the booths should have been prevented by a policy statement in the exhibitors' regulations, policies, and procedures. Each exhibitor should have been required to initial or sign the regulations documents to confirm compliance with these policies. This would have eliminated the issue of music in the booths and given the event manager the necessary tools to enforce these policies.

## CASE QUESTIONS

- What should be included in the exhibitors' policies, procedures, and practices, and regulations?
- How do you design the exhibit floor to avoid crowding, gridlock, and other crowd control issues?
- What do you do if an exhibitor violates regulations?
- How do you communicate effectively with union workers?
- What are some creative solutions to ensure that buyers visit underutilized areas of an exhibit area?

# Attend the Gala!
## (GALA CELEBRATION)

The local county chamber of commerce has produced 74 consecutive annual winter galas. Key stakeholders in this event are the chamber staff, the chamber executives, the local hotel, and chamber members. Over the years, attendance has stagnated. Thus far, neither the chamber staff nor the chamber executives has reacted to this attendance challenge. In fact, the attendance goal always was the prior year's attendance level. The chamber consists of approximately 900 members. The highest gala attendance was one-half of the total membership. The average attendance is about one-third of all members.

To boost attendance, the marketing manager of the chamber considers the following steps:

1. Conducting research to update the target market information and profile.
2. Increasing advertising.
3. Launching new promotions.

The last marketing survey among the members of the chamber of commerce was completed 10 years ago. The marketing manager feels that an updated study is needed. It is also a good opportunity to collect additional data about the members. Until now, information about the gala was provided only in the chamber's newsletter, which was distributed only once a month. Many members may never see this advertisement. The chamber's marketing manager believes that gala information should be put in the form of high-impact advertising. To do this, she wants to place in several local newspapers an ad of one-third of a column showing an elegant man and woman dancing under a sparkling chandelier with the text "Annual Winter Gala—What's all the hype about?" She thinks that this type of advertisement will excite and intrigue members into thinking about attending the gala. The major obstacle with the new advertising campaign is cost. The new ad campaign will raise the gala's costs unless some creative trades with the newspapers are developed.

Up to this point, no promotion campaign has been developed for the annual galas. The marketing manager feels that there may be some positive affect from the promotions; however, she is not sure how the promotions should be conducted. Unfortunately, the marketing manager must decide fast. The chamber of commerce cannot afford to lose money on its galas but cannot cancel the gala either.

## CASE QUESTIONS

- Why it is important to update the members' database? How often should the list be updated? In what forms should the update be conducted?
- Do you support the new advertising campaign?
- What cost-saving agreements can be made with the local media?
- If local newspapers are not flexible, can you come up with alternative advertising partners (radio, TV, Internet)? What are advantages and disadvantages of each?
- Do you agree that promotions can help attendance? How would you design a promotion campaign to maximize the attendance and maximize the revenue?

# Cutting the Ribbon and Healing the Community
## (CIVIC CELEBRATION)

For several weeks the event manager has been inquiring how to get a permit to hold a major municipal parade to celebrate the grand opening of a convention center. Finally, he was introduced to the mayor of the midsized Southern city the night before the parade to celebrate the grand opening of the convention center. "Mr. Mayor," the event manager asked, "how do I get a permit to hold the parade? None of your staff can tell me where to request permission." The mayor smiled, held out his hand and said, "You have my permission." Most event managers know that receiving a parade permit is neither that simple nor that secure. The event manager was lucky to meet the mayor and receive permission, but it would have been much safer to get it in writing or at least to document the conversation.

This municipal celebration offered many other challenges for the novice event manager. First, the convention center was a controversial municipal project and required a great deal of public relations effort to convince the local citizens that this was not just another civic boondoggle. Second, the board of the convention center wanted to be sure that multiple stakeholders were involved and that the programming attracted a wide variety of audience members. Third, the staff of the convention center wanted to showcase their human resources along with the new building. The event manager would have to satisfy all these needs to be successful.

To combat a potential negative public relations reaction, the event manager designed a media luncheon as the first event to introduce the new convention center. At the luncheon the media were captivated by a troupe of singers and dancers who performed an original musical entitled, "Something for Everyone: A Convention Center Now." In the musical a villain named Mr. Sleeze represented downtown before the center was built. The actors encourage the media to boo and hiss Mr. Sleeze and by the end of the musical the entire audience was standing and singing along to the closing lyrics of "Something for Everyone: A Convention Center for Us."

To ensure that multiple stakeholders were involved in the program, the event manager met with dozens of local professional and amateur performing artist organizations. The cast included church choirs, ethnic folk dance troupes, and professional musicians, dancers, and singers. As a result, many audience members were family and friends of the cast and represented the entire rainbow of this Southern city.

Finally, the event manager included in the production schedule for the event two days of customer service training. The entire convention center staff was trained to become members of the cast and were costumed and scripted for the three-day celebration. As a result, many of the media reports commented favorably on the new era of customer service that had arrived at the new convention center.

## CASE QUESTIONS

- How can you determine the public relations challenges for a municipal event and work with your client to mitigate potential problems?
- What type of programming can you incorporate in a municipal event to ensure that you represent every facet of the community as well as to maintain a level of quality and professionalism throughout the program?
- Why is the permanent full- and part-time staff an important consideration at the venue where the event will be held? How can you raise the level of their performance without circumventing their existing training programs?

# Political Campaign on a Shoestring
## (POLITICAL CAMPAIGN)

The city council candidate needed to use event marketing to expand his meager marketing budget. To do this, he used a combination of event public relations, promotions, and stunts. Due to his creativity and consistency of message, he came within 200 votes of winning one of the closest elections in decades. "We may not have much money but we have lots of ideas, let's use them!" roared the city council candidate to his volunteers. They did not know that he was serious when he said "Every day will be a special event in this campaign."

The candidate conducted planning meetings with his staff and volunteers and they developed a series of campaign events that would increase in frequency as the campaign drew to a close. First, the campaign volunteers set up a series of informal "coffee with the candidate" meetings in private homes. Allowing the candidate to listen to the concerns of the 25 to 50 persons who attended each event give him the opportunity to make them feel important, due to the intimacy of each event. Over 1000 persons attended 25 such events.

Next, the candidate's staff made certain that the candidate was featured in a series of municipal events. He served as honorary grand marshal in a parade, judge at a dog show, and honorary coach for a high school basketball game. Over 100,000 persons saw the candidate at these events.

Finally, the day before the election, the candidate literally stopped traffic. For over 20 years the candidate had championed a mass transportation system for the city. So it was natural that he would appear on a busy highway during rush-hour gridlock and hold up a banner that announced, "Vote for Me and You Could Be Home by Now!" Three television stations covered the event live and his picture appeared in color on the front page of the newspaper on election day!

A campaign with very few financial resources was able to compete effectively against an incumbent candidate who had over $1 million to buy advertising and other media support. How did they do this so effectively? First, they realized that events are natural vehicles for charismatic candidates such as theirs. Next, they used a wide variety of events to showcase the candidates' best traits: his warm personal interest in people and his theatrical flair. Finally, they used a signature event that focused on his long and positive record in transportation policy and scored a home run with the media by using creativity to get their message in front of the people.

Although the candidate lost the election, he won the media battle and now over 30 years later the media still occasionally refer to this campaign as one of the most interesting and best media events in the history of their city.

## CASE QUESTIONS

- What kind of sponsors or donors could the campaign managers have solicited to increase the budget?
- What could have been added to campaign events if the event manager had better financial resources?
- How do you make sure that events are consistent with a candidate's message?
- What contingency plans should you devise in case some of events backfire before or during execution?

# Good Luck, Grads!
## (UNIVERSITY)

Sometimes an event has many planners and organizers. This was true in the case of this year's graduation luncheon for a graduate program. Each year for the past three years, a graduate school of a small regional university held an event for its winter graduates. They have held a luncheon on campus to recognize the graduates, give them a chance to assemble, and present them with a small gift as they continue their lives beyond the university. The stakeholders in this graduate luncheon include the new graduates, the university, and the community. In the beginning of November, Chris was given the job of printing the programs. This did not appear to be a difficult task, as he had a sample from the previous year and so didn't begin to work on the job seriously until the beginning of December. As he set to work finalizing the content for this year, Chris quickly began to realize that not only were several people in the department working on different aspects of the luncheon but also that the actual programming of the luncheon was not being taken care of. Specifically, the previous year's luncheon had involved a student speaker and a faculty member who presented the graduation gift. Rather than just including this person's name in the program, Chris learned that one still needed to be nominated. Quickly compiling and mounting an e-mail campaign, he was soon receiving nominations, less than two weeks before the luncheon. Issues of what faculty would be involved in the event also arose and the event manager's job grew to include the task of deciding and scheduling this element of the program.

In the end, a student speaker was selected and included in the program. The luncheon was a total success and the graduates were unaware of the last-minute scrambling. However, an unclear organizational chart can lead to miscommunications and dropped balls. When the structure of the planning group is unclear or unknown, as it was in this case, important details such as student nomination of a graduation speaker can be missed.

### CASE QUESTIONS

- In planning for the luncheon next year, how can the university clearly identify who is in charge of planning the luncheon?
- What type of efficient organizational chart would you recommend for such event in an academic environment?
- What other techniques would be helpful to save, track, and retrieve in the event history?
- How would you create a checklist for the various elements of the event?

# Better Follow-up
## (MOVIE PREMIER)

An event planning company designed the special screening of a major motion picture at one New York theater in the year 2000. The portion of the event that the company was hired for was what can be called the "red carpet event." While the client communicated with the company and specified exactly what was needed and how the design was to be executed, the event planning company missed an opportunity for both research and stronger follow-up.

To begin the research stage, the event organization should have performed a marketing analysis that included both internal and external analysis. Before an event can exceed that of the competition, the organization has to understand the competition's assets and weaknesses as well as their own. However, no marketing research was conducted and no brainstorming was involved. The event organization executed the client's order.

The event organization did not perform these measures, due to the short time frame and because they determined that the event was not large enough. An event is like an actor's performance on stage in that there are no small events, just small event managers. In the organization's defense, the event was cost-efficient and generally satisfied the needs of the client. The client told them what they wanted, and there was not much room for creativity.

During the formal evaluation, the officers of the event organization reported that they really did not conduct a formal evaluation with the client. They just gave the company feedback on how things had gone. Only the event manager in charge that day listened to this feedback and no intercompany database or log was maintained. Sometimes when the crew leaves a site, the client checks in with them and they talk informally about how happy the client is. Then as people come and go within the organization, this is quickly forgotten. The organization is not sure if any better approach is possible for conducting a postevent analysis. Thus far the company has been able to avoid any negative experience, and there is no reason to believe that something should be changed to improve its practices.

## CASE QUESTIONS

- Do you agree that the current practice is the best one?
- If several senior event officers leave the company what affect would it have within this organization on the event management company's performance?
- If you were contracted to target the problems what suggestions do you have for the management?

# Help Wanted!
## (HUMAN RESOURCES)

In the early fall, John Smith, the owner of Events by Stars catering company, came into the service manager's office beaming. "We got the Cameron party," he said enthusiastically while throwing the BEO on Jones' desk. "Great!" Jon exclaimed as he picked up the contract and starting reading. Immediately he realized that the October 28 date was the same as that of four other events for the catering company that night. It was also Halloween weekend, a favorite of the college crowd.

He continued to read the contract and found that he would need 22 staff members and 2 supervisors for the dinner portion of this event alone. His enthusiasm faded. Earlier the same day there were at least two other events, requiring another 38 service personnel. These plus the other 24 for the Cameron dinner put him at 62 service staff needed for one evening. That would be paying for approximately 400 man-hours in one night.

Unfortunately, the events on October 28 were too important just to send warm bodies. A service staff with skills was needed; there was no room for bad service. Where were these people going to come from?

Catering in Charleston is very seasonal and it is very difficult to maintain a full service staff at any given time because the work is so inconsistent. One week someone could work 40 hours, then for a month there would be no hours.

Tourism and hospitality are the top industries in Charleston. There are an enormous number of restaurants and lodging facilities. Charleston is the home of several small universities, one culinary school, one military school, one medical school, and several community colleges. One of the community colleges provides a culinary program and an associate degree in tourism hospitality. The University of South Carolina is 90 miles away and offers a bachelor of science degree in hotel, restaurant, and tourism administration.

There are two hospitality-staffing companies in the area. Neither is typically reliable, providing average, untrained staff. Staff show up in a variety of styles of black and white uniforms, if they show up at all. Working with the staffing companies is kind of like rolling the dice—you never really know what you are going to get. By using a staffing company, the labor expense is increased.

### CASE QUESTIONS

- How does a company maintain part-time staff when there is not enough work to keep them busy all year round?
- What policies and procedures, if any, could be put in place to avoid this situation in the future?

- Is there a way to fully staff these events without negatively affecting the service or budget?
- What is the effect of using untrained staff?
- How do you train temporary staff to get them up to your standards?
- How does a service manager better prepare for such a problem?

# Show Me the Money
(FINANCIAL)

ASEM is a major professional organization dedicated to the science and art of engineering management. The goal of ASEM 2000 conference was to bring together the nation's leading engineering managers, with a special emphasis on evaluation technical leadership in the Washington metropolitan area's vibrant information systems technology sector. This annual conference in Washington, DC is highly respected among technical professionals in the United States. ASEM 2000 was held from October 4 to October 7 in Washington's Marriott Hotel. The main stakeholders included ASEM, the conference management service at one large metropolitan university, engineering managers from high-tech organizations, and other organizations interested in the electronic communication's development.

The annual budget for the conference is close to $100,000 and the organization committee traditionally raised these funds by soliciting contributions from sponsors and by charging participants an attendance fee. The conference organizers had several contracts in place with major vendors: a conference facility, caterers, and a transportation company. These vendor contracts, signed five years ago and not revised since, were fixed-fee contracts.

Approximately ten months before holding the event, the conference committee faced a serious problem. There was a serious deficit of funds to complete the conference organization. Due to a sales decline, one of the conference's sponsors was not able to contribute a pledge this year, and others made clear that they would not be able to cover the gap. During a special meeting held by the organizers, two possible solutions were identified:

1. Generate more revenues by attracting additional sponsorship funds;
2. Reduce the costs of the event by better expense management.

One of the possible solutions is to renegotiate the vendors' contracts. However, the organizers are not sure how to start the negotiations. It is very unlikely that the vendors will agree simply to cut their prices without strong reasoning from the conference organizers' side. You are asked to prepare your recommendations to the organization committee on how to turn around the finances of the conference.

## CASE QUESTIONS

- How would you prepare for the meeting with your vendors?
- What kind of research should be done before any financial contract negotiations?
- What incentive can organizers provide to sponsors and participants earlier to generate cash?
- What other solutions could organizers use to attract funds?

# Hot, Hot, Hot
## (RISK MANAGEMENT)

During the annual fundraising event for a local private school in a small Southern city, the event manager used audiovisual equipment to enhance the evening; however, some of the other enhancements were totally unexpected. Five hundred people attended the gala dinner entitled "A Hot Night in Rio," a silent auction and dance. They ate, drank, and had a good time. Someone donated 20 dozen Krispy Kreme doughnuts and they were served on silver trays by the servers when the coffee bar opened late in the evening. It was fun and successful.

The lighting, sound, food—everything—went well until late in the evening. The music was playing and only 50 guests were left, most dancing on the landing overlooking the ocean. The event manager smelled something similar to hot electrical wiring, so she immediately checked the spotlights and gobos in the hallway and turned off the extra lighting. No one was in the main ballroom, but when the event manager walked in, she could smell something burning in that room.

She checked the lights again and had security and building management check them, and slowly the smell seemed to fade away. Five minutes later, she returned and the entire function room was full of smoke. The smoke was coming out of the vents in the ceiling. An electrical fire had engulfed the ceiling. The event manager immediately notified the building management and they telephoned the fire department.

The remaining guests departed quickly. Surprisingly, the fire alarms did not work, although alarms on all 11 floors should have been signaling the fire department. The alarms may have been disabled due to building renovations.

The electrical fire was the result of a meltdown of the air-conditioning system. The event manager was most fortunate because if the fire had occurred two hours earlier, she would have had 500 people eating dinner with a live auction going on. Although the event was ultimately successful financially, it could just as easily have resulted in a catastrophic loss of lives and property.

## CASE QUESTIONS

- What should the event manager have done before the event to assess this potential risk?
- How could the event manager have verified with the building managers that all fire alarm systems were functioning properly?
- How should the event manager have evacuated the guests?
- If you were to write the incident report for this event, how would you describe the actions of the event manager, the building manager, and the fire department?

# APPENDIX 1

# Organizations and Resources

The event management–related organizations and resources listed in this appendix can help propel your career success.

1. Do your homework and contact listed associations via e-mail and request information about their educational and networking programs and resources.
2. Join a primary organization based on your field of interest. For example, if you are interested in the broad category of event management, the International Special Events Society should be your first choice. However, if your selection is narrowly confined to expositions, you will want to join the International Association for Exposition Management. The primary organization will be where you devote the majority of your time and energy, while the secondary organization is one whose resources and programs can further assist you in developing your career.
3. Set a three- to five-year goal that includes committee involvement and board leadership, and ultimately, serving as one of the officers of the organization's local chapter or national organization. In many industries, the most successful people are those who are also the leaders within their industry's professional organizations.
4. Once you have set your goal, annually keep track of how you are doing. Continually remind those who are more established in the organization of your career goals and seek their help in making sure that you are advancing properly within the leadership of the organization.

In summary, do not merely join and expect success. Success comes naturally from your investment of time and talent.

## Definitions

- *Professional trade associations:* a national or international organization whose purpose is to actively promote the industry within which its members are active.

- *Professional society:* a national or international organization that provides research and educational services for its members and the general public.
- *Regional association:* an organization whose members are located in one regional location.

# Event Management Related Organizations

American Society of Association
  Executives (ASAE)
1575 I Street, N.W.
Washington, DC 20005-1168
(202) 626-ASAE
www.asaenet.org
A professional trade association whose members are executives in professional, trade, and civic associations, as well as those who provide services and products for this industry. The Meetings and Exposition Section is composed specifically of event managers. Allied associations throughout the United States and Europe.

Association for Convention Operations
  Management
965 Flowers Road South, Suite 105
Atlanta, GA 30341
(770) 454-9411
Fax: (770) 458-3314
www.acomonline.org
A professional trade association whose members are employed as convention service managers and in other conference positions.

Association for Fundraising Professionals
1101 Kings Street, Suite 3000
Alexandria, VA 22314
(703) 684-0410
www.nsfre.org

Association of Bridal Consultants (ABC)
200 Chestnutland Road
New Milford, CT 06776-2521
(203) 355-0464

Fax: (860) 354-1404
www.bridalassn.com
A professional trade association that offers educational programs and certification for their members.

Association of Destination Management
  Executives (ADME)
3333 Quebec Street, Suite 4050
Denver, CO 80207
(303) 394-3905
Fax: (303) 394-3450
E-mail: info@adme.org
www.adme.org

Association of International Meeting
  Planners (AIMP)
2547 Monroe Street
Dearborne, MI 48124
(313) 563-0360
A professional trade association whose members organize international meetings.

Connected International Meeting
  Professionals Association
9200 Bayard Place
Fairfax, VA 22032
(703) 978-6287
Fax: (703) 978-5524
www.meetingprofessionals.org
An association of meeting professionals who utilize the Internet as a major tool in their work.

Convention Liaison Council (CLC)
1575 I Street, N.W., Suite 1190

Washington, DC 20005
(202) 626-ASAE
www.assnhg.com
An organization whose members are
associations representing various fields
in the convention industry. The CLC
administers the Certified Meeting
Professional (CMP) designation.

Council of Engineering and Scientific
  Society Executives (CESSE)
2000 Florida Avenue, N.W.
Washington, DC 20009
(202) 462-6900
Fax: (202) 328-0566
www.cesse.org
A professional society whose members
organize meetings in the engineering and
scientific industries.

Council of Protocol Executives (COPE)
101 West Twelfth Street, Suite PHH
New York, NY 10011
(212) 633-6934
www.councilofprotocolexecutives.org
A professional society whose members
are engaged primarily as experts in
protocol.

Foundation for International Meetings
  (FILM)
2111 Wilson Boulevard, Suite 350
Arlington, VA 22201-3058
(703) 908-0707
www.imminetwork.com
A professional association whose
members specialize in organizing
international meetings.

Healthcare Convention and Exhibitors
  Association
5775 Peachtree-Dunwood Road,
  No. 500-G
Atlanta, GA 30342
(404) 252-3663
www.hcea.org

A professional trade association whose
members are exhibitors and others in the
health care industry.

Hospitality Sales and Marketing
  Association International (HSMAI)
1300 L Street, N.W., Suite 800
Washington, DC 20005
(202) 789-0089
www.hsmai.org
A professional trade association whose
members are professional salespeople in
the hotel, convention center, and
hospitality industry and those who
provide services and products for this
industry. HSMAI sponsors a conference
entitled "Affordable Meetings." This
conference provides low-cost resources
for event managers in the convention
industry.

Insurance Conference Planners
  Association
Unit 106260
Esplanade, British Columbia,
V7M 3G7, Canada
(604) 988-2054
www.icpanet.org
A professional association whose
members are planners of conferences in
the insurance industry.

International Association for Exhibition
  Management
5001 LBJ Freeway, Suite 350
Dallas, TX 75244
(972) 458-8002
Fax: (972) 458-8119
www.iaem.org
A professional trade association whose
members manage trade and public
expositions and provide services and
products for this industry.

International Association of Amusement
  Parks and Attractions (IAAPA)
1448 Duke Street
Alexandria, VA 22314
(703) 836-4800
www.iaapa.org

A professional trade association whose members own, manage, market, and consult in the amusement park and attraction industry and provide services and products for this industry.

International Association of Assembly
  Managers
635 Fritz Drive
Coppell, TX 75019
(214) 255-8020
www.iaam.org
A professional trade association whose members own, manage, operate, market, consult, or supply services and products for arenas, auditoriums, stadiums, and other venues.

International Association of Conference
  Centers
243 North Lindbergh Boulevard
St. Louis, MO 63141
(314) 993-8575
www.iacconline.org
A professional trade association whose members own, operate, manage, market, consult, and supply goods and services for conference centers.

International Association of Conventions
  and Visitors Bureaus (IACVB)
2025 M Street, N.W., Suite 500
Washington, DC 20036
(202) 296-7888
www.iacvb.org
A professional trade association whose members manage and market convention and visitors' bureaus for individual destinations and supply goods and services for these bureaus.

International Association of Fairs and
  Expositions (IAFE)
P.O. Box 985
Springfield, MO 65801
(417) 862-5771

Fax: (417) 862-0156
www.iafenet.org
A professional trade association whose members organize and manage fairs and expositions.

International Association of Professional
  Congress Organizers (IAPCO)
40 Rue Washington
B-1050 Brussels, Belgium
Int+ 32 26 40 7105
Fax: +32-2-640-4731
E-mail: iapco@xs4all.be
www.iapco.org
A professional trade association whose members are professional congress organizers.

International Congress and Convention
  Association
The International Meetings Association
Entrada 121
1096 EB Amsterdam, The Netherlands
Int+ 31 20 690 1171
www.icca.nl
A professional trade association whose members are travel agents, congress centers, professional congress organizers, and others involved in the organization and servicing of international meetings.

International Council of Shopping
  Centers (ICSC)
1221 Avenue of the Americas, 41st Floor
New York, NY 10020
(646) 728-3800
Fax: (212) 589-5555
www.icsc.org
A professional trade association whose members own, operate, manage, market, and supply goods and services for shopping centers. ICSC administers the Certified Marketing Director (CMD) exam and designation. This program includes competencies relating to shopping center promotion, including special event management.

International Exhibitors Association
(IEA)
5501 Backlick Road, Suite 105
Springfield, VA 22151
(703) 941-3725
www.tsea.org
A professional trade association whose
members exhibit at international
meetings.

International Festivals and Events
Association (IFEA)
P.O. Box 2950
Port Angeles, WA 98362-0336
(800) 432-4304
www.ifea.com
A professional trade association whose
members own, operate, manage, market,
and supply goods and services for
festivals and events. IFEA in conjunction
with Purdue University administers the
Certified Festival Executive (CFE)
designation/certification.

International Institute of Convention
Management
9200 Bayard Place
Fairfax, VA 22032
(703) 978-6287
www.cimpa.org
A professional trade association whose
members are active in managing
conventions.

International Special Events Society
(ISES)
9202 North Meridian Street, Suite 200
Indianapolis, IN 46260-1810
(800) 688-ISES
www.ises.com
The only umbrella organization
representing all aspects of the special
events industry.

Johnson & Wales University
Dr. Joe Goldblatt, CSEP

8 Abbott Park Place
Providence, RI 02903
(401) 598-4760
www.jwu.edu

Meeting Professionals International (MPI)
1950 Stemmons Freeway, Suite 5018
Dallas, TX 75207-3109
(214) 712-7700
A professional trade association whose
members include corporate, association,
and other meeting planners as well as
those who provide goods and services
for meeting planners.

National Association of Casino and
Theme Party Operations
18914 Des Moines Memorial Drive,
South
Building 4
SeaTac, WA 98148-1928
(206) 241-4777
Fax: (206) 241-6956
www.casinoparties.com

National Association of Catering
Executives (NACE)
5565 Sterrett Place, Suite 328
Columbia, MD 21044
(410) 997-9055
Fax: (410) 997-8834
www.nace.net
A professional trade association whose
members provide on- and off-premises
catering services as well as goods and
services for the catering industry.

National Association of Reunion
Managers
P.O. Box 21127
Tampa, FL 33622
(800) 654-2776
www.reunions.com
A professional trade association for
persons who professionally organize
reunions.

National Ballroom and Entertainment
  Association (NBEA)
2799 Locust Road
Decorah, IA 52101
(319) 382-3871
www.nbea.com
A professional trade association whose
members provide or organize
entertainment.

National Bridal Service (NBS)
3122 West Cary Street
Richmond, VA 23221
(804) 355-6945
www.nationalbridal.com
A professional trade association whose
members consult in the bridal
industry.

National Caterers Association
860 Bay Street
Staten Island, NY 10304
(800) 672-0029
Fax: (718) 420-0025
www.ncacater.org
Founded in 1981, off-premise caterers to
provide education and networking for
caterers.

National Coalition of Black Meeting
  Planners (NCBMP)
8630 Fenton Street, Suite 126
Silver Spring, MD 20910
(202) 628-3952
www.ncbmp.com
A professional trade association whose
members are black meeting planners or
those who provide goods and services
for meeting planners.

National Restaurant Association (NRA)
1200 Seventeenth Street, N.W.
Washington, DC 20036-3097
(202) 331-5900
www.restaurant.org
A professional trade association whose
members own, operate, manage, market,
consult, or supply goods and services to
the restaurant industry.

National Society of Fundraising
  Executives
1101 Kings Street, Suite 700
Alexandria, VA 22314
(703) 684-0410
www.nsfre.org
A professional trade association whose
members are employed in development,
fundraising, or consulting in the
philanthropic field and provide goods
and services for this profession.

Professional Convention Management
  Association (PCMA)
100 Vestavia Office Park, Suite 220
Birmingham, AL 35216
(312) 423-7222
www.pmca.org
A professional trade association whose
members plan and manage meetings and
supply goods and services for meeting
planners.

Public Relations Society of America
  (PRSA)
33 Irvin Place
New York, NY 10003
(212) 995-2230
www.prsa.org
A professional trade association whose
members are involved in public relations
activities or supply goods and services
for this profession.

Religious Conference Management
  Association (RCMA)
One RCA Dome, Suite 120
Indianapolis, IN 46255
(317) 632-1888
www.rcmaweb.org
A professional trade association whose
members are professional meeting
planners for religious organizations and
those who provide goods and services
for this industry.

Resort and Commercial Recreation
  Association
P.O. Box 2437
Aurora, IL 65057

(630) 892-2175
www.r-c-r-a.org
E-mail: rcraone.@aol.com

Society of Corporate Meeting
  Professionals (SCMP)
2965 Flowers Road South, Suite 105
Atlanta, GA 30341
(770) 457-9212
Fax: (770) 458-3314
www.scmp.org
A professional trade association whose
members are involved in corporate
meeting planning and supply goods and
services for this industry.

Society of Government Meeting
  Professionals (SGMP)
908 King Street, Lower Level
Alexandria, VA
(703) 549-0892
Fax: (703) 549-0708
www.sgmp.org
A professional trade association whose
members are involved in planning
government meetings and those who
supply goods and services for this
industry.

Society of Incentive Travel Executives
  (SITE)
21 West 38th Street, Tenth Floor
New York, NY 10018-5584
(212) 575-0910

www.site-intl.org
A professional trade association whose
members organize incentive activities
and supply goods and services for this
industry.

Society of Travel Agents in Government
  (STAG)
6935 Wisconsin Avenue, Suite 200
Bethesda, MD 20815
(301) 654-8595
www.government-travel.org
A professional trade association for
travel professionals involved in
government and those who supply goods
or services for this industry.

Stage Managers Association
P.O. Box 2234, Times Square Station
New York, NY 10180-2020
(212) 543-9567
www.stagemanagers.com
A professional trade association whose
members are theatrical stage members.
Many professional stage managers work
in the event management profession.

Western Fairs Association
1776 Tribute Road, Suite 210
Sacramento, CA 95815-4410
(916) 927-3100
www.fairnet.org
A regional association whose members
organize and manage fairs.

# Miscellaneous Organizations and Resources

Actor's Equity Association (AEA)
165 West 46th Street
New York, NY 10036
(212) 869-8530
www.actorsequity.org
A professional union representing
professional actors, actresses, and
stage managers working in live
theater.

Air Transport Association of America
1301 Pennsylvania Avenue, N.W., Suite
  1100
Washington, DC 20004-1707
(202) 626-4218
www.air-transport.org
A professional trade association whose
members are active in the air transport
industry.

American Federation of Musicians of the
   United States and Canada (AF of M)
1501 Broadway, Suite 600
New York, NY 10036
(212) 869-1330
www.afm.org
A professional union representing
musicians.

American Federation of Television and
   Radio Artists (AFTRA)
260 Madison Avenue
New York, NY 10016
(212) 532-0800
www.aftra.com
A professional union representing
television and radio performers.

American Floral Marketing Council
1601 Duke Street
Alexandria, VA 22314-3406
(703) 836-8700
A trade association that promotes the
floral industry.

American Guild of Variety Artists (AGVA)
184 Fifth Avenue, Sixth Floor
New York, NY 10036
(212) 675-1003
A professional union representing
performers in nightclubs, cabarets,
circuses, and other variety venues.

American Hotel and Motel Association
   (AH&MA)
1201 New York Avenue, N.W., Suite 600
Washington, DC 20005-3931
(202) 289-3100
Fax: (202) 289-3199
A professional trade association
representing owners, managers,
marketers of hotels and motels and those
who provide services and products for
this industry allied organizations.

American Institute of Floral Designers
720 Light Street
Baltimore, MD 21230
(410) 752-3318
www.aifd.org

A professional trade association whose
members represent floral designers and
those who provide products and services
for this industry.

American Pyrotechnics Association
   (APA)
P.O. Box 30438
Bethesda, MD 20824
(301) 907-8181
Fax: (301) 907-9148
www.americanpyro.com
A professional trade association
representing manufacturers, designers,
and producers of professional
pyrotechnics.

American Rental Association
1900 Nineteenth Street
Moline, IL 61265
(800) 334-2177
www.ararental.org
A professional trade association whose
members own and operate rental stores,
including party rental stores.

American Society for Training and
   Development (ASTD)
1640 King Street, Box 1443
Alexandria, VA 22313-2043
(703) 683-8100
www.astd.org
A professional trade association whose
members are trainers and those who
provide services and products for this
industry.

American Society of Composers, Authors
   and Publishers (ASCAP)
One Lincoln Plaza
New York, NY 10023
(212) 621-6000
www.ascap.com
A licensing organization for live and
electronic music.

Broadcast Music International (BMI)
10 Music Square East
Nashville, TN 37203

(615) 401-2000
www.bmi.com

Exhibit Designers and Products
   Association (EDPA)
611 East Wells Street
Milwaukee, WI 53202
(414) 276-3372
www.edpa.com
A professional trade association whose
members design and produce exhibits
for expositions.

Exposition Service Contractors
   Association (ESCA)
2920 North Green Valley Parkway
Henderson, NV 89014
(702) 319-9561
www.esca.org
A professional trade association whose
members provide services for
expositions.

International Association of Speakers
   Bureaus
6845 Parkdale Place, Suite A
Indianapolis, IN 46254-5605
(317) 297-0872
Fax: (317) 387-3387
www.igab.org
A professional trade association whose
members own, operate, and manage
professional speakers' bureaus.

International Communications Industries
   Association (ICIA)
11242 Waples Mill Road, Suite 200
Fairfax, VA 22030
(800) 659-7469
www.icia.org
A professional trade association whose
members provide communications
services.

National Association of Balloon Artists
Katepwa House
Ashfield Park Avenue
Ross-on-Wye, Herefordshire
HR9 5AX, England

01-989-762-204
Fax: 01-989-567-676
www.nabas.co.uk
A professional trade association whose
members provide balloon products and
services.

National Limousine Association
1300 L Street, N.W., Suite 1050
Washington, DC 20005
(202) 682-1426
www.limo.org
A professional trade association for
persons who own, manage, market, and
supply goods and services to the
limousine industry.

National Speakers Association (NSA)
1500 South Priest Drive
Tempe, AZ 85281
(480) 968-2552
www.nsaspeaker.org
A professional trade association whose
members are professional speakers and
those who provide services and products
for the professional speaking industry.

North American Association of
   Ventriloquists (NAAV)
P.O. Box 420
Littleton, CO 80160
(800) 250-5125
www.maherstudios.com
A professional trade association for
people involved in ventriloquism.

Pyrotechnics Guild International (PGI)
3944 Carthage Road
Randallstown, MD 21133
(410) 560-0513
www.pgi.org
An organization comprised of people
engaged in fireworks (pyrotechnics).

Screen Actors Guild (SAG)
5757 Wilshire Boulevard
Los Angeles, CA 90036
(213) 954-1600
www.sag.com

A professional trade union for actors, actresses, and others in the film and television industry.

Society of American Florists (SAF)
1601 Duke Street
Alexandria, VA 22306
(703) 836-8700
Fax: (703) 836-8705
www.safnow.org
A professional trade association for florists and those who provide goods and services for the floral industry.

Special Events Office of the Military
  District of Washington
Fort Lesley J. McNair
Fourth and P Streets, S.W.

Washington, DC 20319-5058
(202) 475-1399
A organization responsible for providing military units such as bands, color guards, and others for special events in the Washington, DC metropolitan area.

Travel Industry Association of America
1100 New York Avenue, N.W.
Washington, DC 20005
(202) 408-8422
Fax: (202) 408-1255
www.tia.org
A professional trade association whose members promote, market, research, and provide information about the travel industry.

# Internet Sites

## Cities and Convention and Visitors' Bureaus

### City Net
A comprehensive guide to communities all over the world.
www.city.net

### ConventionBureaus.com
Directory of official convention bureau and national tourist office Web sites around the globe.
www.conventionbureaus.com

### International Association of Convention and Visitors Bureau
www.iacvb.org

### Tourism Offices Worldwide Directory
Searchable database of offices throughout the world.
www.towd.com

### USA CityLink Project
A directory of U.S. city sites on the Web listed by state. Focuses on two types of cities: tourism sites and sites whose mission is to support their local community.
www.neosoft.com/citylink

## General

### Big Book
Directory of addresses of any business in the United States, as well as maps and restaurant reviews.
www.bigbook.com

### CINET
The database of conventions and expositions managed by the International Association of Convention and Visitors Bureau.
www.iacvb.org

### CNN Financial Network "Be Your Own Travel Agent"
This links to ways to make your own travel reservation on the Web. Hotel, airlines, frequent flyer tips, technology, etc.
www.CNNfn.com/resources/links/travel.html

### DOME
Data on Meetings and Events lists more than 1,000 abstracts of research articles in the meetings, incentives. Convention and exposition-events industry. DOME also collects data (group history) for individual organizations.
www.domeresearch.org

### ExpoGuide
List of trade shows. Allows searches by alphabetical order, date and location, and keyword searches. About 4,800 shows.
www.expoguide.com

### The George Washington University Event Management Program
The gateway to distance learning opportunities for event management students. A live interactive discussion group of event management hot topics. A source for information on the latest event management research from George Washington University.
www.gwu.edu/emp

### The George Washington University Institute of International Tourism Studies
The home page for information regarding graduate and professional programs in tourism studies. The International Institute of Tourism Studies was the first to offer the master's degree in tourism in the United States.
www.gwutourism.org

### The Meeting and Event Planning Center
www.eventplanner.com/mainmenu.htm

### Meetings Industry Mall
Professional connections for meeting planners and suppliers.
www.mim.com

# Hotels and Alternative Venues

### All the Hotels on the Web
www.digimark.net

### All-Hotels.com

### Directory of All Hotels Online
www.hotel.com

### HotelBook
www.utell.com

### The Guide to Campus, Non-Profit & Retreat Meeting Facilities
A site that lets planners search by geographic location for a selection of less customary venues. Free. Over 500 sites listed.

### USAHotelGuide.com


# Online Publications

### Bizbash.com
Resources, discoveries, and news for special event planning, branding, and business entertaining.
www.bizbash.com

### BizTravel
Online magazine for the business traveler from e-publishers.
www.biztravel.com

### Newspage
A clipping service creating news pages for the travel, hospitality, and gaming industry.
www.individual.com

### Successful Meetings
An electronic version of the magazine.
www.successmtgs.com


# Professional Associations/Listservers

### American Society of Association Executives
A membership organization for the association management profession.
www.asaenet.org

### American Travel Association
Carriers that are members of the American Travel Association.
www.air-transport.org/ata/home.htm

## Hospitality Net

Internet home page for the global hospitality industry. Provides a global communication platform for professionals and students, as well as vendors.
www.hospitalitynet.org

## HotelNet

For hospitality professionals in lodging management and hotel food service. Provides a platform for discussing hospitality industry issues; provides relevant electronic information to hoteliers. Access by Telnet:hotelnet.com. Cost is $30 for three months. For more information, see:
www.hotelnet.com

## IAEMNet

Available through the International Association for Exposition Management. For more information, IAEM may be reached at (214) 712-7742.

## Info-tec Travel

A moderated internetwork mailing list dedicated to the exchange of information about information technology in travel and tourism. To subscribe, send an e-mail to Majordomo@igc.apc.org, leaving the subject line blank. In the body of the message, type "subscribe to info-tec travel."

## International Special Events Society

The home page for the International Special Events Society, the only international association serving the events industry.
www.ises.com

## MPINet

Available through Meeting Professionals International on Compuserve. An excellent method for planners and suppliers to network and to get education online via the message sections and library. Conduct real-time conversations, have meetings. For more information, see:
www.mpinet.org

## Tradeshow Listserver

The Tourism and Convention Department at the University of Nevada–Las Vegas operates an e-mail trade show list server. Simply send a message to listproc@nevada.edu, leaving the subject line blank. In the body of the message, type "subscribe trade show (your name)."

## Virtual PCMA

A private broadcast network that delivers news, education courses, and the ability to plan meetings interactively. Similar to a cable television network except that the television is replaced with a personal computer. For more information, call the Professional Convention Management Association at (205) 823-7262.

# Transportation

### Airlines of the Web
www.haas.berkeley.edu/~seidel/airline.html

### Amtrak
Information about Amtrak's rail service.
www.amtrak.com

# Travel Sites

### Expedia.com

### Lowestfare.com

### Priceline.com

### Travelocity.com
Each site provides discounted travel and hotel fares.

# APPENDIX 3

# References

Professional speaker Charles "Tremendous" Jones has been widely quoted as having originated the simple philosophy that many years from now most of us will be exactly the same person we are today except for two things: the books we read and the people we meet along the way.

I encourage you to develop the rigor of reading one new book per week and surveying other written resources daily, such as magazines and newsletters. This will help ensure that you stay current in your profession and provide you with many new ideas to accelerate the growth of your career.

I am often asked, "Where do you get all your ideas?" The questioner assumed that I reach into Pandora's fabled box and divine new wonders of creation. Usually, I reply to this question by stating: "Plato, Aristotle, Shakespeare, Keats, Browning, Hemingway, Dickinson, Stein, Eyre, Barrett, Seurat, Beethoven, Bach, Brahms, Picasso, Vermeer, and other renowned writers, painters, and composers."

The following resources have guided my career and will further ensure your professional success.

## Books Specifically for Event Managers

Adcock, E., D. Buono, and B. McGee (1995). *Premium, Incentive, and Travel Buyers.* New Providence, NJ: Salesman's Guide.

Allen, J. (2000). *Event Planning: The Ultimate Guide to Successful Meetings, Corporate Events, Fundraising Galas, Conferences, Conventions, Incentives, and Other Special Events.* Toronto, Ontario, Canada: Wiley.

American Society of Association Executives (1999). The Law of Meetings, Conventions, and Trade Shows: Meetings and Liability (Washington, DC).

Anderson, N. (1992). *Ferris Wheels: An Illustrated History.* Bowling Green, OH: Bowling Green State University Popular Press.

Association of National Advertisers Event Marketing Committee (1995). *Event Marketing: A Management Guide.* New York: ANA.

Astroff, M. T., and J. R. Abbey (1995). *Convention Sales and Services,* 4th ed. Cranbury, NJ: Waterbury Press.

Badger, R. (1979). *The Great American Fair: The World's Columbian Exposition and American Culture.* Chicago: Nelson-Hall.

Baghot, R., and G. Nuttall (1990). *Sponsorship, Endorsements and Merchandising: A Practical Guide.* London: Waterlow.

Bagley, N. F. (1994). *Reunions for Fun-Loving Families.* St. Paul, MN: Brighton Publications.

Bailey, D. (1999). *American Nightmares: The Haunted House Formula in American Popular Fiction.* Bowling Green, OH: Bowling Green State University Popular Press.

Baldridge, L. (1993). *Letitia Baldridge's New Complete Guide to Executive Manners.* New York: Rawson Associates, Maxwell Macmillan International.

Batterberry, A. R. (1976). *Bloomingdale's Book of Entertaining.* New York: Random House.

Bergen, M. T. (1988). *How to Have Fun at Work: The Complete Employee Services/Recreation Handbook.* Crete, IL: Abbott, Langer & Associates.

Bergin, R., and E. Hempel (1990). *Sponsorship and the Arts: A Practical Guide to Corporate Sponsorship of the Performing and Visual Arts.* Evanston, IL: Entertainment Resource Group.

Berlonghi, A. E. (1990). *The Special Event Risk Management Manual.* Dana Point: CA: Alexander Berlonghi.

Bodde, D. (1975). *Festivals in Classical China.* Princeton, NJ: Princeton University Press.

Boehme, A. J. (1999). *Planning Successful Meetings and Events: A Take-Charge Assistant Book.* New York: AMACOM.

Bowan, J. (1992). *Family Reunions: A Guide to Planning, Organizing and Holding Family Reunions.* Carson, CA: Akila Publishers.

Brashich, C. (1990). *World Manual for Group and Incentive Travel.* Livingston, NJ: Networld.

Brenland, C. (1995). *Wild Planet: 1,001 Extraordinary Events for the Inspired Traveler.* Detroit, MI: Visible Ink Press.

Brody, M., and B. Pachter (1994). *Business Etiquette.* Burr Ridge, IL: Irwin Professional Publishing.

Brown, B. E., and T. Ninkovich (1992). *Family Reunion Handbook: A Guide for Reunion Planners.* San Francisco: Reunion Research.

Brown, R., and M. Marsden (1994). *The Cultures of Celebrations.* Bowling Green, OH: Bowling Green State University Popular Press.

Browne, R. B. (1980). *Rituals and Ceremonies in Popular Culture.* Bowling Green, OH: Bowling Green State University Popular Press.

Browne, R. B., and M. T. Marsden (1994). *The Cultures of Celebrations.* Bowling Green, OH: Bowling Green State University Popular Press.

Calambria, F. M. (1993). *Dance of the Sleep-Walkers: The Dance Marathon Fad.* Bowling Green, OH: Bowling Green State University Popular Press.

Carey, T. (ed.) (1999). *Professional Meeting Management: A European Handbook.* Dallas, TX: Meeting Professionals International.

Cartmell, R. (1987). *The Incredible Scream Machine: A History of the Roller Coaster.* Bowling Green, OH: Bowling Green State University Popular Press.

Catherwood, D. W., and R. L. Van Kirk (1992). *The Complete Guide to Special Event Management: Business Insights, Financial Advice, and Successful Strategies from*

*Ernst & Young, Advisors to the Olympics, the Emmy Awards and the PGA Tour.* New York: Wiley.

Charsley, S. R. (1992). *Wedding Cakes and Cultural History.* New York: Routledge.

Church, B. R., and B. E. Bultman (1987). *The Joys of Entertaining.* New York: Abbeville Press.

Church, B. R. and L. R. Harrison (1993). *Weddings Southern Style.* New York: Abbeville Press.

Colby, L. H. (ed.) (1994). *A Working Guide to Effective Meetings and Conventions,* 6th ed. Washington, DC: Convention Liaison Council.

Cole, H. (1993). *Jumping the Broom: The African-American Wedding Planner.* New York: Henry Holt.

Convention Industry Council (2000). *The Convention Industry Council,* 5th ed. Washington, DC: CIC.

Dance, J. (1994). *How to Get the Most Out of Sales Meetings.* Lincolnwood, IL: NTC Business Books.

Deal, T. E., and A. A. Kennedy (1982). *Corporates Cultures: The Rites and Ritual of Corporate Life.* Reading, MA: Addison-Wesley.

Delacorte, T., J. Kimsey, and S. Halas (1981). *How to Get Free Press: A Do-It-Yourself Guide to Promote Your Interests, Organizations or Business.* San Francisco: Harbor.

De Lys, C. (1989). *What's So Lucky about a Four-Leaf Clover and 8414 Other Strange and Fascinating Superstitions from All Over the World.* East Brunswick, NJ: Bell Publishing.

Devney, D. C. (1990). *Organizing Special Events and Conferences: A Practical Guide for Busy Volunteers and Staff.* Sarasota, FL: Pineapple Press.

Dlugosch, S. E. (1980). *Folding Table Napkins: A New Look at a Traditional Craft,* 9th ed. St. Paul, MN: Brighton Publications.

Dlugosch, S. E. (1990). *Table Setting Guide.* St. Paul, MN: Brighton Publications.

Dlugosch, S. E. (1991). *Tabletop Vignettes.* St. Paul, MN: Brighton Publications.

Dlugosch, S. E. (1989). *Wedding Hints and Reminders.* St. Paul, MN: Brighton Publications.

Dlugosch, S. E. (1993). *Wedding Plans: 50 Unique Themes for the Wedding of Your Dreams,* 3rd ed. St. Paul, MN: Brighton Publications.

Dunkins, M., and J. Gray-Miott (1994). *The Perfect Choice: Wedding and Reception Sites.* Silver Spring, MD: Gray, McPherson and Associates.

Finkel, C. L. (1991). *Powerhouse Conferences: Eliminating Audience Boredom.* East Lansing, MI: Educational Institute of American Hotel and Motel Association.

Flanagan, J. (1993). *Successful Fund Raising: A Complete Handbook for Volunteers and Professionals.* Chicago: Contemporary Books.

Foster, J. S. (1991). *Business Insurance for Independent Planners.* Atlanta, GA: John S. Foster, Esq. Law Offices.

Foster, J. S. (1991). *Choosing a Business Form: What's Best for You?* Atlanta, GA: John S. Foster, Esq. Law Offices.

Foster, J. S. (1995). *Hotel Law: What Hoteliers Need to Know about Legal Affairs Management.* Atlanta, GA: John S. Foster, Esq. Law Offices.

Foster, J. S. (1995). *Independent Meeting Planners and the Law.* Atlanta, GA: John S. Foster, Esq. Law Offices.

Foster, J. S. (1991). *Independent Planner Checklists.* Atlanta, GA: John S. Foster, Esq. Law Offices.

Foster, J. S. (1995). *Meeting and Facility Contracts.* Atlanta, GA: John S. Foster, Esq. Law Offices.

Foster, J. S. (1995). *Meetings and Liability.* Atlanta, GA: John S. Foster, Esq. Law Offices.

Foster, J. S. (1992). *Sample Contract Clauses for Independent Planners.* Atlanta, GA: John S. Foster, Esq. Law Offices.

Freedman, H. A., and K. F. Smith (1991). *Black Tie Optional: The Ultimate Guide to Planning and Producing Successful Special Events.* Rockville, MD: Fund Raising Institute.

Fulmer, D., and N. Eddy (1990). *A Gentleman's Guide to Toasting.* Lynchburg, TN: Oxmoor House.

Gartell, R. B. (1994). *Destination Marketing for Convention and Visitor Bureaus,* 2nd ed. Dubuque, IA: Kendall/Hunt.

Getz, D. (1991). *Festivals, Special Events, and Tourism.*

Giblin, J. C. (1983). *Fireworks, Picnics and Flags: The Story of the Fourth of July Symbols.* Boston: Houghton Mifflin.

Gilbert, E. (1989). *The Complete Wedding Planner: Helpful Choices for the Bride and Groom,* rev. ed. Hollywood, FL: F. Fell.

Global Media Commission Staff (1988). *Sponsorship: Its Role and Effect.* New York: International Advertising Association.

Goldblatt, J., and C. McKibben (1996). *The Dictionary of Event Management.* New York: Van Nostrand Reinhold.

Goldblatt, J. J. (1995). *The Ultimate Party Handbook.* Chevy Chase, MD: Goldblatt Company.

Graham, S., J. J. Goldblatt, and L. Delpy (1995). *The Ultimate Guide to Sport Event Management and Marketing.* Chicago: Irwin Professional Publishing.

Greier, T. (1986). *Make Your Events Special: How to Produce Successful Special Events for Nonprofit Organizations.* New York: Folkworks.

Grimes, R. (2000). *Into the Bone.* Berkeley, CA: Berkeley University Press.

Hall, C. M. (1992). *Hallmark Tourist Events: Impacts, Management and Planning.* New York: Halstead Press.

Hall, S. J. (1992). *Ethics in Hospitality Management: A Book of Readings.* East Lansing, MI: Educational Institute of the American Hotel and Motel Association.

Hansen, B. (1995). *Off-Promise Catering Management.* New York: Wiley.

Harris, A. L. (1988). *Special Events: Planning for Success.* Washington, DC: Council for Advancement and Support of Education.

Heath, A. (1995). *Windows on the World: Multicultural Festivals for Schools and Libraries.* Metuchen, NJ: Scarecrow Press.

Hildreth, R. A. (1990). *The Essentials of Meeting Management.* Englewood Cliffs, NJ: Prentice Hall.

Hoffman, L. J. (1992). *The Reunion Planner: The Step-by-Step Guide Designed to Make Your Reunion a Social and Financial Success.* Los Angeles: Goodman Lauren Publishing.

Holbrook, M. B. (1993). *Daytime Television Game Shows and the Celebration of Merchandise: The Price Is Right.* Bowling Green, OH: Bowling Green State University Popular Press.

Howe, J. T. (1993). *The International Travel Resource for International Meeting and Congress Professionals.* Dallas, TX: Meeting Professionals International.

Howe, J. T., and H. M. Schaffer (1992). *Keeping in Step with Music Licensing.* Dallas, TX: Meeting Professionals International.

Howe, T. H. (1996). *U.S. Meetings and Taxes,* 3rd ed. Dallas, TX: Meeting Professionals International.

Howell, M. D. (1997). *From Moonshine to Madison Avenue: A Cultural History of the NASCAR Winston Cup Series.* Bowling Green, OH: Bowling Green State University Popular Press.

Hoyle, L. H., D. C. Dorf, and T. J. A. Jones (1989). *Managing Conventions and Group Business.* East Lansing, MI: Educational Institute of the American Hotel and Motel Association.

International Association of Business Communicators (1990). *Special Events Marketing (IABC Communication Bank Series).* San Francisco: IABC.

International Association of Professional Congress Planners (2000). *Meeting Industry Terminology,* 4th ed. Brussels, Belgium: IAPCP.

International Events Group (1995). *Evaluation: How to Help Sponsors Measure Return on Investment.* Chicago: IEG.

International Events Group (1995). *Media Sponsorship: Structuring Deals with Newspaper, Magazine, Radio and TV Sponsors.* Chicago: IEG.

International Special Events Society (1993). *ISES Gold.* Indianapolis, IN: ISES.

Jarrow, J., and C. Park. (1992). *Accessible Meetings and Conventions.* Columbus, OH: Association on Higher Education and Disability.

Jewell, D. (1978). *Public Assembly Facilities: Planning and Management.* New York: Wiley.

Jolles, R. L. (1993). *How to Run Seminars and Workshops: Presentation Skills for Consultants, Trainers and Teachers.* New York: Wiley.

Jones, J. (1984). *Meeting Management: A Professional Approach.* Stamford, CT: Bayard Publications.

Jones, J. E., and C. Phypers (1985). *Incentive Travel: The Professional Way.* Stamford, CT: Bayard Publications.

Jones, P., and A. Pizman (1993). *The International Hospitality Industry: Organizational and Operational Issues.* London: Pitman Publishing.

Kahan, N. W. (1990). *Entertaining for Business: A Complete Guide to Creating Special Events with Style and a Personal Touch.* New York: C. N. Potter.

Kaiser, T. A. (1995). *Mining Group Gold: How to Cash in on the Collaborative Brain Power of a Group.* Burr Ridge, IL: Irwin Professional Publishing.

Karasik, P. (1992). *How to Make It Big in the Seminar Business.* New York: McGraw-Hill.

Keegan, P. B. (1990). *Fundraising for Non-profits.* New York: Harper Perennial.

Klausner, S. Z. (1968). *Why Man Takes Chances: Studies in Stress-Seeking.* New York: Doubleday.

Kring, R. (1993). *Party Creations: A Book to Theme Event Design.* Denver, CO: Clear Creek Publishing.

Krueger, C. (1993). *Dream Weddings Do Come True: How to Plan a Stress-Free Wedding.* St. Paul, MN: Brighton Publications.

Kurdle, A. E., and M. Sandler (1995). *Public Relations for Hospitality Managers.* New York: Wiley.

Levi-Strauss, C. (1990). *The Origin of Table Manners, Vol. 3: Mythologies.* Chicago: University of Chicago Press.

Levitan, J. (1994). *Proven Ways to Generate Thousands of Hidden Dollars from Your Trade Show, Conference and Convention.* Vernon Hill, IL: Conference and Exhibition Publisher.

Levy, O., and A. Davidson (1991). *Party Planner.* New York: Langson Press.

Lewis, C. L. (1992). *How to Plan, Produce, and Stage Special Events.* Chicago: Evergreen Press.

Liebold, L. C. (1986). *Fireworks, Brass Bands, and Elephants: Promotional Events with Flair for Libraries and Other Nonprofit Organizations.* Phoenix, AZ: Oryx Press.

Lindsay, D. J. (1994). *Bravo Meeting Planner's Organizer: A Step-by-Step Road Map to Planning a Successful Meeting or Event.* Portland, OR: Bravo Publications.

Lippincott, C. (1994). *Meetings: Do's, Don'ts and Donuts: The Complete Handbook for Successful Meetings.* Pittsburgh, PA: Lighthouse Point Press.

MacCannell, D. (1976). *The Tourist: A New Theory of the Leisure Class.* New York: Schocken Books.

Mack, W. P., and W. Connell (1980). *Naval Ceremonies, Customs and Traditions,* 5th ed. Annapolis, MD: Naval Institute Press.

Mackenzie, J. K. (1989). *It's Show Time! How to Plan and Hold Successful Sales Meetings.* Homewood, IL: Dow Jones-Irwin.

Malouf, D. (1988). *How to Create and Deliver a Dynamic Presentation.* East Roseville, New South Wales, Australia: Simon & Schuster.

Malouf, L. (1999). *Behind the Scenes at Special Events: Flowers, Props and Design.* New York: Wiley.

Mangels, W. F. (1952). *The Outdoor Amusement Industry, From Earliest Times to the Present.* New York: Vantage Press.

Manning, F. E. (1983). *The Celebration of Society: Perspectives on Contemporary Cultural Performance.* Bowling Green, OH: Bowling Green State University Popular Press.

Marsh, V. (1994). *Paper-Cutting Stories for Holidays and Special Events.* Fort Atkinson, WI: Alleyside Press.

Martin, E. L. (1992). *Festival Sponsorship Legal Issues.* Port Angeles, WA: International Festivals Association.

Masciangelio, W. R., and T. Ninkovich (1991). *Military Reunion Handbook: A Guide for Reunion Planners.* San Francisco: Reunion Research.

McDonnell, I., J. Allen, and W. O'Toole (1999). *Festival and Special Event Management.* New York: Wiley.

McGinnis, C. (1994). *202 Tips Even the Best Business Travelers May Not Know.* Chicago: Irwin Professional Publishing.

McIntosh, R. W., and C. R. Goeldener (1990). *Tourism Principles, Practices and Philosophies,* 6th ed. New York: Wiley.

McKinzie, H. (1992). *Reunions: How to Plan Yours.* Los Angeles: McKinzie Publishing Company.

McMahon, T. (1990). *Big Meetings, Big Results.* Lincolnwood, IL: NTC Publishing Group.

Meeting Professionals International and Canadian Council and the Government of Canada, The Department of Human Resources Development (1994). *Meeting Coordinator Standards.* Dallas, TX: MPI.

Meeting Professionals International and Canadian Council and the Government of Canada, The Department of Human Resources Development (1994). *Meeting Manager Standards.* Dallas, TX: MPI.

Miller Brewing Company. *Good Times: A Guide to Responsible Event Planning.* Milwaukee, WI: MBC.

Miller, S. (1991). *How to Get the Most Out of Trade Shows.* Federal Way, WA: Adventure.

Montgomery, R. J., and S. K. Strick (1995). *Meetings, Conventions, and Exposition: An Introduction to the Industry.* New York: Van Nostrand Reinhold.

Morrisey, G. C. (1995). *Morrisey on Planning, Vols. I–III.* San Francisco: Jossey-Bass.

Morrow, S. L. (1997). *The Art of Show.* Dallas, TX: IAEM Foundation.

Morton, A., A. Prosser, and S. Spangler (1991). *Great Special Events and Activities.* State College, PA: Venture Publishing.

Morton, J. (1985). *Jack Morton (Who's He?) Story.* New York: Vantage Press.

Morton, J. (1993). *The Poor Man's Philosopher.* Washington, DC., Jack Morton Worldwide: NY.

Mothershead, A. B. (1982). *Dining Customs around the World: With Occasional Recipes.* Garrett Park, MD: Garrett Park Press.

Museum of Fine Arts (1992). *Wedding Planner.* New York: Rizzoli International Publications.

National Association of Broadcasters (1991). *A Broadcaster's Guide to Special Events and Sponsorship Risk Management.* Washington, DC: NAB.

Neel, S. M., and R. Wray (1995). *Saying "I Do": The Wedding Ceremony. The Complete Guide to a Perfect Wedding.* Colorado Springs, CO: Meriwether Publishing.

Neuhoff, V. (1987). *Scientists in Conference: The Congress Organizer's Handbook: The Congress Visitor's Companion.* Weinheim, Germany: VCH.

Newman, P. J., and A. F. Lynch (1983). *Behind Closed Doors: A Guide to Successful Meetings.* New York: Prentice Hall.

Nichols, B. (1989). *Professional Meeting Management,* 2nd ed. Birmingham, AL: Professional Convention Management Association.

Ninkovich, T. (1991). *Reunion Handbook: A Guide for School and Military Reunions,* 2nd ed. San Francisco: Reunion Research.

Norris, D. M., J. F. Loften, & Associates (1995). *Winning with Diversity: A Practical Handbook for Creating Inclusive Meetings, Events, and Organizations.* Washington, DC: Foundations of Meeting Planners International, Professional Convention Management Association, Association of Association Executives, International Association of Convention and Visitors Bureaus, and International Association of Exposition Management.

Oldenwald, S. B. (1993). *Global Training: How to Design a Program for the Multinational Corporation.* Chicago: Irwin Professional Publishing.

Packham, J. (1993). *Wedding Parties and Showers: Planning Memorable Celebrations.* New York: Sterling Publishing Company.

Petersen, K. (1992). *Historical Celebrations: A Handbook for Organizers of Diamond Jubilees, Centennials, and Other Community Anniversaries,* 3rd ed. Boise, ID: Idaho State Historical Society.

Plessner, G. M. (1980). *The Encyclopedia of Fund Raising: Golf Tournament Management Manual.* Arcadia, CA: Fund Raisers.

Plessner, G. M. (1980). *The Encyclopedia of Fund Raising: Testimonial Dinner and Luncheon Management Manual.* Arcadia, CA: Fund Raisers.

Plessner, G. M. (1986). *The Encyclopedia of Fund Raising: Charity Auction Management Manual.* Arcadia, CA: Fund Raisers.

Polivka, E. (ed.) (1996). *Professinal Meeting Management,* 3rd ed. Birmingham, AL: Professional Convention Management Association.

Post, E. (1991). *Emily Post's Complete Book of Wedding Etiquette,* rev. ed. New York: HarperCollins.

Powers, T., and J. M. Powers (1991). *Food Service Operations: Planning and Control.* Melbourne, Australia: R.E. Krieger.

Price, C. H. (1989). *The AMA Guide for Meeting and Event Planners.* Arlington, VA: Educational Services Institute.

Professional Convention Management Association (1985). *Professional Meeting Management.* Birmingham, AL: PCMA.

Quain, B. (1993). *Selling Your Services to the Meetings Market.* Dallas, TX: Meeting Professionals International.

Ramsborg, G. C. (1993). *Objectives to Outcomes: Your Contract with the Learner.* Birmingham, AL: Professional Convention Management Association.

Ray, C. (2001). *Highland Heritage: Scottish Americans in the American South.* Chapel Hill, NC: University of North Carolina Press.

Reed, M. H. (1989). *IEG Legal Guide to Sponsorship.* Chicago: International Events Group.

Reyburn, S. (1997). *Meeting Planner's Guide to Historic Places.* New York: Wiley.

Reynolds, R., E. Louie, and E. Addeo (1992). *The Art of the Party: Design Ideas for Successful Entertaining.* New York: Viking Studio Books.

Riverol, A. R. (1992). *Live from Atlantic City: A History of the Miss America Pageant.* Bowling Green, OH: Bowling Green State University Popular Press.

Roysner, M. (2000). *Hotel Contracts: A Road Map to Successful Hotel Negotiations.* Dallas, TX: IAEM Foundation.

Rutherford, D. G. (1990). *Introduction to the Conventions, Expositions, and Meetings Industry.* New York: Van Nostrand Reinhold.

Safire, W., and L. Safir (1990). *Leadership: A Treasury of Great Quotations for Everybody Who Aspires to Succeed as a Leader.* New York: Simon & Schuster.

Scannell, E. E., and J. W. Newstrom (1994). *Even More Games Trainers Play.* New York: McGraw-Hill.

Scannell, E. E., and J. W. Newstrom (1991). *Still More Games Trainers Play.* New York: McGraw-Hill.

Schindler-Rainman, E., and J. Cole (1988). *Taking Your Meetings Out of the Doldrums,* rev. ed. San Diego, CA: University Associates.

Schmader, S. W., and R. Jackson (1990). *Special Events: Inside and Out: A "How-to" Approach to Event Production, Marketing, and Sponsorship.* Champaign, IL: Sagamore Publishing.

Schreibner, A. L., and B. Lenson (1994). *Lifestyle and Event Marketing: Building the New Customer Partnership.* New York: McGraw-Hill.

Shaw, M. (1990). *Convention Sales: A Book of Readings.* East Lansing, MI: Educational Institute of the American Hotel and Motel Association.

Sheerin, M. (1984). *How to Raise Top Dollars from Special Events.* Hartsdale, NY: Public Service Materials Center.

Shenson, H. L. (1990). *How to Develop and Promote Successful Seminars and Workshops: A Definite Guide to Creating and Marketing Seminars, Classes and Conferences.* New York: Wiley.

Shock, P. J., and J. M. Stefanelli (1992). *Hotel Catering: A Handbook for Sales and Operations.* New York: Wiley.

Simerly, R. (1990). *Planning and Marketing Conferences and Workshops: Tips, Tools, and Techniques.* San Francisco: Jossey-Bass.

Simerly, R. G. (1993). *Strategic Financial Management for Conferences, Workshops, and Meetings.* San Francisco: Jossey-Bass.

Sinclair, M. T., and M. J. Stabler (1991). *The Tourism Industry: An International Analysis.* Wallingford, Oxon, England: C.A.B. International.

Slocum, S. K. (1992). *Popular Arthurian Traditions.* Bowling Green, OH: Bowling Green State University Popular Press.

Smith, L. J. (1989). *Tourism Analysis: A Handbook.* Harlow, Essex, England: Longman Scientific and Technical.

Soares, E. J. (1991). *Promotional Feats: The Role of Planned Events in the Marketing Communications Mix.* New York: Quorum Books.

Society of Incentive Travel Executives (1990). *The Incentive Travel Case Study Book.* New York: SITE.

Sokolosky, V. (1990). *Corporate Protocol: A Brief Case for Business Etiquette.* Dallas, TX: Valerie and Company.

Sokolosky, V. (1994). *The Fine Art of Business Entertaining.* Dallas, TX: Valerie and Company.

South Australia Department of Tourism (1982). *Planning Festivals and Special Events.* Adelaide, Australia: SADT.

Sowden, C. L. (1992). *An Anniversary to Remember: Years One to Seventy-Five.* St. Paul, MN: Brighton Publications.

Sowden, C. L. (1990). *Wedding Occasions: 101 New Party Themes for Wedding Showers, Rehearsal Dinners, Engagement Parties, and More.* St. Paul, MN: Brighton Publications.

Starsmore, I. (1975). *English Fairs.* London: Thames and Hudson.

Stern, L. (1995). *Stage Management,* 5th ed. Boston: Allyn & Bacon.

Stewart, M. (1988). *The Wedding Planner.* New York: C. N. Potter.

Stewart, M. (1987). *The Weddings.* New York: C. N. Potter.

Storey, B. T. (1997). *One Hundred and One Event Ideas I Wish I'd Thought Of.* Port Angeles, WA: International Festivals and Events Association.

Strick, S. (1995). *Meetings and Conventions.* New York: Van Nostrand Reinhold.

Surbeck, L. (1991). *Creating Special Events: The Ultimate Guide to Producing Successful Events.* Louisville, KY: Master Publications.

Swartz, O. D. (1988). *Service Etiquette,* 4th ed. Annapolis, MD: Naval Institute Press.

Swiderski, R. M. (1987). *Voices: An Anthropologist's Dialogue with an Italian-American Festival.*

Talbot, R. (1990). *Meeting Management: Practical Advice for Both New and Experimental Managers Based on an Expert's Twenty Years in the "Wonderful Wacky World" of Meeting Planning.* McLean, VA: EPM Publications.

Tassiopoulos, D. (ed.) (2000). *Event Management: A Professional and Development Approach.* South Africa: Juta Education: Johannesburg.

Tepper, B. (1993). *Incentive Travel: The Complete Guide.* San Francisco: Dendrobium Books.

The 3M Meeting and Management Team with Jeannine Drew (1994). *Mastering Meetings: Discovering the Hidden Potential of Effective Business Meetings.* New York: McGraw-Hill.

The Reunion Network (1992). *Class Reunions: Lesson 1, A Planner's Guide.* Hollywood, FL: Reunion Network.

The Reunion Network (1992). *Survival Guide for Military Reunion Planners.* Hollywood, FL: Reunion Network.

Thomsett, M. C. (1991). *The Little Black Book of Business Etiquette.* New York: American Management Association.

Torrence, S. R. (1991). *How to Run Scientific and Technical Meetings.* New York: Van Nostrand Reinhold.

Turner, V. (1982). *Celebration: Studies in Festivity and Ritual.* Washington, DC: Smithsonian Institution Press.

Veeck, B. (1972). *Thirty Tons a Day: The Rough-Riding Education of a Neophyte Racetrack Operator.* New York: Viking Press.

Von Bornstedt, M., and U. Prytz (1981). *Folding Table Napkins.* New York: Sterling Publishing Company.

Walford, C. (1968). *Fairs, Past and Present: A Chapter in the History of Commerce.* New York: A.M. Kelly.

Washington, G., Applewood Books Staff (1989). *George Washington's Rules of Civility and Decent Behavior in Company and Conversation.* Mount Vernon, VA: Applewood Books.

Watt, D. C. (1998). *Event Management in Leisure and Tourism.* Harlow, Essex, England: Addison Wesley Longman.

Weirich, M. L. (1992). *Meetings and Conventions Management.* Albany, NY: Delmar Publishers.

Weissinger, S. S. (1992). *A Guide to Successful Meeting Planning.* New York: Wiley.

Wiersma, E. A. (1991). *Creative Event Development: A Guide to Strategic Success in the World of Special Events.* Indianapolis, IN: Elisabeth A. Wiersma.

Wigger, E. G. (1997). *Themes, Dreams, and Schemes: Banquet Menu Ideas, Concepts, and Thematic Experiences.* New York: Wiley.

Wilkinson, D. *A Guide to Effective Event Management and Marketing.* Willowdale, Ontario, Canada: Event Management and Marketing Institute.

Williams, W. (1994). *User Friendly Fundraising: A Step-by-Step Guide to Profitable Special Events.* Alexander, NC: World Comm.; Associated Publishers.

Wilson, J., and L. Undall (1982). *Folk Festivals: A Handbook for Organization and Management.* Knoxville, TN: University of Tennessee Press.

Wisdom, E. J. (1992). *Family Reunion Organizer.* Nashville, TN: Post Oak Publications.

Witkowski, D. (1994). *How to Haunt a House.* New York: Random House.

Wolf, T. (1983). *Presenting Performances: A Handbook for Sponsors.* New York: American Council of the Arts.

Wolfson, S. M. (1986). *The Meeting Planner's Guide to Logistics and Arrangements.* Kansas City,    : Institute for Meeting and Conference Management.

Wolfson, S. M. (1991). *Meeting Planner's Workbook: Write Your Own Hotel Contract.* Kansas City,    : Institute for Meeting and Conference Management.

Wolfson, S. M. (1995). *The Meeting Planner's Complete Guide to Negotiating: You Can Get What You Want.* Kansas City,    : Institute for Meeting and Conference Management.

Wright, R. R. (1988). *The Meeting Spectrum: An Advanced Guide for Meeting Professionals.* San Diego, CA: Rockwood Enterprises.

Zuckerman, M. (1979). *Sensation Seeking: Beyond the Optimal Level of Arousal.* Hillsdale, NJ: Lawrence Erlbaum Associates.

# General Interest Business Books for Event Managers

American Society of Association Executives (1985). *Achieving Goals.* Washington, DC: ASAE.

Axtell, R. E. (1990). *The Do's and Taboos of Hosting International Visitors.* New York: Wiley.

Axtell, R. E. (1991). *Gestures: The Do's and Taboos of Body Language around the World.* New York: Wiley.

Axtell, R. E. (1993). *Do's and Taboos around the World,* 3rd ed. New York: Wiley.

Axtell, R. E. (1994). *The Do's and Taboos of International Trade: A Small Business.* New York: Wiley.

Baker, D. B. (1992). *Power Quotes: 4,000 Trenchant Soundbites on Leadership & Liberty, Treason & Triumph, Sacrifice & Scandal, Risk & Rebellion, Weakness & War and Other Affairs Politiques.* Detroit, MI: Visible Ink Press.

Bartlett, J. (1994). *Familiar Quotations: A Collection of Passages, Phrases, and Proverbs Traced to Their Sources in Ancient and Modern Literature,* 14th ed. Cutchogue, NY: Buccaneer Books.

Davidson, J. P., and G.-A. Fay (1991). *Selling to the Giants: A Key to Become a Key Supplier to Large Corporations.* New York: McGraw-Hill.

Goldsmith, C. S., and A. H. Waigand (1990). *Building Profits with Group Travel.* San Francisco: Dendrobium Books.

Harris, T. L. (1991). *The Marketer's Guide to Public Relations: How Today's Top Companies Are Using the New PR to Gain a Competitive Edge.* New York: Wiley.

Humes, J. C. (1993). *More Podium Humor: Using Wit and Humor in Every Speech You Make.* New York: Harper Perennial.

Kawasaki, G. (1991). *Selling the Dream: How to Promote Your Product, Company or Ideas—and Make a Difference—Using Everyday Evangelism.* New York: HarperCollins.

# Anthropological and Folklore Resources of Interest to Event Managers

Baron, R., and N. R. Spitzer (1992). *Public Folklore.* Washington, DC: Smithsonian Institution Press.

Browne, R. B. (1980). *Rituals and Ceremonies in Popular Culture.* Bowling Green, OH: Bowling Green State University Popular Press.

Cannadine, D., and S. Price (1993). *Rituals of Royalty: Power and Ceremonial in Traditional Societies.* New York: Cambridge University Press.

Jensen, V. (1992). *Where People Gather: Carving a Totem Pole.* Vancouver, British Columbia, Canada: Douglas & McIntyre.

Johnston, W. M. (1991). *Celebrations: The Cult of Anniversaries in Europe and the United States Today.* New Brunswick, NJ: Transaction Publishers.

St. Aubyn, L. (1995). *Rituals of Everyday Life: Special Ways of Marketing Important Events in Your Life.* Buffalo, NY: General Distribution Services.

Visser, M. (1986). *Much Depends on Dinner: The Extraordinary History and Mythology, Allure and Obsessions, Peril and Taboos, of an Ordinary Meal.* Toronto, Ontario, Canada: McClelland and Stewart.

Visser, M. (1991). *The Rituals of Dinner: The Origins, Evolution, Eccentricities and Meaning of Table Manners.* New York: Grove Weinfeld.

# Periodicals

To remain current with the overwhelming amount of event management literature that crosses my desk each month, I prioritize publications into three stacks. The first stack represents information I am currently in need of, and I set aside a specific time each day to review this material. The second stack goes in my travel bag and is read when I have time during travel or other downtime. The third stack is filed under the topic of the article so that when I need the information, I am able to retrieve it quickly.

The periodicals with an asterisk are specifically edited for event managers. The other periodicals are of general interest to event managers.

*Advertising Age.* Weekly; Bill Publications, Chicago, IL. www.advertisingage.com
E-mail: subs@adage.com

*\*Agenda New York.* Annually; Agenda USA, Inc., 686 Third Avenue, New York, NY 10017; (800) 523-1233.

*Amusement Business.* Weekly; Box 24970, Nashville, TN 37202; (615) 321-4250.

*Association and Society Manager.* 825 South Barrington Avenue, Los Angeles, CA 90049.

*Association Management.* Monthly; American Society of Association Executives, 1575 I Street, N.W., Washington, DC 20005; (202) 626-2740.

*\*Association Meetings.* Primedia: 43 L Nason Street, Maynard, MA 01754; (978) 897-5552.

*Association Trends.* Weekly; 7910 Woodmont Avenue, No. 1150, Bethesda, MD 20814; (301) 652-8666.

*Backstage.* Weekly; BPI Communications, 770 Broadway, New York, NY 10003; (212) 764-7300.

*Billboard.* Weekly; Billboard Publications, 770 Broadway, New York, NY 10003. www.billboard.com

*Business Events.* Quarterly; Sullivan Group Corporate Meeting and Event Production, 510 Bering Drive, Suite 455, Houston, TX 77057.

*Business Travel News.* Approximately biweekly; CMP Publications, 600 Community Drive, Manhasset, NY 11030; (516) 562-5000.

*Business TV and Video Guide.* Bimonthly; Business TV, Inc., TeleSpan's Business TV, c/o TeleSpan Publishing Corporation, P.O. Box 6250, Altadena, CA 91003; (818) 797-5482.

*City Business.* Weekly; Stuart Chamblin, Publisher, 5500 Wayzata Boulevard, No. 800, Minneapolis, MN 55416; (612) 591-2701.

*\*Conference and Association World.* Bimonthly; ACE International, Riverside House, High Street, Huntingdon, Cambridgeshire PE18 6SG, England; (0480) 457595; international 011 44 1480 457595.

*Conference and Exhibitions International.* Monthly; International Trade Publications Ltd., Queensway House, 2 Queensway, Redhill, Surrey RH1 1QS, England; (0737) 768611; international, 011 44 1737 768611.

*Conference and Incentive Management.* Bimonthly; CIM Verlag für Conference, Incentive and Travel Management GmBH, Nordkanalstrasse 36, D-20097 Hamburg, Germany; international, 40 237 1405.

*Convene.* Ten times a year; Professional Convention Management Association, 100 Vestavia Office Park, Suite 220, Birmingham, AL 35216-9970; (205) 978-4911.

*Convention Industry: The International Magazine for Meeting and Incentive Professionals.* Monthly; Association Internationale des Palais de Congrès, European Association of Event Centers, and European Federation of Conference Towns Mainzer Landstrabe 251, 60326 Frankfurt am Main, Postfach 200128, 60605 Frankfurt am Main, Germany.

*Conventions and Expositions.* Bimonthly; Conventions and Expositions Section of the American Society of Association Executives, 15751 Street, N.W., Washington, DC 20005; (202) 626-2769.

*Corporate and Incentive Travel.* Monthly; Coastal Communications Corporation, 488 Madison Avenue, New York, NY 10022; (212) 888-1500.

*Corporate Meetings and Incentives.* Bimonthly; Laux Company, 63 Great Road, Maynard, MA 01754; (508) 897-5552.

*Corporate Travel.* Monthly; Miller Freeman, 1515 Broadway, New York, NY 10036; (212) 626-2501.

*Delegates.* Monthly; Audrey Brindsley, Premier House, 10 Greycoat Place, London SW1P 1SB, England; 0712228866.

*Entertainment Marketing Letter.* Twelve times a year; EPM Communications, 488 East Eighteenth Street, Brooklyn, NY 11226-6702; (718) 469-9330.

*Event Solutions.* Monthly; Virgo Publishing, Phoenix, AZ; (602) 990-1101. www.events-solutions.com

*Event World.* Quarterly; International Special Events Society, Indianapolis, IN.

*Events Magazine.* Monthly; 1080 North Delaware Street, Suite 1700, Philadelphia, PA 19125; (215) 426-7800.

*Events USA.* Suite 301, 386 Park Avenue South, New York, NY 10016; (212) 684-2222.

*Festival Management and Event Tourism.* Quarterly; Cognizant Communication Corporation, 3 Hartsdale Road, Elmsford, NY 10523-3701; (914) 592-7720. www.cognizantcommunication.com

*Hollywood Reporter.* Weekly; 5055 Wilshire Boulevard, Los Angeles, CA 90036-4396; (213) 525-2000.

*Hospitality Research Journal.* Three times a year; Council on Hotel Restaurant and Institutional Education, 1200 Seventeenth Street, N.W., Washington, DC 20036-3097; (202) 331-5990.

*IAAM News.* Bimonthly; International Association of Assembly Managers, 635 Fritz Drive, Coppell, TX 75019.

*IEG Sponsorship Report.* Weekly; International Events Group, 640 North Lasalle, Suite 600, Chicago, IL 60610; (312) 944-1727.

*Incentive.* Monthly; Bill Communications, 855 Park Avenue South, New York, NY 10010; (212) 592-6200.

*Insurance Conference Planner.* Bimonthly; Laux Company, 63 Great Road, Maynard, MA 01754; (508) 897-5552.

*In-Tents.* Biannually; Industrial Fabrics Association, 345 Cedar Street, Suite 800, St. Paul, MN 55101-1088; (612) 222-1366.

*International Journal of Hospitality Information Technology.* HITA/HFTP.NAU, Box 5638, Flagstaff, AZ 86011-5638.

*International Meetings News.* Monthly; International Congress and Convention Association, Ashdown Court, Lewes Road, Forest Row, East Sussex RH18 5EZ, United Kingdom; +44 (0) 1342 824044.

*Journal of Convention and Exhibition Management.* Quarterly; Haworth Hospitality Press, 10 Alice Street, Binghamton, NY 13904-1580; (607) 722-5857.

*Journal of Travel Research.* Quarterly; Travel and Tourism Research Association and the Business Research Division, University of Colorado at Boulder, Boulder, CO 80309-0420.

*\*Konferensevarlden.* Monthly; P.O. Box 515, S-611 10 Nykoping, Sweden; + 46 155 21 98 15.

*\*Legal Information Review.* Quarterly; Convention Liaison Council, 1575 I Street, N.W., No. 1200, Washington, DC 20005; (202) 626-2764.

*Leisure Management.* Monthly; Leisure Media Company, Portmill House, Portmill Lane, Hitchin, Hertfordshire SG5 1DJ, England; +44 (0) 1462 431385.

*Lighting Dimensions.* Nine times a year; Entertainment Technology Communications Corporation, 32 West Eighteenth Street, New York, NY 10011-4612; (212) 229-2965.

*Marketing Review.* Hospitality Sales and Marketing Association International, 1400 K Street, N.W., Suite 810, Washington, DC 20005; (202) 789-0089.

*\*Medical Meetings.* Eight times a year; Adams/Laux Company, 63 Great Road, Maynard, MA 01754; (508) 897-5552.

*The Meeting Professional, The* Monthly; Meeting Professionals International, 1950 Stemmons Freeway, Suite 5018, Dallas, TX 75207-3109; (214) 712-7700. www.mpiweb.org

*\*Meeting News.* Monthly; Gralla Publications, 1515 Broadway, New York, NY 10036; (212) 869-1300.

*\*Meeting Planners Alert.* 126 Harvard Street, Brookline, MA 02146.

*\*Meetings and Conventions.* Monthly; Reed Travel Group, 500 Plaza Drive, Secaucus, NJ 07096; (201) 902-1700; subscription service: P.O. Box 5870, Cherry Hill, NJ 08034.

*Performance Magazine.* Weekly; 1101 University Drive, Suite 108, Fort Worth, TX 76107-3000; (817) 338-9444.

*Public Relations Journal.* 845 Third Avenue, New York, NY 10022. www.prsq.org

*\*Religious Conference Manager.* Five times a year; Primemedia (see Association Meetings).

*Rental Management.* American Rental Association, 1900 Nineteenth Street, Moline, IL 61265; (800) 334-2177; (309) 764-2475.

*Research Alert.* Twenty-four times a year; EPM Communications, 488 East Eighteenth Street, Brooklyn, NY 11226-6702; (718) 469-9330.

*\*Reunion Network News, The.* Reunion Network, 2450 Hollywood Boulevard, Suite 301, Hollywood, FL 33020; (800) 775-1945.

*Sales and Marketing Management.* Fifteen times a year; Bill Communications, 355 Park Avenue South, 5th Floor, New York, NY 10010-1706; (212) 592-6200.

*Show Business News.* Weekly; 1501 Broadway, 29th Floor, New York, NY 10036; (212) 354-7600.

*\*Special Events Forum.* Six times annually; Dave Nelson, 1973 Schrader Drive, San Jose, CA 95124.

*Special Events Magazine.* Monthly; Primemedia (see Associations Meetings)

*Stress Free Planning of Special Events.* Quarterly; Patty Sachs, Minneapolis, MN.

*Successful Meetings.* Thirteen times a year; Bill Communications, 355 Park Avenue South, New York, NY 10010; (212) 592-6403.

Tent Rental Report. Tent Rental Division of the Industrial Fabrics Association International, 345 Cedar Street, No. 800, St. Paul, MN 55101; (612) 222-2508.

TLL The Licensing Letter. Twelve times a year; EPM Communications, 488 East Eighteenth Street, Brooklyn, NY 11226-6702; (718) 469-9330.

*Trade Show and Exhibit Manager.* Bimonthly; Goldstein and Associates, 1150 Yale Street, No. 12, Santa Monica, CA 90403; (310) 828-1309.

*Tradeshow Week.* Weekly; 12233 West Olympic Boulevard, No. 236, Los Angeles, CA 90064; (310) 826-5696.

Training. Monthly; Lakewood Publications, 50 South Ninth Street, Minneapolis, MN 55402; (612) 333-0471.

Training and Development Journal. Monthly; American Society for Training and Development, 1640 King Street, Alexandria, VA 22313; (703) 683-8100.

U.S. Association Executive (USAE). Weekly; Custom News, 4341 Montgomery Avenue, Bethesda, MD 20814; (301) 951-1881.

Variety. Weekly; Cahners Publishing Company, 249 West Seventeenth Street, New York, NY 10011; (212) 645-0067.

*World's Fair.* Quarterly; P.O. Box 339, Corte Madera, CA 94976-0339; (415) 924-6035.

Youth Markets Alert. Twelve times a year; EPM Communications, 488 East Eighteenth Street, Brooklyn, NY 11226-6702; (718) 469-9330.

# Directories

Directories are an invaluable resource for event managers. Many libraries stock directories in the reference section. However, for day-to-day use, you will want to own your own copy for quick reference. The directories listed below with an asterisk are specifically for event managers use, and the others are for general business use.

*Academy Players Directory.* Academy of Motion Picture Arts and Sciences, 8949 Wilshire Boulevard, Beverly Hills, CA 90211. List of hundreds of television and film stars and their contact telephone numbers.

*ACCED-I Membership Directory.* Association of Collegiate Conference and Events Directors International, Colorado State University, Fort Collins, CO 80523-8037; (970) 491-5151.

*AFTRA/SAG Talent Directory.* American Federation of Television and Radio Artists/Screen Actors Guild, 1108 Seventeenth Avenue South, P.O. Box 121087, Nashville, TN 37212; (615) 327-2944. List of local performers in the Nashville, Tennessee area.

*Agenda Washington: Special Events Resource Directory* (2001). Agenda Washington. List of special event resources in the Washington, DC area.

*The Almanac of Anniversaries* (1992). By Kim Long. ABC-CLIO, 130 Cremona Drive, Santa Barbara, CA 93117; (805) 368-6868.

*America's Meeting Places* (1984). Facts on File, 11 Pennsylvania Plaza, New York, NY 10001; (212) 967-8800. List of event venues.

*ASAE Convention Themes.* American Society of Association Executives, 1575 Eye Street, N.W., Washington, DC 20005. List and description of successful convention themes.

*The ASAE Meetings and Expositions Section Networking Directory;* annually. American Society of Association Executives, 1575 Eye Street, N.W., Washington, DC 20005-1168; (202) 626-2748. List of meeting and exposition managers.

*Auditorium/Arena/Stadium Guide.* Amusement Business/Single Copy Department, Box 24970, Nashville, TN 37202. List of venues for events.

*Banquet Guide* (1995). Banquet Guide, 8948 Southwest Barbour Boulevard, Suite 132, Portland, OR 97219.

*The Beverly Hills International Party Planner.* Jan Roberts Publications, 139 South Beverly Drive, Suite 312, Beverly Hills, CA 90212. List of resources for events in various cities.

*BIG E, little e, (BIG EVENTS, little events).* The planning directory for events of all sizes. 6300 A Springfield Plaza, Suite 815, Springfield, VA 22150; (703) 866-5112.

*Cavalcade of Acts and Attractions.* Amusement Business/Single Copy Department, Box 24970, Nashville, TN 37202. List of live acts for events ranging from musical performers to circus attractions.

*Chase's Annual Events: Special Days, Weeks, and Months.* Annually; Contemporary Books, 180 North Michigan Avenue, Chicago, IL 60601. List of thousands of annual events.

*CHRIE Member Directory and Resource Guide.* Council on Hotel, Restaurant and Institutional Education, 1200 Seventeenth Street, N.W., Washington, DC 20036; (202) 331-5990. List of scholars and others involved in the hotel and restaurant education field.

*Circus and Carnival Booking Guide.* Amusement Business/Single Copy Department, Box 24970, Nashville, TN 37202. List of circuses and carnivals.

*Culinary and Hospitality Industry Publications Services.* C.H.I.P.S., 1307 Golden Bear Lane, Kingwood, TX 77339; (713) 359-2270. List of books selected specifically for the hospitality industry.

*DC Tech Membership Directory.* Washington, DC Technology Council, 1401 New York Avenue, N.W., Suite 600, Washington, DC 20005; (202) 637-9333.

*Destination: Washington, DC.* Washington, DC Convention and Visitors Association, 1212 New York Avenue, N.W., Suite 600, Washington, DC 20005-3992; (202) 789-7036.

*Directory of City Policy Officials.* National League of Cities, 1301 Pennsylvania Avenue, N.W., Washington, DC 20004; (202) 626-3150. List of people, including event managers, who work for municipal governments.

*The Events Register.* Marilou Stannard Doyle, P.O. Box 98, Hastings-on-Hudson, NY 10706-0098. List of event resources.

*From Day to Day: A Calendar of Notable Birthdays and Events* (1990). Scarecrow Press, 4720 Boston Way, Lanham, MD; (301) 459-3366. List of significant birthdays and other events.

*The Garden Tourist: A Guide to Garden Tours, Garden Days, Shows and Special Events* (1995). Garden Tourist Press. List of events specifically related to garden tours.

*Golden California Special Events 1994.* California Trade and Commerce Agency, Division of Tourism. List of California events occurring in 1994.

*The Government Contracts Reference Book* (1992). George Washington University, National Law Center, Government Contracts Program, Suite 250, 2100 Pennsylvania Avenue, N.W., Washington, DC 20037-3202. Guide to obtaining government events contracts.

*The Guide to Campus and Non-profit Meeting Facilities.* AMARC. List of venues on campus for event managers.

*A Guide to College Programs in Culinary Arts, Hospitality, and Tourism.* International Council on Hotel Restaurant and Institutional Education, Wiley, New York.

*The Guide to Unique Meeting and Event Facilities.* AMARC, P.O. Box 279, 164 Railroad, Suite 250, Minturn, CO 81645; (970) 827-5500.

*Here Comes the Guide: Hawaii* (1994–1995). Hopscotch Press, 1563 Solano Avenue, Suite 135, Berkeley, CA 94707; (510) 525-3379. List of venues for events and weddings in Hawaii.

*Here Comes the Guide: Northern California* (1993–1994). Hopscotch Press, 1563 Solano Avenue, Suite 135, Berkeley, CA 94707; (510) 525-3379. List of venues for events and weddings in northern California.

*Hospitality, Travel and Tourism Catalog.* Delmar Publishers, P.O. Box 15015, Albany, NY 12212-5015; (518) 464-3500.

*The How To of Festivals and Events Membership Directory and Marketplace.* P.O. Box 2950, 115 East Railroad Avenue, Suite 302, Port Angeles, WA 98362; (360) 457-3141.

*ICCA Membership Directory.* International Meetings Association, Entrada 121, NL-1096, EB Amsterdam, The Netherlands; +31-20-398-1919.

*\*IEG Directory of Sponsorship Marketing.* International Events Group, 640 North Lasalle, Suite 600, Chicago, IL 60610; (312) 944-1727. List of individuals and organizations involved in sponsorship marketing.

*\*IEG Guide to Sponsorship Agencies.* International Events Group, 640 North Lasalle, Suite 600, Chicago, IL 60610; (312) 944-1727. List of sponsorship agencies.

*Insurance and Financial Services Directory.* American Society of Association Executives, 1575 Eye Street, N.W., Washington, DC 20005, March 2001.

*International Association of Amusement Parks and Attractions Directory and Buyers Guide.* IAAP, 1448 Duke Street, Alexandria, VA 22314.

*International Association of Assembly Managers, Inc.: Members and Services Directory.* IAAM, 4425 West Airport Freeway, Suite 590, Irving, TX 75062-5835.

*International Association of Conference Centers Global Membership Directory.* www.iccaonline.org

*\*International Handbook.* International Exhibitors Association, 5501 Backlick Road, Suite 105, Springfield, VA 22151; (703) 941-3725. List of international exhibitors.

*\*Locations, etc: The Directory of Locations and Services for Special Events* (1992). Innovative Productions. List of event locations.

*\*The Management Sourcebook.* American Rental Association, Rental Management, 1900 Nineteenth Street, Moline, IL 61265-4198; (800) 334-2177. List of rental resources.

*\*The Meetings Mart. Corporate Meetings and Incentives.* Laux Company, 63 Great Road, Maynard, MA 01754; (508) 897-5552. List of meeting planning resources.

*\*Morris Costumes.* Morris Costumes, 3108 Monroe Road, Charlotte, NC 28205; (704) 333-4653. Annual catalog of inexpensive costumes for events.

*\*MPI Membership Directory.* Annually; Meeting Professionals International, 1950 Stemmons Freeway, Suite 5108, Dallas, TX 75207-3109; (214) 712-7700. List of over 10,000 people involved in meeting planning and related services.

*\*The Original British Theatre Directory* (1990). Richmond House Publishing Company, 1 Richmond Mews, London W1V 5AG, England (01) 437-9556. List of equipment rental for events in Great Britain.

*\*Party Resource* (1994–1995). Directories of America, 14770 Biscayne Boulevard, North Miami Beach, FL 33181; (305) 949-4948. List of local resources for events.

*\*Perfect Places: Northern California,* 2nd ed. Hopscotch Press, 1563 Solano Avenue, Suite 135, Berkeley, CA 94707; (510) 525-3379. List of event venues in California.

*\*Protocol Directory.* Protocol Directory, 101 West Twelfth Street, Suite PH-H, New York, NY 10011. List of resources for protocol throughout the world.

*Publications and Electronic Products.* World Tourism Organization, Calle Capitan Haya, 42, 28020 Madrid, Spain.

*RCRA Membership Directory.* Resort and Commercial Recreation Association, P.O. Box 1208, New Port Richey, FL 34656-1208; (813) 845-7373. List of members and resources for resorts and commercial recreation.

*Sites and Insights: The Special Event Location and Resource Directory.* Site Network, 550 Orange Avenue, Suite 132, Long Beach, CA 90802.

*\*Sourcebook.* Annually; Bill Communications, *Successful Meetings,* 355 Park Avenue South, New York, NY 10010; (212) 592-6403. List of resources for meeting planners.

*State Municipal League Directory.* National League of Cities, 1301 Pennsylvania Avenue, N.W., Washington, DC 20004; (202) 626-3000.

*Tent Rental Directory* (1993–1994). Tent Rental Division of the Industrial Fabrics Association International, 345 Cedar Street, Suite 800, St. Paul, MN 55101-1088; (800) 225-4324. List of resources for tent firms.

*\*Tradeshow and Convention Guide.* Amusement Business/Single Copy Department, Box 24970, Nashville, TN 37202. List of venues and resources for events.

*\*The Tradeshow Week Data Book* (1985). Tradeshow Week, New York, NY, in cooperation with the Trade Show Bureau. List of annual data from the Tradeshow Bureau concerning expositions.

*Travel and Tourism Research Association Membership and Supplier Directory.* Association of Travel Research and Marketing Professionals, P.O. Box 2133, Boise, ID 83701; (208) 429-9511.
www.ttra.com

*UFI Directory of International Fairs and Expositions.* 35 bis, rue Jouffroy d'Abbans F-75017, Paris, France; 33(0) 1-43-67-99-12.

*\*Unique Meeting Places in Greater Washington* (1988). By Elise Ford. EPM. List of unusual venues for events in Washington, DC.

*Washington Speakers Bureau Guide.* WSB, 1663 Prince Street, Alexandria, VA 22314.
www.washingtonspeakers.com

*Who's Who in Association Management.* ASAE Membership directory. American Society of Association Executives, 1575 Eye Street, N.W., Washington, DC 20005; (202) 731-8825. List of association executives (including meeting planners) and their suppliers.

*\*Who's Who in Professional Speaking* (1994–1995). National Speakers Association, 4747 North Seventh Street, Phoenix, AZ 85014. List of over 3000 professional speakers.

*\*Who's Who in Religious Conference Management* (1994–1995). Religious Conference Management Association, One RCA Dome, Suite 120, Indianapolis, IN 46225; (317) 632-1888. List of professional meeting planners employed by religious organizations and their suppliers.

*Worldwide Convention Centres Directory.* Conference and Travel Publications, Ashdown Court, Lewes Road, Forest Row, East Sussex RH185EZ, England; +44(0) 1342-824044.

*\*Your Special Event Planning Guide.* By Patty Sachs. Your Special Event, 2809 Wayzata Boulevard, Minneapolis, MN 55404; (612) 377-9525. List of special event resources and ideas.

# APPENDIX 6

# Audio and Video Resources

Many of the major event management organizations, such as the International Special Events Society (ISES), maintain extensive audio recordings of seminars held at their annual conferences. These audiotapes may be purchased directly from the organization.

The Gelman Library of George Washington University maintains a complete set of all audio recordings from ISES conferences. These recordings may be used within the confines of the library media resources division.

Additionally, the Gelman Library maintain an extensive video collection containing footage of corporate, association, civic, retail, and other types of events, including large-scale programs such as Super Bowl half-time shows and the opening and closing ceremonies of the Olympic Games, the Goodwill Games, and the Olympic Festival. These videotapes may also be viewed within the confines of the library, and with permission of the copyright holder may be duplicated for scholarly or professional use. To receive a complete list of these resources, contact the Gelman Library Media Resources Division, at (202) 994-1000.

Although the resources of the Gelman Library and the Event Management and Marketing Archives are too numerous to list (in fact, each collection has its own finding aid listing dozens of resources), I have a few personal favorites.

First, review the 1988 Super Bowl half-time spectacular produced by Radio City Music Hall Productions. This event is a masterful depiction of logistics, both mechanical and human.

Next, view the Goodwill Games opening ceremonies in Russia. The use of cards by thousands of spectators was so impressive that the television newscaster reporting the games stated that "this was the most memorable moment."

Finally, review the opening ceremonies for the 1984 Olympic Games in Los Angeles, California. This video depicts the transformation of the opening ceremonies from a one-dimensional live event into a multidimensional production staged for a live audience as well as hundreds of millions of television viewers. As a result of this production, the format of the Olympic Games' opening and closing ceremonies shifted to include more spectacular effects.

In addition to these resources, I recommend the following video products for scholarly and professional use:

*The Event Marketing Process* (1988). Produced by Petit Communications, Don Mills, Ontario, Canada. A description of the various competencies involved in event marketing.

IAAPA Training Videotape Series. International Association of Amusement Parks and Attractions, Alexandria, VA; (703) 836-4800.

*Labor Relations: A Partnership for the Future.* IAEM Foundation, 2000. (972) 458-8002. www.iaem.org

*A Matter of Judgement, Conflicts of Interest in the Workplace.* A brief vignette entitled "Special Events Director" dealing with the subject of event managers who receive gifts from hotels and other vendors and the consequences that may follow. This is an excellent way to begin an in-depth discussion of ethics in event management. Ethics Resource Center, Barr Media Group, Irwindale, CA.

*Political Money for Senate Candidates* (1989). Produced by Purdue University Public Affairs Video Archives, West Lafayette, IN. Subject matter deals with raising funds for U.S. Senate candidates.

*Successful Special Events* with Virgil Ecton, CFRE. A lecture by Virgil Ecton, CFRE of the United Negro College Fund, dealing with brainstorming, budgeting, operations, and other factors for helping ensure the success of special events for fundraising purposes. National Society of Fundraising Executives, Alexandria, VA.

# APPENDIX 7

# Software

Using the software listed below may save you time and money. However, remember that part of your investment is the learning curve that must be mastered, and this may require a considerable investment of time. Compare software carefully prior to investment to ensure that you are maximizing your scarce resources with the most efficient software solutions available for your event management practice.

Software is typically divided into four categories. First, software is available for word processing. Second, software is available for financial and data analysis. Third, software is available for publishing, such as the development of diagrams and site plans. Finally, software is available for compiling extensive databases. Whenever possible, try to obtain a software product that combines as many of these functions as possible. In some instances you may wish to purchase a standard product and customize the functions to solve your individual event management business challenges.

*a2zShow.* A Web-based application that helps associations and independent show organizers to market and manage their live trade shows and conferences online. NeoTech Center, 9250 Bendix Road, North, Columbia, MD 21045; (410) 480-7220. www.a2zshow.com

*Advanced Solutions International, Inc.* Special event planning/management package. Alexandria, VA; (703) 765-6380.

*ALERT Computer Systems.* Rental management package. Colorado Springs, CO; (800) 530-8050; (719) 634-7755.

*AlphaSoft, Inc.* Rental management package. Minneapolis, MN; (800) 969-SOFT; (612) 561-7375.

*Automation Plus.* Rental management package. Ft. Lauderdale, FL; (305) 587-1501.

*Business Computer Solutions.* Special event planning/management package. Columbia, MD; (301) 596-5005.

*Campagne Associates: Fundraising Software Solutions.* 195 McGregor Street, Suite 410, Manchester, NH 03102. www.campagne.com

*Catermate.* Catering package. The Event Management Software Co., Indianapolis, IN; (317) 875-5271.

*Codesmiths, Inc. (Printing).* Tent supplier management. Champaign, IL; (217) 352-5510.

*Computer Ease.* Rental management package. Novato, CA; (800) 338-0686.

*Creative Business Services.* Rental management package. Manchester, MO; (314) 227-5190.

*Culinary Software Services.* Catering package. Boulder, CO; (800) 447-1466; (303) 447-3334.

*Dean Evans and Associates Event Management Software.* 5775 DTC Boulevard, Suite 210, Englewood, CO 80111.
www.dea.com

*Devron Integrated Systems Ltd.* Nova Building, Herschel Street, Slough, Berks SL1 1XS, England; +44(0) 1753 701 014.
www.devron.net

*EKEBA International.* P.O. Box 15131, Columbus, OH 43215-0131; (614) 459-7178.

*ErgoSoft, Inc.* Special event planning/management package. Columbia, MD; (800) 346-9484; (410) 381-5599.

*Event Automation Services, Inc.* 3230 Anton Drive, Aurora, IL 60504; (800) 535-1253.
www.wineasi.com

*Event Business Management System.* 87 Hubble, St. Charles, MO 63304; (800) 400-4052.
www.ungerboeck.com

*The Event Edge.* The ultimate event planning tool. ErgoSoft, Inc., Simpsonville, MD; (800) 346-9484.

*EventMaker Pro.* Special events management software. Campagne Associates, Nashua, NH; (800) 582-3489.

*The Event Management System Version 5.3.* Dean Evans & Associates, Englewood, CO; (303) 773-3264.

*Event Planner Plus.* Certain Software, One Daniel Burnham Court, Suite 330C, San Francisco, CA 94109-5460.

*Event Pro Software.* Event scheduling and management software. Saskatoon, Saskatchewan, Canada; (306) 975-3737.

*Event Software.* 520 East Southern Avenue, Suite 101, Tempe, AZ 85282; (480) 517-9990.

*I Do: The Ultimate Wedding Planner.* Touchsoft, Malpetus, CA; (800) 887-8960; (408) 956-0884. (Windows)

*InScribe, Inc.* Calligraphy/printing package. Cambridge, MA; (800) 346-3461; (617) 868-5743.

*International Hospitality and Tourism Database CD-ROM: The Guide to Industry and Academic Resources.* The consortium of Hospitality Research Information Systems. Available through MPI, Dallas, TX; (214) 712-7742.

*MeetingPRO.* Peopleware, Inc., copyright 1987.

*Microchips, Inc.* Function space management. St. Louis, MO; (800) 373-0693; (314) 645-2800.

*Mom 'N' Pops Software.* A shareware company offering party and event planning programs. Springhill, FL; (352) 688-9108.

*MPI Net.* The first global communications network for the meeting industry. Dallas, TX; (214) 712-7742.

*Operation Management System.* Rental management package. Stockton, CA; (800) 767-0280.

*Parsons Technology.* A large company with software for both PCs and Macs. Hiawatha, IA; (800) 679-0670.

*Peopleware, Inc.* Registration package. Bellevue, WA; (800) 869-7166; (206) 454-6444.

*Quality Software Products.* Rental management package. Arvada, CO; (303) 273-9633.

*QuickSilver Software.* Catering package. Sussex, WI; (800) 999-DYNE.

*R.E.N.T.S. Computer Systems.* Rental management package. Sioux Falls, SD; (800) 369-RENT; (605) 338-1800.

*RE: Event (a component of The Raiser's Edge for Windows).* Manufactured by Blackbaud, Inc. Helps planners organize and manage their events. Charleston, SC; (800) 443-9441.

*ROOMER3 Demo.* 1986–1993 by Henry M. Hufnagel. All rights reserved. Portions 1982–1990, Microsoft Corp. All rights reserved.

*Smart-N-Easy Wedding Planner.* Automated Systems; (800) 588-6972; (201) 812-1428. (DOS).

*Social Software.* Calligraphy/printing package. New York; (212) 956-2707.

*Solutions by Computer, Inc.* Rental management package. Springfield, MA; (800) 950-2221; (413) 737-0499.

*Synergy Software International.* Catering package. Arlington, VA; (800) 522-6210; (703) 522-6200.

*Terrapin Systems.* Special event planning/management package. Silver Springs, MD; (301) 933-5599.

*Unique Business Systems.* Rental management package. Santa Monica, CA; (800) 669-4827.

*Venue Technology.* Summitlink, North American Headquarters, Washington, DC. (888) 852-9614.

*The Wedding Planner.* Ninga Software, Calgary, Alberta, Canada; (800) 656-4642; (403) 383-2772. (DOS, Windows).

*Wedding Workshop.* MicroPrecision Software, Santa Clara, CA; (800) 688-9337; (408) 358-8250 (Windows, Macintosh).

*The Woodward Group.* Rental management package. Glendora, CA; (818) 335-6045.

*Zea Software.* Calligraphy/printing package. Alexandria, VA; (703) 379-8201.

# Sample Client Agreement

The client agreement must be reviewed by a local attorney, as each state requires individual language to conform with the code. However, the following template provides event managers with the conceptual framework for a basic client agreement.

**Client Agreement**

Account number: XYZ-1

This agreement is between ABC Event Management Company (hereafter referred to as EVENT MANAGER) and XYZ Firm (hereafter referred to as CLIENT).

### I. EVENT MANAGER agrees to provide:

1. Research, design, planning, coordination, and evaluation of the event entitled "The Night of a Thousand Stars."
2. Research that will commence with the joint execution of this agreement.
3. A professional event that will begin on July 15, 2002 at 8 P.M. central time in the city of Kansas City, Kansas and conclude on the same date at 11:00 P.M central time.
4. A comprehensive evaluation including financial and attitudes and opinions will be submitted to CLIENT by August 15, 2002 at 5:00 P.M central time.
5. Comprehensive general liability insurance with a $1 million limit per occurrence, naming CLIENT as additional insured for the period of the event.

### II. CLIENT agrees to provide:

1. One person as principal contact and decision maker for the EVENT MANAGER.
2. General liability insurance with a $1 million limit per occurrence, naming EVENT MANAGER as additional insured for the period of the event.
3. Decisions in a timely manner as required by the final approved production schedule.
4. Ten (10) volunteers to coordinate registration and guest relations during the event from 7:00 P.M central time to 11:00 P.M central time.

### III. INVESTMENT

The EVENT MANAGER will receive a fee for professional services in the amount of $10,000 exactly. The EVENT MANAGER will receive fees for all direct expenses approved by CLIENT.

### IV. TERMS

The CLIENT agrees to provide the following payments to the EVENT MANAGER as compensation for the services described above.

June 30, 2002:      25% of fee ($2500) plus 50% of direct expenses.

July 15, 2002:      65% of fee ($6500) plus balance of preapproved direct expenses.

August 15, 2002:    10% of fee plus any additional charges approved by client plus the balance of all approved direct expenses.

### V. CANCELLATION

Should the EVENT MANAGER cancel his or her services for any reason other than acts of God, the CLIENT shall receive a refund of all prepaid fees less any costs expended on behalf of the event. Should the CLIENT cancel his or her event, the following payments shall be due:

Cancellation more than 120 days prior to event date: 25% of professional fee and 50% deposit of all direct expenses.

Cancellation less than 120 days prior to event date: 50% of professional fee and 50% deposit of all direct expenses.

Cancellation less than 60 days prior to event date: 75% of professional fee and 100% of all direct expenses.

Cancellation less than 30 days prior to event date: 100% of professional fee and 100% of all direct expenses.

### VI. FORCE MAJEURE

This agreement is canceled automatically if the event is interrupted due to acts of God, including, but not limited to, hurricanes, tornadoes, strikes, war, volcanic eruption, earthquakes, or pestilence.

### VII. ARBITRATION

The American Arbitration Association is designated as the official body for arbitrating any disputes resulting from this agreement.

### VIII. HOLD HARMLESS and INDEMNIFICATION

The EVENT MANAGER and CLIENT agree to hold one another harmless from negligence caused by either party and mutually indemnify one another.

### IX. TIME IS OF THE ESSENCE

The services and related costs described in this agreement are guaranteed through 5:00 P.M central time March 15, 2002. After this date, these services and related costs must be renegotiated.

## X. *THE FULL AGREEMENT*

This agreement and any attachments constitutes the full agreement. Any changes, additions, or deletions to this agreement must be approved in writing by both parties.

## XI. *ACCEPTANCE*

The parties whose signatures are affixed below agree to accept the terms and conditions stated within this agreement.


_____    _____

CLIENT                              DATE


_____    _____

EVENT MANAGER                       DATE

*Note: Sign both copies and return one signed original to the EVENT MANAGER.*

# APPENDIX 9

# Sample Vendor Agreement

Account Number: DEF-1

This agreement is between ABC Event Management Company (hereafter referred to as EVENT MANAGER) and DEF firm (hereafter referred to as VENDOR).

*I. EVENT DATE: July 15, 2002.*

*II. EVENT ARRIVAL TIME: 7:30 P.M. central time.*

*III. EVENT START TIME: 8:00 P.M. central time.*

*IV. EVENT STOP TIME: 11:00 P.M. central time.*

*V. VENDOR shall provide:*

1. Three (3) magicians performing walk-around magic suitable for young children ages 5 to 12 years. Magicians shall wear black tuxedoes.
2. Eight (8)-member top-40 band entitled "Starlight," wearing matching black tuxedoes.
3. Balloon drop of 500 nine-inch silver Mylar balloons. Rigging to be complete by 2:00 P.M. central time and drop to occur between 10:00 P.M. and 11:00 P.M. central time.
4. Comprehensive general liability insurance with a $1 million limit per occurrence, naming EVENT MANAGER as additional insured or period of event.
5. Refrain from distributing promotion literature at event and direct any and all inquiries for future business resulting from event to EVENT MANAGER.

*VI. EVENT MANAGER shall provide:*

1. Complimentary parking for VENDOR and his or her personnel.
2. Two dressing rooms.

3. One lift for rigging balloon drop. Lift to be available from 12:00 P.M. to 2:00 P.M. central time.
4. On-site event coordinator to liaison with VENDOR.

### VII. FEES

EVENT MANAGER shall pay the following fees to VENDOR:
1. Magicians,       $1000
2. Band,            $3000
3. Balloon drop,    $1500
   Total:           $5500

### VIII. TERMS

EVENT MANAGER shall pay a VENDOR 50% deposit ($2750) upon execution of agreement, and the balance net 30 days of event date.

### IX. CANCELLATION

If the VENDOR cancels for any reason, he or she forfeits all funds received or due and shall promptly repay EVENT MANAGER any funds advanced for this event. If the EVENT MANAGER cancels for any reason, he or she must provide the following payments to VENDOR:

| | |
|---|---|
| Cancellation before 120 days of event date: | No fees due. |
| Cancellation up to 90 days of event date: | 15% of total fee. |
| Cancellation of up to 60 days of event date: | 25% of total fee. |
| Cancellation of up to 30 days of event date: | 50% of total fee. |
| Cancellation less than 30 days prior to event date: | 75% of total fee. |

### X. FORCE MAJEURE

This agreement is canceled automatically if the event is interrupted due to acts of God, including, but not limited to, hurricanes, tornadoes, strikes, war, volcanic eruption, earthquakes, or pestilence.

### XI. ARBITRATION

In the event of disagreement pertaining to this agreement, the parties agree to submit to mandatory nonbinding arbitration. The American Arbitration Association is designated as the official body for arbitrating any disputes resulting from this agreement.

### XII. HOLD HARMLESS AND INDEMNIFICATION

The EVENT MANAGER and VENDOR agree to hold one another harmless from negligence caused by that party and to mutually indemnify one another.

### XIII. TIME IS OF THE ESSENCE

The services and related costs described in this agreement are guaranteed through 5:00 P.M. central time March 15, 2002. After this date these services and related costs must be renegotiated.

## XIV. THE FULL AGREEMENT

This agreement and attachments contain the final and entire agreement between the parties, and neither they nor their agents shall be bound by any terms, statements, or representations, oral or written, not contained herein.

## XV. ACCEPTANCE

The parties whose signatures are affixed below agree to accept the terms and conditions stated within this agreement.

_____          _____
CLIENT                                    DATE


_____          _____
EVENT MANAGER                             DATE

*Note: Sign both copies and return to EVENT MANAGER. A fully executed original will be provided once signed by the EVENT MANAGER.*

# Sample Catering Menus

## Menu 1

*Occasions Caterers of Washington, DC is pleased to offer the following proposal:*

Event:          Cocktail Reception and Buffet Dinner
Event Date:     Wednesday, April 25, 2001
Time:           7:00 P.M.–10:00 P.M.
Location:       Phillips Collection, Washington, DC
No. of Guests:  80

*Hors d'oeuvres to be passed in parlors:*

| | |
|---|---|
| Parsley potato crisps | Wafer-thin over baked potato crisps brushed with parsley butter. Offered with sweet garlic aïoli. |
| Blinis with caviar | Fresh blinis topped with crème fraiche and American sturgeon. Garnished with snipped chives. |
| Spicy Thai crabcakes | Miniature crabcakes made of lump crabmeat, blended in an exotic Thai mixture of cellophane noodles, hot peppers, galanga, and cilantro. Pan-griddled and served warm with sweet and sour lemongrass sauce. |
| Mango grilled shrimp | Jumbo shrimp marinated in mango, ginger, lime juice and olive oil and grilled to perfection. |
| Endive with smoked trout and litchii | Endive spears topped with lightly smoked trout, fresh litchii, and a light lemon vinaigrette. Served chilled. |

*To be presented on the buffet table in the music room:*

| | |
|---|---|
| Thyme-roasted lamb chops | Rack of lamb marinated with lemon thyme and red wine. Roasted, cut into individual chops, and presented with a red wine reduction sauce, an apricot-citrus chutney, and a traditional mint sauce. |

| | |
|---|---|
| Veal Wellington | Loin of veal and sauteed mushrooms with shallots wrapped in delicate puff pastry. Served warm with a spring tarragon béarnaise. |
| Sea bass in a mild red curry | Medallions of sea bass seasoned with lemongrass and lime leaves and pan seared. Served in a light coconut-infused red curry sauce with a garnish of crisply fried shallots. |
| Basmati rice | Small-grain Basmati rice simmered in a rich vegetable stock and tossed with sweet butter and cracked pepper. Served warm. |
| Corn soufflé | A savory corn soufflé studded with sweet silver queen corn kernels. Baked to a golden brown and served with tomato relish. |
| Confetti of tournéed potatoes | Hand-turned potatoes in four colors: classic Idaho, Yukon gold, purple, and sweet potatoes. Drizzled with extra virgin olive oil and fresh rosemary. Roasted until crisp. |
| Carrot purée on artichoke bottoms | Delicate purée of carrot folded with whipped egg whites served on freshly poached artichoke bottoms. Served warm. |
| Tomato salad | Chilled salad of garden beefsteak tomatoes, yellow tomatoes, pear tomatoes, and cherry tomatoes. Flecked with fresh basil and dressed with extra virgin olive oil and lemon juice. |
| Baby spinach salad with pancetta | Baby spinach leaves lightly dressed with aged sherry and mustard vinaigrette and crowned with oven-dried Shiitake mushrooms and crisp Pancetta cracklings. |

*Coffee and dessert buffet:*

| | |
|---|---|
| Terrine of chocolate and macaroon | Triangular layered terrine of French almond macaroon with a dark chocolate ganache. Served chilled with a melange of fresh fruit and an apricot sauce. |
| Spring sorbet samplings | A selection of spring sorbet flavors to include tangerine, lychee, cherry, and champagne-peach. Offered in martini glasses with a confetti of fresh fruit. |
| Miniature pastries | Elegant selection of small pastries to include chocolate pistachio opera squares, lemon meringue barquettes, miniature raspberry pavés, chocolate cups filled with hazelnut mousse, and mango and blackberry pâté de fruits. |

| | |
|---|---|
| Selection of colorful fruit | Colorful selection of fresh fruit salads to include orange wheels topped with crimson orange zest, sauterne-splashed melon salad, and a confetti of tropical fruits and berries tossed with a fresh ginger syrup. |
| Coffee, decaffeinated coffee, and tea | To be passed by waiters. |

# Menu 2

*Occasions Caterers of Washington, DC, is pleased to offer the following proposal:*

| | |
|---|---|
| Event: | Gala Dinner |
| Event Date: | Friday, May 11, 2001 |
| Time: | 6:30 P.M.–12:00 A.M. |
| Location: | Great Hall and Mezzanine |
| No. of Guests: | 450 |

*Hors d'oeuvres to be passed during cocktails:*

| | |
|---|---|
| Citrus marinated chicken Tartlets with yogurt | Individual miniature tartlet shells filled with diced citrus-marinated chicken blended with a dab of fresh yogurt. Garnished with fresh cilantro. |
| Roquefort grapes with walnuts | Seedless grapes wrapped in Roquefort, and rolled in chopped toasted walnuts. |
| Tomato and basil "french toasts" | Bite-sized brioches topped with oven-dried tomatoes and fresh basil soaked with fontina custard. Baked until golden and served warm. |
| Assorted sushi | Assorted sushi to include a selection of vegetarian and seafood rolls and individual nigiri. Presented with ginger and wasabi. |
| Miniature beef Wellington | Tenderloin of beef and sauted mushrooms with shallots wrapped in delicate puff pastry. Served with cold béarnaise dip. |

*To be presented on an hors d'oeuvres buffet:*

| | |
|---|---|
| Selection of fine American cheeses | Selection of cheeses to include aged New York cheddar, domestic goat cheese, fontina, and Maytag blue. Presented with a fruit and nut garnish, as well as imported crackers and baguettes. |
| Pesto and sun-dried tomato palmiers | Small palm-shaped puff pastries filled with a savory blend of sun-dried tomato and pesto. |

*First course:*

    All-American seafood cocktail — A luxurious presentation of steamed and cracked lobster, jumbo shrimp, crab salad, and pickled salmon. Served with an icy cucumber sorbet in a gilded compote. Offered with a trio of "cocktail sauces." Served chilled.

    Tomato-dill madeleines — Small, delicate, shell-shaped breads flavored with tomato and fresh dill.

*Main course:*

    "Barbecued" rack of lamb — Rack of lamb marinated with a refined citrus-based barbecue sauce. Grilled over aromatic fruitwoods, sliced in chops, and served on a bed of crisp onion rings with additional barbecue sauce.

    "Macaroni and cheese" in a lacy cheddar tuile — Individual lacy cheddar tuiles filled with a creamy orzo and four-cheese "macaroni and cheese."

    Haricots verts, fiddlehead ferns, yellow wax beans, and carrots — Haricots verts, spring fiddlehead ferns, yellow wax beans, and tourneed carrots are steamed and scented with aromatic bay leaves.

*Salad:*

    Nosegay of colorful lettuces — A small, crisp cracker tuile cone filled with plumes of baby lettuces, slivers of pear, and herb blossoms. Garnished with toasted sunflower seeds and presented with a champagne vinaigrette.

*Dessert:*

    Berry basket — Inspired by baked Alaska: an individual basket crafted of wild strawberry and vanilla bean ice cream and piped with a basketweave of Italian meringue, topped with juicy spring berries and decorated with a lattice basket handle. Offered with a fraises de bois sauce.

    Demitasse coffee

    Chocolate-dipped citrus rind, bittersweet chocolate truffles, and candied ginger — To be passed with coffee.

# APPENDIX 11

# Sample Insurance Certificate

# CERTIFICATE OF INSURANCE

| CERTIFICATE NUMBER |
|---|
| 0016001-00019 |

**PRODUCER**

Marsh USA Inc.
1166 Avenue of the Americas
New York, NY 10036-2774

Alice Prine          (212) 345-6000

THIS CERTIFICATE IS ISSUED AS A MATTER OF INFORMATION ONLY AND CONFERS NO RIGHTS UPON THE CERTIFICATE HOLDER OTHER THAN THOSE PROVIDED IN THE POLICY. THIS CERTIFICATE DOES NOT AMEND, EXTEND OR ALTER THE COVERAGE AFFORDED BY THE POLICIES DESCRIBED HEREIN.

## COMPANIES AFFORDING COVERAGE

| COMPANY A | Name of Insurance Company |
|---|---|
| COMPANY B | |
| COMPANY C | |
| COMPANY D | |

**INSURED**

The Special Event Promoter
229 West 42nd STreet
New York, NY  10036

## COVERAGES

THIS IS TO CERTIFY THAT POLICIES OF INSURANCE DESCRIBED HEREIN HAVE BEEN ISSUED TO THE INSURED NAMED HEREIN FOR THE POLICY PERIOD INDICATED. NOTWITHSTANDING ANY REQUIREMENT, TERM OR CONDITION OF ANY CONTRACT OR OTHER DOCUMENT WITH RESPECT TO WHICH THE CERTIFICATE MAY BE ISSUED OR MAY PERTAIN, THE INSURANCE AFFORDED BY THE POLICIES DESCRIBED HEREIN IS SUBJECT TO ALL THE TERMS, CONDITIONS AND EXCLUSIONS OF SUCH POLICIES. LIMITS SHOWN MAY HAVE BEEN REDUCED BY PAID CLAIMS.

| CO LTR | TYPE OF INSURANCE | POLICY NUMBER | POLICY EFFECTIVE DATE (MM/DD/YY) | POLICY EXPIRATION DATE (MM/DD/YY) | LIMITS | |
|---|---|---|---|---|---|---|
| A | **GENERAL LIABILITY** [X] COMMERCIAL GENERAL LIABILITY   CLAIMS MADE [X] OCCUR   OWNER'S & CONTRACTOR'S PROT | 12345 | MM/DD/YY | MM/DD/YY | GENERAL AGGREGATE | $ 2,000,000 |
| | | | | | PRODUCTS - COMP/OP AGG | $ 1,000,000 |
| | | | | | PERSONAL & ADV INJURY | $ 1,000,000 |
| | | | | | EACH OCCURRENCE | $ 1,000,000 |
| | | | | | FIRE DAMAGE (Any one fire) | $ 50,000 |
| | | | | | MED EXP (Any one person) | $ 5,000 |
| | **AUTOMOBILE LIABILITY** ANY AUTO   ALL OWNED AUTOS   SCHEDULED AUTOS   HIRED AUTOS   NON-OWNED AUTOS | | | | COMBINED SINGLE LIMIT | $ |
| | | | | | BODILY INJURY (Per person) | $ |
| | | | | | BODILY INJURY (Per accident) | $ |
| | | | | | PROPERTY DAMAGE | $ |
| | **GARAGE LIABILITY** ANY AUTO | | | | AUTO ONLY - EA ACCIDENT | $ |
| | | | | | OTHER THAN AUTO ONLY: EACH ACCIDENT | $ |
| | | | | | AGGREGATE | $ |
| | **EXCESS LIABILITY** UMBRELLA FORM   OTHER THAN UMBRELLA FORM | | | | EACH OCCURRENCE | $ |
| | | | | | AGGREGATE | $ |
| A | **WORKER'S COMPENSATION AND EMPLOYERS' LIABILITY** THE PROPRIETOR/ PARTNERS/EXECUTIVE OFFICERS ARE: [ ] INCL [ ] EXCL | 12345 | MM/DD/YY | MM/DD/YY | WC STATUTORY LIMITS [ ] OTHER | |
| | | | | | EL EACH ACCIDENT | $ 500,000 |
| | | | | | EL DISEASE - POLICY LIMIT | $ 500,000 |
| | | | | | EL DISEASE - EA EMPLOYEE | $ 500,000 |
| | **OTHER** | | | | | |

SAMPLE

**DESCRIPTION OF OPERATIONS / LOCATIONS / VEHICLES / SPECIAL ITEMS**

Venue owner is included as an additional insured but only as respects claims arising out of the negligence of the named insured's operations.

## CERTIFICATE HOLDER

Venue Owner Name
Address

## CANCELLATION

SHOULD ANY OF THE POLICIES DESCRIBED HEREIN BE CANCELLED BEFORE THE EXPIRATION DATE THEREOF, THE INSURER AFFORDING COVERAGE WILL ENDEAVOR TO MAIL __30__ DAYS WRITTEN NOTICE TO THE CERTIFICATE HOLDER NAMED HEREIN, BUT FAILURE TO MAIL SUCH NOTICE SHALL IMPOSE NO OBLIGATION OR LIABILITY OF ANY KIND UPON THE INSURER AFFORDING COVERAGE, ITS AGENTS OR REPRESENTATIVES.

Marsh USA Inc.
BY:

JHMM1 (2/98)          VALID AS OF:     4/17/01

# Sample Incident Report

*Note: The incident report should be completed as soon as possible after an incident has occurred. Copies of this form should be easily accessible to all event personnel.*

1. Name of event: _____

2. Name of venue: _____

3. Report of incident: (check one) _____ Injury _____ Theft _____ Lost person _____ Lost property _____ Violent activity _____ Other _____
   Describe_____ .

4. Location of incident: _____ .

5. Date and time of incident: _____ .

6. Date and time of report: _____ .

7. Exact location of incident: _____
   _____ .

8. Complainant: _____
   _____ .

9. Gender/race of complainant: _____ .

10. Complainant address:_____
    _____ .

11. Complainant city, state, zip code:_____
    _____ .

12. Complainant telephone contact: (Home)_____
    (Office) _____ (Fax)_____

**13.** Additional means to contact complainants/reporting persons:

_____

_____ .

**14.** Illness/injury received: _____

_____ .

**15.** Description of illness/injury: _____

_____ .

**16.** _____ Admitted for treatment

**17.** _____ Released
Property code: V, vehicle from which theft occurred; S, stolen; R, recovered; L, lost; I, impounded; E, evidence; F, found; O, other.

**18.** _____

| Code | Items | ID# | Value Estimated by Complainant | Purchase Date | Value Estimated by Reporter |
|------|-------|-----|-------------------------------|---------------|-----------------------------|
| Example: | | | | | |
| S | Purse | 12/31/02 | $100 | 12/15/02 | $75 |
| _____ | _____ | _____ | _____ | _____ | _____ |
| _____ | _____ | _____ | _____ | _____ | _____ |
| _____ | _____ | _____ | _____ | _____ | _____ |

**19.** Description of automobile:
Year: _____ Make: _____ Model: _____
Color: _____ Body: _____ Tag/state/year: _____
Vehicle identification number: _____

**20.** Suspect description:
Race: _____
Gender: _____
Age: _____
Height: _____
Weight: _____
Eye color: _____
Hair color: _____
Complexion: _____
Scars: _____
Hat: _____
Coat: _____
Jacket: _____
Pants: _____
Shirt: _____

**21.** Narrative. Describe and state the action taken by the event manager.

_____

_____

_____

**22.** Reporting person: _____

**23.** Status:

_____ Open

_____ Closed (List date and if closed by arrest list arrest
number): _____

**24.** Internal review: (Describe supervisor's findings below):

_____

_____

_____

# Sample Purchase Order

*Note:* To control payments, the purchase order must be issued to vendors prior to authorization of purchase. The purchase order is not an invoice; rather, it is an official order to the vendor to provide your event organization with specific goods and services. The vendor's invoice will serve as the agreement and therefore must be inspected carefully to ensure that it meets the specifications of the purchase order.

**Purchase Order**

Tracking number: XYZ-1

   I. Event name:_____

  II. Event date:_____

 III. Vendor name: _____

 IV. Vendor address: _____

  V. City, state, zip: _____

 VI. Vendor telephone: _____

VII. Vendor facsimile: _____

| VIII. Quantity | Item Description | Cost per Unit | Total Cost |
|---|---|---|---|
| Example: | | | |
| 32 | Black derbies | $1.00 | $ 32.00 |
| 10 | Red garters | 0.50 | 5.00 |
| 100 | Red bandanas | 3.00 | 300.00 |
| Subtotal: | | | $337.00 |

 IX. Applicable taxes (if tax exempt, attach appropriate documentation): Tax exempt

  X. Total amount authorized for this purchase: _____$337.00

XI. Terms: Net 30 days upon receipt of invoice.

XII. Delivery date and time: _____

XIII. Delivery address: _____

XIV. Delivery contact person (receiving agent): _____

XV. Telephone number at delivery site: _____

XVI. Note to vendor. No substitutions or changes may be made to this order without the written consent of the purchaser.

XVII. Name of event management organization _____
Address _____
Telephone _____

XVIII. _____
Authorized signature

# Sample Event Evaluations

## Quantitative Survey

**ISES Survey on Educational Programs**

1. *Please select only ONE discipline that best describes your company's products and/or service.*
   - ❏ Event planning and coordination
   - ❏ Design, decor, and graphics
   - ❏ Technical services and products
   - ❏ Entertainment
   - ❏ Food service and products
   - ❏ Travel and transportation services
   - ❏ Event public relations and marketing
   - ❏ Other (specify) _____

2. *How many years have you been in the special event industry?*
   - ❏ Less than 1 year  ❏ 1–4 years  ❏ 5–10 years  ❏ 10 or more years

3. *What is your highest level of education? (Check only ONE.)*
   - ❏ Some high school
   - ❏ High school diploma
   - ❏ Some college
   - ❏ Undergraduate degree
   - ❏ Graduate degree

4. *Have you previously attended ISES DC chapter educational seminar(s)?*
   - ❏ Yes
   - ❏ No

   If yes, when and on what topic(s)? _____

   If no, please indicate a reason for nonattendance and **skip to question 6.** _____

5. *How satisfied are you with the overall quality of the seminar(s)?*
   - ❏ Very satisfied
   - ❏ Fairly satisfied
   - ❏ Not too satisfied
   - ❏ Not satisfied at all

6. *Please mark ALL the seminar topics that you would like to attend in the future.*
   - ❏ Strategic planning
   - ❏ Fundraising

❑ Building your own business
❑ Legal, ethical, and risk management
❑ Creating effective proposals
❑ Technology
❑ Marketing through Internet
❑ Marketing through print promotion
❑ Design and creative concept generating

❑ Corporate sponsorship
❑ Budgeting and financial planning
❑ Recruitment, motivation, and coordination of volunteers
❑ Cross-cultural event management
❑ Strategic entertainment
❑ Other (specify) _____

7. *What ONE time is the most convenient for you to attend such educational seminars?*
   ❑  Morning          ❑  Afternoon          ❑  Evening

8. *Who would you like to hear as a guest speaker at a monthly meeting?* _____

9. *What location(s) would you suggest for future meetings? (Identify a specific location.)*
   _____

   If you can, please list the contact person at the location (name and telephone number)
   _____
   _____

10. *Would you volunteer to be a speaker in your area of expertise at an ISES meeting?*
    ❑  Yes                              ❑  No
    On what topic? _____
    If you answered **yes,** we would be happy to know your name and contact telephone _____

11. *Are you currently an ISES member?*
    ❑  Yes                              ❑  No

*Thank you very much for your cooperation! Someone will collect your completed questionnaire.*

# Quantitative Survey, Likert Method

**Road Financing and Road Fund Management Workshop Evaluation Survey**
**Kiev, Ukraine**

*Please fill out the questionnaire below and drop it at the registration desk on your way out. In appreciation for your feedback we have a small souvenir for you that you can exchange for a completed questionnaire.*

1. *Do you believe that you have learned something new during this workshop?*
   ❑  Yes                              ❑  No

2. *Do you believe that the workshop was applicable to the current road situation in Ukraine?*
   ❑  Yes                              ❑  No

3. *On a scale of 10, how strongly did the workshop influence your vision of road financing and road fund management?* (1, did not influence at all; 10, greatly influenced)

   1   2   3   4   5   6   7   8   9   10

4. *Which, if any, message(s) were in your opinion communicated throughout the workshop? (Please check all that apply.)*
   ❑  Importance of having an autonomous road agency
   ❑  Managing the road agency along commercial lines
   ❑  Involving road users to win public support for increased road financing
   ❑  There is a need to manage the road fund more actively

5. *Which presentation did you find most useful for your future work? (Please check ONE box only.)*
   ❑  EBRD Consultant Study              ❑  South African Road Experience
   ❑  EU Accession Criteria              ❑  Latvian State Road Fund Experience
   ❑  Commercially Managed Road Funds

6. *Which presentation did you find least useful for your future work? (Please check ONE box only.)*
   ❑  EBRD Consultant Study              ❑  South African Road Experience
   ❑  EU Accession Criteria              ❑  Latvian State Road Fund Experience
   ❑  Commercially Managed Road Funds

7. *On a scale of 10, how would you evaluate the quality of translation?* (1, poor; 10, excellent)

   1   2   3   4   5   6   7   8   9   10

8. *On a scale of 10, how would you evaluate facilitation of the discussions?* (1, poor; 10, excellent)

   1   2   3   4   5   6   7   8   9   10

9. *Would you be interested in attending similar workshops in the future?*
   ❑  Yes                              ❑  No

10. *You can identify the organization that you are representing at this workshop as (please check ONE box only):*
    ❑  Governmental     ❑  Engineering          ❑  Other (please specify)
    ❑  Association       ❑  Research
    ❑  Commercial        ❑  Regional governmental    _____

*We encourage you to use the back of this questionnaire for any comments or suggestions that you might have regarding the workshop.*

*Thank you very much for your cooperation!*

# Qualitative Event Evaluation Methods

## FOCUS GROUPS

The following steps should be utilized to conduct an effective focus group or panel.

1. Qualify 9 to 12 persons who have one or two homogeneous characteristics. For example, they may be both men and women but all have a college degree. Or they may all be midlevel managers or between the ages of 35 and 50.
2. Use a survey instrument or interviews to qualify participation.
3. Distribute a confirmation letter to the qualified participants listing the date, time, location, and topics for the focus panel.
4. Offer a reward or gift for their participation, such as a book.
5. Make certain that you recruit 15 to 25 percent more participants than you will actually need to allow for attrition.
6. Appoint a trained focus group facilitator. A good facilitator will be skilled at remaining neutral during the focus group session and probing to elicit the most valid responses from the participants.
7. Call the participants the day before the focus group session to remind them and reconfirm their participation.
8. At the beginning of the focus panel you should announce the agenda and format. Encourage the participants to express themselves fully even if they wish to speak to one another.
9. Record using an audio recorder or video recorder the focus panel.
10. Transcribe the recording and notes from the focus panel.
11. Analyze the focus panel transcription and note areas of agreement as well as areas of dissonance among the participants.
12. Submit your final report, including your recommendations based on the focus group comments.

## KEY INFORMANT INTERVIEWS

The following steps will assist you in targeting key informants to provide high-quality information about your event.

1. Identify those persons with the highest level of expertise.
2. Request an interview that will last no more than 15 minutes.
3. Prepare up to 10 questions to ask the key informant.
4. Use a quantitative approach for some of the questions, such as "How would you rate the potential location for this event on a 1–5 scale, 1 being unacceptable and 5 very acceptable?"
5. Use open-ended questions such as "How would you describe the overall quality of the event?"
6. Probe to extract more information for the key information using questions such as "Tell me more about this" or "Why do you feel this way?"
7. Reduce your field notes from the interview questions to a short written report using initials for the key informants responses and the letter "Q" for your questions.

8. Summarize and analyze the report, listing the key points that were identified by the key informant and how you will use these recommendations to resolve the issues associated with the event or improve overall performance.

## ETHNOGRAPHIC STUDIES

The ethnographic study is an excellent research tool to employ when seeking in-depth knowledge of the event environment. The ethnographic researcher participates and observes the stakeholders who are associated with the event to report on subtle nuances and unspoken issues. The purpose of ethnographic research is to identify meanings associated with event behaviors. Use the following steps to conduct effective ethnographic studies for your event.

1. Establish an outline and timeline for the study.
2. Request permission from event stakeholders to conduct the study.
3. Utilize a trained field researcher.
4. Develop interview questions for the various stakeholder groups.
5. List the events, programs, and meetings that the field researcher should attend to participate and observe the critical activities of the stakeholders.
6. Record in the field notes not only the verbal responses but also the physical behavior of the stakeholders.
7. Analyze the field notes to identify trends, patterns, and ultimately meanings of stakeholder responses and behaviors.
8. Reduce your findings to a short written report that describes your finding and offers recommendations for using this information to develop the event strategically.

# ISES Code of Ethics

Each member of ISES shall agree to adhere to the following:

1. Provide to all persons truthful and accurate information with respect to the professional performance of duties.
2. Maintain the highest standards of personal conduct to bring credit to the special events industry.
3. Promote and encourage the highest level of ethics within the profession.
4. Recognize and discharge by responsibility, to uphold all laws and regulations relating to ISES policies and activities.
5. Strive for excellence in all aspects of the industry.
6. Use only legal and ethical means in all industry activities.
7. Protect the public against fraud and unfair practices, and attempt to eliminate from ISES all practices which bring discredit to the profession.
8. Use a written contract clearly stating all charges, services, products, and other essential information.
9. Demonstrate respect for every professional within the industry by clearly stating and consistently performing at or above the standards acceptable to the industry.
10. Make a commitment to increase professional growth and knowledge by attending educational programs recommended, but not limited to, those prescribed by ISES.
11. Contribute knowledge to professional meetings and journals to raise the consciousness of the industry.
12. Maintain the highest standards of safety, sanitation, and any other responsibilities.
13. When providing services or products, maintain in full force adequate or appropriate insurance.
14. Cooperate with professional colleagues, suppliers, and employees to provide the highest quality service.
15. Extend these same professional commitments to all those persons supervised or employed.
16. Subscribe to the ISES Principles of Professional Conduct and Ethics and to abide by the ISES Bylaws.

The great law of culture is: Let each become all that he was capable of becoming.

Thomas Carlyle

# Index